GODFATHER

GODFATHER

The Intimate
Francis Ford Coppola

Gene D. Phillips

With a Foreword by
Walter Murch

THE UNIVERSITY PRESS OF KENTUCKY

Publication of this volume was made possible in part by a grant
from the National Endowment for the Humanities.

Copyright © 2004 by The University Press of Kentucky

Scholarly publisher for the Commonwealth,
serving Bellarmine University, Berea College, Centre
College of Kentucky, Eastern Kentucky University,
The Filson Historical Society, Georgetown College,
Kentucky Historical Society, Kentucky State University,
Morehead State University, Murray State University,
Northern Kentucky University, Transylvania University,
University of Kentucky, University of Louisville,
and Western Kentucky University.
All rights reserved.

Editorial and Sales Offices: The University Press of Kentucky
663 South Limestone Street, Lexington, Kentucky 40508-4008
www.kentuckypress.com

04 05 06 07 08   5 4 3 2 1

Library of Congress Cataloging-in-Publication Data

Phillips, Gene D.
Godfather : the intimate Francis Ford Coppola / Gene D. Phillips.
p. cm.
Includes bibliographical references and index.
ISBN 0-8131-2304-6 (alk. paper)
1. Coppola, Francis Ford, 1939- I. Title.
PN1998.3.C67P48 2004
791.4302'33'092—dc22
2003024590

This book is printed on acid-free recycled paper meeting
the requirements of the American National Standard
for Permanence in Paper for Printed Library Materials.

Manufactured in the United States of America.

 Member of the Association of
American University Presses

For
Stanley Kubrick,
the ultimate
Hollywood maverick

Contents

Part Three Artist in an Industry

Part Four The Vintage Years

Photographs follow page 172

Foreword

Collaborating with Coppola

Walter Murch,
film and sound editor

It disappeared long ago, but in 1972 the Window was still there, peering through milky cataracts of dust, thirty-five feet above the floor of Samuel Goldwyn's old Stage 7. I never would have noticed it if Richard hadn't suddenly stopped in his tracks as we were taking a shortcut on our way back from lunch.

"That . . . was when Sound . . . was King!" he said, gesturing dramatically into the upper darknesses of Stage 7.

It took me a moment, but I finally saw what he was pointing to: something near the ceiling that resembled the observation window of a 1930s dirigible, nosing its way into the stage.

Goldwyn Studios, where Richard Portman and I were working on the mix of *The Godfather*, had originally been United Artists, built for Mary Pickford when she founded U.A. with Charles Chaplin, Douglas Fairbanks, and D. W. Griffith in the early 1920s. By 1972, Stage 7 was functioning as an attic—stuffed with the mysterious lumbering shapes of disused equipment—but it was there that Samuel Goldwyn produced one of the earliest of his many musicals: *Whoopee* (1930), starring Eddie Cantor and choreographed by Busby Berkeley. And it was there that Goldwyn's director of sound, Gordon Sawyer, sat at the controls behind the Window, hands gliding across three Bakelite knobs, piloting his Dirigible of Sound into a new world . . . a world in which Sound was King.

Down below, Eddie Cantor and the All-Singing, All-Dancing Goldwyn

Girls had lived in terror of the distinguished Man Behind the Window—
and not just the actors, but musicians, cameramen (Gregg Toland among
them), the director, the producer (Florenz Ziegfeld), even Sam Goldwyn
himself. No one could contradict it if Mr. Sawyer, dissatisfied with the quality
of the sound, leaned into his microphone and pronounced dispassionately
but irrevocably the word "Cut!"

By 1972, forty-five years after his exhilarating coronation, King Sound
seemed to be living in considerably reduced circumstances. No longer did
the Man Behind the Window survey the scene from on high. Instead, the
sound recordist was usually stuck in some dark corner with his equipment
cart. The very idea of his demanding "Cut!" was inconceivable. Not only
did none of those on the set fear his opinion, but they hardly consulted him
and were frequently impatient when he did voice an opinion. Forty-five
years seemed to have turned him from king to footman.

Was Richard's nostalgia misplaced? What had befallen the Window?
And were sound's misfortunes all they appeared to be?

There is something about the liquidity and all-encompassing embrace
of sound that might make it more accurate to speak of her as a queen rather
than a king. But was she then perhaps a queen for whom the crown was a
burden and who preferred to slip on a handmaiden's bonnet and scurry
incognito through the back passageways of the palace, accomplishing her
tasks anonymously?

Neither Richard Portman nor I had any inkling on that afternoon
when he showed me the Window that the record-breaking success of *The
Godfather* several months later would trigger a revival in the fortunes of
the film industry in general and of sound in particular.

Three years earlier, in 1969, I had been hired to create the sound effects for—and mix—*The Rain People*, a film written, directed, and produced by Francis Ford Coppola. He was a recent film school graduate, as
was I, and we were both eager to make films professionally the way we had
made them at school. Francis had felt that the sound on his previous film
(*Finian's Rainbow*) had bogged down in the bureaucratic and technical in-
ertia at the studios, and he didn't want to repeat the experience.

He also felt that if he stayed in Los Angeles he wouldn't be able to
produce the inexpensive, independent films he had in mind. So he and a
fellow film student, George Lucas, and I, and our families, moved up to San
Francisco to start American Zoetrope. The first item on the agenda was the
mix of *The Rain People,* to be done in the unfinished basement of an old
warehouse on Folsom Street.

Ten years earlier, this would have been unthinkable, but the invention of the transistor had changed things technically and economically to such an extent that it seemed natural for the thirty-year-old Francis to go to Germany and buy—almost off the shelf—mixing and editing equipment from K.E.M. in Hamburg and to hire me, a twenty-six-year-old, to use it.

Technically, the equipment was state of the art, and yet it cost a fourth of what comparable equipment would have cost five years earlier. This halving of price and doubling of quality is familiar to everyone now, after thirty years of microchips, but at the time it was astonishing. The frontier between professional and consumer electronics began to fade away.

In fact, it faded to the extent that it now became economically and technically possible for one person to do what several had done before, and that other frontier—between the creation and mixing of sound effects—also began to disappear.

From Zoetrope's beginning, the idea was to try to avoid the departmentalism that was sometimes the by-product of sound's technical complexity and that tended too often to pit mixers (who came mostly from engineering—direct descendants of the Man Behind the Window) against the people who created the sounds. It was as if there were two directors of photography on a film, one who lighted the scene and another who photographed it, and neither could do much about countermanding the other.

We felt that there was now no reason—given the equipment that was becoming available in 1968—that the person who designed the sound track shouldn't also be able to mix it and that the director would then be able to talk to one person, the sound designer, about the sound of the film the way he was able to talk to the production designer about the look of the film.

At any rate, it was against this background that the success of *The Godfather* led directly to the green-lighting of two Zoetrope productions: George Lucas's *American Graffiti* and Francis Coppola's *Conversation*—both with very different but equally adventuresome sound tracks where we were able to put our ideas to work.

Steven Spielberg's *Jaws* soon topped the box office of *The Godfather* and introduced the world at large to the music of John Williams. The success of *American Graffiti* led to *Star Wars* (with music by the same John Williams), which in turn topped *Jaws*. The seventy-millimeter Dolby release format of *Star Wars* revived and reinvented magnetic six-track sound and helped Dolby Cinema Sound obtain a crucial foothold in film postproduction and exhibition. The success of the two *Godfather* films would allow Francis to make *Apocalypse Now,* which broke further ground in originating, at the end of the 1970s, what has now become the standard film sound format: three channels of sound behind the screen, left and right surrounds behind the audience, and low-frequency enhancement.

The Window is long gone, and will not now return, but the autocratic temporal power that disappeared with it has been repaid a hundred—a thousand—times in creative power: the ability to freely reassociate image and sound in different contexts and combinations.

This reassociation of image and sound is the fundamental pillar upon which the creative use of sound rests and without which it would collapse. Sometimes it is done simply for convenience (walking on cornstarch, for instance, happens to record as a better footstep-in-snow than snow itself). But beyond any practical consideration, I believe this reassociation should stretch the relationship of sound to image wherever possible. It should strive to create a purposeful and fruitful tension between what is on the screen and what is kindled in the mind of the audience.

This metaphoric distance between the images of a film and the accompanying sounds is—and should be—continuously changing and flexible, and it often takes a fraction of a second (sometimes even several seconds) for the brain to make the right connections. For instance, the image of a light being turned on accompanied by a simple click is a basic association that is fused almost instantly and produces a relatively flat mental image.

Still fairly flat, but a level up in dimensionality is the image of a door closing accompanied by the right "slam"—this can indicate not only the material of the door and the space around it but also the emotional state of the person closing it. The sound for the door at the end of The Godfather, for instance, needed to give the audience more than the correct physical cues about the door. It was even more important to get a firm, irrevocable closing that resonated with and underscored Michael's final line: "Never ask me about my business, Kay."

That door sound was related to a specific image, and, as a result, it was "fused" by the audience fairly quickly. Sounds, however, that do not relate to the visuals in a direct way function at an even higher level of dimensionality and take proportionately longer to resolve. The rumbling and piercing metallic scream just before Michael Corleone kills Solozzo and McCluskey in a restaurant in The Godfather is not linked directly to anything seen on screen, and so the audience is made to wonder—at least momentarily, if perhaps only subconsciously—"What is this?" The screech is from an elevated train rounding a sharp turn, so it is presumably coming from somewhere in the neighborhood (the scene takes place in the Bronx).

But precisely because it is so detached from the image, the metallic scream works as a clue to the state of Michael's mind at the moment—the critical moment before he commits his first murder and his life turns an irrevocable corner. It is all the more effective because Michael's face appears so calm and the sound is played so abnormally loud. This broadening tension between what we see and what we hear is brought to an abrupt end with the pistol shots that kill Solozzo and McCluskey: the distance between what we see and what we hear is suddenly collapsed at the moment that Michael's destiny is fixed.

This moment is mirrored and inverted at the end of *Godfather III*. Instead of a calm face with a scream, we see a screaming face in silence. When Michael realizes that his daughter Mary has been shot, he tries several times to scream—but no sound comes out. In fact, Al Pacino was actually screaming, but the sound was removed in the editing. We are dealing here with an *absence* of sound, yet a fertile tension is created between what we see and what we would expect to hear, given the image. Finally, the scream bursts through, the tension is released, and the film—and the trilogy—is over.

The elevated train in *The Godfather* was at least somewhere in the vicinity of the restaurant, even though it could not be seen. In the opening reel of *Apocalypse Now*, the jungle sounds that fill Willard's hotel room come from nowhere on screen or in the "neighborhood," and the only way to resolve the great disparity between what we are seeing and hearing is to imagine that these sounds are in Willard's mind: that his body is in a hotel room in Saigon, but his mind is off in the jungle, where he dreams of returning. If the audience members can be brought to a point where they will bridge with their own imagination such an extreme distance between picture and sound, they will be rewarded with a correspondingly greater dimensionality of experience.

The risk, of course, is that the conceptual thread that connects image and sound can be stretched too far, and the dimensionality will collapse: the moment of greatest dimension is always the moment of greatest tension.

The question remains in all of this, why we generally perceive the product of the fusion of image and sound in terms of the image. Why does sound usually enhance the image and not the other way around? In other words, why does King Sight still sit on his throne and Queen Sound haunt the corridors of the palace?

In his book *AudioVision*, Michael Chion describes an effect that he calls the acousmêtre, which depends on delaying the fusion of sound and image to the extreme by supplying only the sound—most frequently a voice—and withholding the revelation of the sound's true source until nearly the end of the film. Only then, when the audience has used its imagination to the fullest, is the identity of the source revealed. The Wizard in *The Wizard of Oz* is one of a number of examples, along with the mother in *Psycho* and Hal in *2001* (and although Chion didn't mention it, Wolfman Jack in *American Graffiti* and Colonel Kurtz in *Apocalypse Now*). The acousmêtre is—for various reasons having to do with our perceptions—a uniquely cinematic device: the disembodied voice seems to come from everywhere and therefore to have no clearly defined limits to its power.

And yet . . . there is an echo here of our earliest experience of the world: the revelation at birth that the song that sang to us from the very dawn of consciousness in the womb—a song that seemed to come from everywhere and to be part of us before we had any conception of what "us" meant—that this song is the voice of another and that she is now separate from us and we from her. We regret the loss of former unity—some say that our lives are a ceaseless quest to retrieve it—and yet we delight in seeing the face of our mother: the one is the price to be paid for the other.

This earliest, most powerful fusion of sound and image sets the tone for all that are to come.

Acknowledgments

First of all, I am grateful to Francis Ford Coppola, who was willing to talk with me at the Cannes International Film Festival, for reading the précis from which this book was developed and for reading through all of his published interviews to check for factual errors. In addition, I would also like to single out the following among those who have given me their assistance in the course of the long period in which I was engaged in remote preparation for this study: Tennessee Williams, for sharing his thoughts with me about *This Property Is Condemned,* a film that Coppola co-scripted; film director Fred Zinnemann for discussing with me the parallels between the Johnny Fontane character in *The Godfather* and Frank Sinatra in his film *From Here to Eternity.* Actors Shirley Knight (*The Rain People*), Terri Garr (*The Conversation, One From the Heart*), the late Elizabeth Hartman (*You're a Big Boy Now*), and the late Richard Conte (*The Godfather*); and producer Albert Ruddy (*The Godfather*) for speaking with me about working with Coppola.

Many institutions and individuals provided research materials. I would like to specifically mention: the staff of the Motion Picture Section of the Library of Congress and the staff of the Film Study Center of the Museum of Modern Art. Research materials were also provided by the Paramount Collection of the Margaret Herrick Library of the Motion Picture Academy of Arts and Sciences; the Research Library of the University of California at Los Angeles; the Warner Brothers Collection in the Archive of the Library of the University of Southern California; the Script Repositories of Warner Brothers, Paramount, Universal, and United Artists; Musette Buckely, Vice-President of Production Resources, Warner Brothers; Vincent LoBrutto, research professor of the School of Visual Arts, New York City; Lieutenant Robert Clarke, U.S.M., for discussing Coppola's two Vietnam films with me; film expert Edin Dzafic, who helped track down Coppola's amateur films; and Raymond Baumhart, S.J., Professor of Management in the Loyola University School of Business Administration, for discussing *Tucker: The Man and His Dream* with me.

The essay by Walter Murch, which appears as the foreword of this volume, is reprinted from the *New York Times* (1 October 2000, sec. 2, pp. 1, 24–25, copyright 2000 by Walter Murch) by permission of the author.

The interview with S. E. Hinton, which is quoted in this book, is reprinted from the *New York Times* (20 March 1983, sec. 2, pp. 19, 27, copyright 1983 by the New York Times Co.).

Some material in this book appeared in a completely different form in the following publications: *The Movie Makers: Artists in an Industry* (Chicago: Nelson-Hall, 1973, copyright 1973 by Gene D. Phillips); "Francis Coppola," *Films in Review* 40, no. 3 (March 1989, pp. 155–60, copyright 1989 by Gene D. Phillips); *Conrad and Cinema: The Art of Adaptation* (New York: Peter Lang, 1995, copyright 1995 by Peter Lang, used with permission).

Chronology for Francis Ford Coppola

1939   Born April 7 in Detroit, Michigan, to Carmine and Italia Coppola.

1957   Attends Hofstra University on a drama scholarship.

1960   Earns a Bachelor of Arts degree at Hofstra and enters the film school of the University of California at Los Angeles, where he studies on campus for two years.

1962   Is hired by Roger Corman, an independent producer, and works on *Battle Beyond the Sun, The Young Racers,* and other films.

1963   Directs his first feature, *Dementia 13,* a low-budget movie made for Corman. The assistant art director is Eleanor Neil, whom Coppola marries after completing the movie.

1966   As scriptwriter for Seven Arts, an independent production unit, Coppola is given a screen credit for co-scripting *This Property Is Condemned* and *Is Paris Burning?*

1967   Directs *You're a Big Boy Now,* his first film for a major studio; it enables him to earn his Master of Arts degree at UCLA, which is conferred the following year.

1968   *Finian's Rainbow,* a musical with Fred Astaire.

1969   *The Rain People* wins the Grand Prize and the Best Director Award at the San Sebastian International Film Festival. Inaugurates American Zoetrope, an independent production unit in San Francisco.

1970   *Patton,* for which he coauthors the screenplay, wins him his first Academy Award, for Best Screenplay.

1972   *The Godfather* wins him an Academy Award for coauthoring the screenplay of the film, which he also directed; the picture is also voted the Best Picture of the Year.

1974   *The Conversation* wins the Grand Prize at the Cannes International Film Festival. *The Great Gatsby,* the last picture for which he wrote a script without directing the film, is released. *The Godfather Part II* wins him Academy Awards for Best Director and for coauthoring the screenplay; the film becomes the only sequel up to that time to be voted Best Picture of the Year.

1979   *Apocalypse Now,* which had an unprecedented shooting period of 238 days, wins him his second Grand Prize at the Cannes International Film Festival; one of the first major films to deal with the Vietnam War.

1980   Inaugurates Zoetrope Studios in Hollywood.

1982   *One from the Heart,* a commercial failure, forces him to close his independent studio in Hollywood; he continues to run an independent production unit, American Zoetrope, in San Francisco, producing films for release by major studios in Hollywood.

1983   *The Outsiders* and *Rumble Fish* are made back-to-back in Oklahoma.

1984   Assumes direction of *The Cotton Club,* a film with a troubled production history up to that point.

1985   "Rip Van Winkle," a telefilm, is first broadcast.

1986   *Peggy Sue Got Married* becomes a major hit.

1987   *The Gardens of Stone,* his second film set during the Vietnam War.

1988   *Tucker: The Man and His Dream,* after some false starts, is finally made.

1989   *New York Stories,* an anthology film with segments by Martin Scorsese, Woody Allen, and Coppola.

1990   *The Godfather Part III,* the final sequel to *The Godfather.*

1991   Fax Bahr and George Hickenlooper's feature-length documentary *Hearts of Darkness,* about the making of *Apocalypse Now.*

1992   *Bram Stoker's Dracula* is a commercial success; Coppola receives a Golden Lion as a Life Achievement Award at the Venice International Film Festival.

1995   The National Film Registry of the Library of Congress, which preserves films of enduring quality, includes *The Godfather, The Godfather Part II,* and *The Conversation* in its collection.

1996   *Jack,* a vehicle for Robin Williams.

1997   *The Rainmaker,* from the John Grisham novel.

1998   Recipient of the Life Achievement Award, the highest honor that can be bestowed by the Directors Guild of America. A jury orders Warner Brothers to pay him $80 million for reneging on a deal to film *Pinocchio*—the largest victory by a film-maker over a major studio up to that time.

1999 American Zoetrope, Coppola's production unit, releases *The Virgin Suicides,* written and directed by his daughter Sofia.

2000 Coppola edits (uncredited) the release version of *Supernova,* after the director, Walter Hill, departs the project.

2001 Theatrical release of *Apocalypse Now Redux,* with fifty minutes of additional footage added to the film as originally released. Release on DVD of *The Godfather Trilogy,* with a documentary about the making of the three films.

2002 Gala tribute by the Film Society of Lincoln Center of New York for his lifetime achievement in the cinema, May 7. American Zoetrope releases *CQ,* written and directed by Coppola's son Roman. *Sight and Sound*'s international poll of film directors and film critics chooses Coppola as one of the top ten directors of all time and *The Godfather* and *The Godfather Part II* among the top ten films of all time.

2003 *Premiere* magazine conducts a nationwide poll for the one hundred greatest films, and *The Godfather Part II* leads the list in first place. The American Film Institute honors the best one hundred heroes and villains in cinema history with a TV special aired on June 3, including Michael Corleone in *Godfather II* as a legendary villain. The Motion Picture Academy sponsors a screening of *One from the Heart,* with Coppola leading a discussion of the film. Francis Coppola serves as an executive producer for American Zoetrope on Sofia Coppola's second feature, *Lost in Translation.*

2004 A nationwide poll published by *Premiere* magazine lists *The Godfather* as one of the seventy-five most influential films of all time, because it raised the gangster film to the level of a cinematic epic.

Prologue

Artist in an Industry

Isn't Hollywood a dump—in the human sense of the word? A hideous town, full of the human spirit at a new low of debasement. This is no art, it's an industry.

—F. Scott Fitzgerald

This isn't a business, it's a racket.

—Harry Cohn, producer

At 7:00 PM on the evening of May 7, 2002, Francis Ford Coppola took his place in a special box overlooking the auditorium of Avery Fisher Hall in New York City's Lincoln Center for the Performing Arts. The occasion was a gala tribute sponsored by the Film Society of Lincoln Center honoring Coppola's lifetime achievement as a filmmaker. Several cinema artists associated with his career were on hand to pay tribute to him, and these same individuals will be cited throughout this book. But Coppola himself was the main attraction.

One of the reasons that Coppola's career is so fascinating is that, despite the wide diversity of genres in which he has worked, all of his films reflect in varying degrees the artistry of the director who made them all, as I shall endeavor to show in the course of this study. Coppola himself has declared that a good director does not make a group of separate films—

rather each film that he makes is a series of installments in the same film. As he puts it, "Why do we continue to think in cinema that one makes one film, then another? . . . I prefer to think that my films are the same film. You know, if you take all of my films from first to last, it is all the same film."[1]

This is another way of saying that it is the director more than anyone else involved in the production of a film who leaves his personal stamp on a motion picture. Filmmaking, it is true, is a corporate effort, to which a whole host of individuals, from actors to technicians, must make their contribution. But it is the director who must create a unified work of art from all of these varied contributions.

Indeed, the premise of this book is precisely that the director alone can confer artistic unity on a motion picture. The director, after all, is the single controlling influence during the production of a motion picture. It is up to him to blend all of the varied contributions of cast and crew into a unified whole.

Only the director, then, can create a unified work of art out of the corporate effort that characterizes the making of a motion picture. In describing the central role of the director in the production of a movie, another critic has said that the director's function is that of quarterback, orchestra leader, trail boss, company commander, and, at times, lion tamer. When the role of the director is viewed in this fashion, moreover, as the guiding light of film production, it is clear that he is the true author of a film in much the same way that a writer is the author of a novel.

The auteur theory, which proposes that the director is the center of the filmmaking process, can be readily applied to European directors working in relatively small industries, such as those in Sweden or France, where they can with relative ease control every aspect of the production of a film from beginning to end. At first glance, however, it seems much less apparent that an American director like Francis Coppola, working in a much larger and more complex industry, could gain a similar artistic control over his films.

On closer examination, however, it is clear that Coppola has been able with a fair degree of consistency to give his movies the imprint of his own personal vision and style in much the same fashion as his European colleagues have done, regardless of the diversity of genres in which he has worked. Indeed, one suspects that the "factory system" in Hollywood studios presented him with a challenge to his artistic creativity that sharpened his determination to turn out a succession of films over the years that he could in a real sense call his own.

Filmmaking, it is true, involves a whole host of individuals, from actors to technicians, who collaborate with the director on a movie. Yet genuine auteurs are directors who have nevertheless been able to impress their films with their personal trademark, regardless of the number of collaborators involved with them on a given picture, by systematically influencing every phase of the production process—from script to scoring—as Coppola has done.

Richard Schickel observes about film critics and scholars that, with few exceptions, "we are all auteurists now. The reason is self-evident: Directors are responsible for the movieness of movies. This is to say, they are in change of all the things that are unique to film as an expressive form. As the senior officer present on any picture, the director gets most of the credit or blame for its success or failure."[2]

In fact, Geoffrey Chown states in his book, *Hollywood Auteur: Francis Coppola,* that Coppola's career demonstrates that the auteur theory is still a valid approach to film criticism. As he puts it, while writing his book on Coppola he acquired "a new appreciation of the value of the auteur theory."[3]

Other commentators on Coppola's films have willingly conferred auteur status on him. Chuck Kleinhans calls Coppola one of the more celebrated examples of auteurism, given the manner in which his work has evolved from the 1970s onward. Although Coppola has worked within the commercial system, he has made a number of films that seem personally important to him "and that were highly regarded as cinematic art"—films that demonstrated both his "artistry and personal vision, from *The Godfather* to *Bram Stoker's Dracula.*"[4]

Expatiating on this point, Coppola biographer Michael Schumacher adds that Coppola is equally adept at creating small personal films like *The Conversation,* as well as huge productions like *Dracula.* Hence, he is "as close to being an auteur as could be found in American film."[5] As such, Coppola has helped to make possible the individualism and independence that are hallmarks of today's new breed of directors. Consequently, Mast and Kawin conclude in their history of film that Coppola is "the single most important film figure of his generation."[6]

Coppola himself personally agrees with the fundamental tenets of the auteur theory concerning the pivotal role of the director in the filmmaking process. "The auteur theory is fine," he states, "but to exercise it you have to qualify, and the only way you can qualify is by having *earned* the right to have control."[7] Coppola has certainly earned that right.

The present study is designed to provide a complete critical study of Coppola's career. Therefore, it focuses not only on his most celebrated achievements—like the *Godfather* movies, which together compose a supreme cinematic epic, and *Apocalypse Now,* a great antiwar film—but it gives equal time to Coppola's other important pictures, which have not received the critical attention they deserve in previous studies of his work. These movies include *Peggy Sue Got Married,* a charming comedy-fantasy, and *The Rainmaker,* a superior courtroom drama. In addition, I have made an effort to reassess those Coppola films that have been accorded neither critical nor popular acceptance, such as *The Cotton Club* and *Tucker: The Man and His Dream.* Surely these neglected and underappreciated movies warrant the reconsideration offered here.

In surveying the previous books on Coppola, I am obliged to note that a number of them, like Schumacher's *Francis Ford Coppola* and Peter Cowie's *Coppola,* are biographies and thus offer relatively little critical insight into the director's movies. By the same token, books on individual films, like Harlan Lebo's *The Godfather Legacy* and Cowie's *The Apocalypse Now Book,* are mere production histories of the films in question. Moreover, the critical studies published in the 1970s and 1980s, such as Robert Johnson's *Francis Ford Coppola* and Chown's book, are obviously incomplete and out of date, since Coppola continued making movies throughout the 1990s.

My procedure has been to interview Coppola and others associated with his films, to read the screenplays and the director's production journals, and to weigh the evaluations of other commentators on his work with my own. In this manner I have sought to achieve a balanced consensus.

The present volume, then, represents an attempt to demonstrate, by analyzing all of his motion pictures, that Francis Coppola is a genuine cinematic artist who is also a popular entertainer. As a matter of fact, the very popularity of his movies is reason enough for some critics to write him off as a mere crowd pleaser rather than recognize him as an authentic artist of the cinema. That a director can be both is suggested by the fact that Coppola's finest films—for example, *The Godfather* and *Apocalypse Now*—are also among his most popular.

The following pages, in sum, pay tribute to a filmmaker who has been able through his resourcefulness to place on his films, not the stamp of the studio, but the stamp of his own directorial style. The present study is, therefore, intended not only for the cinema specialist but also for those filmgoers who have enjoyed Coppola's movies, in order to provide them with a context by which they can appreciate his work more fully.

Part One

Hollywood Immigrant

1

Point of Departure

The Early Films and Screenplays

I was convinced in the beginning that there must be some discoverable method of working in pictures, which would not be completely stultifying to whatever creative talent one might happen to possess. But like others before me, I discovered that this was a dream.

—Raymond Chandler

"Hollywood's like Egypt," the late producer David O. Selznick once remarked, "full of crumbled pyramids. It will just keep crumbling until finally the wind blows the last studio prop across the sands. . . . There might have been good movies if there had been no movie industry. Hollywood might have become the center of a new human expression if it hadn't been grabbed by a little group of bookkeepers and turned into a junk industry."[1]

These are bitter words indeed to come from the man responsible for producing films like *Gone with the Wind* (1939). Nonetheless, Selznick has accurately expressed the perennial problem that has vexed motion picture makers since the movies developed from their humble beginnings into a full-scale industry: the problem of trying to make motion pictures that are personal, unified works of art a director can truly call his own despite the fact that he is working in a complicated commercial industry. Yet many a filmmaker has succeeded in this hazardous enterprise, and Francis Ford Coppola is one of them.

"The trouble with American filmmaking is that producers don't allow the risk of failure. If a good film can't risk being a failure, it won't be really good." So said Francis Ford Coppola when he spoke with me at the Cannes Film Festival, one of the international festivals at which a movie of his had won a prize. Add to that the five Academy Awards he has received during his career and one can see that Coppola's penchant for making films that, in his words, "depart somewhat from the ordinary Hollywood fare" has often paid off. When I talked with Coppola in Cannes, I noticed that his stocky build and full beard make him an imposing figure. Yet I found him cordial and cooperative when he shared with me some of his reflections about his movies. The festival, of course, attracts film directors from around the world, but Coppola was as unmistakably American as the Queens section of New York where he grew up and went to school. As a matter of fact, he has kept his New York accent over the years despite his living most of his adult life on the West Coast. The material I gleaned from our conversation can be found throughout this book.[2]

Early Years

Francis Ford Coppola was born in Detroit, Michigan, on April 7, 1939, to Carmine and Italia Coppola. He received his middle name because he was born in the capital of the American automobile industry, in Henry Ford Hospital. Furthermore, his father was flautist and assistant conductor for the "Ford Sunday Evening Hour" radio concerts. He has used his full name professionally for most of his career, although he temporarily suppressed his middle name in the early 1980s when he heard that people tend to dismiss as an upstart someone who calls himself by three names. (His director's credit on The Outsiders reads "directed by Francis Coppola.") But he eventually reinstated "Ford" at the behest of distributors who wanted him to keep his full name for consistency's sake.

Young Francis was raised in a second-generation Italian American family. He was the second of three offspring, with an older brother, August, and a younger sister, Talia. He attended no less than twenty-two schools, necessitated by his father's travels around the country at various times conducting the pit band for touring stage shows. But his childhood was spent mostly in Queens, and he thus has always considered his roots to be in New York.

Because his family moved around so much, Francis was all too often the new kid on the block. He was skinny and awkward and describes himself in those days as an ugly duckling, comparing himself to Ichabod Crane, the graceless, scrawny central character in Washington Irving's *Legend of Sleepy Hollow.* (Perhaps he recalled this childhood memory when he served as executive producer on a film adaptation of *Sleepy Hollow* in 1999.)

While Francis was enrolled at New York City School P.S. 109 (the same school attended by the hero of *You're a Big Boy Now,* his first Hollywood studio film), he suffered a great misfortune. In 1949, when he was nine, there was a polio epidemic in the New York area. After a Cub Scout outing in which the troop got caught in a deluge, Francis was dispatched to Jamaica Hospital in Queens with a stiff neck. The hospital did not have room for all of the polio cases, so there were racks of youngsters billeted in the corridors, he among them. The next day he tried to get out of bed only to fall on the floor. He could no longer move his arms and legs. Francis was paralyzed for a year, which he spent in his bedroom at home.

No other children came to visit, because polio was a contagious disease. But nearly half a century later, when he made *Jack,* a film about a freakish kid with no friends, he remembered when, as a polio victim, he longed to play with other children. Still, some of his relatives brought him presents to cheer him up. "I had a television, an 8 mm movie projector, a tape recorder, a ventriloquist's dummy, and puppets," he recalls; "I became a ventriloquist and a puppeteer. I watched television a lot."[3] After nine months, young Francis began to recover, and he went back to school.

The experience had been traumatic for Francis, who was left permanently with a slight limp. Indeed, the memory of this childhood episode surfaces in a monologue delivered by the hero of his film *The Conversation,* who remembers being paralyzed as a child. Significantly, the gadgets Francis had been given to occupy his time while he was quarantined continued to interest him, thereby beginning a lifelong preoccupation with technology. He cut together 8 mm home movies that his family had shot and invented stories out of them—tales in which he would always come out as the hero. Francis employed his tape recorder to add sound to these movies. He would then show his synchronized films to the neighborhood kids and charge admission. "I had a little movie company there on 212th Street in Queens," he says.[4]

Coppola realizes in retrospect that these home movies were the genesis of his ambition to become a filmmaker, someone who could bring together scenery, lights, dramatic action, and music to tell a story on film. His interest in movies was further sparked by his brother August, who took him to matinees at a movie theater on Queens Boulevard. He loved adventure films with Errol Flynn and horror movies—like the Bela Lugosi classic *Dracula,* which he would remake some four decades later.

Talia Shire, his younger sister, recalls that, for her generation, Italian American parents wanted their sons to enter one of the professions, like law or medicine. Therefore, when Francis asked his mother for money to direct a home movie with a little Kodak camera, she refused. Francis recalls going "to the janitor, who gave me a quarter to help me."[5]

At age fifteen Francis won a scholarship to play the tuba in the band at the New York Military Academy at Cornwall-on-Hudson, where he transferred in his junior year of high school. Still the awkward, sickly adolescent, he hated what he termed the "phoney baloney" regime at the military school, with its overemphasis on sports, from which he was excluded because of his limp. Finally, when the script and lyrics he wrote for a school musical were revised by the faculty without his consent, he angrily quit the academy. Francis knocked around New York City for a few days and experienced some little adventures that he would later recall when he was making *You're a Big Boy Now*—in which the hero rambles around New York and gets into trouble. He transferred in due course to Great Neck High on Long Island, from which he graduated in 1956.

His heartfelt performance in the title role of Rostand's *Cyrano de Bergerac,* plus some plays he had written, secured for him a drama scholarship for Hofstra University, in Hempstead, New York, where he majored in Theater Arts. Since Coppola had not attended any one high school long enough to make friends, Hofstra was important for him in that he developed a circle of friends among the theater majors.

Two of his classmates, Ronald Colby and Robert Spiotta, would later be involved in producing some of his films. James Caan, who would appear in *The Godfather* and other Coppola pictures, was another classmate, as was Lainie Kazan, whom Coppola would cast in *One from the Heart.* Coppola participated in a variety of activities while attending Hofstra: He contributed short stories and one-act plays to *The Word,* the student magazine, thereby developing his skills as a creative writer. And he directed successful student productions of Eugene O'Neill's one-acter, *Rope,* and Tennessee Williams's *A Streetcar Named Desire.* Coppola's productions were much admired for the technical proficiency with which he mounted them, and he finally won the Hofstra Award for outstanding service to the Hofstra Theater Arts Department, conferred on him by the chair of the department.

Nevertheless, he was still fascinated by cinema and founded the Hofstra Cinema Workshop, a club that screened 16 mm prints of classic films. After watching *Ten Days that Shook the World* (1928, a film about the Russian Revolution), *Ivan the Terrible* (1946), and other movies made by the legendary Russian director Sergei Eisenstein, Coppola wanted more than ever to be a movie director. "On Monday I was in the theater," he remembers. "On Tuesday I wanted to be a filmmaker." Still he continued to devote himself to stage projects for the time being. "I was dying to make a film," he explains, but he followed Eisenstein's example by gaining experience in the theater before devoting himself to a film career.[6] Coppola learned how to build and light sets, as well as how to direct actors for stage productions, because that is precisely how Eisenstein began. In due course he sold his car to purchase a 16 mm movie camera. He attempted to make a short film about a mother whose children disappear mysteriously during a trip to the country, but he possessed neither the experience nor the technical expertise to complete the project. Nevertheless, he had acquired a well-rounded experience in theater production while at Hofstra.

Hoping to gain the expertise necessary to be a bona fide filmmaker, Coppola enrolled in the master's program in film at the University of California at Los Angeles (UCLA) after his graduation from college in 1960. At the time that Coppola entered the graduate program in film at UCLA, attending a film school had not yet become fashionable on university campuses. Film was simply not considered a serious academic major. Indeed, the UCLA film school was housed in wooden Quonset huts left over from World War II, which were situated in a wooded area that was isolated from the rest of the campus and the rest of the student body. Most of the film students were older than Coppola, and he experienced none of the camaraderie that he fondly remembered from the Hofstra Theater Arts Department. Carroll Ballard, who would later direct *The Black Stallion* (1979) with Coppola as his producer, states that the atmosphere was "competitive and ego-driven" and hence not very congenial—many of the students pictured themselves as the next Stanley Kubrick.[7]

"All they knew," adds Coppola, "was how to criticize the lazy ways of Hollywood film producers," implying that they alone would be capable of making great motion pictures. Still, he made a few friends, including Steve Burum (who would photograph both *The Outsiders* and *Rumble Fish* for Coppola in the years ahead), Dennis Jakob (who subsequently served as a consultant on Coppola's *Apocalypse Now*), and Jack Hill (who worked with Coppola on his early low-budget films).

For the most part Coppola was disenchanted with the quality of the teaching and the limited filmmaking facilities at the UCLA film school: "We were given minuscule amounts of 8 mm film. We were put in a field and told to bring back a film."[8] Gradually, the students were taught to work with sound. They occasionally had access to a 16 mm camera and eventually to a Moviola to edit the footage they had shot. Furthermore, Coppola found the curriculum too close to that of a vocational training school. Since he had been schooled in the theater at Hofstra, he yearned to learn more about acting and directing, not just about the technical side of cinema.

Coppola did manage to put together a promising featurette while at UCLA, a slight comedy entitled *Aymonn the Terrible*. It included a reference to Eisenstein's *Ten Days That Shook the World,* which contains a striking shot of a huge bust of the former czar. Coppola's scenario centers on Aymonn, a narcissistic sculptor who creates a twelve-foot bust of himself. The picture was photographed in part by Steve Burum, who was considered the best cinematographer in the film program.

One of the faculty was former film director Dorothy Arzner (*Craig's Wife,* 1936), the best-known woman director in Hollywood in the 1930s. She was impressed with Coppola's student films and encouraged him to pursue a career as a commercial film director. Nonetheless, the notion of entering the movie business by way of one's film school training was simply unheard of at the time. The common practice in the Hollywood studios was for an aspiring movie director to serve an apprenticeship in a film studio, where he would have to work his way up to the status of director by way of lesser jobs. So Coppola's prospects for carving out a career as a Hollywood director were not very promising at that point.

Meanwhile, Coppola was perennially broke. He could barely exist on the ten-dollar-a-week allowance his father sent him, and he also had to pay his tuition. He finally saw some light at the end of the tunnel when some friends of his suggested that he make a nudie film. He wrote a script and shopped it around until he managed to raise two thousand dollars to shoot the picture. At age twenty-one Coppola was entering the film business on the very bottom rung of the ladder by making a short entitled *The Peeper.* It was the only chance he had, Coppola explains, to actually "fool around with a camera and cut a film."[9]

The movie had a "cute" little premise, he recalls. Benjamin Jabowski, a would-be voyeur, hears about a photographer who is shooting pin-up pictures in the building next door to his apartment. The flimsy plotline deals with Ben's efforts to sneak a peek at the photo sessions. But all of his attempts to do so backfire in a farcical fashion. For example, he laboriously hauls a gigantic telescope up to his room and focuses it on the window of the photographer's studio across the way, but the lens is so powerful that all he glimpses is a belly button.

Undeterred, Ben then peeks at the girls through the skylight on the roof above the studio. But he becomes so distraught when the photographer catches him in the act that he falls through the skylight into the studio below. Slapstick episodes like this in the movie prompt Coppola to describe *The Peeper* as a sort of "Tom and Jerry" cartoon. Actually the film may be looked upon as implicitly foreshadowing *The Conversation,* which deals very seriously with another kind of eavesdropping—that of a professional surveillance technician.

Coppola constructed some simple, minimal sets in an abandoned department store in Venice, a town near Los Angeles. The sets consisted of four flats with pictures hung on them. "I had so little money, that I had no place to sleep, except on the set," he remembers. It was very depressing to shoot scenes with a girl cavorting on a bed during the day "and then have to sleep in the same bed at night."[10]

When he sought a distributor to release *The Peeper,* Coppola found no takers for his soft-core, slapstick flick. Finally he showed it to a small-time distributor who already had a rather silly Western skin flick on hand called *The Wide Open Spaces.* This little item was about a drunken cowpoke who gets conked on the noggin by a rock. Afterward he sees naked girls instead of cows sauntering around the prairie. The company asked Coppola to intercut his film with theirs in order to have a saleable commodity. Coppola accordingly devised some new material in order to combine *The Peeper* with the topless Western. He then had to raise an additional three thousand dollars to shoot the new scenes. One of the backers balked at kicking in more funds for the new version of the film. According to Coppola's classmate Frank Zuniga, who helped with the editing of the film, Coppola then slumped to the floor and began clutching his stomach as if he were having some sort of seizure. With that, the backer anted up more money for the project. This was not the last time that Coppola would manage to get an associate on a film to see things his way by what appeared to be a sudden attack of illness.[11]

The plot gimmick that Coppola dreamed up to provide the narrative frame for the two stories he was knitting together into one film is built around a character from each film who shares his tale with the other. The resulting movie, eventually entitled *Tonight for Sure,* was first released in 1961. In it two crusty codgers, Benjamin Jabowski (Karl Schanzer) and Samuel Hill (Donald Kenney), fancy themselves moral crusaders. They meet in a tawdry strip joint on Sunset Strip called the Harem Club, where they plan to stage a protest about the lurid shows presented there.

Each of them recounts in flashback how he arrived at his present up-standing moral stance. They are really hypocrites who furtively ogle the strippers on stage with feigned disapproval while they are ostensibly plot-ting their protest demonstration against such lascivious shows. (One of the strippers is dressed as a cow girl and, thus, prefigures one of the Playboy Bunnies who is similarly attired while performing in a USO show in Vietnam in *Apocalypse Now.*) Coppola later described the expanded version of his original film as "an inane comedy, in which you saw a couple of boobs once in a while."[12] Some commentators on Coppola's work who have not seen *Tonight for Sure* have assumed that there is full frontal nudity on display in the film, which is certainly not the case. The picture qualifies as a "nudie" because of the succession of topless girls who parade through the movie. Consequently, it comes across as an extended version of a bawdy burlesque skit rather than a porno flick.

Although both the Cowie and Schumacher biographies of Coppola assert that *Tonight for Sure* is a black-and-white movie, all of the footage is in color (albeit muddy, dingy color), with the color photography for the Coppola segments shot mostly by his classmate Jack Hill. Carmine Coppola (listed in the credits as Carmen) supplied the jazzy score for the picture and would score other Coppola films in the future.

Coppola was so eager for screen credits at the beginning of his career that in the film's opening credits he generously gave himself sole credit as director of the entire movie—although he estimates that only about half of the complete film was his work.

After completing *Tonight for Sure*, Coppola was commissioned to work on another skin flick. A producer had bought the American distribution rights to a 1958 German picture entitled *Mit Eva Fing Die Sünde* (*Sin Began with Eve*), which had already been dubbed into English. He commissioned Coppola to interpolate some nudie footage in color into the black-and-white film, in much the same way he had amalgamated *The Peeper* and *The Wide Open Spaces* into a single film. The final film was retitled *The Bellboy and the Playgirls* (and not *The Belt Girls and the Playboy*, as Chaillet and Vincent erroneously assert).

Since this was the only Coppola movie I had not seen at the time I interviewed him, I asked him about it. He answered that this picture got him a few days' work, "adding five three-minute nudie sketches in color to a stupid German movie that had been shot in black-and-white," amounting to fifteen minutes of additional footage.

The Bellboy and the Playgirls was long thought to be lost after its initial release on the grind circuit in 1962 and a subsequent brief exposure on videotape. So no previous commentator on Coppola's work had apparently seen it. But one print of the film, owned by a private collector of Coppola memorabilia, surfaced recently, and I was able to view it. Having now seen the movie, I can attest that Coppola's recollections of it are faulty.

Since Coppola's color footage is easily identifiable in the finished film, it is possible to state that the five Coppola sequences add up to nearly fifty minutes of screen time, thereby accounting for about half of the total ninety-four-minute running time of the finished product. This is about three times more footage than Coppola remembers.

At any rate, Al Locatelli once more designed the sets for the Coppola segments, and Jack Hill returned as cinematographer on the picture. The color sketches feature Playboy Bunny June Wilkinson. In one of them, Coppola recalls, there were five girls sitting at dressing tables in a hotel room in various stages of undress. During filming one of the girls took Coppola aside and confided, "I'm only seventeen, and my father is going to kill me." He replied, "Well, you can keep your bra on." Since the girls were hired and paid to do these scenes, the producer reprimanded Coppola for making this accommodation to one of the girls when he saw the completed footage.

Because this movie is virtually inaccessible today, I shall describe it in some detail as an example of Coppola's apprenticeship in the movie business. The original German film, directed by Fritz Umgelter, stars Willy Fritsch, an enduring actor in the German cinema for four decades. His career was winding down when he made *Mit Eva*. On the other hand, the career of Karen Dor, his co-star, was just taking off, and she would later appear in two James Bond films.

The plot of the German portions of the present film concerns Dinah (Karen Dor), a young actress who refuses to do a seduction scene during rehearsals for a stage play. She claims that she is too "old-fashioned" to appear in such a compromising scene on stage before a live audience. Gregor, the director (Willie Fritsch), endeavors to loosen her up and take away her inhibitions by telling her randy stories about sexual relations throughout the centuries. There is a flashback to ancient Greece in which a young maiden is advised by a Don Juan with a wink, "Men believe that wives are for procreation and mistresses are for recreation." Another flashback, to the Middle Ages, shows a lascivious knight seducing a damsel while her husband is away at the Crusades. Gregor eventually coaxes Dinah into going through with the love scene in the play.

Into the German film's tedious plot Coppola inserts a naughty storyline about George (Don Kenney), the bellboy from the Happy Holiday Hotel next door to the theater. George, addressing the camera, informs the viewer that he is taking a correspondence course in how to be popular with women. He is observing the rehearsals of Gregor's play from the catwalk in the rafters above the stage in order to learn how the young man in the play ingratiates himself with his unwilling girlfriend. He then goes back to the hotel and seeks to gain entrance to room 299—which is occupied by Madame Whimplepoole (June Wilkinson) and her Pink Lace Girls—in order to make time with the girls.

The madame assures George that she is a designer of exotic ladies' lingerie and that the scantily clad girls merely model the undies for retailers. In one of the doubles entendres with which Coppola has laced these scenes, Madame points to one of the girls wearing a diaphanous nighty and declares, "This is one of our very best bedroom accessories." Similarly, George adds in a voice-over, "These girls are hiding something, and I must uncover it."

George is unconvinced by the madame's explanation. Masquerading as a telephone repair man, he attempts to install surveillance equipment in room 299 (shades of Coppola's later feature *The Conversation*). As in *Tonight for Sure,* this erotic romp at times slides into slapstick. At one point the girls, who are fed up with George's obsession with them, stage a free-for-all in which they pelt George with dollops of cold cream from the jars on the dressing tables. The scene recalls the pie-throwing fights from the era of silent comedy. They finally manage to discourage George's attentions by luring him to participate in a game of strip poker—after they have stacked the deck against him. So it is George who loses his clothes. He flees from room 299 in his shorts after wrapping himself in a window curtain.

At the fade-out the chastened George is watching the lovemaking on the theater stage below as he sits once more in the rafters. Once again addressing the camera, he says that he is aware that he has failed to become a Lothario—for now at least—but he is going to continue his correspondence course in how to be popular with women.

Fritz Umgelter's stilted handling of the action in the German film makes for fairly stiff performances from his cast, and no amount of creative manipulation of the two story lines on Coppola's part could salvage the film as a whole. Still Coppola provides plenty of door slamming and misunderstandings, after the manner of old-fashioned French farce, for his segments of the movie.

Coppola does not apologize for his exploitation films. "It was the only way for me to work with a camera and actually make a movie," he explains. He may have gained experience by working on *The Bellboy and the Playgirls,* but it did not enrich his bank account. In fact, Jack Hill received an exposure meter worth twenty-five dollars for his efforts, and Coppola himself did not get much more. He was still officially a student at the UCLA film school, and he was severely criticized by his classmates "for deciding to go into exploitation films," as he puts it. "I was called a cop-out because I was willing to compromise."[13]

Tonight for Sure was reissued in 1983, presumably to cash in on Coppola's celebrity. *Variety* at the time dubbed the sixty-six-minute exercise in primitive filmmaking "disreputable" and "ridiculous," adding that because of the absence of "below-the-belt frontal nudity" it would no doubt have received an R rating if it had been submitted for classification by the industry film censor at its re-release. In any event, it is not the stag movie its title seems to suggest. In fact, by today's standards, the film has no more nudity than an R-rated commercial film is allowed, as *Variety* points out.

The next phase of Coppola's apprenticeship as an aspiring young filmmaker began with his accepting employment from independent producer-director Roger Corman, known as the "King of the B's" along Hollywood's Poverty Row, which churned out low-budget pictures. These small-time studios were also known as "Gower Gulch" because some of them were located on Gower Street. Corman's aim was to exploit the youth market, which still flocked to drive-ins to see his cheaply made, sensational, action-packed movies. Corman's B pictures typically ran seventy-five minutes or less and were based on weak scripts. They were shot in two weeks or so without stars or even many accomplished actors in the casts, and they employed minimal, inexpensive sets and locations.

When Corman was looking for an assistant who would work for peanuts, he approached Dorothy Arzner, Coppola's mentor at UCLA, for suggestions, and she immediately put Corman on to Coppola, her most promising student.

Coppola in turn phoned Corman's office and was told by the office manager to send over some samples of his screenwriting efforts and that she would get back to him. He had recently been notified by the phone company that his phone was to be shut off because he had not paid the bill. He remembers sitting by the phone, praying, "Please don't cut off!" In a stroke of luck, the lady called back with a job offer only a couple of hours before his phone was disconnected.[14]

Coppola was the first of several young filmmakers to whom Corman provided an entry into the film business in Hollywood, a roster that includes Martin Scorsese (*Raging Bull*), Jonathan Demme (*Silence of the Lambs*), and Peter Bogdanovich (*The Last Picture Show*). To his credit, Corman showed his fledgling filmmakers the ropes and taught them his efficient penny-pinching methods for making a movie on the double and on the cheap.

Corman actually thought it propitious that Coppola had been exposed to the soft-core porn market, because it meant he had already had some experience in cutting corners while making a low-budget picture. Having been trapped temporarily in the skin flick racket, Coppola comments, "I started to move up the exploitation film ladder." He was willing to do any kind of production work to learn his craft, and Corman provided him with ample opportunities to do just that.[15]

In his autobiography Corman recounts that Coppola's first assignment involved a Russian intergalactic space picture originally entitled *Nebo Zowet* (*The Heavens Call*, 1959), which "I had acquired rather inexpensively from Mosfilm." He asked Coppola to edit the picture "and to write and loop English dialogue, so it made sense to an American audience," and then to shoot and insert some special effects into the science-fiction picture. The film was released in the United States as *Battle Beyond the Sun* (1963). In Corman's autobiography Coppola is cited as saying "Roger's thinking" was that he could "jazz it up for American audiences. I had to translate the images into an English storyline" with dialogue that "fit the actors' mouth movements." Coppola did not understand a word of Russian, so he simply watched each scene and made up what he guessed the characters might be saying to each other and then dubbed in the new English dialogue in place of the original Russian dialogue on the sound track. "I'd stay up most of the night to do the sci-fi [special effects]," Coppola adds. In order to impress Corman with his industry, he would catch a few hours' sleep at the editing table; so, when Corman arrived in the morning, he would find Coppola slumped over the Moviola, asleep.[16]

In one scene a Russian astronaut has a vision in which a golden astronaut holding a golden torch materializes on a crag. The vision is apparently meant to signify hope, Coppola explains. But Corman instructed him to replace the golden astronaut with "a vision of two moon monsters . . . battling it out." Coppola accordingly manufactured the monsters out of foam rubber and latex for the scene: "I shot that for him and cut it into the film." The result, Coppola comments laconically, was a violent scene "where the Russians had the Golden Astronaut of Hope."[17] At any rate, Coppola declines to comment on the results of his handiwork—he never bothered to see the finished product.

Corman did not want American filmgoers to know that they were watching a recycled Russian movie, so he told Coppola to invent fictitious American names for the individuals listed in the movie's opening credits. Consequently, the picture's cast was ostensibly headed by "Edd Perry and Arla Powell," while the director was said to be "Alexander Kozyr." The only authentic names in the credits belonged to Francis Coppola, who signed the film as associate producer, Roger Corman, who was listed as producer, and Carmen Coppola (Carmine), who was credited as composer of the underscore. Francis Coppola, of course, was gratified to have gotten a screen credit at last on a legitimate commercial film rather than on an underground skin flick.

The plot Coppola concocted for this retread of a Russian sci-fi picture revolves around rival space missions to Mars staffed by astronauts from two antagonistic powers, North Hemis and South Hemis (the astronauts were Russian and American in the original film). Reviewers found this low-rent space opera absurd and suggested that Corman should have left it in the Russian cin bin where he found it. But Coppola recalled that at least one reviewer thought the special effects—including Coppola's rubber space monsters—were good enough to keep the kids at the drive-ins from setting fire to the concession stand.

Corman was pleased that the picture turned a profit, while Coppola, for his part, was pleased that Corman had provided him with a small office and editing room as a reward for his work on the movie—although Coppola had netted only $250 for six months of labor on the project. Corman "started to see me as an all-purpose guy," Coppola says.[18] The producer would call Coppola whenever he was in need of a low-priced assistant, usually paying Coppola $400 a week at this point—a king's ransom for a graduate student in film school. He was gaining experience, moreover, as a dialogue director, a script doctor, and a second unit director at various times.

Working for Corman, Coppola explains, "I felt as if I were climbing the ranks of the cinema industry." His peers at UCLA, as ever, regarded his employment as Corman's "roustabout" as treason. They insisted that they would never stoop to working on exploitation films for the youth market and snidely predicted that Coppola would wind up a Hollywood hack. "I was prepared to do anything in order to make more films," Coppola counters, and the best opportunity afforded him at the time was under the aegis of Roger Corman, who, after all, possessed a good deal of commercial savvy when it came to turning out pictures on the studio conveyor belt.[19] In short, working for Corman amounted to an intensive practical course in the mechanics of film production.

In the meantime, UCLA's film school was conducting a script competition, offering a two-thousand-dollar prize to the winner of the Samuel Goldwyn Award for the best student screenplay. In a single marathon working session Coppola expanded the scenario of an earlier short film, *The Two Christophers,* into a seventy-page screenplay entitled *Pilma, Pilma,* while consuming innumerable mugs of coffee. The story concerns an extreme case of sibling rivalry, whereby a deeply disturbed youngster who is obsessively jealous of his older brother plots to murder him. According to Coppola, it was pure Tennessee Williams Southern Gothic, filled with the sort of lurid violence that characterizes Williams's plays. Corman was exceedingly proud when his protégé was the winner of the prestigious Goldwyn Award, and he took ads in the trade papers announcing Coppola's prize.

One day Corman inquired if Coppola could recommend a sound engineer he could hire for *The Young Racers* (1963), a movie he planned to direct about sports car racing that would follow the Grand Prix racing circuit across Europe and incorporate footage from various racing meets. With youthful bravado Coppola volunteered, "I'll do the sound." With that, he says in Corman's autobiography, "I immediately got the Nagra sound recorder out of the closet at the office and went home to read the manual." The first step was, "Push button A . . .," and Coppola proceeded from there to master the art of sound recording.

"I had always thought a Grand Prix film would be fun to shoot with the races and the crowds," says Corman.[20] Robert Towne, who would later write some major scenes for *The Godfather,* also served as an assistant to Corman on the movie. Coppola was not only sound man but second unit director as well. Coppola betrayed his amateur standing as a sound recordist, however, when Corman screened rushes of the first day's footage. Cinematographer Floyd Crosby (*High Noon*) commented that the dialogue was inaudible and scornfully blamed the tyro sound man. Coppola unabashedly blamed Crosby for allowing the noise of the camera to be picked up on the sound track. Corman feels that, because Coppola did not hesitate to talk back to the older and more experienced film technician, he showed that he had guts.

In retrospect, Coppola explains that the movie was being shot with a camera that was somewhat noisier than the average motion picture camera (Corman never could afford state-of-the-art equipment). And yet the camera was not equipped with a blimp, a device that blankets the camera noise, since Corman's itinerant caravan was traveling with a minimum of equipment. As a result, it was not possible to shoot the movie and muffle the camera noise on the sound track. "So we had to redupe the dialogue for the whole picture," Coppola concludes. Mark Damon, who played a retired racing driver, was not available when the redubbing was done, and so his lines were spoken by William Shatner.[21] In the end Corman says that he was satisfied with the sound track of the picture (although Coppola inexplicably received no screen credit as sound man).

"Working as a team for the races was quite exhilarating for me," Coppola comments. "I was soundman and second unit director."[22] In the latter capacity he shot most of the actual racing footage that was incorporated into the picture. According to William Campbell, who played a champion racer in the picture, Coppola would go out onto the race track in the middle of a race with his hand-held camera, "shooting pictures of these damn racing drivers, driving past him within six feet!"[23] As a matter of fact, Coppola's exploits were somewhat less perilous than Campbell imagined. He would take his camera to trackside, lie on the ground, and photograph the racing cars as they whooshed by him, but he was not lying on the track, as Campbell suggests.

When the movie was released, the critics basically felt that in making the movie Corman had aimed merely to make a routine low-budget actioner and had not even accomplished that minimal goal. *Variety* summarized "the hackneyed story" as having to do with Joe Machin (William Campbell), a daredevil Grand Prix champion and womanizer, "with a girl in every pit stop," who turns out to have "a heart of gold beating beneath the grease and goggles."[24] But the feeble plotline about Joe's multiple affairs is soft-pedaled in favor of following him from one racing event to the next. The movie engages the viewer's attention only intermittently, when it thrusts the spectator into the cockpit with the driver to go careening around the race track at championship speeds—thanks to Coppola's hand-held camera. So there were just enough thrills and spills amid the atmosphere of screeching tires and roaring crowds to satisfy the drive-in trade.

After the location shooting for *The Young Racers* had been completed in England with the Grand Prix at Liverpool, Corman remembers, "I decided to finance a second film." After all, he had already paid the travel expenses of the cast and crew to bring them to Europe for the first film. Therefore, shooting two movies back-to-back and employing the same crew and some of the same actors would really be a money-saving enterprise.

Corman had brought over to Europe a Volkswagen minibus that he had outfitted with the technical equipment needed to shoot a film. "We had the minibus with the cameras, lights, and dollies," Corman continues. "What we didn't have was a work permit. The most logical place to shoot the film was Dublin, because we could just ferry the minibus over from Liverpool. Ireland was much looser with labor permits." Corman wanted to keep the film's budget to twenty thousand dollars, the amount he had left over from shooting *Racers*. He told Coppola that "if he could come up with an idea for a film in Ireland, he could direct it."[25]

Coppola was enthusiastic about the prospect of directing a feature film all his own. He told Corman, "Let me take a camera and some of the equipment and staff, and make a low-budget psychological thriller." That night he came up with the concept of a "Hitchcock-type" horror scene and pitched it to Corman the following day.

Dementia 13 (1963)

Coppola described to Corman the following scene, in which, he says, he had included "everything I knew Roger would like:"[26] "A man goes to a pond and takes off his clothes, picks up five dolls, ties them together, goes under the water, and dives down, where he finds the body of a seven-year-old girl with her hair floating in the current. . . . Then he gets axed to death." Corman responded enthusiastically, "Change the man to a woman, and you've got a picture, kid!"[27] Coppola willingly complied. Coppola now concedes that at that juncture he had no clear idea about who the woman was or what she was doing in the pond. So he arrived in Ireland with no script but with a secretary Corman had sent along to accompany him after Corman himself had returned to Hollywood. She was mandated by Corman to see to it that the young Coppola stayed within the stipulated budget. But Coppola sweet-talked her into allowing him to transfer the entire twenty thousand dollars that Corman had allocated for the movie into his personal bank account.

Moreover, in Ireland Coppola met a British producer, Raymond Stross (*The Fox*). Coppola recalls that Stross was mightily impressed with the young director's description of his movie as a slasher-type picture, which was obviously designed to cash in on Hitchcock's highly successful *Psycho*, "with a lot of people getting killed with axes, and so forth."[28] Stross matched Corman's $20,000 with another $20,000 of production capital in exchange for the British distribution rights to the picture. Corman got to hear how Coppola by some adroit wheeling and dealing had managed to swell his own bank account with $40,000 of production money and was accountable to no one as to how he spent it. The producer accordingly wanted to withdraw his half of the money from the production—to no avail, since the entire amount was in Coppola's own account.

Coppola then settled down to write a screenplay, working virtually non-stop for three frantic days and nights. He developed his original concept into a full-length script, which he typed directly onto mimeograph stencils for immediate distribution to cast and crew. He had initially intended to call the movie *Dementia,* but Corman soon discovered that that title had been preempted by an hour-long 1955 film that depicted the Freud-ian fantasies of a troubled woman. So Coppola added the legendary un-lucky number to his title and came up with *Dementia 13*.

To shoot the picture, Coppola was allowed to use the facilities of Ardmore Studios in Dublin for free, since Raymond Stross was part owner of the studio. Coppola, with his minimal crew of nine, shot for nine days at Ardmore—which was the length of time decreed by Corman for principal photography. In addition, Coppola did some additional location work in the country for a couple of days, thereby going over-schedule slightly. He still completed principal photography in record time, but he did not shoot the picture in three days as some commentators on the film have asserted.

Once production was underway, Corman sent Coppola frequent tele-grams urging him to include generous helpings of sex and violence in the picture to satisfy Corman's drive-in following, and Coppola did his best to comply. He had, after all, observed how some young filmmakers would try to straddle the fence between making an art house film and an exploitation film and would end up with some sort of hybrid "that wasn't good enough for an art film or funky enough as an exploitation film."[29] In short, Coppola had no illusions about what sort of movie Corman expected him to make and attempted to meet his producer's expectations.

A group of Coppola's fellow students from the UCLA film school came over to Dublin at their own expense to help out with the production. John Vicario, the camera operator, was accompanied by his girlfriend, Eleanor Neil, who had a degree from UCLA's Art Department. When she arrived at the farmhouse that was Coppola's production headquarters on location, she found Coppola, who had been up all night, shirtless and disheveled, pounding out some pages of the script on mimeo masters. She was im-pressed with his dedication. Eleanor Neil assisted the art director, Albert Locatelli, and eventually earned a screen credit as a set decorator. Mean-while, her relationship with Vicario cooled as she and Coppola became an item. They eventually married after the picture was completed, in Las Ve-gas on February 2, 1963.

The cast of *Dementia 13* not only included some of the actors from *The Young Racers,* such as William Campbell and Patrick Magee, but also some of the members of Dublin's distinguished Abbey Theater, such as Eithne Dunn, whom Coppola coaxed into playing character parts.

The plot that Coppola conjured up for *Dementia 13* initially centers on John Haloran and his wife Louise. While John rows Louise, a brassy blonde, on a pitch-dark lake they argue about his mother's will, which stipu-lates that Louise will profit from Lady Haloran's will only as long as John, who has a weak heart, remains alive. John, exhausted from the strain of rowing as well as from the quarrel, abruptly succumbs to a heart attack before they return to shore. The cruel Louise, after watching her husband expire, actually slaps his face in irritation at the thought of his jeopardizing her claim to part of his mother's estate by his ill-timed death. The scheming Louise pushes John's corpse overboard in order to hide his death and subsequently informs Lady Haloran (Eithne Dunn) and her other two sons, Richard (William Campbell), a sculptor, and Billy (Bart Patton), that John has flown to New York on business.

Lady Haloran, who presides over Castle Haloran, continues to mourn morbidly for her deceased daughter Kathleen, seven years dead, who perished in the lake as a child. Louise plots to drive Lady Haloran mad so that she can break the aging woman's will in the event that John's body is eventually discovered. In pursuing her plan, she ties some of Kathleen's nursery dolls together and dives into the lake, leaving them at the bottom of the lake, with a view to their eventually surfacing as an eerie reminder to Lady Haloran of Kathleen's death. While under water, Louise spies a life-sized replica of Kathleen's body lying next to a gravestone on the lake's floor. When Louise rises to the lake's surface close to the shore, she is bludgeoned to death by an unseen attacker. This episode, of course, is a revised version of the scene that Coppola originally pitched to Corman as the basis of his film.

Lady Haloran pays a visit to Kathleen's dollhouse, which she has turned into a musty shrine to her dead daughter. There she discovers the effigy of Kathleen—it apparently floated to the surface of the lake, was retrieved by the psycho loose on the estate, and was placed in Kathleen's playhouse. Just then the ax-wielder appears and savagely smashes the dollhouse to pieces. Lady Haloran flees the premises and narrowly escapes being murdered.

Richard's fiancée Kane (Mary Mitchel) endeavors to convince him to leave the doom-ridden estate, particularly after Simon (Karl Schanzer), an old friend of the Halorans, is dispatched by an ax after he discovers Louise's corpse hidden in the woods. Justin Caleb, the family doctor (Patrick Magee), then devises a scheme to smoke out the killer.

Dr. Caleb orders the lake to be drained, and a gravestone turns up, bearing the inscription "Forgive me, Kathleen dear." Caleb recalls that Billy has been suffering from nightmares ever since Kathleen's death, so the doctor strongly suspects that Billy knows more about Kathleen's death than he has ever divulged. Accordingly, at the wedding reception for Richard and Kane on the lawn of the estate, Caleb confronts Billy with the ubiquitous wax figure of Kathleen's corpse, which had turned up in the dollhouse earlier.

He forces Billy to admit that he accidentally pushed Kathleen into the pond when they were scuffling about, playing a children's game on the shore. In fact, the effigy of Kathleen is really a wax doll Billy made to "relieve his guilt for her death," as the doctor puts it. With that, Billy goes berserk and is thereby revealed to be a homicidal maniac whose obsession with death has led him to murder Louise and others. Just as he is about to attack Kane with an ax lying conveniently on the lawn, Dr. Caleb shoots him dead. Caleb then melodramatically buries Billy's hatchet in the skull of the effigy, to dramatize the fact that the curse on the Haloran family has been shattered at last.

It is easy to pick flaws in *Dementia 13*. For one thing, Dr. Caleb's explanation of Billy's psychosis is "cookbook Freud," a bizarre elaboration on Freud's theory of neurotic guilt. The screenplay has an interesting premise, but the ending is too abrupt and hence unsatisfactory. For another thing, the performances are uneven: while some of the cast underact, Patrick Magee gives an unbridled performance and well nigh chews up the scenery. In addition, Karl Schanzer turns in a performance as Simon that is just as amateurish as the one he gave as the Peeping Tom in *Tonight for Sure*.

On the other hand, veteran actress Eithne Dunn as the disturbed matriarch steals nearly every scene she is in. Another point on the positive side is that the limited budget and short shooting schedule inspired Coppola to improvise practical solutions to production limitations in a rather inventive manner. For example, because most of the scenes took place at night or in murky interiors, Coppola photographed many scenes in deep, jarring shadows. He was therefore able to get away with simple, sparsely furnished settings because they were shrouded in shadows and, in this fashion, to conceal the film's meager production values. More importantly, the murky, darkened sets were perfectly attuned to the grim atmosphere of a horror picture. Another plus for the film is that the pace never lags, since the suspenseful story is punctuated with not only scenes of violence but smatterings of piquant sex. At one point Richard and Kane are shown embracing passionately on the grounds of the estate while the camera pulls back to reveal Lady Haloran spying on them from her window.

Nevertheless, Corman was not satisfied with Coppola's rough cut. When the director showed it to him back in Hollywood, Corman lambasted the picture immediately after the screening. He criticized the shallow, inept script, which presented a pinwheeling series of murders without enough transitional material to link them together into a coherent narrative. After a stormy shouting match, Coppola convinced Corman that he could film some additional material along with some voice-over narration by various characters on the sound track in order to plug up the holes in the plot. He then shot some additional footage, with Griffith Park in Los Angeles standing in for the Irish countryside.

But Coppola drew the line when Corman insisted on another ax murder to bolster the picture's commercial potential for the drive-in trade. When Coppola adamantly refused to oblige him, Corman commissioned Jack Hill, who had worked on *Tonight for Sure* with Coppola, to write and film a couple of additional scenes to accommodate him. "Roger wanted some more violence, which he got—though not from me," Coppola states laconically.[30] Corman expressed his gratitude to Hill by giving him a screen credit that reads, "Second unit written and directed by Jack Hill."

Not yet finished tinkering with the movie, Corman saddled the picture with a five-minute prologue called the "D-13 Test," in which an actor impersonating a psychiatrist tested filmgoers to ascertain if they were emotionally stable enough to view the movie. The questions he asked the viewers to consider included: "Are you afraid of death by drowning? . . . Have you ever attempted suicide?" This opening, which was presumably part of Hill's second unit work, was used only for the movie's original theatrical release and was jettisoned when *Dementia 13* was released on TV and on videocassette. Finally, in an effort to beef up the film's ad campaign, the sensational posters warned, "Do not see this film alone, or if you have a weak heart."

The majority of film critics ignored *Dementia 13* when it opened in New York in September 1963. Even *Variety,* which normally reviewed lesser Corman efforts like *The Young Racers,* overlooked it. The few reviewers who did notice it dismissed the picture as the sort of teen-oriented "axploitation movie" that was typical of the Corman film factory, made on a microbudget with a shooting schedule to match. One critic opined that the characters were mostly cardboard cutouts and that the plot was drowned in blood. Another reviewer quipped that he was not interested in learning about the fate of the first twelve demented lunatics referred to in the movie's title—number thirteen was quite enough. He added that the wooden dialogue at times seemed muffled and that that, after all, might be a blessing.

Be that as it may, *Dementia 13* did show a modest profit and has been judged more benignly by film historians who have reassessed it over the years. Thus, after it was released to video, *American Film* commented in 1990 that Coppola's skill in portraying cinematic violence in *The Godfather* was already operative in *Dementia 13,* "in which the finest scenes are decidedly the bloodiest"—for example, the "tabloid-lit" scene in which the murderer slaughters Louise, "who should have known better than to take a mid-picture swim in her underwear."[31]

In addition, Cowie sees the picture as a bellwether of Coppola's future career and astutely observes that *Dementia 13* prefigures Coppola's later work by introducing his interest in the family as a source of strife and tragedy—from the neurotic Lady Haloran's endless mourning for her dead daughter Kathleen to her criminally insane son Billy's multiple homicides. Looking back on the movie, Coppola seems satisfied with it. "I think it showed promise; it was imaginative," he comments, appraising it as more than a mere accumulation of clichés. "In many ways it has some of the nicest visuals I have ever done."[32] He may well have in mind the convincing atmosphere of dread created by the shots of the forbidding castle with its shadowy passageways, which is effectively employed to suggest a disquieting atmosphere of fear and foreboding. It is worth noting that there is a homage of sorts to the film in an episode of *The Sopranos* (2001), a TV series about the Mafia. In it the daughter of a Mafia don and her date attend a screening of *Dementia 13* at a New York revival house and are appropriately frightened.

Shortly after Coppola finished his chores on *Dementia 13,* he decided to sever his relationship with Corman. He appreciated the firsthand experience he had obtained as a tyro filmmaker while working under Corman's tutelage, but he was still disgruntled about the additional scenes Corman had insisted that Hill add to the picture. So, in the early winter of 1963, when Coppola was offered a job as screenwriter at $375 a week by Seven Arts, an independent producing organization that later amalgamated with Warner Brothers, he took it. Seven Arts had expressed interest in Coppola on the basis of his winning the 1962 Samuel Goldwyn screenwriting award, a coup that Corman had publicized in the trades while Coppola was in his employ.

Coppola was still a graduate student at UCLA at this point, and he recalls that "the day I got my first job as a screenwriter, there was a big sign on the film school's bulletin board saying, 'Sell out!'" Although some of his fellow students encouraged him to work in the film industry and even came over to Ireland to help him make *Dementia 13*, others treated him with a resentment grounded in jealousy. "I was making money," he explains. "I was already doing what everybody was just talking about."[33]

The Early Screenplays

Seven Arts was in the business of packaging film productions: preparing a first-draft script, obtaining commitments from stars and a director, and then selling the production package to a major studio, which would then finance and produce the movie in question. In 1963 Seven Arts had an option on Carson McCullers's controversial novella, *Reflections in a Golden Eye,* an exercise in Southern Gothic dealing with homosexuality, nymphomania, and other lurid topics. No screenwriter had as yet been able to come up with a viable script from this shocking material. With the option on the book running out, the front office decided to let Coppola, their newest acquisition, take a crack at it. Seven Arts was pleased with the decent screen adaptation of the novella that Coppola was able to turn out in six weeks, and so was John Huston (*The Maltese Falcon*), who was set to direct. But Huston's previous commitments forced him to postpone the venture, and when he finally made the picture he ultimately used a screenplay by Chapman Mortimer and Gladys Hill. The film as finally released endeavors to conjure up some dark melodrama, only to wind up chasing its own tail amid a slew of unlikely plot twists. So Coppola was fortunate not to have his name associated with the final product.

Meanwhile, Seven Arts was still impressed with his version of the script, for his screenplay for *Reflections* showed that he could tackle a job on order and for hire and do it well. So they raised his salary to five hundred dollars a week for the next three years. Coppola eventually worked on eleven scripts, but he only received an official screen credit on three of them, and it is those three films that will be highlighted at this point. To begin with, Coppola received a screen credit as co-writer on two 1966 films on which he worked for Seven Arts: *This Property Is Condemned* and *Is Paris Burning?*

This Property Is Condemned is a one-act play by Tennessee Williams that can be acted on the stage in about twenty minutes. Coppola was familiar with the play, since he had directed it on the stage at Hofstra. The play simply presents a thirteen-year-old girl named Willie Starr who has been deserted by her parents. Willie recounts for a lad named Tom the sad story of her sister Alva, who took care of her until Alva's untimely death from lung cancer. And so it is Alva whom Willie idolizes and wants to imitate. Unfortunately, since Alva was a prostitute in her mother's boarding house/ brothel for railroad men, Willie naively but firmly believes that the kind of life Alva led is the only truly glamorous existence for any girl. Consequently, there is little doubt by play's end that Willie is condemned to take up her sister's sordid way of life.

An enormous amount of expansion was imposed on the play's slender plot to bloat it into nearly two hours of screen time, which is fairly obvious when one views the movie, directed by Sydney Pollack (*Out of Africa*). The three principal authors of the 1966 film version—Fred Coe, Edith Sommer, and Coppola—elaborated Williams's slender little tale far beyond his original conception. The basic format the screenwriters hit upon was to make Williams's play the framing device for the picture. Accordingly, they broke the one-act play roughly in half, presenting the first portion as a prologue to the film and the remaining segment as an epilogue. In this way they utilized almost all of the play's original dialogue in their screenplay. In the prologue of the film, Willie, played by Mary Badham (*To Kill a Mockingbird*), describes her family and present situation to the boy Tom, and in the epilogue she wraps things up by telling Tom what happened to each of them. The scriptwriters then had to devise a full-blown story told in flashback to fit between the prologue and the epilogue. Several of the characters in the picture are derived from people to whom Willie refers in the one-act play.

The one character who is cut from whole cloth in the movie, and who has no discernible counterpart in the play, is Owen Legate (Robert Redford). He is a railroad inspector who hopes to marry Alva (Natalie Wood). But before Owen can make an honest woman of Alva, her life is tragically cut short by lung cancer. Williams told me in conversation that he was understandably disappointed in the finished product. Indeed, he accurately assessed the film as a "vastly expanded and hardly related film with the title taken from a very delicate one-act play. The movie was hardly deserving of the talents of Robert Redford and Natalie Wood." Or, one might add, the talents of Sidney Pollack and Francis Coppola.

It was not uncommon in Hollywood for a platoon of writers to work on the same script. As writer-director Preston Sturges (*The Miracle of Morgan's Creek*) once quipped, writers worked in teams, like piano movers. This was a system Coppola deplored. He estimates that after the script he had prepared with Coe and Sommer was submitted to the front office an additional dozen script doctors tinkered with the screenplay before it was finally completed. And the meandering continuity of the finished film demonstrates that too many cooks well nigh spoiled the broth. The final shooting script was not very good, he recalls in *On the Edge,* "not that our version was much better." Yet Ray Stark, Coppola's immediate boss at Seven Arts, continued to see him as competent and dependable, and raised his salary to a thousand dollars a week. He became known around Seven Arts as a "clutch writer, a troubleshooter salvaging movies that were teetering on the brink of catastrophe."[34]

One project that certainly fit that description of his talents was the war film *Is Paris Burning?,* a joint American-French coproduction to be directed by French director René Clément (*Purple Noon*) and released by Paramount. In early 1965 Stark sent Coppola to Paris to collaborate with the ailing screenwriter Anthony Veiller (*The Night of the Iguana*). Stark saw Coppola as Seven Arts' insurance policy—in the event of the aging Veiller's demise, Coppola was to take over for him. "I was to take the pencil from his hand when it fell out," Coppola states.[35] Veiller was not aware of Coppola's private arrangement with Stark. He saw Coppola as a mere neophyte screenwriter who was to learn his trade from Veiller. "For five weeks, I would go to him every morning at his hotel, and he would mock my work," Coppola recalls.[36] Finally, just as Coppola got fed up with bickering with Veiller, the elderly screenwriter did expire, and Coppola found himself saddled with a mammoth project—a bewildering, multistoried account of the liberation of Paris in 1944, a bloated war epic with an all-star cast, including Charles Boyer, Orson Welles, and Kirk Douglas.

Screenwriter Gore Vidal (*Suddenly Last Summer*) was brought in to help Coppola finish the script, since it was clear that it was too much for a young writer to cope with alone. Like Veiller, Vidal saw their collaboration as a junior-senior relationship, Coppola remembers, but Vidal was much more gracious than Veiller. He would have him work out a scene and then they would go over it.

The film's French producer, Paul Graetz, had made an agreement with the city officials in Paris that the historical events would be depicted in the screenplay in a manner that pictured General Charles de Gaulle as a gallant French leader. In return, they would allow the film unit to shoot on location all over Paris. At this juncture de Gaulle, as president of France, was still a world figure. Therefore, to ensure that he would not be offended in any way by the movie, some French screenwriters, including Claude Boulé, Jean Aurenche, and Pierre Bost, were appointed to kibitz on the script at the behest of government bureaucrats. (Aurenche and Bost had co-scripted Graetz's most celebrated film, *The Devil in the Flesh* [1947].)

As it happened, Clément's contract did not give him control over the script, and so, with Graetz's support, the French writers usually overruled Clément's ideas about improving the screenplay. The script conferences inevitably deteriorated into shouting matches. The whole affair, in Coppola's view, had degenerated into what he termed an insane mess. He ultimately realized that it was hopeless to endeavor to pacify the Gaullist writers on the film, who staunchly maintained that every Frenchman was a hero. In the end no less than ten screenwriters worked on the screenplay. The intransigence of the French writers contributed in no small way to the fact that the script of *Is Paris Burning?* turned out to be fragmented and lacking in continuity. The final shooting script was principally a collation of the work of Coppola, Vidal, Brulé, Aurenche, and Bost. The Screenwriters Guild in Hollywood, however, awarded sole screen credit to Coppla and Vidal. As a result, several critics blamed Coppola and Vidal because the script bulldozed the complexities of the historical events the movie presented.

Veiller was not the only casualty during the period the film was being made. Producer Graetz, worn out from all of the infighting, suffered a heart attack and died during the final days of shooting. As for Coppola, he and Seven Arts decided to part company in the wake of the debacle that was *Is Paris Burning?* Coppola recounts that he both quit and was fired at the same time.

Kirk Douglas did a cameo in *Is Paris Burning?* as General George S. Patton, who was involved in the liberation of Paris. This proved to be a harbinger of Coppola's next major assignment as a scriptwriter. In May of 1965, Twentieth Century-Fox offered him fifty thousand dollars to write a script for a full-scale screen biography of the legendary General Patton, whose men had named him "Blood and Guts."

Patton (1970)

Producer Frank McCarthy had rejected several script drafts submitted by other writers and decided to infuse the project with some new blood by hiring Coppola, who would hopefully bring some fresh ideas to the project. Moreover, given the months he labored on *Is Paris Burning?*, Coppola explains in Johnson's book, he was seen by the studio moguls as "a Second World War specialist." (Obviously the failure of that film was not laid at his door by industry insiders.) However, since his military experience in actual fact consisted of a stint in military school, Coppola devoted himself to researching the life of the controversial general.[37]

Coppola gradually realized that "Patton was obviously out of his mind." On the one hand, if he wrote a script glorifying Patton as a great American hero, as some of the previous scriptwriters had done, it would be laughed at. On the other hand, if he wrote a script that condemned Patton as a heartless martinet, the screenplay would be rejected out of hand. Consequently, Coppola opted to combine both approaches and focus on the duality of Patton's character—to show him as a medieval knight living in the wrong century, "a man out of touch with his time, a pathetic hero, a Don Quixote figure." The people who disapproved of Patton could say, "He was crazy; he loved war," while the people who believed him to be a hero could say, "We need a man like that now." Coppola concludes, "And that is precisely the effect the movie [*Patton*] had, which is why it was successful."[38]

The most celebrated scene in the entire film, which was directed by

Franklin Schaffner (*The Best Man*), is the opening, in which Patton, standing before an enormous American flag, addresses an unseen gathering of troops. Coppola comments that he was experimenting with the concept that if a character just stands in front of the audience and talks for five minutes "the audience would know more about him than if you went into his past and told about his family life." In one memorable line, the outspoken Patton warns his men, "You do not prove your patriotism by dying for your country; you make the other poor bastard die for his country." Coppola composed this monologue by quoting from three of Patton's speeches and later opined that "it was the best scene in my script."

After devoting six months to the screenplay, which is dated December 27, 1965, Coppola moved on to other projects. In typical Hollywood fashion, his screenplay was passed on to other writers who altered it substantially. When the title role was offered to George C. Scott, he remembered having read Coppola's screenplay earlier. He stated flatly that he would accept the part only if they used Coppola's script. "Scott is the one who resurrected my version," says Coppola.[39] Screenwriter Edmund North then made some modifications in the Coppola version, but the shooting script is essentially Coppola's work.

Coppola depicts both the triumphs and trials of the aggressive, eccentric general, just as he said he would. Thus the film presents Patton's decisive victory over German Field Marshall Rommel in the African campaign. But it also encompasses the scene in which Patton, while visiting a medical outpost near the war zone, accuses a whimpering soldier suffering from shell shock of malingering, calls him a "gutless coward," and slaps his face. The episode becomes notorious enough to reach Supreme Commander Dwight Eisenhower, who demands that Patton apologize in front of his troops.

In brief, the movie presents a portrait of this intriguing, complicated figure in an ambiguous fashion, showing him as a legendary commander committed to serving his country and as a military leader who thirsted for fame and glory as the reward for his exploits on the battlefield. Accordingly, critics applauded the script for examining both the virtues and the faults of the general, without leaning too much in either direction—and that is precisely what Coppola intended to do from the start.

This spectacular war epic (nearly three hours long), as it happened, did not reach the screen until 1970, when it won the Academy Award as the Best Picture of the Year as well as Oscars for Schaffner and Scott and Coppola and North, who shared the official screen credit for the screenplay.

Coppola wrote only one more script for a film that he did not personally direct. After the successful launching of *The Godfather* in March 1972, Robert Evans, Paramount's production chief, asked him to compose the screenplay for the film adaptation of F. Scott Fitzgerald's celebrated novel of the Roaring Twenties, *The Great Gatsby,* which would be directed by Jack Clayton (*Room at the Top*). It seems that the muddled script submitted by Truman Capote, filled with confusing dream sequences and flashbacks, was not acceptable. In fact, Evans, in his autobiography, termed Capote's screenplay "a miscarriage" and moaned that "we're back at starting gate without a jockey." Evans wanted Coppola to provide a more straightforward rendition of the plot.[40]

The Great Gatsby (1974)

Coppola took on the task in order to provide himself with a change of pace from working on *The Godfather* and hammered out a serviceable script in five weeks. He followed a procedure he had employed in adapting *The Godfather* for film: he began by pasting each page of the novel into a large notebook and summarizing the action in the margin. This notebook was the road map that guided him in writing each scene. Then he spent several mornings pecking away on a portable typewriter in a New York hotel room as he committed the script to paper. Each afternoon he would dictate what he had composed in the morning to a secretary, who produced a clean copy.

In the story, Jay Gatsby (Robert Redford) crystallizes the American Dream for himself in Daisy (Mia Farrow), the girl he lost to millionaire Tom Buchanan a few years earlier. Gatsby, of course, is deeply hurt by Daisy's rejection. But he eventually decides to mount a campaign to win her back by attempting to amass a fortune by racketeering. Nonetheless, Gatsby is doomed never to win Daisy away from Tom. He is eventually killed by a lunatic who mistakenly assumes that Gatsby is responsible for his wife's death. Evans remembers that "Coppola delivered a screenplay that really worked."

"Francis came in and did an absolute miracle job," Clayton has said, adding that he made only minor alterations in the screenplay that Coppola turned over to him. Clayton did admit to removing some passages from the script that he thought were superfluous, however, and to putting into the screenplay some material from the book that Coppola had not originally included. But anything that was added to the film, Clayton emphasized, "was *always* in the book." Yet it is precisely Clayton's additions to his screenplay that Coppola afterward contended were responsible for extending the duration of the finished film to the point where the movie seemed, in his estimation, "interminable."[41] One salient example will suffice to illustrate Coppola's point. On the one hand, Coppola had included in his script the scene from the novel in which Gatsby's father, Henry Gatz, comes to town for his son's funeral. He included this scene because he thought it important for the viewer to see that, ironically enough, in the eyes of at least one person, Gatsby had really grown up to be the great Gatsby, for, as far as Henry Gatz could tell, his son had become a distinguished man of business who had possessed at the time of his death an enormous estate complete with all the luxuries that money could buy. On the other hand, Coppola did not believe that the film should continue on to depict the funeral itself, in spite of the fact that that scene is in the book, because he felt that playing out such a scene in detail would needlessly protract the running time of a film he was hoping could be kept down to a manageable length. Coppola had planned instead to have the movie conclude with a further touch of irony. As Coppola describes the final scene as he envisioned it, Gatsby's father, while looking around his son's bedroom, "sees the picture of Daisy, and he says, 'Who's the girl?'" That, Coppola maintains, should really have been the end of the movie.

Had Mr. Gatz's remark about the photograph been used to conclude the film, Coppola continues, it would have neatly tied in with the shot of this same photograph of Daisy that appears in the course of the movie's opening credits. In this manner the movie would have both begun and ended with the picture of Daisy, Gatsby's most cherished possession and the symbol of his dreams and ambitions. "So what I had set up at the beginning," Coppola concludes, would have gone "all the way to the end."[42] By adding the lengthy funeral sequence to the script as a replacement for his own much more terse finale to the movie, Coppola contends that Clayton made the closing scenes of the movie that follow Gatsby's death seem less like an epilogue than an anticlimax.

Regardless of which side one takes in the matter of Clayton's adding the funeral episode to Coppola's script, it must be conceded that all of the interpolations Clayton made in the screenplay, taken together, eventually resulted in a motion picture that in the last analysis seems at times slow paced and overlong. To that extent, it seems that Coppola's complaints about Clayton's revisions of his screenplay were ultimately justified.

Despite the fact that some Hollywood wags had dubbed the film "The Great Ghastly," Redford's box-office appeal made the movie a commercial success. But that did not alter Coppola's negative opinion of the final film. He then moved on to write and direct *The Conversation*.

Looking back on the time that he spent writing screenplays for other directors, Coppola reflects, "I don't enjoy the directing process; and if you had asked me the question, whether I was a writer or a director before *Gatsby,* I would have said I was a writer and I just direct sometimes." But when he saw the way that Clayton spent time "fidgeting" with his screenplay for *Gatsby* without his knowledge or consent, he realized the strong influence a director has on the way a film turns out.[43] Coppola therefore resolved regularly to direct the scripts he wrote.

Novelist-screenwriter Raymond Chandler (*Lady in the Lake*) holds a similar view about the way a writer's screenplay is altered after being written: "Too many people have too much to say about a writer's work. It ceases to be his own." On this point an upcoming Hollywood screenwriter says, "I don't feel the position of writers in Hollywood has changed much over the years," since Chandler's time. "We know no script is going to start shooting without some changes being made, but there's this idea in the studios that everybody should be allowed to contribute to the process, that the script should please everybody."[44] Coppola certainly could attest to the prevalence of this attitude.

Still, whatever Coppola's gripes about the studio system, he worked conscientiously at the craft of screenwriting while he was employed by the studios as a screenwriter. When adapting another author's work for film, Coppola endeavored to be true to the thematic intent of his literary source, as in the case of *Gatsby,* for which he stuck as closely as possible to Fitzgerald's novel. Musing about the role of the screenwriter in the filmmaking process, Coppola ultimately resolved that he would never again entrust a screenplay he had written to another director.

2

Going Hollywood

You're a Big Boy Now and *Finian's Rainbow*

Hollywood is a surreal place. The first time I saw a crane plant-
ing a full-grown tree in a garden, I realized that Hollywood is
not organic; nothing grows or develops naturally there.

—John Schlesinger

The making of a motion picture is an endless contention of tawdry egos, almost none of them capable of anything more creative than credit-stealing and self-promotion.

—Raymond Chandler

The collapse in the 1960s of Hollywood as the center of mass entertainment in America was precipitated by the advent of television, which became America's principal source of entertainment for the mass audience.
The big Hollywood studios became aware that they must make an effort to
present audiences with fresh material, not just a rehash of old commercial
formulas long since overfamiliar to moviegoers.

Coppola had written a screenplay while he was still working for Seven
Arts that was a fresh and inventive take on the usual "coming of age" movie,
and he thought he could interest a studio in the property. The script was
based on David Benedictus's novel *You're a Big Boy Now,* about a nineteen-
year-old male working in a London shoe store. The book was brought to

Coppola's attention by Tony Bill, a young actor who hoped to play the lead if Coppola made the movie. "But I also suggested Peter Kastner to him," Bill remembers, "because I had seen a little Canadian film he was in called *Nobody Waved Goodbye* (1965) about a troubled teenager. As it happened, Bill did not play the lead but, instead, the hero's buddy.[1]

Coppola had optioned Benedictus's novel for a thousand dollars and set about transplanting the story to New York City because he had always wanted to portray the life of a teenager living in New York, where he had grown up. Coppola had actually written his screen adaptation in his spare time in Paris while he was collaborating with Gore Vidal on the script for *Is Paris Burning?*—in order to "stay sane," as he quipped. When Seven Arts got wind of the fact that Coppola had composed the script while he was in their employ, they claimed, quite rightly, that they owned the rights to any material Coppola had written while on their payroll as a screenwriter. He shrewdly pointed out to the front office that he owned the rights to the novel from which the screenplay was derived and they owned the script: "Therefore, I own one half and you the other. So let's do it together."[2]

You're a Big Boy Now (1967)

At this time Seven Arts was merging with Warner Brothers, and Phil Feldman, business manager at Seven Arts for the past four years, had decided that the time was right for him to break with Seven Arts and become an independent producer. Feldman had faith in Coppola, and Coppola convinced him to produce *You're a Big Boy Now*. They began the preproduction phase for the film before they had obtained financial backing for the project. "We were shelling out our own money," Coppola recalls, "using credit cards and what have you."[3]

Feldman finally negotiated a deal with Seven Arts that would resolve the dispute over the ownership of the screenplay: Ray Stark, Coppola's former boss at Seven Arts, would pay Coppola no fee for the script (which technically belonged to Seven Arts), but he would pay Coppola $8,000 for directing the movie on a twenty-nine-day shooting schedule. Stark, in return, got the newly formed Warner Brothers-Seven Arts to make the picture. "Why did I make *Big Boy* for just $8,000?" Coppola comments. "I would have done it for nothing."[4]

Coppola explains his strategy with Warners-Seven this way: "I don't ask anybody if I can make a movie." He simply informs a studio that he is ready to go into production, "and if they're wise, they'll get in on it." In the motion picture business very few executives can resist getting in on a project that is already a going concern. So he and Feldman advised Warners-Seven that they were going ahead with the picture and that it was almost too late to get in on the ground floor. The moguls simply said, "Well, we might as well make this movie."

But Warners-Seven only offered Coppola a measly $250,000 budget because the plot centered on a nineteen-year-old and there were few bankable teenaged stars. As a result, Coppola decided to cast relative unknowns in the key roles and to get better-known actors for the supporting cast. He accordingly cast as the young hero and heroine Peter Kastner, the promising Canadian actor, and Karen Black, a graduate of the Actors' Studio with one Broadway play, *The Playroom,* to her credit. In addition, he cast as the young femme fatale Elizabeth Hartman, who garnered an Academy Award nomination for playing a blind girl in *A Patch of Blue* (1965), her first film.

Hartman had appeared in a couple of other pictures, usually as a mousey, inhibited girl. In giving her an unsympathetic role Coppola was exemplifying his willingness to cast an actor against type. The late Elizabeth Hartman told me during a brief conversation that when Coppola phoned and asked her to play the sexy Barbara Darling she nearly cried. "Do you know what I look like?" she asked. He did, and he stuck to his choice.

Coppola took the bull by the horns and bypassed the agents of the experienced actors he wanted for supporting roles and contacted the actors directly. He phoned Julie Harris and Rip Torn and his wife Geraldine Page himself and coaxed them into reading the script. Geraldine Page spoke for the others when she said, "I get scripts daily, but this one really made me laugh." She thought Coppola was a marvelous young talent and trusted him implicitly.[5] (She eventually got an Oscar nomination for playing the hero's dotty mother.) When all of these distinguished actors agreed to be in the movie, Warners-Seven raised Coppola's budget to eight hundred thousand dollars, still a meager budget by studio standards.

Some Hollywood insiders thought the studio was imprudent in bankrolling Coppola's film. One publicist described Coppola's conferences with the studio officials this way: "All these stuffy executives were sitting around a conference table, offering the moon" to this kid "with a beard and blue jeans."[6] In actual fact, Warners-Seven was wise to finance Coppola's picture, since allowing the twenty-seven-year-old aspiring director to make a low-budget film for a mainstream studio would enable him to demonstrate what he could do. In addition, a young talent, anxious to prove himself, would not command a large salary but would very likely finish the film on time and on budget.

Coppola had always been fascinated by the young people, called pages, who get books for patrons at the New York Public Library on Fifth Avenue by sailing down the eighty miles of library stacks on roller skates, and so he gave that job to his hero rather than making him a shoe clerk as in the novel. But library officials were not pleased that Coppola had inserted into the script the suggestion that the library had a secret vault stocked with exotic pornographic books and *objets d'art*. They also feared that Coppola and his film crew would interrupt the library's daily routine. After the library board denied him permission to film on the premises, Coppola pointed out to Mayor John Lindsay that Lindsay had a policy of encouraging film crews to work on location around New York City as a goodwill gesture to the film community. Lindsay acquiesced and issued a permit for Coppola to shoot in the library, overruling the library board's veto.

In Coppola's screenplay Bernard Chanticleer (Peter Kastner) works in the stacks at the New York Public Library, where his father, Humphrey Chanticleer (Rip Torn), is curator of rare books. Bernard's raffish friend Raef (Tony Bill), who also is employed at the library, often attempts to make the naive Bernard a bit more worldly in his outlook on life. Humphrey Chanticleer, over the protests of his wife Margery (Geraldine Page), decides that Bernard should move out of their Long Island home and into an apartment of his own in New York City. Bernard apologizes to "Mummy" and "Daddy" for his failure to live up to their expectations in the past, thereby indicating that he is still in essence their little boy—he is not a big boy yet.

The apartment house Mummy and Daddy choose for him is presided over by the sexually repressed Miss Nora Thing (Julie Harris), who readily agrees to Margery's request that she report to Bernard's parents any partying Bernard indulges in with the opposite sex. Another tenant is a burly cop called Francis (after the young director), who likewise keeps a suspicious eye on Bernard, whom he views as a young punk. As things develop, Bernard becomes interested in Amy Prentiss (Karen Black), a co-worker at the library. But he soon transfers his attachment to Barbara Darling (Elizabeth Hartman), one of the library's patrons. Given the fact that Barbara is a go-go dancer at a Greenwich Village discotheque and an actress in offbeat, off-Broadway plays, it is hard to imagine her as a regular library patron—but no matter. In any case, the promiscuous Barbara eventually sheds Bernard for the more attractive Raef.

To his dismay Bernard learns that his father, who maintains a respectable facade, is really a lecher who has made a pass at Amy and has even endeavored to work his wiles on Miss Thing when he corners her in the secret library vault he has filled with erotic art. Disenchanted with his father, Bernard defies Humphrey by stealing a prized Gutenberg Bible from his father's rare book collection. After a chase led by Humphrey through lower Manhattan, Bernard is captured and jailed—and bailed out by Amy.

Benedictus's novel concludes with Bernard having lost both Barbara and Amy, but Coppola's screenplay reunites Bernard with Amy. Benedictus points out that his book concludes with Bernard living a solitary life, whereas Coppola supplied a happy ending: "Instead of being scarred for life by this sadistic Barbara Darling, the young hero will get a nice girl in the end. . . . Still I think there have been fewer concessions to public taste than in most American films." As a matter of fact, Coppola's script does have a serious dimension underlying the plot, despite the happy ending. Like the novel, the script presents a young fellow on the brink of manhood who matures by finally summoning the gumption to defy his overbearing parents and outgrow their influence.

Coppola prepared a rehearsal version of the screenplay and had the actors rehearse in a Manhattan warehouse without benefit of scenery or costumes as a way to familiarize them with their roles. This procedure was a carryover from his days rehearsing plays at Hofstra. After ten days of rehearsing with the cast, Coppola explains, "We played the entire script all the way through before a live audience." In this manner the actors were able to evolve their roles to performance level, "and I was able to get a sense of what my picture was going to look like before we started shooting."[7] (In the years ahead Coppola would continue to hold rehearsals prior to the start of principal photography.) Coppola then gave the actors a final shooting script just before filming commenced.

It is true that Coppola had already gained some experience in directing by making a low-budget film for Roger Corman. Nevertheless, he was still diffident at the prospect of shooting the present film on location in New York City with some gifted and well-known character actors, with a real union film crew, and on a limited schedule. He was scared when he walked on the set he had never seen before on the first day of shooting, and when cinematographer Andrew Laszlo inquired what the first camera setup would be, Coppola froze. He looked at the nine actors and the crew of forty and abruptly decided to dismiss them for half an hour, while he blocked out the scene. He could not function with forty-nine people watching to see if he knew what he was doing.

When he was shooting on location in the streets of New York, Coppola utilized Eastman's high speed color film, which enabled him and Laszlo to film with natural light, even at night. One location sequence recalls an incident from Coppola's youth: after he had run away from military school, he wandered around Manhattan trying to summon the courage to go home and face his parents. Similarly, in the film, Bernard roams around Broadway and Times Square just after he moves into his own apartment. The scene is photographed with documentary-like realism as Laszlo's handheld camera follows Bernard while he is window-shopping around the 42nd Street porno shops and penny arcades.

This sequence reaches its climax when Bernard drifts into a peep show parlor. While looking at a raunchy filmstrip, Bernard gets his tie caught in the rickety viewing machine. Amy, who happens to spot him from the street and follows him into the store, snips his tie off with fingernail scissors she is conveniently carrying. The wholesome Amy, of course, represents a marked contrast to the lewd creature in the filmstrip that Bernard had been watching. In fact, the awkwardness Bernard displays in the porno emporium he visits implies that raw sex is not really attractive to him—he is looking for love. This scene accordingly prefigures how Bernard will ultimately prefer love with Amy over a mere sexual relationship with Barbara.

At any rate, once outside the porno parlor, Bernard and Amy chat with each other on the telephones in adjoining phone booths on the street, an act that serves as a metaphor for their attempt to connect with each other. Indeed, they discover that, among other things, they both attended P.S. 109 in New York City (the same school Coppola attended).

A stand-out location sequence in *Big Boy* begins in Humphrey's office, where nearly all of the principals in the cast (even Barbara) meet for a showdown. It is at this point that Bernard impulsively steals the Gutenberg Bible and is pursued down Fifth Avenue by a posse led by his father. En route, they wind up in Macy's department store. Coppola explains that he wanted to see what would happen when this "madness" hit Macy's at 11:00 AM, with no one outside the film's cast and crew having the remotest idea of what was transpiring. Three cameras were concealed in delivery carts and shopping bags. Coppola and Laszlo, as usual, filmed the scene with the natural light available, in this case a mixture of the fluorescent lights overhead and sunlight coming in through the windows. Kastner and his pursuers were running up and down the aisles, "and they started a riot," Coppola remembers—"some kids started ripping Peter's clothes off" (footage which did not make the final cut). "My only regret is we didn't have thirty cameras to get everything down on film."[8]

The chase ends when Barbara finally corners Bernard in a room where the department store mannequins are kept and clobbers him with the leg of a dummy. This shot is apparently a homage to one of Stanley Kubrick's early films, *Killer's Kiss* (1955), in which the hero slugs it out with the villain in a warehouse stored with department store mannequins.

Chown observes that Coppola photographed the movie in a rather showy fashion, with frenetic handheld camerawork during the chase in Macy's and ostentatious dolly shots in the library as Bernard skates through the stacks. The freewheeling cinematography, he continues, is marked by the wild camera movement and gaudy colors reminiscent of TV commercials and, hence, draws attention to itself. Coppola, commenting on his style of cinematography in the picture, told me, "*You're a Big Boy Now* is a flashy movie to some extent. I have since been more subtle than that. But flashy films do attract attention, and that was what I wanted to do when I was making my first film for a studio." In fact, he has often thought of the movie as the first underground film ever made for a major Hollywood studio by a tyro moviemaker.

At times the flashy photography pays off, as when Bernard takes Amy on a date to a psychedelic disco in the Village where Barbara is appearing. Coppola's canny camera captures the garish atmosphere, all dazzling lights and glittering decor. To top it off, gory scenes from Coppola's own *Dementia 13* are being projected on one of the walls just to add to the bizarre setting.

Barbara, a typical 1960s swinger dressed in a miniskirt and plastic boots, is gyrating to the music in a cage suspended from the ceiling. Bernard looks up at her adoringly, as if she were an inaccessible goddess on a pedestal. By the same token, Barbara looks down at Bernard like a goddess eyeing with disdain one of the mortals who worships her.

This scene incorporates some excellent visual imagery, some of which has just been described. In addition, there is the shot, shortly afterward, when Bernard kisses Amy while they are walking in Times Square. As they embrace Bernard fantasizes that a gigantic neon sign above them is spelling out "Barbara, you're on my mind" in bright lights. Thus Coppola indicates visually that Bernard is preoccupied with Barbara, even while he is kissing Amy! Another fine visual symbol occurs when Bernard and Raef are flying a kite in Central Park, with Raef all the while advising Bernard to give up his dream of winning the unattainable Barbara. The kite gets caught in a tree, and Bernard cannot reach it when he tries to retrieve it—a metaphor for how a young man's romantic dreams all too often elude his grasp.

Indeed, when Barbara finally invites Bernard to her apartment for a sexual escapade, the experience is an unqualified disaster. Barbara, who was seduced by a middle-aged therapist when she was a youngster, is a castrating female who despises men. Little wonder that Bernard fails to perform at the climax of the scene. When he expresses his shame to her, Barbara, the bitch-goddess, smirks with her usual condescension, "There is nothing wrong with you that a firing squad couldn't fix." As already suggested by Bernard's embarrassed tour of the porno shops earlier, he is not satisfied by sex without love—which is all that Barbara can offer him, and he cannot respond to it. He subconsciously yearns for the kind of genuine love that Amy represents. So much for Barbara as Bernard's dream girl.

At the film's denouement Bernard is jailed for stealing the Gutenberg Bible. While he is behind bars he admits to a guard that he has been imprisoned by his domineering parents, who have caused him to be "filled with self-doubt, frustration, and perpetual guilt. I've been in my parents' custody all my life. From now on I'm going to be in my own custody." Significantly, it is Amy who bails Bernard out. She not only liberates him from prison but ultimately helps to free him from his parents' control.

The picture ends with the couple merrily romping through a pretzel factory (Bernard had earlier opined that what this country needs is a good five-cent pretzel). They are accompanied by the 1960s rock group the Lovin' Spoonful singing, "Go on and take a bow, cause you're a big boy now," while a conveyor belt sends a cascade of nickel pretzels toward the camera.

You're a Big Boy Now reflects Coppola's theme, already enunciated in *Dementia 13,* that the family is a source of strife and emotional problems. He states, "I'm fascinated with the whole idea of family." In his work, "it is a constant."[9] Indeed *Big Boy* is the first of his movies to explore a father-son relationship, a theme that would surface prominently in films like *The Godfather.*

Big Boy was taken seriously by the film community. It was chosen as the only official U.S. entry at the Cannes International Film Festival and gained Geraldine Page an Academy Award nomination. Still the picture merited a mixed bag of reviews, both at Cannes and in the American press. Some critics noticed positively that the movie is crisply paced and has a refreshing story that turns somersaults and zigzags off in unexpected directions. They conceded that it is hard not to warm to the director's brash, invigorating style. As one reviewer put it, when the camera is capturing city life off the cuff, the picture has energy and charm. By contrast, the movie was criticized for its anarchic, "custard-pie plot" (a reference to the slapstick chase through Macy's department store, with its resonance of the Keystone Cops' silent comedies).

As for the acting, on the one hand, the supporting cast headed by Julie Harris, Geraldine Page, and Rip Torn, were complimented for giving their roles a dizzy spin. On the other hand, the naysayers pointed out that their performances at times came close to caricature, as when Margery Chanticleer or Miss Thing screeched at Bernard for chasing girls. It is true that the characterizations of some of the minor figures are somewhat superficial and even border on the grotesque, as certain critics maintained, but Bernard himself is drawn in some depth. At times he seems to be traveling a road without signposts in his journey toward maturity. He seems a feckless outsider, the sort of innocent whose luggage an airline is bound to lose. Kastner gave the most memorable performance in the picture as the harried young man.

All in all, *You're a Big Boy Now* is a winning amalgam of quirky comedy and serious drama that offers glimpses into complicated lives, and that keeps it from becoming merely an inflated situation comedy. The picture is in some ways slight and slender, but it nevertheless indicates the stirrings of a major directorial talent. Goodwin and Wise cite critic Joseph Morgenstern as stating that not since Orson Welles went riding out of town "has any young American made a film as original, spunky, and just plain funny as this one."[10] Charles Champlin, critic of the *Los Angeles Times,* delivered the ultimate accolade to Coppola by acknowledging that the young writer-director already deserved to be termed an auteur.

Asked at the time of the film's American release how the movie's box-office performance would affect his career, Coppola replied stoically, "If the movie's a bomb it won't destroy my reputation as a director because I don't have any," adding that he could always go back to being a screenwriter for the time being.[11]

Although budgeted at $800,000, the picture eventually cost closer to $1 million, which it never recouped during its original release. The film was not a commercial success because, besides the mixed reviews, the two leads were unknowns who had not yet established themselves in the movie world, and the supporting players likewise lacked marquee value for the youthful filmgoers at whom the film was targeted. When *Big Boy* failed to attract ticket buyers in its initial New York and Los Angeles runs, Warners-Seven gave it only a limited distribution across the rest of the country. The upshot was that the movie did not break even until it was sold to television.

The young principals in *Big Boy* continued to pursue film careers. Elizabeth Hartman's career never really got off the ground, and she finally took her own life in 1987. Although *Big Boy* was not a moneymaker, Warners-Seven was sufficiently impressed with Coppola's handling of the film and the positive reviews it received in some quarters to ask the promising young director to make *Finian's Rainbow,* a movie musical with Fred Astaire.

Finian's Rainbow (1968)

The merger of Warner Brothers and Seven Arts had reached the point where Jack Warner, the venerable Warners production chief, finally sold his stake in the studio to Seven Arts. Earlier, when Joseph Landon, producer of *Rainbow*, had broached Coppola's name to Warner as a possible director for the film, Warner dismissed Coppola as too young and inexperienced for a big musical (George Cukor was a sexagenarian when Warner picked him to direct *My Fair Lady* in 1964). After Warner's departure, however, Eliot Hyman was named chief executive officer of the company. Hyman, in turn, appointed his son Ken as production chief ("the son also rises," as one wag quipped), and Ken Hyman was interested in nurturing young talent in a way that Jack Warner, a scion of the old Hollywood, was not. So Ken Hyman authorized Landon to consider Coppola for the director's chair for *Finian's Rainbow*.

The new administration at Warners-Seven Arts had some very practical reasons for setting their sights on Coppola. To begin with, the studio had not allocated a huge budget for *Rainbow*, despite the fact that at the time it was customary to assign a generous budget for a large-scale musical, such as *Funny Girl* (1968). But Warners-Seven wanted *Rainbow* to be made quickly in order to cash in on the wave of musicals initiated by the blockbuster *Sound of Music* (1965) before the trend waned, and they wanted to do so at bargain prices. Hence, instead of the $10 million budget usually set aside for a musical in those days and a six-month production schedule, the studio wanted *Rainbow* to be made for a thrifty $3.5 million on a three-month schedule. Consequently, the front office really wanted Coppola to helm *Rainbow*, not only because they knew a young director would not command a substantial salary, but also because he had proved with the low-budget *You're a Big Boy Now* that he could bring in a picture on time with a shoestring budget. They also hoped he could give the picture the vigor that *Big Boy* had.

By this time Coppola had taken some office space and commenced writing the first draft of a screenplay that would eventually become *The Conversation*. Landon phoned him and cagily sent up a trial balloon by inquiring of Coppola if he knew anyone who could direct *Rainbow*. "I thought about it," Coppola remembers, "and I gave him some suggestions and hung up." Coppola did not suggest himself because he had promised himself not to make another film for a major studio unless he was assured of a reasonable degree of artistic freedom as director. The next day Landon phoned again and this time asked him flat out, "What about you?"[12]

Coppola pondered Landon's offer for a few days and initially turned it down after reading the hackneyed script that had been derived from the old-fashioned 1947 Broadway show. Nevertheless, Coppola eventually changed his mind because, for a start, Ken Hyman had let it be known that he planned to attract up-and-coming directors by giving them more artistic control of their films than had been the case under the old regime at Warners.

In addition, "musical comedy was something that I had been raised with in my family, and I thought frankly that my father would be impressed."[13] Carmine Coppola had conducted the pit orchestra for the road companies of several Broadway musicals when Francis was a lad, and young Francis got a chance to see some of them. Moreover, Coppola had written the script and lyrics for a musical while he was still in high school and had directed a musical show at Hofstra in his college days. Then too, making *Finian's Rainbow* afforded Coppola the opportunity of directing one of the screen's legendary hoofers, Fred Astaire. But what finally clinched the deal for Coppola was the score lyricist E. Y. Harburg (who had written the lyrics for *The Wizard of Oz*), and composer Burton Lane had served up in *Rainbow*: a score that boasted a bumper crop of songs like "Old Devil Moon" and "If This Isn't Love." Several of these songs had become standards, and they went a long way in explaining why the musical had racked up 725 performances on Broadway. In fact, Coppola judged the score one of the best ever composed for the American musical theater, and so he was essentially persuaded to make the picture "by the goddamn thought of doing all those wonderful musical numbers."[14]

Still Coppola had to contend with the screenplay, adapted from the script of the stage play. *Finian's Rainbow* takes place in Rainbow Valley, Missitucky, a mythical Southern village. Finian McLonergan (Fred Astaire) and Sharon, his daughter (Patricia Clark), have fled to America from Glocca Mora, Ireland, to elude Og, a leprechaun (Tommy Steele), whose magical pot of gold Finian has stolen. Woody Mahoney (Don Francks), a sharecropper, sells Finian a plot of land, on which Finian buries the pot of gold that has the power to grant three wishes to whoever possesses it.

Sharon uses one of the wishes to teach a lesson to the racist Senator "Billboard" Rawkins (Keenan Wynn). She temporarily transforms him into a black man to let him experience racial bigotry. Sharon uses the second wish to restore the senator to his status as a white man. Meanwhile, Howard, a black friend of Woody's, has invented a way of growing menthol tobacco, which brings prosperity to Rainbow Valley when he and Woody form the Tobacco Cooperative with the black and white sharecroppers. Og the leprechaun eventually becomes human so that he can woo Susan the Silent, Woody's mute sister (Barbara Hancock). Og himself invokes the third and final wish that the crock of gold can grant in order to give Susan the power of speech. By then Woody has fallen in love with Sharon, and they are married. At the fade-out Finian departs, continuing to "follow the rainbow" wherever it will lead him. The theme of the story seems to be that gold is merely a base metal, while people constitute the world's true wealth—a rather banal notion not calculated to keep the moviegoer up nights pondering it.

As noted, Coppola was appalled when he read the "cockamamie" script. The creaky plot of the twenty-year-old formula musical simply did not hold up. One of the principal elements of the plot concerns the blustering Senator Rawkins who threatens to disrupt the racially integrated community of sharecroppers. The social commentary implied in this situation was at odds with the never-never-land atmosphere of the rest of the story, which revolved around Og, the fanciful leprechaun whose crock of gold can make people's dreams come true. The two strands of the story had been combined in what was nothing less than a shotgun marriage. As Coppola put it, "A lot of liberal people were going to feel it was old pap" because its civil rights stance seemed woefully outdated in the wake of the intervening two decades of racial struggle. It was a white man's patronizing approach to civil rights. Conversely, "the conservatives were going to say it was a lot of liberal nonsense" when it came to a racially integrated group of sharecroppers. "I knew I was going to get it from both ends." He therefore overhauled the screenplay in an effort to "make it acceptable for contemporary audiences" and yet remain faithful to the spirit of the original show. Thus the film ends with emphasis on the whites and blacks working together with good old American know-how, raising mentholated tobacco and bettering their communal existence in the bargain. In sum, Coppola thought *Rainbow* was a marvelous show of yesteryear: "I tried to make it work on its own terms and not get fancy." He endeavored to give it a "timeless" dimension so that the period in which the story is set is never really defined.[15]

Coppola did his best to turn out a respectable movie musical within the limitations of schedule and budget imposed on him. He was granted three weeks of rehearsal time prior to shooting. Following the same procedure he used on *You're a Big Boy Now,* he took over a small rehearsal hall on the lot and ran through the whole show without scenery or costumes, with Astaire and the rest of the cast accompanied by Carmine Coppola on the flute with a pianist and a drummer. And, just as he did on *Big Boy,* he had a run-through before an audience in a theater-in-the-round format, which admittedly looked more like an Omaha high school production than the makings of a movie musical. (Coppola's father stayed on to help in orchestrating the score.) "We rehearsed for about three weeks and shot it in just twelve weeks," Coppola remembers. "It was not a luxury production."[16]

Coppola had petitioned the studio brass to permit him to shoot the picture on location in Kentucky, but they refused. They wanted him to film the movie on the backlot and to employ an enormous forest set they had spent a lot of money to build for an earlier musical, *Camelot* (1967). It would stand in for rustic Missitucky, thereby enabling the studio to get its money's worth out of the forest set. In effect, that meant that the dancers had to perform on soft grass and muddy earth—instead of on the hard surfaces of a proper dance floor—as Astaire led the jolly inhabitants of Rainbow Valley in merry dances through fields and streams. This situation became a bone of contention between Coppola and dance director Hermes Pan. Since the issues that led to the falling out between the director and the choreographer have not been explored in detail in previous discussions of *Finian's Rainbow*, it is appropriate that I do so here.

Pan, a veteran of several vintage Astaire musicals like *Blue Skies* (1946) and *The Barkleys of Broadway* (1949), had been hired at Astaire's behest. He maintained that he could only stage dance numbers properly on the carefully prepared surfaces of a dance floor and that the soft, grassy turf of the rural outdoor sets on the backlot was inadequate for his purposes. Coppola rejoined that they had to make do with the sets they had at their disposal, notably the *Camelot* forest set. They reached an impasse. Coppola was not satisfied with Pan's choreography, and Pan contended that it was the best he could do with a principal set that had not even been designed for the present film. He asked to have more rehearsal time, but Coppola could not grant his request since there was no margin in the tight production schedule.

"The choreography was abysmal; let's be honest," says Coppola bluntly. "We fired the choreographer halfway through the picture." Coppola staged most of the musical numbers eventually. To give Hermes Pan "equal time," it is appropriate to record his remarks about Coppola, whom he thought "a real pain. He knew very little about dancing and musicals." Pan observed that "these schoolboys who studied at UCLA think they are geniuses, but there is a lot they don't understand."[17] Obviously Pan shared the attitude of the old Hollywood toward the generation of young filmmakers coming out of university film programs who had not done an apprenticeship in the studios. Pan could console himself, however, that he still retained an official screen credit as choreographer on the movie—although it is doubtful that he would have wanted to be held responsible for what passed for choreography in the production numbers Coppola staged.

Coppola, after all, would be the first to admit that he was no dance director. Nevertheless, he did develop a concept for each number in the wake of Pan's departure from the film. "I dreamed up the way the numbers were going to be done," he explains. For example, for "Something Sort of Grandish" Coppola decided, "I'll shoot it on a hill and have Petula Clark hanging white bed sheets" on a clothesline while she warbles a duet with Tommy Steele. "If this Isn't Love" would be done with children's games. "On that Great Come-and-Get-It Day" the sharecroppers "are going to throw away all their old furniture in big piles," looking toward the day when the Tobacco Co-op begins to pay off.[18]

Be that as it may, the bulk of the production numbers were filmed without any set choreography once Pan had walked off the picture. Coppola would play back the music for a dance routine and instruct the dancers to "move with the music" while he directed them from behind the camera. Astaire, who was accustomed to plotting out each dance routine in meticulous detail with a choreographer, had to make do with Coppola telling him, "We'll put the camera here; Fred, go over there and do something. Then let's have two girls block in this space."[19] Astaire, old trouper that he was, would then oblige with a little impromptu soft shoe routine as he danced his way around a rustic backyard or shuffled off down a country road.

Coppola would shoot about eight takes of a musical number and have Astaire and the other dancers improvise their way through the number each time, so that each take varied somewhat from all the others. During editing Coppola then pasted together the best bits from each take into the final version of the number.

In some of the production numbers Coppola sought to get by with no choreography at all by substituting a montage of quick cuts. For example, "If This Isn't Love," which, as mentioned, is structured around children's games, opens with Woody singing as he rides atop the hood of a truck, followed by a series of jump cuts showing Woody in a tug-of-war, running in a sack race, playing leapfrog and blind man's bluff, and dancing around a maypole.

In the end Warners-Seven permitted Coppola to shoot on location for a scant eight days. This footage was carefully interspersed throughout the film to enliven the bulk of the footage that was shot at the studio. It was used to particularly good advantage in the opening credit sequence. Coppola assigned Carroll Ballard, a fellow film school alumnus, to do second-unit photography for the title sequence. During the opening credits the camera roams over a field of flowers and then pans up to Finian and Sharon hiking through the fields. The camera then takes in a rainbow as Sharon sings, "Look to the Rainbow" (recalling Harburg's lyrics for a song in *The Wizard of Oz,* "Over the Rainbow"). There follows a succession of quick shots, wherein the pair pass several legendary American landmarks, including the Statue of Liberty, Mount Rushmore, the Golden Gate Bridge, and Glacier National Park, in the course of their journey to Rainbow Valley, where they arrive at the close of the credits. Coppola shot the rest of the location exteriors in Modesto, Monterey, Carmel, and San Francisco, with cinematography that is clean and handsome.

Besides the paucity of location footage in the movie, there were other drawbacks for the production, one of which was that some of the actors did not meet Coppola's expectations. Don Francks, a former lounge crooner, never improved much as an actor, Coppola remarks, while Tommy Steele tended to overplay his role with too much exuberance, which was in keeping with his stage persona. "I felt the leprechaun should be more shy and timid and bewildered," Coppola complains. "I wanted him to be an introvert leprechaun, a guy who speaks in a quiet voice and finally becomes a human being." At Coppola's insistence Steele began to tone down his performance during rehearsals, but "somehow during the actual shooting, little by little he slipped back into his familiar character," mugging and pulling faces. Only when serenading Susan the Silent with "When I'm Not Near the Girl I Love, I Love the Girl I'm Near" was his delivery less mannered and more subdued. In short, Steele did not scale down his performance for the camera, but acted broadly, as if he were playing to the last row in the balcony from a theater stage. (Steele took such a drubbing from the critics that he acted in only one more film.)

Finally, Keenan Wynn was fine as the bombastic Senator Rawkins in his early scenes—until the senator is transformed into a black man. At that point Wynn's over-the-top performance smacks all too much of a comedian doing a blackface routine in a minstrel show.

Yet, despite the movie's stringent budget and tight schedule, *Finian's Rainbow* was being groomed by the studio brass to be a roadshow attraction, with reserved seat performances at advanced prices, complete with an overture and an intermission. It would therefore have to compete with more lavish, expensive musicals like *Funny Girl,* to its own disadvantage. The studio even opted to blow up the film to 70 mm for the roadshow engagements, and the wide screen ratio dictated that the top and the bottom of the frame had to be cropped, thereby cropping off the feet of Astaire and the other dancers while they were dancing. When the film was processed in

70 mm, Coppola moans, "no one bothered to check the top and bottom of the frame."[20]

At all events, the skimpy production numbers, coupled with the dated storyline (with the racist senator experiencing a miraculous change of heart), coalesced to make the movie decidedly not a favorite with audiences or with critics. Coppola's brave effort to yoke liberal social attitudes about Southern racism to a quaint, threadbare Irish fable about leprechauns just did not come off. Even the tune-bank of charming songs could not save the picture.

Pauline Kael writes, "For the sake of some rather pretty songs," one must endure "the three fairy-tale wishes and the race-relations paradise," i.e., the racially integrated Tobacco Co-op, as well as the "hypertense Tommy Steele's Puckish leprechaun." Yet Kael adds sympathetically, "With this kind of decaying material that reeks of old Broadway, . . . the best Coppola can hope for is to keep the show moving, and he manages to do that."[21] Coppola simply shrugs, "I was brought in to direct a project that had already been cast and structured."[22] He had done the best he could to sell a tale drenched in sentiment to an audience of supposedly world-weary cynics. At its best, *Rainbow* is an amiable if lightweight musical filled with simple, goodhearted rustics. Nevertheless, Fred Astaire understandably termed *Finian's Rainbow* overall the biggest disappointment of his long career. Not surprisingly, it was the sixty-eight-year-old Astaire's last appearance as a lead in a musical.

One unexpected dividend that did come out of Coppola's travails in making the picture was that it provided him with the opportunity of meeting George Lucas, with whom he would collaborate in the years ahead. Lucas, a University of Southern California film student, had won a scholarship that entitled him to an internship at Warners-Seven Arts, whereby he could observe a film in production for six months. Since *Rainbow* was the only film being filmed on the Warner lot at the time, Lucas showed up daily on Coppola's set. He was aware that Coppola was the first film school graduate to go big time and wanted to make a good impression on him.

They sensed that they were kindred souls from the outset. Lucas recalls, "We were the only two people on the set who were under forty or fifty and who had beards" and who had both gone to film school.[23] Adds Coppola, "I was very grateful to have someone of my own generation around to discuss what I was trying to do as opposed to what I was able to do."[24] He told Lucas, "Look, kid, you come up with one good idea a day and you can actually do stuff for me." Coppola made Lucas his administrative assistant on the picture. One of his tasks was to take Polaroid snapshots of the sets in order to check the lighting. Later on, Coppola invited Lucas to kibitz in the editing room.

"We became very close friends," Lucas remembers, "because in every single way we're opposite, two halves of a whole. Coppola's very Italian and compulsive," whereas Lucas is Scandinavian, "conservative and plodding."[25] Lucas was a fledgling filmmaker and Coppola was his mentor, and this relationship would continue on Coppola's next film, *The Rain People.* "We respect each other," Lucas has said, "but at the same time we are totally different personalities. He says he's too crazy and I'm not crazy enough. Francis spends every day jumping off a cliff and hoping he's going to land okay. My main interest is security. . . . But the goals we have in mind are the same. We want to make movies free from the yoke of the studios."[26]

3

Nightmares at Noon

The Rain People and *The Conversation*

Things have a way of turning out so badly.

—Tennessee Williams

Warners-Seven Arts was satisfied with Coppola's direction of *Finian's Rainbow*, particularly his filming of the musical numbers. What's more, although the picture was not a box-office bonanza, it earned $5.5 million in its initial run, and Coppola had brought the picture in on a budget of $3.5 million. The front office was therefore interested in the movie he wanted to make next, a modest production based on an original scenario of his own entitled *The Rain People*. Production chief Kenny Hyman was continuing to pursue his policy of encouraging young directorial talent at Warners-Seven, and with good reason.

As noted before, Hollywood was faced with the rise of television. Instead of trying to upgrade the quality of their films, the studios first turned to technical innovations as a possible way of saving their audience. Thus Hollywood seemed convinced that a wider screen with the old traditional plots acted out on it would do the trick. That was certainly the studio's thinking behind the making of *Finian's Rainbow*. But movie audiences continued to defect to television, as they all too often found the average Hollywood product stuck in familiar grooves. The studios began turning to the new breed of young directors who wanted to depart from the conventional formulas of past Hollywood movies. Francis Coppola was one of the crop of budding auteurs who wanted to get away from Hollywood and make movies his own way. So he invested some of the money he had earned for directing *Finian's Rainbow* in eighty thousand dollars' worth of state-of-the-art technical equipment. He purchased, among other things, a German-made Steenbeck editing machine, which was a significant improvement over the clumsier Moviolas still in general use in Hollywood. His fellow film school alumni, Coppola remembers, said that he should "take the money and run." That is, a young director should make one studio film "and then make a personal film; but when they get the money, they're too terrified to do it. If you're not prepared to risk some money when you're young, you'll never risk it."[1] Coppola, as we shall see, never hesitated to gamble his bank account on a pet film project.

His own savings, of course, were not enough to float even a low-budget film version of *The Rain People*. Hence, he got Warners-Seven to provide financial backing to the tune of $750,000. The scenario had its antecedents in 1960, says Coppola: "I had started to write a long screenplay entitled *The Gray Stationwagon*; I eventually changed the title to *Echoes*." It dealt with three women, all of whom decide to leave their respective husbands. He soon realized that it was far too ambitious an undertaking for a twenty-one-year-old aspiring filmmaker. "I never finished it," he told me in Cannes.

Nearly a decade later, when he wanted to make another personal film based on a script he had written himself (which is what *You're a Big Boy Now* was), he turned again to that old manuscript. "I decided to do the story of just one of these women." And that was the genesis of *The Rain People*.

The Rain People (1969)

When Coppola took *You're a Big Boy Now* to the Cannes International Film Festival, he met Shirley Knight, the star of *Dutchman* (from the Le Roi Jones play), which was also entered in the festival. In *Dutchman*, Knight plays a racist prostitute who humiliates a black man on a subway train and finally stabs him. Knight was crying because some journalist had spoken rudely to her. Asked about this episode, Shirley Knight told me that one of the international press corps quite gratuitously assumed that the actress shared the racist attitude of the harlot she played in the film and berated her for it. She recalls that Coppola, who had always wanted to write a film tailored to a particular actor, said to her, "Don't cry. I'm going to write a film for you." Knight was delighted at the prospect of someone writing a part especially for her. "Oh, really?" she replied. "That's nice."

The original idea of *Rain People* was suggested to Coppola by an episode from his childhood. His mother Italia, after a horrendous quarrel with her husband Carmine, disappeared for three days. Coppola later learned that she took refuge with her sister, "but at the time she told me that she had stayed in a motel," he says. "It just clicked with me, the idea of a woman just leaving and staying in a motel."[2]

The plot of this tragic drama concerns Natalie Ravenna (Shirley Knight), a depressed young housewife with a child on the way who impulsively decides to walk out on her husband one rainy morning and to make a cross-country trek in her station wagon. She takes this rash course of action in the hope of getting some perspective on her life. Natalie at this juncture feels stifled by the responsibilities of married life, epitomized by the prospect of having a child. "She gets married and suddenly starts feeling her personality being eroded, because marriage restricts her personality," Coppola explains, "and she's pregnant—that's the final straw."

As she drives along the highway, she occasionally thinks of happier times, as when we see flashbacks to her Italian wedding, foreshadowing the opening wedding scene of *The Godfather*. In the course of her journey she picks up a hitchhiker, an ex-football player named Jimmy "Killer" Kilgannon (James Caan), who turns out to be mentally retarded as a result of a head injury he suffered in his final game. In effect, Natalie now has yet another "child" on her hands, and, almost in spite of herself, she gradually comes to care for him more and more as they travel along together.

"So it's a story of a human being becoming more and more responsible toward another human being. It's like a woman sitting next to the kid she's going to have."[3] In brief, Jimmy becomes the surrogate for the child Natalie is carrying.

In a sense both Natalie and Jimmy qualify to be numbered among the rain people of the film's title. The rain people are tender, vulnerable types who, as Jimmy himself describes them at one point, are "people made of rain; when they cry they disappear, because they cry themselves away." Like the rain people, Natalie and Jimmy are easily hurt, and, sadly, they will both end up wounding each other deeply. The rain glistening on the deserted sidewalks in the opening credits takes on new meaning when Jimmy tells Natalie about the rain people.

Coppola actually had gotten the ball rolling for the picture in late 1967, when he took his production assistant George Lucas, coproducer Bart Patton (who played the slasher in *Dementia 13*), and James Caan (a fellow Hofstra alumnus) to the Hofstra campus over the Thanksgiving weekend to film some footage at a football game that would serve for flashbacks to

Kilgannon's days as a college football star. This was even before Coppola had struck a deal with Warners-Seven, and he used these sequences to convince Kenny Hyman to back the movie.

When the studio was considering the project, Coppola presented the movie to the executives as a *fait accompli*—he affirmed that the film was ready to go into production, as evidenced by the fact that he already had the football game footage in the can. He simply told them on Friday, "Look, I'm starting to shoot in earnest on Monday, and I need money; and if you don't give it to me, I'll get it from someone else." This, we remember, is precisely the approach he had employed to get Warners-Seven to finance *You're a Big Boy Now*, and it worked again. The studio officials anted up the money, "and I never showed them the script."[4] Lucas, admiring Coppola's method of bluffing studio bosses, quipped that Coppola could sell ice to the Eskimos. After meeting with Coppola, Hyman was really convinced that seventy-five thousand dollars was not a huge risk for a director of Coppola's talents.

Barry Malkin was selected by Coppola as editor for the movie. He was a boyhood acquaintance of the director's from Queens. "We lived in the same neighborhood as teenagers," says Malkin, but they had not seen each other for years. Malkin visited fellow editor Aram Avakian while the latter was working on *You're a Big Boy Now*, and he noted that the screenplay bore the name of Francis Ford Coppola. "I used to have a friend when I was a kid named Coppola," he exclaimed. "I wonder if it's the same guy."

When Avakian got around to inquiring if Coppola knew Malkin, he answered, "I knew a guy named Blackie Malkin," which was Malkin's nickname as a youngster. Coppola eventually asked Malkin to edit *Rain People*. "It was my opportunity to edit a class feature film," Malkin states, after working on a forgettable programmer called *Fat Spy* (1966). *Rain People* was being released by a major studio. Coppola and Malkin went on to collaborate on several features thereafter, because Malkin found Coppola an easy director to work with: "For starters, we don't have discussions about which take to use; our tastes are similar, and there is a mutual trust."[5]

In the spring of 1968 Coppola assembled a hand-picked cast and crew to make the movie, which he planned to shoot entirely on location. Together they formed a caravan consisting of five cars, as well as a Dodge Travco minibus that had been remodeled to carry their technical equipment. Making the film while traveling cross-country reminded Coppola of his experience of working on Roger Corman's *Young Racers*, which was shot while the crew were migrating across Europe in a minibus (see chapter 1).

They traveled for four months through eighteen states, filming as they went. Coppola did not set out with a finished screenplay in hand. He took with him a draft dated February 7, 1968, but he continued filling it out as shooting progressed. When he spied a setting that appealed to him along the way, the group would stop, and he would work out a scene for the actors to play. Thus, while in Chattanooga, Tennessee, Coppola heard tell of an Armed Forces Day parade and incorporated it into a sequence.

George Lucas went along as production manager. Coppola wangled some money from Warners-Seven to enable Lucas to shoot a documentary about the making of *Rain People,* entitled *filmmaker: a diary by George Lucas.* The crew also numbered cinematographer Bill Butler, administrative assistant Mona Skager, and editor Barry Malkin—the film was edited en route on the Steenbeck, which was on board the Dodge minibus. In addition to Shirley Knight and James Caan, Robert Duval came along to play the key role of Gordon, a motorcycle cop with whom Natalie gets involved. In all, there were twenty actors and crew members in Coppola's entourage.

The footage shot each day was regularly sent to a New York laboratory for processing and returned within three days. Malkin edited the footage in the Dodge minibus, as noted before. He taped a sign on the outside of the Dodge, christening their mobile movie unit "The Magical Mystery Tour." The Steenbeck at which he worked, he recalls, was wedged into the original kitchenette space of the mobile home, which also doubled as the dressing room.

The last two months of shooting were in Nebraska, so Coppola took over an abandoned shoe shop in Ogallala and transformed it into his command post. The production team occupied an empty store, says Malkin, and flew in additional editing equipment from the Warners-Seven stockpile. He started a full-scale editing of the footage into a preliminary rough cut at this point. Coppola was convinced that making *Rain People* 15,500 miles away from the Hollywood studio "shark pool" was the prototype of how he would like to make movies in the future. If he could operate out of a store front in a one-horse town in Nebraska, there was no reason why he should have to live and work in the Hollywood film colony thereafter.

George Lucas thought of his half-hour documentary *filmmaker* as a cinematic journal that "offers a personal viewpoint on the daily tension and stress occurring during a film production."[6] The documentary records the odyssey of Coppola and his convoy of actors and technicians, living out of suitcases as they traveled through New Jersey, Pennsylvania, West Virginia, Tennessee, Kentucky, and, ultimately, Nebraska. Coppola, of course, had to keep in touch with the studio brass back at Warners-Seven. *Filmmaker* includes a shot of Coppola pacing back and forth during a heated discussion over the long-distance wire with a studio executive who fears that Coppola is drifting further and further out of studio control as he continues his cross-country trek. Coppola finally loses patience and issues a sweeping condemnation of the hidebound studio system. "The system," he barks into the phone, "will fall by its own weight!" adding that he is determined to finish the picture on time and on budget—and on his own terms.

At other times in the course of the documentary Coppola confesses to his colleagues his doubts about reaching journey's end successfully, as when he frantically rewrites a portion of the screenplay to work in the Armed Forces Day parade in Chattanooga. Late in the documentary, when the going gets especially rough at one point, Coppola confesses, still on camera, "I am tired of being the anchor when I see my world crumbling."

Lucas remembers the whole production experience as the best of times and the worst of times. He affirms that the cast and crew shared some good times during the trip. "It was difficult, but for the young clowns that we were, it was fun." By contrast, the twenty people involved in the expedition spent countless nights in cheap motels in the middle of nowhere, and "that was nervewracking."[7]

One of the difficulties posed by shooting the film entirely on location was that the director of photography, Bill Butler, had to make do with the minimum of lighting equipment that had been brought along in the minibus. Butler came from Chicago TV and was shooting his first Hollywood feature. He was in his forties, making him the oldest member of Coppola's production unit on the picture. His experience in making TV documentaries had taught him how to shoot quickly and efficiently with a small crew. "I told Coppola I could shoot just about any kind of scene that he could dream up," Butler says. Coppola followed the same procedure on the present film as he had on *You're a Big Boy Now,* filming the location scenes as much as possible with the natural light available at the location site.

Gordon, the motorcycle policeman to whom Natalie is sexually attracted, lives in a trailer park, and Butler had to light a night sequence there. For an interior scene in the trailer, he simply screwed photoflood lamps into the lighting fixtures already available in the trailer in order to provide sufficient lighting for shooting the scene. For exterior shots, as the characters walked around the trailer park at night, Butler hid lights behind bushes on the grounds in order to provide illumination for shooting. "It's a real challenge when you have a minimum number of lights to work with," he comments. "You really have to be inventive." He liked working with Coppola on this film and on *The Conversation* because "he gives you a lot of freedom. He lets your creativity work for him."[8]

The screenplay, we know, was not in final form when Coppola's caravan hit the road to begin filming. Consequently, Coppola was constantly revising the script, changing any dialogue that no longer fit the flow of the shooting as it progressed. He was carefully modifying the dialogue by improvising with the actors during rehearsals in order to make the dialogue fit the action of the scene satisfactorily. Coppola found shooting the film on location to be stimulating. In the controlled environment of the studio, he told me, "you lose the random, unpredictable things that can energize a scene." A case in point is the Armed Forces Day parade in Chattanooga. In the scene Jimmy, temporarily separated from Natalie, wanders dazed and confused among the spectators and the youngsters in the high school bands as they march down the street, as if he were a little boy who has lost his mother.

Like the shoppers in Macy's department store, where Coppola shot the climax of *You're a Big Boy Now*, neither the spectators nor the band members had any idea that a movie was being shot. So they were baffled by this stranger intruding on the parade. All in all, it was a touching scene, all the more noteworthy since it was written to order on the spot. In short, there was nothing haphazard about the use of improvisation to revise the screenplay. The rewrites were not scribbled on the back of an envelope with no concern for narrative coherence, as a wag back at Warners-Seven had opined.

As filming continued and the script was further developed, it became evident to Coppola that Natalie's attitude toward Jimmy was coming more clearly into focus. For her part, Natalie is touched by Jimmy's disarming vulnerability, but she is also wary of his growing emotional dependence on her and wants to break off their burgeoning relationship. She consequently secures him a job on an animal farm they happen to come across during their trip in order to be able to move on without him. Jimmy obviously does not want her to leave him behind. When the proprietor of the farm asks him sarcastically, "Is she your mother?" He responds, "She's my best friend."

But the childlike Jimmy spoils everything by releasing all the animals from their cages, because he simply cannot stand to see them penned up. Jimmy is fired, of course, and Natalie is enraged at him for continuing to be attached to her. She accordingly abandons him on the road and forthwith takes up with Gordon, a state highway patrolman (Robert Duvall). Gordon, whose wife is dead, invites her back to the trailer park where he lives with his young daughter, Rosalie.

Jimmy surreptitiously follows Natalie to Gordon's trailer and furiously bursts in on them in order to save her from Gordon's advances. Rosalie also shows up unexpectedly. When she sees the hulking "Killer" Kilgannon attacking her father, she frantically grabs his patrolman's pistol and shoots Jimmy. The movie ends abruptly, with Natalie sobbing inconsolably as she cradles the mortally wounded Jimmy in her arms, futilely promising to care for him from now on. "I'll take you home and we'll be family," she murmurs as Jimmy expires.

The screenplay, which is on file in the Script Repository at Warner Brothers, contains an epilogue that follows the death of Jimmy Kilgannon. Natalie meets Vinny at the airport (he has flown out to meet her and escort her back home). They are reunited at the fade-out. Coppola wisely opted to end the film instead with Jimmy's demise. Following that dramatically powerful scene with the reunion of Natalie and Vinny would have been nothing short of an anticlimax.

Throughout the shooting period Coppola had to cope with his increasing disagreements with Shirley Knight. She stated in conversation that she preferred to work in the more structured environment of a studio and grew weary of the vagabond existence on the road. Moreover, she found Coppola's improvisational technique of working out scenes tedious and trying.

To make matters worse, Coppola was not satisfied with how Shirley Knight was interpreting the role of Natalie as filming continued. They clashed often while he was rehearsing various scenes with her and the rest of the cast. The character of Natalie, as he had conceived it, is a headstrong, reckless individual, he explains. But she also has "a tremendously compassionate side." On the one hand, Natalie becomes fed up with Jimmy's emotional dependence on her. On the other hand, she is aware that she is a mother figure for Jimmy. "I didn't feel I was getting that from Shirley. I would get the high-strung, nervous intensity" more than anything else— she was too abrasive.

Coppola saw Natalie as a young woman driven to panic and despair at the prospect of having a child and frustrated by her attempts to cope with the mentally retarded Jimmy, who becomes increasingly possessive in making demands on her—he is not as passive as he at first appeared. He even rips out the telephone wires when Natalie endeavors to phone her husband, in an obvious demonstration of childish jealousy. At such times Coppola wants the audience to sympathize with her plight. Yet he sensed that Knight too often portrayed Natalie as self-centered and almost cruel, thereby making it hard for filmgoers to feel sorry for her. For example, after Jimmy breaks the phone connection between Natalie and her husband,

Natalie scratches his face vindictively. Coppola remarks, "I don't know how much I liked that character," as Knight played her, "whereas I liked the character I had written."[9]

The tensions between director and star are on display in one segment of *filmmaker,* wherein Coppola and Knight bicker about whether or not Natalie should carry a purse in an upcoming scene. If Coppola comes across as somewhat controlling, Knight seems equally intransigent. Despite her creative differences with the director, however, Knight gives a compelling performance as Natalie.

To be fair to Knight, there was some merit in her complaints that Coppola's rewriting of the script while they were shooting the film made inroads on the screenplay's continuity. Because the script for *The Rain People* was developed in this piecemeal fashion, the story does not hang together as coherently as one would like. As a matter of fact, Coppola is the first to concede that the killing that climaxes the movie is a kind of *deus ex machina* he concocted in order to resolve the movie's plot. The lack of a tightly constructed plotline made for a slow-moving film, and, therefore, *The Rain People* did not win over the critics or the mass audience.

Still there are some fine things in the film—for example, the key scene in which Jimmy liberates the animals from their captivity is a symbolic reminder that Natalie at this point still feels cooped up by circumstances and likewise yearns to be set free from the emotional entanglements in her life. A similar point is made in the scene in which she phones her husband for the first time, from a phone booth on the Pennsylvania Turnpike. Natalie seems trapped in a cage as she is photographed through the glass of the telephone booth, desperately confessing to Vinny that she is not sure she knows what it means to be a wife, much less a mother. This image of entrapment is ironic: although Natalie embarked on this journey to regain her freedom, she still remains shut in with her unresolved emotional conflicts.

Another neat Coppola touch is having Gordon live in a mobile home, an indication of the transient nature of his life since he lost his wife and, by the same token, a foreshadowing of the sort of rootless existence Natalie is opening herself to if she opts to forsake her husband for good. Indeed, the desolate small towns, the bleak, endless turnpikes, the seedy motels, and shabby roadside diners visually underscore this point. It is a world in which a woman with a past can encounter a man with no future in the depressing atmosphere of a tawdry trailer park.

Significantly, Coppola's overriding theme, which centers on the importance of the role of a family spirit in people's lives, is clearly delineated in this film. Thus, as Robert Johnson notes in his book on Coppola, Natalie takes to the open road to escape the responsibilities of family life, only to find that she has taken them with her. This fact is strikingly brought home to her when she reflects that her unborn child, the very emblem of her marriage, is always with her, accompanying her wherever she goes. And this reflection in turn ultimately leads her by the end of the picture to reconcile herself to her responsibilities as a wife and mother, for she realizes that in trying to escape the obligations of family life she has brought nothing but misery to herself and others. Hence the movie ends, Coppola emphasizes, with an implicit "plea to have a family."[10]

Coppola finished the film on schedule and for $740,000, slightly under budget. When the convoy got back to Los Angeles in the fall of 1968, George Lucas suggested Walter Murch, a fellow film student of his at USC, as sound engineer to mix the sound track of the film. Murch was aware that Coppola had gone to film school at UCLA, across town from its rival film school, USC. Like Lucas, Murch very much wanted to work with Coppola, who was already making an impact on the industry while still in his late twenties.

Coppola accepted Murch on Lucas's recommendation, and Murch viewed the rough cut of *Rain People* with Coppola only once. Then Coppola installed Murch in the cellar of a warehouse on Folsom Street in San Francisco, where Coppola had a Nagra sound recorder and the Steenbeck editing machine set up. And so Murch mixed the sound track for the film far removed from the watchful eyes of the studio authorities in Hollywood.

Furthermore, Murch had to work away from the studio not only to forestall any meddling on the part of studio officials but because—like many recent film school graduates—he was not yet a member of a union. "I was frightened that it would be found out that somebody non-union was editing the sound, and I'd lose this chance to work on a feature," Murch explains.[11] He was even afraid to visit the studio to make use of the sound library, which housed endless shelves of prerecorded sound effects. So he had to create all of the sound effects himself.

Murch, who up to this point had only worked on short films, was pleased with the trust Coppola placed in him to do his job properly. Like Bill Butler, who is cited above, he believes that Coppola gives to each of his collaborators authority to operate with a great deal of freedom in their own domain. "It's paradoxical; by giving so much freedom and authority to you, you feel much more beholden to him" and want to do the best job possible, Murch says.[12] Murch would continue to work with Coppola on subsequent films, as is clear from his foreword to this book.

Moreover, Coppola was building a small band of collaborators with whom he would continue to work in the future. He found that one way of placing his personal stamp as an auteur on his films was precisely to assemble a production team that went from picture to picture with him. As time went on, creative collaborators like Barry Malkin and Walter Murch could almost intuit what Coppola wanted from each of them as a picture was being shot.

Although *The Rain People*, like *You're a Big Boy Now,* drew mixed reviews, some of the favorable notices were enthusiastic, noting how impressive acting and direction had triumphed over a weak script. Indeed, the positive reviews affirmed that the director displayed an eye for detail keen enough to compensate for the deficiencies of the material. This is not, after all, an independent film cobbled together with secondhand furniture and secondhand talent. It has expert cinematography and the glossy look of a film made in a Hollywood studio rather than by an itinerant band of film-makers filming all over the country, as was actually the case.

Pauline Kael heaped both praise and blame on Coppola for *Rain People*, as she had done on *Finian's Rainbow.* "There's a prodigious amount of talent in Francis Ford Coppola's unusual, little-seen film," she writes, "but the writer-director applies his craftsmanship with undue solemnity to material that suggests a gifted college student's imitation of early Tennessee Williams."[13] Interestingly enough, Coppola has said that he did have in mind Williams's brand of Southern Gothic melodrama when penning his early screenplays, especially *Pilma, Pilma,* the unproduced script that won him the Goldwyn Award while he was still at UCLA. Furthermore, in retrospect, he thought that the bloody finale of *Rain People* did recall Williams's more lurid melodramas.

Shirley Knight was applauded for presenting Natalie as a complicated human being attempting to navigate her way through a serious emotional crisis. It is worth noting that one of her last films was Antonio Tibaldi's *Little Boy Blue* (1997) in which she took to the road yet again. This time she played a character moving from one motel to another in the South as she searched for her kidnapped son. So, in making another "road movie," Knight's career had come full circle.

James Caan was recognized by some critics as playing Jimmy not merely as a pathetic simpleton but as a mentally handicapped individual trying desperately to relate to others. Caan gives an off-kilter, on-target performance as a mental retardate. Up to this point in his career he had, quite frankly, been in more turkeys than Stove Top dressing, as the saying goes. Therefore *Rain People* added some depth to his resumé.

Moreover, Coppola could take some solace in the fact that the picture captured both the Grand Prize and the best director award at the San Sebastian International Film Festival. Nevertheless, the critical consensus on *Rain People* was fairly negative, and the picture died at the box office. It finally found on network TV and in its release on videocassette the audience it deserved. What's more, the reputation of the film has improved over the years, possibly because of its exposure on television and on videotape. It is now seen as an early feminist film portraying in unsentimental terms a picture of a young woman seeking to find liberation from a marriage that she fears is stifling her. In this regard Coppola states, "I sensed that there must be married women who were expected to accomplish something, and who were in fact dying inside. I thought it would be an interesting affirmation for one of them to simply get up and leave."[14] As a feminist film, then, the movie is now recognized as being years ahead of its time. More than one feminist critic has singled out *Rain People* as one of the first films to come out of Hollywood that addressed the constricting role of the housewife in modern society. Furthermore, *Rain People* is now viewed as one of the deepest examinations of the conflict between independence and responsibility that American cinema has given us.

American Zoetrope

Francis Coppola's experience working out of a production office in Ogallala, Nebraska, during the last two months of filming *Rain People* convinced him that he did not have to be based in the Hollywood film colony to make movies. When he and George Lucas drove back to Los Angeles from Nebraska in the fall of 1968, they passed through San Francisco, where they encountered filmmaker John Korty, who was finishing his third independent feature, *Riverrun* (1970), in a garage at Stinson Beach. Coppola was much impressed. He said, in effect, to Korty, "If you can do it, I can do it too!" At that moment, according to Lucas, Coppola crystallized his determination to lift his filmmaking operation out of Hollywood.

"We wanted a little studio where we could mix and edit our films," Lucas recalls. They wanted a base of operations where they could function as they did in that makeshift production office in Ogallala. Looking around San Francisco, Coppola considered it to be a beautiful place to live, with a bohemian artistic tradition congenial to young independent filmmakers. Standing in the lobby of the Mark Hopkins Hotel, Coppola exclaimed, "This is great; let's move!"[15]

Another advantage of San Francisco was that it was close enough to

Los Angeles to allow Coppola to draw talent from there. Coppola points out that the motion picture industry at the time was "a closed shop, employing men in their fifties who had worked in the studio system."

Lucas gleefully decided to join Coppola in San Francisco and shortly afterward inquired if Walter Murch, who had originally signed on only as sound engineer on *The Rain People,* wanted to be part of their new independent film unit. Murch replied that he thought it was a great idea—he did not plan to spend the rest of his life in Hollywood under any circumstances. So in April 1969 "we all decamped," says Murch, who drove a van filled with the technical equipment Coppola had acquired so far from Los Angeles to San Francisco. Coppola had by this time taken a long-term lease on the three-story warehouse at 827 Folsom Street in an industrial area of downtown San Francisco—the same place where Murch had mixed the sound track of *Rain People.* There were disused warehouses in the district that were now empty, Murch explains, and Coppola and company were able to lease one fairly inexpensively.

Coppola went to a film trade fair in Cologne, Germany, around this time and promptly invested in another eighty thousand dollars' worth of new state-of-the-art, high-tech editing equipment, which he did not have the funds to pay for at the moment. He then had it installed in the dingy warehouse that was being renovated to serve as a filmmaking facility.

Coppola's new independent producing unit, born in a warehouse loft, was christened American Zoetrope. The zoetrope, a viewer invented in the nineteenth century by William Horner, was a harbinger of the cinema. It was a cylinder circumscribed with images. When the drum on which the images were drawn was rotated rapidly, it gave the illusion of motion from still images. Coppola named his company after the zoetrope because it was a traditional symbol for the cinema. He had received one as a gift, and he liked to point out that the Greek root of zoetrope means "the movement of life," a reference in his mind to the dynamic young filmmakers who had started the new film organization. Besides Lucas and Murch, other film school alumni were enlisting in Coppola's little band of moviemakers, including directors-to-be John Milius and Martin Scorsese. Lucas, who was five years Coppola's junior, said that they all saw Coppola as the great white knight who gave them hope that they could make films far from the Hollywood factory system.

The Rain People was the first film to be released under the banner of American Zoetrope, although technically the new producing company was only a gleam in Coppola's eye when that film was being made in 1968. American Zoetrope was officially incorporated as a film organization in San Francisco on November 14, 1969, with Coppola as its president and sole stock-holder, Lucas as vice president, and Mona Skager, production manager on *Rain People*, as secretary-treasurer. On December 13, 1969, Coppola held a full-dress press conference with the mayor present to announce the formation of American Zoetrope. At the press conference he declared that he was gratified to have created a film facility in San Francisco. In Los Angeles, he observed, filmmakers talk about making deals, in San Francisco they talk about making films.

He issued a press release that proclaimed, "The main objective of this company will be to undertake film production in several different areas by collaborating with the most gifted and talented young people, using the most contemporary and sophisticated equipment available."[16]

One of Coppola's assistants quipped that those working at American Zoetrope felt that they were clocking in at a factory every day, "but, in any case, it was our factory."[17] In fact, Coppola and his comrades saw themselves as an autonomous guild of filmmakers, quite distant from the Hollywood studios. Coppola was really following Roger Corman's lead in bringing together aspiring filmmakers from the UCLA and USC film schools who were eager to learn their craft. But they enjoyed much more autonomy at Zoetrope than Coppola did when he was serving his apprenticeship with Corman (see chapter 1). Coppola would give a camera to a street cleaner who was interested in Zoetrope, Lucas says wryly. Lucas was only half-joking. Always conservative in business matters, he was genuinely concerned that Coppola would allow just about anyone to handle Zoetrope's expensive equipment, regardless of their lack of experience in filmmaking.

For his part, Coppola envisioned Zoetrope as an alternative movie organization "where he could get a lot of young talent," according to Lucas. They would make movies, "hope that one of them would be a hit," and eventually build up a thriving independent film unit that way.[18]

Viewing American Zoetrope as the wave of the future, Coppola was clearly the driving force behind the company. He implicitly saw American Zoetrope as a way of putting the auteur theory into practice by setting up a filmmaking operation in which moviemakers could place on each of their films, not the stamp of a Hollywood studio, but the stamp of their own cinematic style and personal vision. In short, Zoetrope reflected Coppola's utopian vision of how movies could be made outside the traditional Hollywood factory system.

Coppola went to Warners, which had produced three of the films he had directed, and offered them a package of seven movie projects. The studio had once again changed hands and was now owned by Steve Ross, the head of Kinney National Service. Ross had started his firm, a limousine service, by borrowing his father's funeral parlor limousines. Kinney's interests ranged from a chain of parking lots to a talent agency. Ted Ashley, who had been associated with the talent agency, was now studio chief. Warner Brothers was now known officially as Warner Communications Inc. Coppola employed the same bluff he had used to get Warners to back both *You're a Big Boy Now* and *The Rain People*: he telegrammed Ashley that Zoetrope had its first project ready to go into production, and this was the studio's only chance to get in on the ground floor.

The film in question was *THX 1138,* which Lucas was to direct from his own screenplay. It was, in fact, an expanded version of a prizewinning student featurette that Lucas had submitted as his master's thesis to USC. Part of the exclusive deal that Coppola was presenting to Warners-Seven included his proposal for *The Conversation,* a thriller about a surveillance expert. For good measure, he also threw in *Apocalypse Now,* a concept for a movie about the Vietnam War that had been hatched by Lucas and Milius.

As Coppola had anticipated, Ashley gave the green light to *THX 1138,* but he saw it as a B picture and assigned it a budget under $1 million. As for the other six projects, Ashley decreed that the studio would put up $300,000 in seed money for script development for them. Ashley also agreed to lend Coppola an additional $300,000 to establish the fledgling Zoetrope company as a functioning business concern.

But Ashley drove a hard bargain. He was not investing in American Zoetrope—he was merely loaning money to Coppola's organization. If the scripts Coppola eventually submitted to Warners-Seven did not meet the studio's expectations and the studio wanted out of the deal, Warners would have to be reimbursed in full for the $600,000 that Coppola had borrowed. Coppola accepted these stiff terms largely because Ashley had agreed to finance *THX 1138,* and Coppola was aware that, with one movie definitely set to go into production, American Zoetrope was actually in business. Besides, if only one or two of the other projects were developed into successful films, neither Coppola nor Warners-Seven would lose on the deal. To Coppola that seemed to be a safe bet.

When Coppola enthusiastically related to Lucas the terms of the deal he had made with a major studio, Lucas was naturally glad about the prospect of getting *THX* made, but he resented the fact that Coppola had included *Apocalypse Now,* which had originated with himself and Milius, in the package deal without consulting him. But he was willing to swallow his displeasure at the time. Like Coppola, he was euphoric that American Zoetrope now seemed to be established on a firm footing. As Lucas puts it, "we young filmmakers were going to conquer the world."[19]

The future seemed bright. Coppola planned to spend a good deal of Warners' advance funds, not only for reconstruction of the warehouse site, but also to pay for the expensive high-tech equipment he was steadily acquiring. American Zoetrope would have seven editing rooms, equipped with Keller sound editing equipment and Steenbeck film editing machines, as well as 35 mm and 16 mm cameras.

What's more, *THX* seemed a promising venture for Zoetrope's maiden voyage into feature filmmaking. The personnel involved in the Lucas picture included some veterans of past Coppola movies. Lucas himself—whose previous directorial credit was on *filmmaker,* his documentary short about the making of *Rain People*—was directing *THX* as his first feature. He had co-written the screenplay with Walter Murch, the sound engineer on *Rain People,* who was functioning in the same capacity on *THX*. And Robert Duvall, who had a featured role in *Rain People,* had the lead in Lucas's film.

Everything was rosy until Coppola went to Warners several months later with the rough cut of *THX* and the scripts for the other six film projects Zoetrope was offering the studio. Coppola delivered to Ashley's office a huge box containing the screenplays, each of them in a handsome black binder proudly bearing the Zoetrope imprimatur. The studio executives who viewed *THX 1138* with Ashley included business manager Frank Wells, known in the industry as a tough customer. When the lights came up at the end of the screening, the executives present declared emphatically that they were appalled by the austere futuristic tale of robotlike creatures living in a society where sex is outlawed. Ashley and his cohorts found the plot hard to follow and the bleak atmosphere of the movie, with its bleached costumes and pale decor, downright depressing.

Dale Pollack, in his book on George Lucas, states baldly that Warners-Seven rejected out of hand the group of scripts from American Zoetrope that Coppola had brought with him on the same day as the screening of the rough cut of *THX*. On the contrary, the documentation in the Warner Brothers archive indicates that the studio moguls were not quite as precipitous as that. Coppola left the box of proposed scripts with Ashley and scheduled a meeting to discuss them after he returned from a trip to Europe. So Coppola did not get the studio's verdict on the scripts he had submitted to them a few hours after the screening of *THX*, as Pollack mistakenly asserts.

When Ashley and Wells finally met with Coppola, they advised him that, since Warners-Seven had bankrolled the making of *THX 1138*, the studio was committed to releasing the picture. But Ashley was personally so thoroughly upset by Lucas's anti-utopian saga that he consequently rejected in turn, with Wells's firm support, each of the other six Zoetrope scripts Coppola had submitted to the studio. At this final meeting Ted Ashley told Coppola flatly that Warners-Seven was pulling the plug on their deal with American Zoetrope altogether. Adding insult to injury, he informed Coppola that Zoetrope must repay not only the $300,000 the studio had loaned Coppola for refurbishing and outfitting with equipment Zoetrope's headquarters, but Zoetrope must also reimburse Warners-Seven for the additional $300,000 the studio had spent developing the scripts. In effect, the studio was making Coppola buy back his own scripts. "Warners not only pulled the rug out from under Francis," Murch said later, "they tried to sell it back to him."[20]

Coppola had no choice but to capitulate. "They had all the marbles," he commented afterward.[21] At all events, Coppola's final confrontation with Ashley and Wells concluded with Coppola being sent packing, along with his box of scripts, back to San Francisco. Film historian Peter Biskind reports that, as a parting shot, Coppola, sensing that he had nothing more to lose, shouted on his way out the door, "I'm an artist; you're fucking Philistines."

Lucas later hazarded that the projects Coppola had presented to Warners, including his own *THX*, were too adventurous for their conventional tastes. In addition to *THX* there was a screenplay that took a controversial stance toward the Vietnam War (*Apocalypse Now*) and a script for an intricate, subtle psychological thriller about a neurotic wiretapper (*The Conversation*). Over and above the studio's displeasure with the Zoetrope projects, Warners' decision to cancel the deal with Zoetrope altogether was motivated to some degree by the fact that, by this time, it was abundantly clear that *You're a Big Boy Now* and *The Rain People*—both of which had originated with Coppola, had finished their respective theatrical runs out of the money. This, of course, was a factor of which Wells, as the manager of the studio's finances, would have been particularly aware. At any rate, the date of Coppola's final confrontation with Warners-Seven, November 19, 1970 (just one year after Zoetrope was officially inaugurated as an independent film organization), would forever after be known in Zoetrope lore as "Black Thursday"—a reference to Black Tuesday, the day that the stock market crashed in 1929.[22]

When Warners released *THX* (with some minor cuts) in 1971, it was not a moneymaker, although it has acquired a cult following over the years. Coppola drew some consolation from the fact that once he eventually paid back the money he had borrowed from Warners-Seven he would own the rights to all of the unproduced Zoetrope scripts—including two that he would eventually direct himself, *The Conversation* and *Apocalypse Now*. But that was in the unforeseeable future.

For now Zoetrope was bankrupt. As one of Coppola's associates joked, Coppola's office was down to one miniskirted secretary and a jar of instant coffee, which had replaced Coppola's beloved espresso machine. Although Coppola's staff was not as meager as that, Zoetrope was operating in the red. Furthermore, there had been other losses besides those incurred by the breakup with Warners. Some rookie filmmakers had, without authorization, borrowed and not returned a lot of expensive film equipment. As noted before, this was just the sort of thing that the cautious George Lucas had feared might happen when he had warned Coppola that American Zoetrope was not being run efficiently. For the record, during the first year of operation, forty thousand dollars' worth of cameras and other equipment disappeared. "It was tremendously irresponsible" on their part to take advantage of his goodwill, Coppola complains. He had spent that whole time plus all the money he could muster setting up a film facility, "and things got stolen and Zoetrope was picked clean." It was becoming a "fraternity house" for tyro filmmakers, a free-for-all.[23]

Coppola became increasingly aware that even a small film facility needs capital to survive, and he was actually afraid at one point that the sheriff would put a chain across the front door and close the whole operation down. Things got even worse, Lucas remembers: "We were not only broke, but we were blackballed in the industry." Warners had spread the word that he and Coppola were not responsible parties, and neither of them could get a feature picture off the ground.[24]

But the resilient Coppola promptly reorganized and diversified Zoetrope in order to pay his debts. He began producing educational films, industrial documentaries, and television commercials. He also rented out Zoetrope's first-class postproduction facilities, which boasted the latest editing equipment, to other filmmakers.[25]

In the long run it was short-sighted for Ashley and company to jettison Zoetrope and all of its talent with a sweeping vote of no-confidence. Biskind goes so far as to say that it was a colossal blunder for them to alienate Coppola, who would in the not-too-distant future turn out to be an important director. In fact, both Coppola and Lucas would soon become two of the most outstanding filmmakers of the 1970s, and they would rarely work for Warner Brothers again.

The fact remains that, as Lucas notes above, Coppola was experiencing some difficulty in launching another film project—until the release of *Patton*, which Coppola had co-scripted just before he made *You're a Big Boy*

Now (see chapter 1). He won an Academy Award for co-writing the epic World War II movie. The film was so long in incubation before it was finally produced that it was not released until 1970. Since Coppola's stock had suddenly risen in the film industry, Paramount decided to entrust him with the direction of a gangster picture about the Mafia entitled *The Godfather* that they were going to make based on the bestselling novel by Mario Puzo.

When Warners got to hear about this, one bigwig there, Frank Wells, phoned Paramount and advised the studio chief that he might as well turn over Coppola's check directly to them. As a matter of fact, after the subsequent success of *The Godfather,* Coppola recalls, "I paid them the $300,000 loan," which he had used for renovating the Folsom Street warehouse and for outfitting the film facility with production equipment. But he asked Warners-Seven to reconsider their demand for the additional $300,000 seed money that Ashley had allocated for script development for the projects Coppola had offered to Warners-Seven in his original package. Coppola countered their demand for this additional fee by emphasizing that there was simply no precedent in the movie industry for a studio to be reimbursed for money that they had spent on developing scripts that they ultimately rejected—something both Lucas and Murch had pointed out early on in discussing Black Thursday with Coppola. It is, after all, standard procedure for a studio to invest money in the development of scripts "on spec" and to absorb the development costs, whether or not the studio eventually accepts or rejects the finished products.

Warners responded characteristically that no precedent was necessary—a deal was a deal. So Coppola and Warners had reached a stalemate. When Coppola was preparing to direct *Godfather II* in 1974 Warners again notified Paramount that they should turn over his salary to them. Paramount, tired of being pestered by Warners, paid up so that Coppola could get on with *Godfather II,* but they subsequently deducted the sum from Coppola's earnings on that picture. But the cloud had a silver lining: "Because of the reimbursal," Coppola concludes, "American Zoetrope had got back the script rights," including those for *The Conversation* and *Apocalypse Now.* He had in essence been forced to buy back the scripts in question, and they now belonged unequivocally to Zoetrope. The two scripts that he himself later filmed enhanced his reputation considerably: *The Conversation* garnered some Oscar nominations and became a cult film; *Apocalypse Now* became an established cinema classic, as we shall see.[26]

Coppola made *The Conversation* between *The Godfather* and *Godfather II.* In order to treat the *Godfather* trilogy as a unit in this book, it seems appropriate to deal with *The Conversation* at this point in order to avoid interrupting the discussion of the three *Godfather* films. Moreover, *The Conversation,* like *The Rain People,* was derived from an original screenplay by Coppola and, as such, deserves to be discussed in tandem with the earlier film.

From the beginning of his career as a director, Coppola had wanted to develop projects of his own rather than merely hire himself out to various studios to direct the films they wanted him to make. *You're a Big Boy Now* was a project Coppola had initiated himself, although it was not an original screenplay but was based on a novel. He took some pride in the fact that *The Conversation,* like *Dementia 13* and *The Rain People,* was an original script. As novelist-screenwriter Raymond Chandler used to say, "Original screenplays are almost as rare in Hollywood as virgins."[27]

After the exhausting experience of making *Finian's Rainbow,* Coppola asserted that he was thinking of pulling out of Hollywood and making cheaper movies—like *The Conversation*—that he would write himself: "If it means I've got to make $6,000 movies in San Francisco, then I guess that's what I have to do."[28] *The Conversation,* of course, would cost more than $6,000, but it would still have a modest budget by studio standards, and it would be filmed in San Francisco.

As a result of the success of *The Godfather,* Paramount was prepared to finance *The Conversation.* As George Lucas commented at the time, artistic independence comes at a price. "If you're going to use your own resources and not rob a bank," a director has to figure out a way to obtain financing for the personal films he wants to make. "Francis couldn't have made *The Rain People* if he hadn't made *Finian's Rainbow.*" By the same token, he had to make *The Godfather* "in order to make *The Conversation,* his next film."[29]

The Conversation (1974)

The phenomenal success of *The Godfather* gave Coppola the leverage not only to make *The Conversation* but also to make American Zoetrope solvent again. "I was always fighting utter bankruptcy," says Coppola, "so the notion of having excess money was new."[30] It was around this time that Coppola joined forces with fellow directors Peter Bogdanovich (*The Last Picture Show*) and William Friedkin (*The French Connection*) to form the Directors Company, an independent film unit separate from American Zoetrope. The Directors Company was the brain child of Charles Bludhorn, chairman of Paramount's parent company at the time, Gulf and Western.

Bludhorn wanted to secure the services of these talented directors "and was willing to offer them creative autonomy," Anita Busch and Beth Faski have written.[31] Accordingly, Bludhorn empowered Frank Yablans, president of Paramount, to negotiate the deal with the trio of directors: They could make any movie they chose that cost no more than $3 million, and they also had final cut on each of their pictures.

But soon resentment began to build among the three filmmakers. Neither Coppola nor Friedkin was happy with Bogdanovich's choice of *Daisy Miller,* an old-fashioned Henry James period piece. Friedkin, in turn, thought *The Conversation* was likewise an unpromising project. Furthermore, Bogdanovich signed a separate three-picture agreement with Warners-Seven, and Friedkin similarly made a separate two-picture deal with Universal. None of these films would be made for the Directors Company. Nor would *Godfather II,* which Coppola had committed himself to before the Directors Company was formed.

Coppola acknowledges the technical issues created by the directors' choices of more personal films like *The Conversation.* The studios were really not looking for small personal projects. Rather, they were looking for gigantic spectacles concerned with torching office towers or sinking ocean liners. In reality, Paramount was reluctant to finance the personal films that the three directors came up with. There was trouble in paradise, and the Directors Company proved to be a short-lived business venture, with the result that Coppola's partnership with Bogdanovich and Friedkin was soon dissolved. The only contribution that Coppola made to the Directors Company was *The Conversation,* to which he still owns the rights. This movie once more proved Coppola's capabilities as a first-class filmmaker, and Coppola continued his association with Paramount, if not with the Directors Company.

In the fall of 1972 Coppola turned his full attention to *The Conversation.* Coppola saw *The Godfather* as a strictly commercial venture, a gangster flick, and he was anxious to confirm his reputation as a serious artist by filming an original screenplay of his own, as well as by writing the screen adaptation of F. Scott Fitzgerald's distinguished classic novel, *The Great Gatsby* (see chapter 1).

He first conceived the idea for *The Conversation* in the mid-1960s, while listening to director Irvin Kershner (*The Flim Flam Man*) discuss espionage and state-of-the art surveillance tactics, which fascinated him. He told Coppola about long-distance "shotgun" microphones that looked like rifles. They were so powerful that when they were aimed at the mouth of each speaker they could actually record a conversation between two individuals, even in the midst of a crowd. (This is precisely what happens in the opening sequence of *The Conversation*: the movie begins with a couple having a conversation in a public square in downtown San Francisco, which is being monitored by a wiretapper.)

In looking back on his conversation with Kershner, Coppola was struck anew by the idea that a film about an expert wiretapper could make an interesting movie. He was especially fascinated by the concept that "bugging was a profession, not just some private detective going out and eavesdropping with primitive equipment." Before composing a full-scale screenplay for the movie, Coppola collected information of all kinds about the technology involved in clandestine surveillance procedures and incorporated much of it into the script. He also read voraciously about expert wiretappers. The movie's main character, Harry Caul, was based in part on Bernard Spindel, a legendary surveillance expert who was so fascinated with intrigue and espionage that he became obsessed with his craft, as does Harry Caul. Kershner had sent Coppola some documentation about surveillance wizard Hal Lipset, a native of San Francisco, early on, and Coppola in due course enlisted him as a technical consultant on *The Conversation*. Indeed Lipset in some ways also served as a model for Harry Caul (and is even mentioned in the film's dialogue).

To flesh out the personality of Harry Caul, the film's central character, Coppola enriched Caul with elements of his own background. As mentioned in chapter 1, Coppola had been interested in gadgets from childhood, as had Harry. Coppola also embellished Harry's background with his own bout with polio as a child and with his Catholic upbringing. (In fact, Harry goes to a priest for sacramental confession at one point.)

As the character of Harry Caul began to take shape in his mind, Coppola saw him as someone who was considered an oddball in high school because he spent so much of his time tinkering with his gadgets. Harry was the sort of "techno-freak" who was the president of the school's radio club. Coppola owns himself to be that type: he was president of the radio club, and his nickname in high school was "Science." As a teenager young Francis even planted a network of hidden microphones behind the radiators in his home so he could eavesdrop on family conversations and possibly learn what gifts he was going to receive for his birthday. He recalls having a sense of power in possessing the ability to listen to private conversations without being detected.

Coppola had actually started working on the screenplay for *The Conversation* toward the end of 1966, while he was finishing up postproduction on *Big Boy,* but he had put it aside to do *Finian's Rainbow*. His approach to the material had not changed in the intervening time. He still envisioned the film, he said, as centering on a nightmarish situation that had developed in our society, "a system that employs all the sophisticated tools that are available to intrude upon our private lives."[32] Recall that a preliminary draft of the script was part of the package that Coppola had submitted to Warners in 1970. Coppola had subsequently revised the screenplay in the version on file in the Paramount Script Repository, dated November 11, 1972, just two weeks before principal photography began.

Not surprisingly, Coppola invited the gifted Walter Murch, who had first joined Coppola's "filmmaking family" when he served as sound engineer on *The Rain People,* to work on the film. Coppola needed an inventive sound technician like Murch because several scenes in the movie were sound-oriented. He desired, he said, to "free the sound from the tyranny of the image," because *The Conversation,* by the very nature of its subject, was a film for which the sound track was of immense importance.[33] (Coppola also got Robert Duvall—another member of Coppola's "repertory company" of artists and who had appeared in *Rain People*—to do an uncredited cameo in the present film.)

The budget Paramount provided for the picture was $1.6 million— not a king's ransom, but considerably more than he had for his previous films (such as *Rain People*). At first he hired cinematographer Haskell Wexler (*In the Heat of the Night*) as director of photography, but the headstrong Wexler did not get along with the equally strong-minded Coppola. When the director complained that the painstaking Wexler was taking too long to set up a shot, Wexler shot back that Coppola had chosen some locations— such as the opening sequence in a crowded public square—that were well nigh impossible to light and to shoot. Coppola responded that, if Erich Von Stroheim could shoot *Greed* in the streets of San Francisco in 1924, he did not see why he could not shoot *The Conversation* in the streets of San Francisco in 1972.

Coppola finally shut down the picture for ten days, during which he sent word to Wexler that his services were no longer required and secured another cinematographer. He eventually replaced Wexler with Bill Butler, who had done yeoman's service in photographing *You're a Big Boy Now* in the streets of New York City. At any rate, Coppola privately welcomed the ten-day hiatus because it gave him one last opportunity to fine-tune the screenplay.

One can understand Wexler's problems with the sequence that took place in Union Square at high noon. When principal photography commenced there on November 26, 1972, Coppola and Wexler had to photograph the two lovers, Ann (Cindy Williams) and Mark (Frederic Forrest), while they walk around Union Square surrounded not only by extras but by innumerable passersby on their lunch break. This sequence required six cameras, plus a battery of long-distance microphones. Coppola instructed the cameramen to keep their cameras trained at all times on the two principals, lest the pair get lost in the crowd.

Like the participants in the Chattanooga parade in *Rain People,* the pedestrians in Union Square were not aware that a movie was being shot. Indeed, the police were not always sure what exactly was going on, even though they knew that Coppola and company were shooting a scene. A couple of sound men stationed on different rooftops overlooking the square with shotgun mikes resembling rifles were arrested as snipers, suspected of attempting to assassinate Coppola. Meanwhile, although Coppola and Wexler endeavored to keep the cameramen in the square out of sight, occasionally one cameraman walked into the camera range of another. "Half of our crew were in the shots" filmed in the square, jokes Coppola, "cameras photographing cameras."[34] After filming was completed in Union Square, with its elaborate multicamera setup, Wexler became increasingly disgruntled with Coppola's choice of locations around town, until Coppola finally gave him his walking papers.

Still the opening scene was worth all the trouble. It starts out with a slow, three-minute overhead zoom shot that gradually moves in on the milling crowds in Union Square then finally zeroes in on Ann and Mark, who are conversing about Ann's husband, the wealthy director of a corporation (Robert Duvall). Ann fears the Director (as he is referred to throughout the movie) will find out about her adulterous relationship with Mark.

Harry Caul (Gene Hackman), who has supervised the surveillance operation, takes the tapes of Ann and Mark's conversation back to his workshop, a loft in an otherwise empty warehouse. As a matter of fact, the warehouse used in the film was conveniently located only five blocks away from the warehouse where American Zoetrope was situated for some years. Harry ascends to his quarters in a cagelike elevator, which reflects how he, himself, is shut in his own private world. Coppola states in his commentary on the DVD of *The Conversation* (released in 2000) that "the warehouse where Harry does his work is like a citadel, with fence like partitions separating the high security areas where he keeps his personally designed technological devices locked away from the rest of the workshop," so that no one, not even his assistant, Stan (John Cazale), can enter there.

Harry labors assiduously to clean up the sound of the crucial conversation on the tapes in order to produce a clean, audible master tape for the

Director. When Harry delivers the tape to the Director's offices in San Francisco's huge Embarcadero Center, Martin Stett (Harrison Ford), the Director's enigmatic assistant, attempts to intercept the package. Harry suspects foul play and accordingly refuses to relinquish the tape to Stett, who warns him not to meddle in this affair. But Harry remains adamant and returns to his lair to scrutinize all of the tapes of the conversation more carefully.

Harry obsessively replays and refines all of the tapes, systematically filtering out the background noise, until he is ultimately able to make audible a segment of the conversation that was previously inaudible: Mark is overheard to say, "He'd kill us if he got the chance." Harry finds this revelation very disturbing.

Since Harry is a Catholic, he heads for his parish church, where he goes to Confession, a religious ritual whereby a Catholic tells his sins to a priest in order to obtain spiritual nourishment. He confesses to the priest that he still feels some lingering moral guilt about an earlier case in which two people were murdered as a result of his disclosures to his client, even though he was not legally responsible for their deaths. Now he feels that he should intervene in his present case in order to save two young people from being murdered and, thus, atone for the previous deaths. It is evident that Harry is ambivalent about the morality of spying on people.

On the one hand, Harry strives to see himself as an unobtrusive observer who remains detached from the people he eavesdrops on, claiming that his work is morally neutral. On the other hand, he knows by experience that the result of the work he does can bring harm to others. So, as a Catholic, Harry feels the need for sacramental confession and absolution. Coppola comments that Harry's practicing a profession about which he has misgivings "seemed very Catholic to me, to do one thing and yet believe another."[35]

Coppola comments on the DVD that Harry's confessing his sins to the priest "is another form of surveillance": Harry expresses his feelings to the priest who is "eavesdropping on Harry's life," though, of course, with Harry's knowledge. The Catholic ritual of Confession "is an age-old way of learning someone's private thoughts."

Harry attends a convention for surveillance experts and invites some of them back to his loft for a party. Meredith, a call girl, also comes along and lingers after everyone else is gone. Harry and Meredith inevitably bed down together. After he falls asleep Harry dreams that he meets Ann in a foggy park and attempts to explain himself to her, even describing some painful youthful experiences of his to her. When he awakens, Meredith and the tapes are gone.

Back in his apartment, Harry gets a phone call from Stett, who admits that he had the tapes stolen because he feared that Harry might destroy them. Harry then remembers that on the tape Ann and Mark make reference to a rendezvous at 3 PM in room 773 of the Jack Tar Hotel on the following Sunday. On that day, Harry—intent on protecting them from the wrath of Ann's husband, who may show up to confront them—occupies the room next to the one where their meeting is to take place.

As resourceful as ever, Harry drills a hole in the wall between the two rooms and inserts a bug, thereby penetrating the fateful meeting that is taking place in the adjoining room. He overhears a quarrel between Ann, Mark, and the Director, which escalates into a shouting match. Finally, when it is apparent that a violent struggle is in progress in the adjacent room, Harry leaps into bed, pulls the blankets over his head, and claps his hands over his ears in a futile attempt to insulate himself from the mayhem taking place next door that he feels powerless to stop.

Harry eventually summons the courage to break into the room, which on the surface seems neat and clean. Still Harry is suspicious because the room seems to have been tidied up too carefully, as if to sweep the sordid facts about what has transpired there under the rug. While examining the bathroom, he flushes the toilet—only to have it disgorge bloody rags and paper towels, which spill out all over the floor.

As mentioned, Coppola made use of his own boyhood memories in building the character of Harry Caul. But this particular incident in the movie was suggested to him by Walter Murch, who drew on an episode from his own youth. "When I was a kid, I got some porno magazines," Murch recalls in his commentary on the DVD of *The Conversation*. "When my parents came home unexpectedly, I tried to flush them down the toilet, but the toilet blocked up, and the porno magazines came gurgling up out of the toilet when my father flushed it. So in this scene in *The Conversation*, the toilet likewise regurgitates the evidence of guilt. It slowly overflows with blood. The guilty pair had tried to force the evidence of the murder down the toilet in order to clean up the hotel room, but it came flooding back up like an accusing finger." Coppola adds that this scene is a homage to Alfred Hitchcock's *Psycho* (1960) in which Norman Bates enters the bloody bathroom where a brutal stabbing has taken place and cleans up the mess in order to destroy the evidence of what has transpired.

After the toilet in *The Conversation* has vomited blood all over the bathroom, Harry hastens to the Director's office complex. He is startled when outside the building he spies a newspaper headline declaring that the Director has been killed in an auto accident. In a flash he realizes that he totally misinterpreted the conversation on the tapes. He assumed that the Director had been plotting to kill Ann and Mark when in reality it is Ann and Mark who have murdered the Director. It seems that the Director, when he learned from the master tape of their rendezvous at the Jack Tar Hotel, decided to surprise them in order to have a showdown with his unfaithful wife and her inamorato. Stett, who was in cahoots with her and Mark all along, prepared them for this eventuality. They had counted on the Director invading their hotel room once he had heard the tape. They arranged to slay him and to disguise his death as a traffic accident so that they could possess his wealth and power.

Too late Harry realizes that he had misunderstood Mark's statement on the tape, "He'd *kill* us if he got the chance." He now understands that Mark had really said, "He'd kill *us* if he got the chance"—meaning that they would murder the Director before he got the opportunity to slay them.

Completely shattered by this revelation, Harry withdraws to his apartment and seeks solace in playing his saxophone. He receives one last telephone call from Stett, who warns Harry, "We know that you know, and we are watching you." Aware that his own living quarters have now been bugged, Harry frantically dismantles the whole apartment, futilely looking for the wiretapping device. Always the conscientious Catholic, Harry hesitates to smash the plaster statue of Mary, the mother of Christ, but finally does. Still, he dismembers his apartment to no avail.

The film ends with Harry in despair, playing a mournful melody on his sax. Harry, an intensely private and lonely man, retreats from his profession as a wiretapper to his hobby as a musician—from being someone preoccupied with recording devices to someone absorbed in the music of his own tenor sax. Coppola's rotating camera slowly encircles Harry, as if the camera itself were a surveillance device. He is imprisoned in his own apartment and is being monitored by the conspirators who liquidated the Director. Furthermore, Foster Hirsch observes, "Harry is trapped from within by the coils of his own unravelling psyche."[36]

Coppola observes on the DVD that he has often been asked where the bug was planted in Harry's apartment. "I always imagined that it was in the strap of his saxophone, which was hanging around his neck and was fastened with a clasp to his sax. Harry often forgot to take the strap off after he finished playing," so he absentmindedly wore it around his neck like a necklace that he was unaware of.

Another question that Coppola has sometimes been asked is how Harry Caul got his rather odd last name. "I dictated the script into a tape recorder and a secretary transcribed it. I called him Harry Call, but she had typed Caul. When I saw what she had typed, I decided to keep the spelling, since I knew what a caul is." It is the membrane that surrounds a fetus until it is born. Through most of the movie, Coppola continues, Harry wears a translucent plastic raincoat, a visual symbol that he is still insulated inside a caul. At one point "Harry lies down on the bed next to his mistress Amy [Teri Garr] without removing his transparent raincoat," says Coppola. "When she asks him personal questions about himself, he bristles. She equivalently wants to look through the transparent raincoat at the man underneath," and he accuses her of prying.

Another metaphor in the movie also came about by chance. The scenes in the apartment house where Harry lived in the film were shot on location in a neighborhood that was being torn down for redevelopment. "Through Harry's window we see a building across the way being demolished," Coppola says on the DVD. "The notion of tearing down the walls that protect the people inside from the view of others is thematically related to a film about surveillance. The lives of the inhabitants of the building are being exposed to the light of day" and to the gaze of others.

As quoted earlier, Walter Murch notes that Coppola gives his collaborators a great deal of leeway in performing their functions on a film. This was particularly true of Murch's work in making the final cut for the present film. Since Coppola had to begin preproduction on *Godfather II* immediately after he finished shooting *The Conversation,* he appointed Murch as both film editor and sound engineer on *The Conversation* and left Murch to supervise postproduction on his own. This meant that the director was not around on a daily basis to confer with him as a director normally does with an editor during postproduction.

Murch was really "a full collaborator on the film," says Coppola. He edited the picture, assisted by Richard Chew, and mixed the sound track. Although Murch had already served as sound engineer on other movies, this was his first assignment as a film editor on a feature motion picture. "Essentially Francis left me on my own," says Murch. About once a month Murch would invite Coppola to come by the editing room for a progress report.[37] Murch would screen the rough cut for Coppola, who would make suggestions, which Murch then would implement.

Naturally, Murch found the task of sifting through the mountains of footage daunting. Postproduction took nearly a year. "In the process Murch invented some new plot connections and rediscovered others that had been temporarily overlooked," Goodwin and Wise write.[38]

One narrative link that Murch made during editing concerned Meredith, the call girl, and the theft of the tapes. In the screenplay "Meredith slept with Harry and simply disappeared the next morning," Murch comments on the DVD. In a separate scene Harry discovered that the tapes had been snatched by some minion of Stett, the Director's chief assistant. "I thought that, if we insinuated that Meredith took the tapes, it would make things hang together better." It would be more interesting to identify the thief as the call girl, rather than make the thief some anonymous henchman of Stett's. Hence Murch combined the two incidents, so that it is evident that Meredith seduced Harry in order to steal the tapes for Stett. "But that tie-up was constructed during editing," Murch concludes. "That was not in the script."

Another modification of the scenario that Murch made during editing centers on the dream sequence in which Harry imagines that he sees Ann in a park engulfed in a misty fog and attempts to talk to her. In the screenplay this incident is not a dream at all. Harry follows Ann into the park and tries to explain himself to her. He says he had polio as a child and almost drowned in the bathtub when his mother was not around. "I was disappointed that I survived," he explains. "You see, I'm not afraid of death, but I am afraid of murder." He urgently calls after her as she recoils from him and disappears in the swirling fog. "He'll kill you if he gets the chance." After Coppola had filmed this scene, he was inclined to scrap it, since he did not think it held up. "It remained for Walter Murch's creativity in the editing room," Coppola says on the DVD, to employ the scene as a dream sequence that shows Harry's anxiety for Ann, whom he still sees at this point as someone he wants to save from danger.

Murch made an even more significant contribution to the film while he was mixing the sound track. He discovered a crucial bit of tape that he had previously overlooked: it was an alternate reading of the line in the opening sequence in which Frederic Forrest as Mark altered the emphasis from "He'd *kill* us if he got the chance" to "He'd kill *us* if he got the chance." Murch decided to employ both readings of the line in the film at different points—the more innocuous one in the first scene, and the more sinister one when Harry later hears the remark again late in the movie. Coppola completely agreed with Murch when the latter pointed out that it was the only way to clench the idea for the audience that Harry had finally uncovered the truth (i.e., that Mark and Ann were planning to murder her husband, and not vice versa). Murch explains that he wanted to clarify for the audience that the first time Harry hears Mark's statement, Harry thinks of Mark and Ann as two potential victims who need his protection. But when Murch employed the second reading of the line with a different inflection, which emphasizes *us* rather than *kill*, he wanted to indicate to the filmgoer that the phrase now takes on a new emphasis for Harry. As Murch puts it, "Harry hears the line in his mind as it must have been all along": "He'd kill *us* if he got the chance." This implies: If he is going to kill them, they should kill him first. At last Murch dug out the old recording of Forrest's reading of the line that he had disregarded months before and used it.[39]

In the course of mixing the sound track Murch noticed the significance of Coppola arranging to have a single piano to provide the underscore for the film. The background music was composed and played by David Shire, who at that time was married to Coppola's sister Talia Shire. *The Conversation* is one of the few mainstream Hollywood films to have a background score played by a solo instrument (the zither accompaniment for Carol Reed's *The Third Man* [1949] also comes to mind). Because the background music was scored for piano alone, the music has a lonely and haunting sound: "a single instrument for a film about a single, lonely man," says Murch on the DVD.

Although Gene Hackman turned in a superb performance as Harry Caul, Coppola has described the actor as feeling miserable inside Harry's emotional straightjacket. "He was really a constipated character," comments Hackman. It was a difficult role to play because it was so low key.[40] Harry's bruised professionalism and sense of weary detachment as he leads his shadowy existence are evidence of a complex personality. He believes emotions are a nuisance during business hours, and all his hours are business hours. Many critics still consider Harry Caul to be Hackman's most virtuoso performance.

The Conversation is sometimes compared to Michelangelo Antonioni's *Blow-Up* (1966), which is about a photographer who thinks he spies evidence of a murder in the background of one of his photos, but the evidence mysteriously disappears from his studio. On the contrary, Coppola probes the mind of his hermetic, guilt-ridden hero much more deeply than Antonioni does in his film. The characterization of the photographer in *Blow-Up* is superficial by comparison to the in-depth portrait of the surveillance expert Hackman played in Coppola's picture.

Asked to name his favorite among his films, Coppola indicated to me that it was *The Conversation,* because "it is a personal film based on my own original screenplay." Recently he confirmed that *The Conversation* remains his best movie in his opinion, since "it represented a personal direction where I wanted to take my career" (i.e., he always preferred to create his own story material, rather than make films derived from literary sources).[41] Coppola's predilection for the film is understandable, for the movie is rarely less than accomplished, its every frame polished and gleaming in the director's best manner. In summary, it is a masterwork.

The Conversation proved to be a prestige picture for Paramount. It won the Palme d'Or, the grand prize, at the Cannes International Film Festival. It also copped two major Academy Award nominations, for best picture of the year and for best original screenplay. Nonetheless, audiences did not show up for the movie, either here or abroad, since it was generally considered to be too slow-moving and cerebral for a thriller. Although the picture had gotten into the black by 1975, it was still considered a flop as far as its initial theatrical run was concerned.

You're a Big Boy Now met the same fate in 1966. At that time Coppola made a trade-off with Warners-Seven. He directed *Finian's Rainbow* in exchange for the studio financing *The Rain People,* a film that eventually also failed commercially. So Coppola decided that he must be very careful about what he did next after *The Rain People.* As a result of his winning an Oscar for co-scripting *Patton,* Paramount offered him what looked like a formula gangster picture based on a pulp novel about the Mafia. As such, it did not seem to him a very promising venture at all.

Part Two

The Mature Moviemaker

4

In a Savage Land

The Godfather

You can get a lot more done with a kind word and a gun than with a kind word alone.

—Al Capone

I've never made a movie as good as *The Godfather,* and I don't have the ambition to try.

—Steven Spielberg

When Francis Coppola first considered filming Mario Puzo's novel *The Godfather,* he perused the book and found it a rather sensational, sleazy crime novel. But, then, Puzo was not aspiring to create a work of literature. When he conceived it, as he confesses in *The Godfather Papers,* he had already published two novels that did have literary pretensions, but they went largely unread. He decided to write a novel about the Mafia because this time around he was determined to turn out a bestseller. And that accounts for the liberal doses of sex and violence in the book, which are precisely what turned Coppola off. Deeply in debt, Puzo decided that "it was time to grow up and sell out, as Lenny Bruce advised."[1]

Progress was slow because Puzo had no direct links with the underworld; therefore, his knowledge of the Mafia was derived totally from research. In the spring of 1968 he met with Robert Evans, production chief at

Paramount, and offered him the screen rights for his as yet unfinished opus. "From a rumpled envelope he took out fifty or sixty even more rumpled pages," Evans remembers. Puzo explained that his novel, tentatively titled *Mafia,* was going to give the inside story on organized crime. An inveterate gambler, Puzo confided to Evans that he had a $10,000 gambling debt that he had to pay off pronto, and hence he would consider any reasonable advance that Evans proposed. "I've just optioned *Mafia* for $12,500," Evans immediately replied. He did not know it then, Evans adds, but for that paltry sum, he now owned the rights "to the Hope diamond of literature."

Evans's high hopes for the project were not shared by others at Paramount. "Sicilian mobster films don't play," the head of distribution told him. He pointed to *The Brotherhood* (1968), a Kirk Douglas vehicle that fizzled.[2] Evans figured that *The Brotherhood* failed because almost none of the creative personnel connected with the picture were of Italian descent. The director, Martin Ritt, and the star, Douglas, were both Jewish. Bernard Dick writes that, like Douglas, most of the cast were Sicilian "in make-up only." It was an ordinary crime movie "with a few Italian touches thrown in for good measure."[3]

Despite the misfire with *The Brotherhood,* Evans thought that interest in the Mafia was growing in the United States. To begin with, Senator Estes Kefauver's Committee on Organized Crime was convened in 1950. The hearings were televised and acquainted the nation with mafiosi like Frank Costello, who testified before the Committee. In addition, in the fall of 1963 Senator John McClellan's committee investigating organized crime likewise received nationwide attention. The country was ready for a Mafia movie, Evans reasoned.

The Godfather, as the book was finally titled, appeared in April 1969. After briefly considering non-Italian directors like Elia Kazan (*A Streetcar Named Desire*) to direct the picture, Evans became increasingly convinced that only an Italian American director could supply the creative tissue to make a Mafia movie work. "It must be ethnic to the core," he said. "[Y]ou must smell the spaghetti. That's what brought the magic to the novel—it was written by an Italian."[4]

Peter Bart, a Paramount vice president and Evans's chief assistant, suggested Francis Coppola as a director of Italian ancestry who could fill the bill. Evans recalled the flashbacks in *Rain People* to the heroine's Italian wedding and decided to go for Coppola. "He knew the way these men ate their food, kissed each other, talked. He knew the grit."[5] Coppola could, for example, get across to the mass audience the Mafia's unswerving allegiance to the Sicilian code of silence (*omertà*) about the inner workings of the organization, which dictates that a member pay with his life for violating it. That is why most members prefer to call the organization *La Cosa Nostra* (our affair), signifying that the family business is not to be shared with outsiders.

Furthermore, Evans deplored earlier attempts to portray Italian gangsters on the American screen, which had merely resulted in stereotypical portrayals of Italian immigrant-criminals. In this regard filmmaker Martin Scorsese (*Mean Streets*) singled out Howard Hawks's *Scarface* (1932), in which Paul Muni plays a mobster modeled on Al Capone. Muni's mugging for the camera and his phony Italian accent were embarrassing, says Scorsese. His performance exemplified the "Mama Mia" school of acting. "No one talks that way."[6] (As a matter of fact, Coppola affirms that mafiosi born in New York and not in the old country have New York accents, not Italian accents.) It would be up to Coppola, Evans concluded, to show the Italian American community in an authentic manner—how they treated their families and celebrated their rituals.

But Coppola was not hired just because he was Italian American, he points out, but because he had recently made a flop for Warners, *The Rain People*. Coppola guessed that Paramount thought that he was young enough and chastened enough by his recent box-office failure to be pushed around by the studio officials. On the credit side of the ledger, Bart was impressed that Coppola made *Rain People* on a meager budget and that he had the reputation of a director who could make a film economically. And, more important, he knew that Coppola had coauthored the Academy Award–winning screenplay for *Patton* (1970) (see chapter 1).

When Coppola was invited to make *The Godfather,* he got around to reading the book for the first time, but he never got past page 50. He dismissed it as "pretty cheap stuff." He was offended by some sensational subplots, which Puzo admittedly concocted to boost sales (e.g., Sonny Corleone's tempestuous affair with Lucy Mancini). Moreover, Coppola thought the book read like a lurid potboiler by the likes of Irving Wallace (*The Chapman Report*)—books that he considered below the belt and beneath discussion. Besides, Coppola wanted to avoid doing formula pictures. He believed that he had taken a left turn when he had agreed to make a commercial picture like *Finian's Rainbow* (see chapter 2). He did not want to make another big studio project, this time a gangster movie.

A few weeks later Bart decided to phone Coppola again and tracked him down at George Lucas's home in Mill Valley, where Lucas was editing the final cut of *THX 1138*. Lucas remembers that Coppola covered the receiver with his hand and asked, "George, should I make this gangster movie?"

Lucas reminded Coppola that American Zoetrope was foundering (see chapter 3). "Francis, we're in debt," he said; "you need a job. I think you should do it. Survival is the key thing here."[7] So Coppola took Paramount up on its offer and went back to reading *The Godfather* through to the end.

When he got further into the book, Coppola saw that it was "the story of a family, this father and his sons; and I thought it was a terrific story, if you could cut out all the other stuff." So, once he had scraped away the dispensable subplots, he concluded that "it wasn't a piece of trash."[8] His father, Carmine, confirmed his decision to make the movie, pointing out that making a successful commercial film would enable him to finance his more personal projects. Coppola accordingly informed Bart that he would make the movie so long as it was not merely a film about an organization of gangsters but a family chronicle.

The Godfather (1972)

When the film's producer, Albert Ruddy, gave Puzo the news about Coppola, Puzo was working on a draft of the screenplay. Ruddy advised him that Coppola would be collaborating on the script as well as directing, and Puzo suggested to Coppola that they work together. "Francis looked me right in the eye and said no. That's when I knew he was really a director."[9]

Coppola spent his mornings working on the screenplay at a secluded table in the Café Trieste in San Francisco, while Puzo toiled in an office in Los Angeles. Coppola says in the documentary that accompanies the DVD of the *Godfather Trilogy* (released 2001), "I did my own version of the screenplay, then I contacted Mario and we collaborated." Puzo adds in the same documentary, "We wrote separately. I sent my stuff to him, and he sent his stuff to me. Then he made the final decision as to what would be in the shooting script."[10] Coppola was able to whittle Puzo's gargantuan novel down to a screenplay of 163 pages for a film of about three hours.

Before getting down to work on the screenplay, Coppola went through a preliminary procedure that would ensure that all of the key events of the novel would find their way into the script. He began by tearing the pages from a copy of Puzo's novel and pasting each page into a large stage director's notebook. He then summarized the action with handwritten notes in the margin of each page. Coppola explains in the documentary, "I would indicate what the core of each scene was. This became the master document that I would work from while directing the film. I would refer to it in addition to the script while filming. This was for me a multi-layered road map to direct the picture."

Coppola never backed off from indicating in the script that the mobsters were of Italian descent. He wished to show the Italian American community with understanding and candor, to indicate that Don Corleone, the godfather of the title, was convinced that organized crime was the passport to the American dream for downtrodden immigrants. In order to give some historical perspective on the way organized crime developed in the United States, the movie would suggest that the lack of career opportunities open to unskilled immigrants from Italy, Ireland, and other European countries made racketeering, in their view, one of the few lucrative avenues of opportunity open to immigrants. The mobs gained power through patronage of corrupt politicians and thereby made more inroads on legitimacy. In short, the Mafia grew out of the anarchy in the inner city itself, in the face of social injustice.

In apportioning credit for the shooting script, Coppola explains that, on the one hand, Puzo created the characters and the plot and, on the other hand, Coppola himself chose which episodes from the book would be in the film and which incidents would be bypassed. He also added some elements to the film that moviegoers assumed were in the book but that were not. "The art of adaptation," he told me, "is when you can do something that wasn't in the literary source but is so much like the source that it should have been."

Coppola added a minor but telling incident early in the film, when one of Don Corleone's capos, Peter Clemenza (Richard Castellano), is leaving home to arrange the murder of Paulie Gatto, the don's treacherous bodyguard who is in the pay of another mob. Coppola had Clemenza's wife say to him, "Don't forget to bring home some cannoli." Then in the scene where Clemenza has a hit man liquidate Paulie in a car on a remote country road, Clemenza says to him, "Leave the gun. Take the cannoli." Clemenza's thinking about the dessert his wife told him to bring home—immediately after a killing—provides a chilling moment in the film. Edward Rothstein comments that this scene brings into relief that "at the heart of the movie is a forthright assertion of ethnic identity as a source of strength. That is where we find the human side of the mob; the warmth, the loyalty, the love of cannoli. Aside from the nature of the family business, the plot could be about an immigrant family trying to preserve its ethnic traditions."[11]

It is evident that Puzo provided Coppola with a roaring good plot, Pauline Kael writes. He gave Coppola "a storyteller's outpouring of incidents and details to choose from." She also observes that Coppola refined the crudities of the novel: "The movie starts with a trash novel," Kael states, but one that is "gripping and compulsively readable." From this raw material Coppola "salvaged Puzo's energy and lent the narrative dignity," performing a job of alchemy in turning Puzo's novel into art on the screen. The abundance is from the book, "the quality is from Coppola."[12]

When the screenplay was finished, Ruddy met with Coppola to inform him that Paramount had sustained heavy losses on some recent flops like the Julie Andrews vehicle *Darling Lili* (1970). The studio was therefore not willing to gamble on a big budget gangster picture. It was generally known that Ruddy had a reputation for bringing B pictures in on budget. Since he was more adept at saving money than making it, Coppola was not surprised that Ruddy had been selected to produce *The Godfather* on a modest budget.

More specifically, Evans had declared that *The Godfather* was to be a low-budget movie, shot at the studio and using the back lot. Moreover, it was to be set in the present, rather than after World War II (which is the time frame of the book) in order to avoid the extra expense of making a period picture. The movie, in brief, was designed to be made on the double and on the cheap for $1 million.

Coppola balked at these restrictions. To begin with he maintained that the story simply would not work if set in the present. For example, mob members no longer shot each other in the streets like rabbits the way they did during the gang wars in the old days. "I made a big point of saying to the studio that the story was immersed in the postwar period and had to take place there," he says in his DVD documentary. He insisted that the film be set after World War II like the book, with the feeling of the 1940s. Evans responded that that would add another $1 million to the budget and was out of the question.

Undaunted, Coppola also lobbied to have the picture shot on authentic locations rather than on the studio back lot, whose "New York" street was familiar to moviegoers from countless Paramount pictures. That petition was likewise rejected as too costly.

It was while Coppola was negotiating with the studio about the production values of the film that, much to everyone's surprise, the novel began its steady climb to the top of the bestseller charts. When the book became a runaway hit with the public, Coppola, who was turning out to be a good deal less tractable than the front office had anticipated, strongly urged the studio to upgrade the production to an A picture, as benefitted the movie adaptation of a bestseller.

He ultimately succeeded in getting the studio to change its tune: The picture was to be set in period and he would be allowed to film the bulk of the picture on location in New York, and even to shoot the scenes set in

Sicily on location in Sicily. When the budget was finally increased to $6.5 million, it was evident that Coppola had begun to dominate the decisions made about the production. Recalling the pitched battle he had with Evans and the studio brass, Coppola says that a great deal of the energy that went into the making of the movie was expended on just convincing the people who held the power, whom he referred to as "the suits," to let him do the film his way. Puzo reflected, "Francis is heavy-set, jolly, and is usually happy-go-lucky. What I didn't know was that he could be tough about his work."[13]

Once the word got out that Paramount was making a movie about the Mafia, to be shot largely in New York City, the studio was plagued with protests from the New York–based Italian American Civil Rights League, which claimed a movie about the Mafia would be disparaging to all Americans of Italian descent. Ironically, the league was spearheaded by New York Mafia chieftain Joseph Columbo. For all practical purposes the league was a smoke screen to keep the law from prying into Columbo's underworld activities. Albert Ruddy told me, during a brief conversation after a screening of one of his subsequent movies, that Evans got an anonymous phone call from a mobster who warned him not to make a movie about "the family" in New York City. Otherwise, they would disfigure his "pretty face." Evans, never one to mince words, responded, "Fuck you, buddy. If you have a problem, you should take it up with Al Ruddy, the producer."

After Ruddy's car was found riddled with bullets, he decided to hold a meeting with the league. He promised to take out all the references to the Mafia in the script and to see to it that the screenplay preserved Italian honor. The league, in turn, pledged its cooperation in the making of the film. Puzo has written, "I must say, Ruddy was a shrewd bargainer, because the word *Mafia* was never in the script in the first place."[14] Instead of referring to the Mafia or to La Cosa Nostra in the script, the New York mobs were called "the five families." Ruddy further emphasized to the league that *The Godfather* was focusing on a group of fictitious Italian criminals and not defaming the entire Italian community.

Evans learned that some mob members had initially planned to picket the New York locations when Coppola would be shooting in the Italian neighborhoods. He phoned a friend of his, attorney Sidney Korshak. To the FBI, Korshak was "the most important contact that the mob had to legitimate business and labor in Hollywood and Las Vegas."[15] A couple of phone calls from Korshak and all previous threats of picketing the film unit evaporated.

When the question of casting came up, both Coppola and Puzo agreed that their first choice to play Don Vito Corleone, the sixty-five-year-old godfather, was Marlon Brando. Indeed, Puzo had written the character with the forty-seven-year-old Brando in mind. The part called for an actor who possessed the sort of magnetism and charisma that this pivotal role in the movie required. "The mystique Brando had as an actor amongst other actors would inspire precisely the right kind of awe in working with the legendary Brando and would translate on film into awe for the powerful godfather."[16]

Nevertheless, Evans rejected Brando out of hand since the actor had a reputation for being temperamental and cranky on the set. His recent pictures, including *Candy* (1968) and *The Night of the Following Day* (1969), had reportedly gone way over budget because of delays during shooting caused by Brando's incessant feuds with his directors, and neither film turned a profit. Still Coppola would not consider any other actors, and so he and Evans reached an impasse.

Evans scheduled a meeting with Coppola, Ruddy, and Stanley Jaffe, the thirty-year-old president of Paramount, to discuss casting. When the issue of casting Brando was raised, Coppola made an eloquent appeal on the actor's behalf. "I pleaded as if I were a lawyer pleading for someone's life," he recalls. Jaffe interjected, "As president of Paramount Pictures, I assure you that Marlon Brando will never appear in this motion picture." With that, Coppola suddenly clutched his stomach and fell down on the carpet, apparently in a fit of convulsions. Coppola explains that he collapsed on the floor as if to say, "How can I deal with this kind of stubborn attitude?" He continues, "My 'epileptic fit' was obviously a gag, but they got the point. Finally they recanted and told me I could consider Brando."[17]

Coppola had employed this gambit of faking a seizure years before, in his student days, to compel a backer to cough up the additional funds he needed to finish *Tonight for Sure,* and the ploy worked equally well with Jaffe and the other executives. Jaffe relented to the extent that he approved of Brando as a candidate for the role of the don, provided that Brando submit to doing a screen test. This was the joker in the deck, as far as Jaffe was concerned, since it was common knowledge that Brando refused to be tested for any role. So Jaffe assumed that Brando would turn down the part.

Coppola recalls in his DVD commentary that he diffidently phoned Brando, without mentioning the possibility of a screen test. "I suggested that I do a make-up test at his house," since Don Vito was an elderly man close to seventy. Much to Coppola's relief, Brando agreed. Coppola went to Brando's house accompanied by a photographer with a video camera and Salvatore Corsitto, an Italian barber, whom Coppola had already chosen to play Bonasera, the undertaker who asks the godfather for a favor at the beginning of the film.

Brando emerged from his bedroom wearing a kimono, Coppola says, and he gradually began to slide into the character. He put on a rumpled shirt and jacket, then he took some shoe polish and dabbed on a moustache. Next he stuffed Kleenex in his jaws, saying "The godfather should have the face of a bulldog." Then he said, "In the story Don Vito is shot in the throat, so I think he should talk as if it never quite healed." He added that when Frank Costello appeared at the televised Kefauver hearings he had a raspy voice, which he wanted to imitate. At this point Brando and Corsitto improvised an impromptu scene. As soon as Coppola started filming, he could see Brando slipping into the godfather's skin, and Coppola marveled at the transformation. Coppola flew to New York and showed the test to Charles Bludhorn, the tough Austrian immigrant who was head of Gulf and Western, Paramount's parent company. Bludhorn was so impressed, concludes Coppola, that "he allowed us to use Brando on his authority."

But Coppola's casting troubles were just beginning. He went on to campaign, with Puzo's support, for Al Pacino to play Michael Corleone, the don's son and heir apparent. (Michael is the most Americanized of the Corleone sons, having gone to college.) Once again Evans objected to what he considered Coppola's penchant for unorthodox casting: Pacino was too short, looked too scruffy, was too intense—and forgot his lines during the screen test. Besides, he had mostly stage rather than film experience.

Pacino says in the documentary that he tested poorly because "I didn't like testing for a part where I knew the studio didn't want me. It was Francis's tenacity that got me the part." In the face of Evans's opposition, Coppola kept repeating, "A good actor is a good actor," said Puzo.[18] Actually Coppola held out for Pacino because he believed Pacino had the map of Sicily on his face. In reading the book, Coppola explains in his DVD commentary, "it was Pacino's face that I saw in the scenes where Michael sojourns in Sicily, and that is why I was so persistent." Finally, after Pacino's third screen test, Evans told Coppola that he could use the "little dwarf" (!) if he wanted to.

When Evans cast Coppola's sister Talia Shire as the don's only daughter Connie without consulting him, it was Coppola's turn to object. Aware that some disgruntled studio executives were fed up with fencing with Coppola about production and casting decisions, Coppola sensed that some of them would like to be rid of him. That thought impinged on the casting of Talia Shire. She recalls in the documentary that Coppola said to her, "The last thing you need when you are making a movie and your job is in jeopardy is your sister." She adds that it was Mario Puzo who said, "Let her have a chance, Francis." Finally Coppola decided that he had caused so much conflict over the casting of the picture that it was time to make a concession to Evans, who liked her in the part.

Fortunately Coppola had little difficulty with the studio in casting two veterans of his previous pictures in *The Godfather*: James Caan (*Rain People*) was to play Michael's volatile brother Sonny, and Robert Duvall (*Rain People* and *Conversation*) was cast as the don's adopted Irish son and consigliere (the family's legal adviser), Tom Hagen.

Coppola concedes that many of the actors he cast were not stars who were familiar to the public. He explains that he was not interested in marquee names: "I was looking for people like Pacino who would be believable as real Italian-Americans," so as not to repeat the mistake made with the casting of *The Brotherhood*.[19] Thus Coppola hired Richard Conte, a distinguished actor of Italian origin, to play Don Barzini, a cunning, sadistic rival of Don Corleone. He had in fact played a similar role in the classic film noir *The Big Combo* (1955). "Barzini is a real snake in the grass," Conte told me when I encountered him at the London premiere of the film. "Barzini is secretly determined to bring down the Corleone crime family." Conte said he enjoyed working with Coppola, and Conte played Barzini to perfection. Indeed, critics pointed to Conte as a prime example of how Coppola packed the picture with talented supporting players.

As mentioned, Coppola suspected that his clashes with the front office might ultimately lead to his being dismissed as director. Furthermore, as the picture evolved into a more elaborate production, Evans and other executives wondered if the young director was too inexperienced to handle such a huge undertaking. In fact, Evans coolly suggested that perhaps Coppola should be replaced by a more established director like Elia Kazan, who had proved adept at handling Brando's shenanigans on the set of three previous pictures. Coppola heard through the grapevine that Evans had actually made an overture to Kazan about substituting him for Coppola. This bit of news caused Coppola nightmares. Later on Evans told an interviewer that Kazan had urged him to stick with Coppola, but Coppola did not know that at the time.

After principal photography commenced on March 23, 1971, at the old Filmways Studio in New York, Paramount still harbored doubts about continuing with both Coppola and Pacino. When the studio brass saw the rushes of Pacino's first scenes, "they thought I was dull," Pacino says in the documentary. Even the camera crew tittered at times when he was on camera.

"Pacino embarked on his most famous role with such elegant minimalism that it was nearly taken from him," writes Karen Durbin.[20] Watching Pacino's cool, unreadable young Sicilian in the rushes, "Paramount executives hounded the director to fire him, backing off only after viewing the scene in which Michael avenges his father" and commits his first two murders.

The scene was shot at the Café Luna in the Bronx, where Michael kills Sollozzo, a mobster who had tried to kill his father, and the rogue cop who is his bodyguard. The studio bosses were much impressed both with Coppola's direction of the scene and Pacino's performance. "You look pretty good when you shoot people," is Pacino's laconic rendition of their change of heart.[21] "This scene certainly saved me," Coppola notes in his commentary. "And it won a lot of admiration for Al. He really showed his stuff—his concentration and intensity were riveting."

But there was still dissonance in the ranks about Coppola's competency as a director. Gordon Willis, the director of photography, did not cotton up to Coppola from the get-go. The director had what he terms in his commentary "a touch-and-go relationship" with Willis on *The Godfather*. "To him I was just some kid," while Willis saw himself as a seasoned veteran, with films like *Klute* (1971) behind him. Willis assumed quite gratuitously that Coppola, who was, after all, an alumnus of the UCLA graduate program in film, knew little about the technical aspects of moviemaking. Coppola found Willis "a grumpy guy" to work with.[22]

A major bone of contention between them was Coppola's penchant for encouraging the actors to improvise during rehearsals, with a view to making some last-minute revisions in the script before finally shooting a scene. As Dean Tavoularis, the production designer, quips in the documentary, "For Francis a script is like a newspaper. A new one comes out every day." Willis grew increasingly impatient waiting around for Coppola to finish lengthy rehearsal periods before he could finally photograph a scene.

"I like to lay a thing out and make it work with discipline," Willis explains. Whereas, in his mind, Coppola spent an exorbitant amount of time improvising with the actors on the outside chance that he might improve the scene as written. "You can't shoot the whole movie, hoping for happy accidents," he concludes. "[W]hat you get is one big, bad accident."[23]

While conceding that Willis is "a genius and a complicated guy, who has much wisdom," Coppola states that Willis failed to comprehend that when a director experiments with different ways to play a scene during rehearsals some unpredictable things can emerge that will improve the whole scene, as he found on his previous pictures, particularly *Rain People* (see chapter 3). "Sometimes you catch lightning in a bottle."

When Willis pointed out that the film was falling behind schedule because of the extra time Coppola was spending on improvising during rehearsals, Coppola replied that he had requested an eighty-day shooting schedule and was given fifty-five days by Evans. It was therefore inevitable that he would fall behind schedule. (In point of fact, the shooting period was finished in sixty-two days.)

Camera operator John Chapman, who would later be a cinematographer (*Taxi Driver*), remembers what he calls "the marvelous operatic fights" between Willis and Coppola.[24] The camera crew knew that Willis had small confidence in Coppola. He appeared insecure to the tough New York crew. They even made snide remarks about him that he sometimes overheard. "They made me feel like an outsider. I remember sitting in the restroom near the sound stage, hidden in a stall, when two guys walked in," he recalls in the documentary. One of them said, "Coppola will never make another big picture. Everyone agrees that he doesn't know what he's doing. He's overwhelmed by the job." Coppola continues, "I was so embarrassed that I lifted my shoes up, so they couldn't tell who was in the stall. I didn't have a lot of confidence in myself. I was only thirty years old. I was just hanging on by my wits."

One day Coppola and Willis had an especially acrid disagreement about a particular camera setup. It degenerated into a shouting match that peaked with Willis bellowing at Coppola, "You don't know how to do anything right!" With that, he retreated to his trailer and refused to come out. When Coppola decided to go ahead and shoot the scene, Willis was nowhere to be found. The camera crew froze. He asked Chapman to take over, but Chapman declined to shoot the scene in Willis's absence. He was not prepared to get caught between two higher-ups. Coppola was beside himself. "Fuck this picture!" he shouted. "I've directed four movies without anyone telling me how to do my job." He then stalked off the set. Shortly afterward, a resounding bang reverberated from the direction of Coppola's office. "Oh my God!" the assistant director exclaimed. "He's shot himself!!"[25] In actual fact Coppola, while blowing off steam, had kicked a hole in his office door, and he was sitting inside when the production manager came to investigate. To smooth things over, the crew took a picture of the ruined door and gave it to Coppola as a gag gift.

An uneasy truce was established between the director and the cinematographer, and filming went on. Gradually both men gained a modicum of respect for each other's talents, but Coppola says in his commentary that they did not really get along well until *Godfather II*. Despite their differences, they did work well together. "I agreed with Gordy on how the film should look," states Coppola in his commentary. For example, in order to evoke the films of the 1940s, the movie's time frame, they used grainy film stock like old period photographs. Willis says the overall look of the picture is a sort of "1940s New York grit." What's more, they devised a sinister, shadowy atmosphere for the interiors in which dangerous people like the godfather are only partially visible.

Thus in the opening scene the godfather sits in his office doing business shrouded in darkness, while his daughter's wedding reception is in progress in the rainbow-hued garden outside. "The idea was that this was a character who didn't always let you know what he was thinking," says Willis. So sometimes he was sitting in the shadows where one could not see the expression on his face. The low-level lighting emphasizes the deception and secretness of this dark underworld. The don is the personification of evil, says Willis, so he wanted to keep him in menacing shadows.

The murky, under-lit look of these scenes was daring and unconventional at the time. As the rushes were shipped to the studio in Hollywood, the report came back, "The camera is always focused on the dark." Studio moguls, accustomed to ultra-bright lighting in films, were disturbed by such scenes. "I got a lot of criticism because of the juxtaposition of the bright, kodachromy stuff for the wedding reception with the dark office where sinister things were happening," Willis concludes. One of the executives said that the murky photography made him think that he had worn sunglasses to view the rushes. "But in my mind and in Francis's mind the contrast between the happiness outside" and what was going on inside "was quite clear."[26]

Unlike Willis, Dean Tavoularis, who was responsible for set design, had a harmonious relationship with Coppola. *The Godfather* was his first Coppola film, and he went on to design the two sequels, as well as *Apocalypse Now*. Tavoularis was glad that Coppola had held out for setting the movie in the postwar period, because he finds period films challenging— he has to be vigilant, so that every detail of the sets fits the historical setting of the story. In fact, Tavoularis's attention to historical detail gave the film the authentic look of the decade covered by the story, from 1945 to 1955. "You can't, for example, just put a can of soup on a shelf," he says in the documentary. "It has to be the right can of soup." Being a stickler for detail and thus vividly creating the historical era in this film and his subsequent Coppola films placed Tavoularis at the head of his profession.

During the course of the three-month shooting schedule, most of the time was spent on the 102 New York locations. Another two weeks were spent in Taormina, Sicily, a village near Palermo, which represented Corleone, the birthplace of Vito Corleone. Coppola's stock with the suits at

Paramount steadily rose and fell in the course of production as he sought to appease the people in power—who were monitoring his progress during production—while still attempting to make the movie his own way. For example, he steadfastly refused to have Willis use more light in the don's dark study.

Moreover, through the grapevine he learned of what he considered to be a palace revolution in the making. He was convinced that film editor Aram Avakian, with the support of assistant director Steve Kestner, was fomenting a conspiracy to have him ousted as director. Avakian's defection from Coppola's camp was a real blow for the director, since Avakian had edited his first mainstream feature, *You're a Big Boy Now*. Avakian put out the word that the footage Coppola was giving him to edit would not cut together. That is, there was not enough footage shot from different angles to enable the editor to assemble a coherent sequence in the editing room. With Kestner's encouragement, Avakian phoned Evans from New York. "Bob, shot-by-shot it looks great," he said, "but it cuts together like a Chinese jigsaw puzzle." He continued, "The guinea [Coppola] doesn't know what continuity is."[27]

For the record, Coppola did not always feel the need to supply the editor with a great variety of surplus footage in order to ensure sufficient material for the editor to assemble a scene in final form. But he always saw to it that he gave the editor enough footage to cut together a coherent sequence.

By contrast, Avakian favored the kind of director who tended to shoot a scene from every possible angle and then allowed the editor to decide which takes to use when he assembled the whole thing in the cutting room. But Coppola consistently maintained that he wanted to make the movie on the set and not allow the editor to remake it in the editing room. Be that as it may, gossip around the set was that Avakian, who had already directed two features, was angling to replace Coppola as director and that was the real source of his complaints about him.

Evans examined all of the footage that Coppola was shipping to the west coast with another editor, Peter Zinner. Together they replied to Avakian that they were satisfied with Coppola's work. Evans sensed that "Avakian wanted at all costs to derail Francis, knowing that, with him out, he would have a good shot to take over."[28] He accordingly authorized Coppola to fire the insubordinate Avakian and his ally Kestner. "Like the godfather, I fired people as a preemptory strike," Coppola says in his DVD commentary. "The people who were angling the most to have me fired, I had fired." Avakian was replaced by Zinner and William Reynolds, Kestner by Fred Gallo.

Coppola felt that he had won a battle, but he had not won the war since some studio officials still harbored misgivings about the young filmmaker. Given the pressure he was under, Coppola sometimes felt like throwing in the towel just to get the ordeal over with. He recalls in his commentary that his secretary told him, "Don't quit—let them fire you." He explains laconically, "If I quit, I wouldn't get paid. If they fired me, I would." Marlon Brando, who knew about the effort of Avakian and others to unseat him as director, told the studio "that he would not continue to work on the picture if I was fired." Brando, Coppola emphasizes, really saved his neck.[29]

Still Coppola continued to be demoralized by the unsettling feeling that he had to keep proving himself to the powers that be. "My history with *The Godfather* was very much the history of someone in trouble," he recalls. Even in the best of circumstances directing a major film "is like running in front of a moving locomotive. If you stop, if you trip, if you make a mistake, you get killed. And *The Godfather* was worse than most."[30] One evening at the end of an arduous day of filming, he outlined for one of his assistants the foolproof way to direct a movie: "Have the definitive script ready before you shoot"; keep rewrites to an absolute minimum; and "work with people you trust and feel secure with." Upon reflection, he added, "I have managed to do neither of these things on this film."[31]

Although there was no longer any question of the studio taking Coppola off the picture, Evans complained that Coppola was too timid in portraying violence in what was, after all, a gangster picture. Coppola was distressed to hear that Evans was going to send a second unit director to the set to beef up the violence in the action sequences yet to be shot. It was at this point that a scene came up in the schedule in which the pregnant Connie's brutish husband Carlo (Gianni Russo), a cheap bookmaker, beats her during a domestic quarrel. In order to satisfy Evans that this scene was sufficiently violent, Coppola surreptitiously went to the set on a weekend with his sister Talia Shire and his nine-year-old son Gio, who was standing in for Russo, to stage the scene.

"We worked out as much of the action as we could think of," Coppola recalls in his DVD commentary. "My son was whipping his aunt with a belt, and she was breaking dishes." Talia Shire notes in the documentary that one of the ideas that cropped up while they were blocking out the scene was that "we thought how pitiful it would be that she was pregnant, and she tried to hide behind the flimsy curtain as Carlo beat her." Coppola says that they laid out the scene on Saturday and filmed it on Monday. "So this scene was directed by a filmmaker who knew an action director was arriving on the set unless he got plenty of action into the picture." At all events, when principal photography wrapped on July 2, 1971, Coppola was still at the helm.

The movie opens with Connie's wedding reception in the sun-drenched garden of the don's estate. As noted earlier, it offers a sharp contrast to the somber scene in his study, where the godfather sits in the dark recesses of his inner sanctum, stroking his cat and listening to petitions being presented to him by his associates. He is following an ancient custom that dictates that a godfather must seriously consider any request for help made to him on such a festive occasion. From the first the film establishes the two "families" depicted in the movie: the outer family of wives and children in a congenial atmosphere of family occasions and celebrations, and the inner family comprising the men who conduct the family's dirty business in secrecy. William Reynolds, who edited the opening sequence, says, "It was an interesting problem to keep the wedding and the indoor scenes going at the same time."[32]

Vito Corleone is a calculating man who has always run his empire of crime with the efficiency of a business executive. Whenever he encountered resistance from someone with whom he wanted to make a deal, the don simply extended to him what he ominously terms "an offer he couldn't refuse" and got what he wanted.

The filmgoer is afforded a salient example of how the don implements this policy in the episode in which Don Corleone intimidates Hollywood producer Jack Woltz (John Marley) into giving a part in a picture to singer-actor Johnny Fontane (Al Martino), one of the don's "godsons." He does so by arranging to have the producer's prize stallion decapitated, and its head placed in Woltz's bed.

"In the book the horse's head was on the bedpost," Coppola points out in his commentary, "but I thought it would be more horrible if he at first sees some wet blood on the bedsheets and fears that *he* has been stabbed. Then he pulls back the blankets and sees the horse's head." Coppola's staging of this scene is an improvement on the manner in which Puzo handled it in the book, as the novelist was the first to admit.

"Actually I did get a lot of complaints from animal lovers about the horse's head," Coppola observes. "But we got the head packed in dry ice from a dog food company after the horse had already been slaughtered. So my reply at the time to all of the angry pet lovers was that it was *their fault*—the horse was killed to feed their puppies and not because of my movie.[33] Furthermore, Coppola still cannot understand why people were more outraged by the head of a dead horse in the movie than by the three dozen people murdered in the picture.

There was another problem associated with the Woltz sequence. When the novel was published, it was widely rumored that the Johnny Fontane character was based on Frank Sinatra. When Johnny entreats Vito to get him a part in a war movie that he needs to resuscitate his ailing career, many readers thought of how Sinatra lobbied to get the role of Maggio in Fred Zinnemann's film *From Here to Eternity* (1953) in order to revive his fading career. Sinatra personally berated Puzo, when he encountered him in a restaurant, for apparently implying that he got the role he wanted in *From Here to Eternity* through the intervention of the Mafia.

Director Fred Zinnemann told me that he cast Sinatra in that picture because he admired Sinatra's acting skills. Indeed, Sinatra won an Academy Award for the film. "At no time was a horse's head involved in the casting decision," he affirms. "The author of *The Godfather* was using poetic license." Coppola confirms in his DVD commentary that "Mario concocted a fictionalized picture of Sinatra in the book."

The awesome Don Vito is the object of the envy and the hatred of some other mafiosi, who fear that he is becoming too powerful. Accordingly an assassination attempt is made on his life, which leaves him incapacitated for some time. Sonny, his oldest son (James Caan), rules in his stead for the duration of his illness. Michael, Don Vito's youngest son (Al Pacino), just home from serving in the army during World War II, is anxious to prove himself to his father. He gets the chance to do so when he convinces Sonny to let him even the score with the family's enemies by killing the two individuals responsible for the attempt on their father's life: drug kingpin Virgil "Turk" Sollozzo (Al Lettieri) and Captain McCluskey (Sterling Hayden), a corrupt cop.

In one of the most riveting scenes in the picture, Michael successfully carries out his plan to gun down both men in a Bronx restaurant. Sound engineer Walter Murch (*Rain People*) remembers that Coppola wanted musical accompaniment to this scene only after Michael has committed the murders and is leaving the restaurant. So, as Murch notes in his foreword to this book, he decided to add a sound effect just prior to the murders. He was aware of the elevated train tracks near the restaurant, so he employed the "screeching effect as the train turns a difficult corner" to symbolize Michael's state of mind. He is irrevocably turning a difficult corner: "This is the first time he has killed anybody face-to-face."[34] In short, the grating sound of the train's brakes is a metaphor for Michael's anxiety, implying his apprehension as the moment of the massacre draws near. Murch's superior work on *The Godfather* and other Coppola films placed him at the head of his profession.

Before Michael shoots the two men at close range, "he tries to summon the nerve to stand up and start firing," writes Karen Durbin. "Pacino's dark eyes dart around frantically in his otherwise immobile face. His whole future—his rise to power and his incalculable loss of humanity—is anticipated in that moment."[35] Little wonder that this scene helped to convince the Paramount bosses that perhaps both Coppola and Pacino knew what they were doing.

After he liquidates Sollozzo and the rogue cop, Michael escapes into temporary exile in Sicily in order to be out of the reach of reprisals. While in Sicily Michael meets and marries Apollonia, a beautiful peasant girl. Despite the bodyguards that surround Michael and his new bride, Apollonia dies in an explosion that had been intended to kill Michael. Embittered and brutalized by this never-ending spiral of revenge, Michael returns to America, where his tough methods of dealing with other mafiosi continue to impress his father, and he gradually emerges as the heir apparent of the aging Don Vito.

Friction between the Corleones and the other Mafia clans continues to mount, and the volatile Sonny is gunned down as the result of a clever ruse. He is lured into making a hurried trip to New York from the Corleones' compound on Long Island without his bodyguard. En route he stops to pay the toll on a causeway, where he is pulverized by an execution squad with submachine guns. A barrage of bullets blasts Sonny's Lincoln Continental and riddles Sonny's body as he writhes in agony.

The tollgate massacre was inspired by the death of the outlaws Bonnie Parker and Clyde Barrow in Arthur Penn's film *Bonnie and Clyde* (1967). Penn depicted the ambush of Bonnie and Clyde by police officers as a montage sequence, which became known as "the ballet of blood," and Coppola's tollgate ambush is equally stunning. "My Dad used to say, 'Only steal from the best,'" says Coppola in his commentary.

Coppola was not satisfied with the last conversation in the movie between Vito Corleone and Michael in the don's garden, which occurs just before the don's demise. In it Vito passes on the leadership of the Corleone family to his son. The scene as originally written appears in the shooting script dated March 29, 1971, which is on file in the Paramount Script Repository. It fails to convey clearly the transition of power from one generation to the next. Coppola turned to Robert Towne, a renowned script consultant, to rewrite the scene.

"Towne needed to create new material that combined . . . a subtle transfer of power, expressions of love, respect, and parental regret," Lebo explains. "Vito is obliged to pass the cup, and Michael is obliged to take it."[36] Towne's rewrite, as it appears in the published version of the screenplay, includes Vito's explanation to his son of the life that the don has lived:

"I never wanted this for you. I worked my whole life—I don't apologize—to take care of my family. . . . I thought that, when it was your time, you would be the one to hold the strings: Senator Corleone, Governor Corleone, something." Michael responds affectionately, "We'll get there, Pop."[37] Despite the brevity of this three-minute scene, Towne created a pivotal moment in the film.

Brando's time on the film was running out, and Coppola still had to do the don's death scene. So the front office decreed that it would have to be done immediately or not at all—they were not prepared to pay the star overtime for staying on to do the scene after his contract ran out. As Coppola prepared to shoot the scene, he recalls, "We were already losing the light," so it had to be filmed quickly. In the course of the scene Vito is playing with his grandson Anthony in his tomato patch.[38]

While rehearsing the scene Brando said, "I have a little game I sometimes play with kids." He made fangs out of an orange peel, wedged them in front of his teeth, and growled like a bear. Coppola set up two cameras in order to be sure that he captured the scene. "Brando shoved the orange peel into his mouth, and the lad playing his grandson really got scared." Here was the godfather "dying as a monster!" says Coppola, for shortly afterward the old man keels over and expires among the tomato plants. It is a touching scene, he concludes, "and it came close to never being shot."[39]

When the ailing Don Vito dies, the Corleone family closes ranks under Michael's leadership, and the new don effects the simultaneous liquidation of their most powerful rivals by having them all killed on the same day and at the same hour. Coppola intercuts these murders with shots of Michael acting as godfather at the baptism of his little nephew. The ironic parallel between Michael's solemn role as godfather in the baptismal ceremony and the stunning "baptism of blood" he has engineered to confirm his position as godfather of one of the most formidable Mafia clans in the country is unmistakable.

Coppola told me that it was his idea to include the baptism in the film. When Puzo said the script lacked real punch at the end, Coppola responded, "We'll have Michael's enemies murdered while his nephew is being christened." Elsewhere he explains, "I decided to include some Catholic rituals in the movie, which are part of my Catholic heritage. Hence the baptism. I am familiar with every detail of such ceremonies, and I had never seen a film that captured the essence of what it was like to be an Italian-American."[40]

William Reynolds was assigned to cut the first half of the picture and Peter Zinner to edit the second half. Accordingly Coppola worked closely with Zinner to create the baptism scene. "Intercutting the baptism with the slaughter was not in the script," Coppola explains. The two sequences were to be presented separately. When he opted to intercut the two sequences, Peter Zinner suggested that they add the powerful organ theme, which then became the unifying force that tied the two sequences together musically. In short, the montage choreographed mayhem with religion by intercutting multiple murders with the baptism of Michael Corleone's godson, Michael Rizzi, the son of Connie and Carlo.

The scene starts with the baptism liturgy, along with the organ playing solemn tones. The escalating organ music builds to a frenzied crescendo with the wave of killings. Thus the blaring organ accompanies the priest who asks Michael, according to the baptism liturgy, if he renounces Satan and all his works, and Michael, speaking for his godson, responds that he does renounce them. "The effect," says Sragow, "sealed the movie's inspired depiction of the Corleones' simultaneous dueling rituals—the sacrament of Church and family, and the murders."[41]

As for the killings, Moe Greene (Alex Rocco), a casino owner who refused to sell his holdings to the Corleones, looks up from a massage table, puts on his glasses, and stares at his killer, who shoots directly into Greene's glasses. The lens cracks as the bullet goes into his eye and blood pours out. Another enemy of the Corleone clan is gunned down while trapped in a revolving door, and his blood splatters the glass in the door.

The baptism sequence illustrates the immeasurable gap between the sacred rituals of the Church and the unholy rites of the murderous Corleone mob—"in the end the gap between good and evil," writes Naomi Greene. And the sacrilegious lies Michael utters demonstrate "how far he has fallen from grace, how binding is the pact he has made with the devil" he claims to renounce.[42]

One of the casualties of Michael's purge is Carlo Rizzi, who, besides mistreating Connie, had sold out to Barzini's rival Mafia family. Connie accuses Michael of killing her husband, but he coolly denies it. By this time Michael has married again, and his second wife Kay (Diane Keaton) likewise demands to know if he has murdered Carlo. Michael again lies and declares that he did not murder his brother-in-law.

The movie ends with Kay standing in the doorway of the study where Don Vito once ruled, watching the members of the Corleone Mafia family kissing Michael's hand as a sign of their loyalty to him. The camera draws away and the huge door of Don Michael's study closes on the scene, shut-

ting out Kay—and the filmgoer—from any further look at the inner workings of the Mafia.

Sound designer Walter Murch emphasizes in his foreword to this study
the importance of the shutting of that door. He accompanied the image of
the door closing not with a simple click but with a slam. "It was even more
important to get a firm, irrevocable closing that resonated with and underscored Michael's final line, 'Never ask me about my business, Kay.'" By the
end of the picture, Kathleen Murphy notes, Pacino has seamlessly morphed
from the clean-cut Marine veteran at the wedding reception into a "Satur-
nine, Machiavellian, masked Mafia assassin, . . . given to molten rage."[43]

During postproduction the musical score was added to the sound
track. Coppola commissioned Nino Rota, the distinguished composer of
several film scores for Italian director Federico Fellini—like *La Dolce Vita*
(1960)—to furnish the underscore for *The Godfather*. (Carmine Coppola
composed the incidental music for the dance band at the film's wedding
reception.) In his score Rota utilized a symphonic structure to comment
on characters and situations. Evans initially feared that the score was too
highbrow and operatic, but Coppola as usual stuck to his guns and insisted
that the Rota score be used in the film.

Subsequent critical reaction to Rota's music was unanimously positive. "The score was laced with intricate melodies, Italian-tinged passages,
and hauntingly tragic themes," Lebo comments.[44] Some of the themes are
among the most memorable in film history— for example, "The Godfather Waltz," first played by a lone trumpet during the opening credits and
repeated throughout the film in various combinations of instruments.

Coppola's principal concern about the rough cut of the picture during editing was the running time, as he says in his DVD commentary. "Bob
Evans said that, if it was over two hours, I would have to cut the film at
Paramount in Los Angeles," meaning that the studio brass would supervise the shortening of the rough cut, probably with a meat cleaver. Coppola
had originally envisioned a three-hour film, but he assured Evans he would
comply with his dictum. The director started out with five hundred thousand feet of footage (about ninety hours), which he had to whittle down to
a reasonable running time. Reynolds and Zinner had done a preliminary
edit of each scene as it was filmed, and now Coppola had to supervise the
assembly of a full-scale rough cut. In all, Coppola spent five months editing the rough cut.

"My first cut was in fact three hours, so I cut all the footage that wasn't
germane to the story and got it down to two hours and twenty minutes." It
was safely below the outside limit of three hours, so that the studio would

not have an excuse to fire him and take over the editing of the film. He shipped the rough cut to Evans, who soon phoned him in a fit of rage. Coppola continues: Evans called the short version "a two hour trailer" for the movie. "You've cut all the human stuff out, and you've only got the plot left. All the best stuff is gone!"

So Evans ordered Coppola to bring the rough cut down to Paramount in Los Angeles and restore the footage he had eliminated from his first cut. "Basically I simply put back everything that I had cut from my first version," which was three hours. Peter Bart, Evans's right-hand man in those days, goes so far as to say that because Evans was dissatisfied with Coppola's short version, he personally supervised Coppola's editing of the long version, "transforming a superbly shot but ineptly put-together film into a masterpiece."[45]

Coppola flatly denies that Evans actually oversaw his reediting of the film. Coppola on his own methodically reinstated "all that wonderful stuff" he had cut originally at Evans's behest in order to bring the film in at two hours and twenty minutes. "It's true that Evans realized that a lot of the human texture, the family warmth, had been taken out in the shorter version. But there was no problem about my simply putting it all back, because it had all been there in the first place."

A decade after the release of the film Coppola read an interview with Evans in which Evans again claimed that he personally masterminded the final edit of *The Godfather*. Coppola shot off a vehement telegram to Evans dated December 13, 1983, stating in part: "Your stupid blabbing about cutting *The Godfather* comes back to me and angers me for its ridiculous pomposity." Evans replied in a telegram dated the following day that he did not deserve "the venomous diatribe."[46]

The consensus of those involved in the release of *The Godfather*, including Frank Yablans, who had succeeded Stanley Jaffe as president of Paramount, was to side with Coppola. Indeed, Yablans remembers Evans lobbying with him in support of Coppola's three-hour version of the film, but he affirms pointedly: "Evans did not save *The Godfather*; Evans did not make *The Godfather*. That is a total figment of his imagination."[47] Ruddy assured me in conversation that the release version of *The Godfather* "was Francis's cut, frame for frame."[48]

Brett Morgen and Nanette Burstein's documentary on Robert Evans's life, *The Kid Stays in the Picture*, premiered at the 2002 Cannes Film Festival; in it Evans continues to maintain that he had an artistic influence on *The Godfather*. In the directors' commentary included on the DVD of the documentary, Morgen acknowledges that Coppola contests Evans's claims about his role in shaping *The Godfather*. But, he adds, "This is Bob Evans's film; it's told from his point of view. It's the world according to Bob."

Some of the scenes Coppola excised from the rough cut during postproduction were not reinstated. All of these deleted scenes can be viewed in a special section of the DVD. The only one that I wish that Coppola might have found a place for in the final cut of the film is the scene in which Kay is praying for Michael in church—a scene that Coppola had originally intended to use as the ending of the film. It shows Kay lighting a candle and praying for her husband's lost soul. Puzo favored this ending since this is the way the book ends. But Evans and others thought that the ending would be more effective if the picture concluded with Michael closing the door on Kay as he takes his place as the head of the Corleone dynasty, and Coppola eventually went with that ending. Still the brief scene of Kay praying fervently in church might have been inserted elsewhere in the film, since it proves a significant contrast to Michael's hypocritical participation in the baptism ceremony.

On its release, *The Godfather* was criticized in some quarters for subtly encouraging the audience to admire the breathtaking efficiency with which organized crime operates and for celebrating the violent means by which the mafiosi achieve their goals. Coppola counters in his commentary that it was never his intention to present a cosmeticized study of organized crime or to glamorize violence. "In fact, there's very little actual violence in the film. It occurs very quickly," he maintains, as when Carlo Rizzi is murdered while he is sitting in the front seat of a car. He is garroted by an assassin who is in the back seat. The camera watches impassively as his shoes flail about and finally smash through the windshield as he dies.

Moreover, Coppola feels that he was making an especially harsh statement about the Mafia at the end of the film, when Michael makes a savage purge of all of the Corleone crime family's known foes. He points out that the violence in this scene was derived from real-life gangland killings. The death of Moe Greene, for example, was suggested by the murder of Las Vegas racketeer Bugsy Siegel, who was the target of a Mafia hit. In Coppola's defense John McCarty contends that Coppola was correct in not portraying the mafiosi as obviously menacing criminal types: "The members of the underworld are not all eye-rolling, saliva-dripping goons," like the stereotypical mobsters in the old gangster pictures.[49] The film rightly shows how the Mafia has become comfortably ensconced in a veneer of respectability, says Andrew Dickos. Thus the Corleone crime family has adopted "a sophisticated capitalistic approach," as crime organizations like the Mafia operate more and more "like a corporation in a corporate society."[50]

Coppola's status as an auteur is confirmed by the fact that his ongoing theme is clearly evident in this movie (i.e., his continuing preoccupation with the importance of family in modern society is once again brought into relief in the present picture).[51] As a matter of fact, the thing that most attracted Coppola to the project in the first place was that the book is really the story of a family. It is about "this father and his sons," he says, "and questions of power and successions."[52] In essence, *The Godfather* offers a chilling depiction of the way in which Michael's loyalty to his flesh-and-blood family gradually turns into an allegiance to the larger Mafia family to which they, in turn, belong, a devotion that in the end renders him a cruel and ruthless mass killer.

The family, John Cawelti states, is the unifying principle of the film. It is a tale of a family, recounting the rise of Michael as son and heir "and reaching a climax with his acceptance of the power and responsibilities of godfather." Most of the characters are members of the Corleone family, and the key scenes are events in the family history: the marriage of a daughter, the death of a son and then of the father. But the movie extends the family symbolism beyond the actual progeny of Don Vito's immediate family "to the members of the organization of which he is leader," and they constitute his extended family. In brief, family is the thematic core of the entire film.[53]

With this film Coppola definitely hit his stride as a filmmaker. He tells the story in a straightforward, fast-paced fashion that holds the viewer's attention for close to three hours. Under his direction the cast members, without exception, give flawless performances, highlighted by Brando's Oscar-winning performance in the title role. His performance lends strength and coherence to the film and transcends genre. *The Godfather* also received Academy Awards for the best picture of the year and for the screenplay, which Coppola coauthored with Puzo. Furthermore, the picture was an enormous critical and popular success.

Later on, the picture received Italy's David Donatello Award as the best foreign film of the year. As Italy's top prize for an international motion picture, the Donatello Award demonstrated that Italy itself had no quarrel with the fashion in which Italian Americans were represented in the movie.

The Godfather went on to set box-office records that are among the highest in cinema history. By the time its first run was completed, the movie had amassed an unprecedented $134 million in domestic rentals alone.

Pauline Kael speaks for the majority of critics when she calls *The Godfather* a groundbreaking film that raised the gangster picture to the level of cinematic art. As William Pechter puts it, *The Godfather* is "bigger, longer and more richly upholstered than any other treatment of its subject."[54] Moreover, when the American Film Institute honored the best one hundred American films made during the first century of cinema in 1998, *The Godfather* headed the list.

Still, despite the hosannas lavished on the film, Coppola was disturbed at the time of the film's release by the notices that unfairly chastised him for celebrating and sentimentalizing the Mafia. If some reviewers and moviegoers missed the point he was trying to make about organized crime, he looked upon the sequel, which Paramount had asked him to make, as "an opportunity to rectify that," for in the sequel Coppola would see to it that Michael was shown to be manifestly more cold-blooded and cruel than his father had ever been.[55]

5

Decline and Fall

The Godfather Part II and *The Godfather Part III*

> I grew up in a neighborhood where organized crime was a way of life. I never knew these people as criminals. To me they were fathers and sons, childhood friends that I went to school with and sat next to in church.
>
> —Bo Dietal, a policeman in
> the film *One Tough Cop*

> I no doubt deserve my enemies.
>
> —Walt Whitman

When *The Godfather* became a runaway hit, Coppola's earnings from the film's profits amounted to a small fortune. So he could now afford to move the offices of American Zoetrope, his independent film production unit, from the old Folsom Street warehouse in San Francisco to more ample quarters. He took over the eight-story Sentinel Building at 910 Kearney Street, which had survived the San Francisco earthquake of 1906. The edifice, which was painted sea green, was topped by a blue and gold dome that he christened "Coppola's cupola." He remodeled the new home of American Zoetrope to encompass a penthouse office-studio, from which he could look out on the Golden Gate Bridge, and a high-tech postproduction facility, not to mention an espresso machine (no more instant coffee as in his austere, pre-*Godfather* days).

It was from the new office complex of Zoetrope that Coppola continued to develop film projects, which he arranged to finance and release through the distribution setups of various major studios in Hollywood. Thus *The Conversation* was a Zoetrope production, financed and distributed by Paramount (see chapter 3).

At the outset, Coppola was not enthusiastic about making the sequel to *The Godfather*. It seemed to him too much like reheating last week's stew. He joked that he would only direct the sequel if he could make it along the lines of a farce called *Abbott and Costello Meet the Godfather* (a reference to the series of Abbott and Costello comedies like *Abbot and Costello Meet Frankenstein*). He was inclined to return to making small personal films like *The Conversation,* even if he was reduced "to making them on Super 8."[1]

Charles Bludhorn would not hear of any other director but Coppola taking on the sequel, Coppola says in his DVD commentary on *Godfather II*. Bludhorn told him, "Francis, you've got the recipe for Coca-Cola, and you don't want to manufacture any more bottles of Coke!" Paramount offered Coppola a handsome salary and a generous slice of the profits, but Coppola was especially interested in artistic control of the production. In negotiating with the studio he demanded that Robert Evans, with whom he feuded constantly on *The Godfather,* was to have "zero to do with the film" at any phase of the production. This stipulation was not a problem, since, as Biskind states frankly, Evans "was getting deeper into drugs" and eventually "stopped coming to the office."[2]

An early scenario proposed to Coppola dealt with the death of Michael Corleone, and he declined to consider it. "I did not want to see him assassinated by his rivals or go to jail," he explains. "I wanted to take Michael toward what was in fact his destiny. . . . After winning all the battles and overcoming all of his enemies, I wanted him to be a broken man, a condemned man."[3]

What finally convinced him to take on the project was his conviction that the public had not morally condemned Michael at the end of *The Godfather*. He got to hear that some filmgoers actually applauded when the door of Michael's office was slammed in Kay's face at the film's final fadeout. Showing Michael Corleone to be the ruthless, cold-blooded criminal that he has become would provide Coppola with the lead-in to the sequel. He decided to call the film *The Godfather Part II,* a title that occurred to him when he remembered Russian filmmaker Sergei Eisenstein's *Ivan the Terrible Part II* (1945). "*Godfather II* was the first American film that did not have a special title for the sequel," Coppola says in his DVD commentary. For example, a sequel to *In the Heat of the Night* (1967) was called *The*

Organization (1971). "Calling the sequel to a Hollywood film *Part II* began with *The Godfather.*"

The Godfather Part II

Once Coppola had finally agreed to do the film, Paramount gave him a fairly tight schedule to work on because the studio wanted this movie to open during the lucrative Christmas season in 1974. A novelist takes two years to finish an ambitious novel, Coppola says. "I looked at the calendar and realized that I had three months to write a two-hundred-page screenplay for *Godfather II,* and then go right into pre-production."[4] He was making a $13 million movie as if it were a quickie for his former boss Roger Corman (see chapter 1).

In approaching the screenplay, Coppola explains, "I believed that the family would be morally destroyed, and it would be a kind of Götterdämmerung. Moreover, I thought it would be interesting to juxtapose the ascension of the family under Vito Corleone with the decline of the family under his son Michael," to show in flashback how the young Vito Corleone was building this crime family in America, while his son in the present is presiding over its disintegration.[5]

In the documentary that accompanies the *Godfather Trilogy* on DVD, Coppola notes, "I had always wanted to write a screenplay that told the story of a father and a son at the same age. They were both in their thirties, and I would integrate the two stories." Young Vito Corleone's early life as an Italian immigrant would be set during World War I, while the later life of the Corleone family presided over by his son Michael would be updated to the 1950s. The modern story would depict the family as "beset by Byzantine intrigues, marital discord, fraternal rivalry, and internal decay."[6] Consequently, *Godfather II* covers nearly sixty years of American history, from the immigrants coming to America in the early 1900s all the way up to the post–World War II period. It is evident that he definitely did not want *Godfather II* to be a rehash of *The Godfather*: "In order not to merely make *Godfather I* over again, I gave *Godfather II* this double structure by extending the story in both the past and in the present." He was fascinated by the concept of a movie that would move freely back and forth in time. In short, he was interested in making a sequel that was "more ambitious, more advanced than the first."

Paramount had commissioned Mario Puzo to prepare a preliminary draft of the screenplay before Coppola came on board, and Coppola incorporated some incidents from it in his version of the screenplay. Puzo also contributed some additional material to the shooting script along the way, but the bulk of the screenplay was composed by Coppola. By burning a lot of midnight oil, he finished the script on time.

Most of the events in the modern story were invented by Coppola. Some of them were suggested by contemporary newspaper accounts. There is, for example, the incident in which Michael frames Nevada Senator Pat Geary by having a dead prostitute found in his bed in a sleazy bordello run by the Corleones in order to ensure the Senator's continued patronage of the Corleone enterprises. This episode was inspired by a sensational newspaper exposé of Nevada brothels.

The flashbacks to young Vito's life in New York's "Little Italy" were drawn from material left over from Puzo's novel—historical background for which there had been no room in the first film. In fact, Book III of the novel is a thirty-page description of the roots of the Mafia in Sicily and Vito Corleone's subsequent rise to power as a Mafia leader when he immigrates to the United States.[7] Puzo chronicles how Vito becomes a Mafia godfather who is a sort of Italian-immigrant entrepreneur in Little Italy. Coppola simply plucked historical incidents from Book III of the novel and wrote them into the script.

These flashbacks in essence depict the experiences of immigrants like Vito Corleone coming to this country and trying to realize the American dream of success in their lives. But they were reduced to laboring in sweat shops and dwelling in slums, so they found self-esteem and cash by joining street gangs, which they saw as brotherhoods.

The immigrants had a tradition of violence born of their resistance to the rural landlords who had exploited them back in Sicily. When they came over to America they formed gangs and secret societies, just as they had done in the old country. As historian Luc Sante states in the ABC-TV documentary *The Real Gangs of New York* (2003), "Crime became a necessary means of survival in the lawless slums," which were therefore a fertile ground for the growth of gangs in the United States.

"My heart was really in the Little Italy sequences," Coppola remembers, "in the old streets of New York, the music, all that turn-of-the century atmosphere."[8] To that extent, Coppola the auteur sees *Godfather II* as a personal film in which he addressed his own ancestry and ethnic heritage. In one flashback Vito and his friend Genco attend an Italian musical drama in a neighborhood music hall. The operetta, *Sensa Mamma,* was actually composed by Coppola's grandfather Francesco Pennino, after whom he was named. It is about an immigrant who left his mother behind in Italy when he came to New York, and was quite popular in its day.

As the characters took shape in the script, Coppola's thoughts turned to considering who would play the various parts. Many of the actors from *The Godfather* reprised their roles in *Godfather II*: Al Pacino, Talia Shire, Diane Keaton, John Cazale, and Robert Duvall all returned. As for new members of the cast, Coppola was at pains to find the right actor to play Vito Corleone as a young man. He tested Robert De Niro (*Mean Streets*). "I thought De Niro could be the young Brando," Coppola says in his DVD commentary. "De Niro had a sort of stately bearing, as if he really was the young Vito who would grow into that older man who was Marlon Brando in *Godfather I*. He had grace." As a matter of fact, De Niro had spent some time in his apprenticeship days as a young actor studying Brando's acting style and was able to recreate in *Godfather II* Brando's measured gestures and calm, convincing voice.

"Al Pacino suggested Lee Strasberg to play crime syndicate treasurer Hyman Roth," an aging Jewish racketeer. Strasberg was the head of the renowned Actor's Studio in New York, where he had been Pacino's mentor. Coppola admits, "I was intimidated by Strasberg. Here was this great teacher of acting, and I would be in the position of having to direct him. But he was very responsive to direction and would easily put himself into whatever mood the scene called for." Strasberg made Roth a wily financial wizard who was a worthy opponent for Michael. Roth ostensibly treats Michael as an ally, but covertly plots to overthrow him. He was modeled on the notorious Jewish gangster Meyer Lansky. Like Lansky, Roth lives in a modest bungalow in Florida, which belies his stature as a wealthy, powerful kingpin of organized crime. When the septuagenarian Strasberg became ill during the shoot, Coppola modified the script in order to make Roth an ailing man. Playwright Michael V. Gasso (*A Hatful of Rain*) was likewise an important casting choice in the role of small-time Mafia crook Frankie Pantangeli. Both Strasberg and Gasso received Academy Award nominations for this film. Other interesting additions to the cast were G. D. Spradling, a former politician, to play Senator Pat Geary; and Troy Donahue, a former teen idol, to play Merle Johnson, Connie's fiancé. Coppola had gone to military school with Donahue, whose real name was in fact Merle Johnson. Coppola's brilliant strokes of casting demonstrated why there is more first-rate acting in even the smallest roles in this film than in most other American movies.

Coppola brought back some of the creative personnel that had worked on *The Godfather* or other Coppola films: cinematographer Gordon Willis (*The Godfather*), film editor Barry Malkin (*Rain People*), film editor Peter Zinner (*The Godfather*), production designer Dean Tavoularis (*The Godfa-*

ther), sound engineer Walter Murch (*Rain People, The Godfather*), and composers Nino Rota and Carmine Coppola (*The Godfather*). As for Willis, Coppola's nemesis on *The Godfather,* "I got along with Gordy Willis on this film," Coppola says in his DVD commentary. "I didn't feel I was up against this crotchety school marm who wanted things done his own way. Of course, I was producer as well as director, so I really had no one to answer to but myself."

Working with Willis, Coppola conceived a visual scheme to keep the two plotlines in the picture distinct: The flashbacks to Vito's youth would be photographed in what Willis terms nostalgic "golden amber" tints, to give these scenes a period flavor as they portray Vito as a "Lower-East-Side Robin Hood" who steals from the rich and gives to the poor (in cahoots with Peter Clemenza [Bruno Kirby], a young hood who was an order man in *The Godfather* and was played there by Richard Castellano). In the flashbacks, says Willis, "the imagery is softer and not as sharply defined." The scenes about Michael set in modern times would be filmed in a spare realistic color scheme featuring cool blues and grays in order to suggest how Michael becomes colder and more ruthless as time goes on.[9]

Principal photography for *Godfather II* began on location at Lake Tahoe, high in the Sierras, on October 23, 1973. Coppola commandeered the elaborate Fleur de Lac estate, constructed in 1934 by Henry Kaiser, to serve as the Corleone compound at Lake Tahoe. By mid-November the production unit moved on to Paramount studios in Hollywood for five weeks of filming interiors. On January 2, 1974, Coppola and company were on their way to Santo Domingo in the Dominican Republic, where Gulf and Western owned a good deal of property that they put at Coppola's disposal. Santo Domingo was the site chosen for the scenes set in Cuba, where Michael attends a high-level conference with other leaders of organized crime. During the Batista regime in Cuba the Mafia was involved in the gambling casinos and other rackets there. But their holdings would soon be lost in the wake of the overthrow of Batista's dictatorship by Fidel Castro, which is portrayed in this sequence.

Pacino, who was already suffering from exhaustion brought on by playing the demanding role of Michael Corleone, came down with pneumonia in Santo Domingo and was ordered by his physician to take a month's sick leave. Due to Pacino's illness, Coppola transplanted the film unit to New York City to shoot the flashbacks with De Niro. When Coppola was asked if he was overwhelmed by the shifts in period during the production from the modern story to the flashbacks, he replied, "No, because basically you still do one day at a time, one shot at a time."[10]

The film unit moved on to New York City in late January, where Dean Tavoularis cordoned off East Sixth Street in Lower Manhattan, between Avenues A and B, and systematically transformed it into Little Italy in 1918, with old-fashioned store fronts and a dirt road replacing the pavement of later times. Tavoularis would deservedly win an Academy Award for his production design on *Godfather II*.

Since the studio kept its promise to leave him alone during filming, Coppola confesses in his DVD commentary that the only problems he had were personal ones. "I was in the middle of a vulnerable time in my marriage" during the New York shoot, he says. He had taken on Melissa Mathison as his production assistant and protégée. She was young, intelligent, and, by all accounts, devoted to the director. Indeed, they were seen together off the set often enough to become an item in the gossip columns, much to the displeasure of Coppola's parents, who visited the New York location. Coppola had the Little Italy set on Sixth Street wired for sound so that he could easily communicate with Willis and the camera crew. On one occasion Coppola got into a quarrel with his mother, Italia Coppola, over his relationship with his assistant, and their argument was amplified over the production unit's public address system all along Sixth Street. Coppola, who had made a film about wiretapping (*The Conversation*), had inadvertently bugged himself. "You're a good Catholic boy," his mother remonstrated. "What do you mean carrying on with that girl?" Furious that a private family argument had gone public, he shot back, "It's none of your business; I'm a grown man."[11] Eleanor Coppola remembers crying a lot during that period, but the marriage survived.

The film unit then journeyed overseas to shoot on European locations. As in *The Godfather*, the village of Taormina again served as the town of Corleone, the home of the Corleone family (it would be used again in *Godfather III*). An enormous fish market in the Italian seaport of Trieste was chosen by Tavoularis to stand in for the Immigration Arrival Center on Ellis Island, where Vito, while still a child, waits for admission into the United States. Coppola opted to film this scene in Italy because he wanted the eight-hundred extras to look like European immigrants entering the United States. The extras in New York City would have looked too American. Once again Coppola favored shooting on location over filming in the studio. Shooting outside the insulated atmosphere of a film studio gives a scene a sense of actuality, Coppola comments: "it is rewarding for the director because there is a sense of reality that he and his actors can dig into."

By May 1974, *Godfather II* had completed more than eight months of principal photography on a budget of $13 million. "The film was shot in

104 days, as opposed to 62 days for *Godfather I*," Coppola says in his DVD commentary. But the shooting schedule involved extensive location work in both Europe and the Dominican Republic as well as in New York, "so it was an efficient shoot." By the end of filming Coppola was worn out by the grueling shooting schedule at far-flung locations. Asked by a journalist what he was looking forward to after finishing *Godfather II*, Coppola quipped, "retirement."

But surcease from labor was nowhere in sight since he had to pare down the huge accumulation of footage into a feature film of reasonable proportions in time for the premiere on December 12. So supervising the editing of the film became a race against the clock for Coppola, but by November the rough cut had been shaved down to three hours and twenty minutes.

The studio was worried that audiences would get lost in the complicated plot, which glided back and forth between past and present. "As I view the film now, I realize how audacious it was," Coppola comments on the DVD. Some studio officials thought "the modern story was enough, and that we didn't need the old world story."

By this time George Lucas and Coppola had gone their separate ways, but they still continued to consult with each other about their work. Lucas, who viewed an early assembly of the footage, expressed strong doubts about Coppola's concept of a dual plotline for *Godfather II*. "Francis, you have two movies," said Lucas ruefully. "Throw one away; it doesn't work."[12]

Not to be deterred, Coppola soldiered on. "I knew I could never top *Godfather I* in terms of financial success," he says, "but I did want to make a film that topped it as a really moving human document." He believed that in moving back and forth in time at significant moments in the lives of father and son he had linked their lives together and showed how each dealt with problems that faced the family.[13] In switching back and forth from a scene in Michael's time to Vito's young manhood, Coppola was at pains to provide smooth transitions between present and past that would suggest the affinities between Michael and his father. Thus Michael gazes down on his sleeping son in his Tahoe mansion, and the scene slowly dissolves to Vito gazing at his first-born son in the same ancient fashion in a New York tenement.

With the film's premiere in mid-December fast approaching, Coppola had a sneak preview in San Francisco, which turned out to be a total disaster. "We made a lot of changes after that preview," he recalls, "because it was hard for the audience to follow the two story lines. They wrote preview cards saying the picture was cold and confused," especially in the last hour.[14]

Coppola previewed the picture again in San Diego, where it played much better, but still the audience began to fidget noticeably as the movie unspooled. Walter Murch, who worked closely with Coppola during postproduction, explains in the DVD documentary, "In the version shown in San Diego the two stories were intercut very often, i.e., each story interrupted the other very often: there were twenty cuts back and forth" between the modern story and the flashbacks. During the San Diego screening Coppola muttered notes to himself into a pocket tape recorder. At a roundtable discussion with his postproduction team, held after the preview, he ironed out the difficulties, as he notes in his DVD commentary: "I found that the audience had trouble staying with the film if the segments were too short. When we went back and forth between the modern era and the past era too quickly, we were leaving each segment too soon." Hence he concluded that "the audience would feel more comfortable if they could watch a section of the movie for a longer duration. Each segment would then come to a resolution before it was interrupted to go to the other level of the story." Consequently, in the final cut he shifted back and forth between the present and the past only eleven times—instead of the twenty shifts in the previous cut.

One of the assistant editors working on the final cut said at the time, "I was amazed at Francis's total lack of proprietary ideas." If people on the postproduction staff said they did not like the way a scene was cut, he would say, "Okay, try something else." "He wants the movie to be good, and he doesn't care whose ideas make it good; and that's what gets people excited about working with him."[15] Barry Malkin, Peter Zinner, and Richard Marks were the principal film editors. Malkin recalls: "We were working day and night to get the final mix finished. I remember sleeping on the floor of the editing room, just getting catnaps." Malkin says that Coppola made no substantial alterations in the film at this juncture: "it was mostly a lot of tightening up."[16] Coppola's office complex in San Francisco contains state-of-the-art editing equipment, and the end credits of *Godfather II* state that the film was made "with the production facilities of American Zoetrope."

Nevertheless, Coppola managed to pull together a final cut of *Godfather II* just days before it opened. One critic marveled, "Doesn't Coppola always bring his pictures in at the last minute—a surgeon delivering the baby like a parcel, in a dead run, double-parked?"[17] Coppola had managed to create a vast epic reflecting the historical development of organized crime in the United States in terms of the Italian-immigrant past.

As Pauline Kael says, "We only saw the middle of the story in the first film; now we have the beginning and the end"; The second *Godfather* film not only chronicles Michael's later career as head of the "family business," but it also presents in flashback Don Vito's early life in Sicily, as well as his rise to power in the Mafia in New York City's Little Italy after his immigration to the United States.[18]

The parallel structure of the film brings into relief the symbiotic relationship between Vito and his son Michael. The child Vito Corleone, who arrives alone at Ellis Island, will grow up to forge a crime family that will "subvert the American dream to attain criminal wealth," and his son Michael will follow in his footsteps.[19] To that extent, *Godfather II* can be called Coppola's requiem for the American dream.

Godfather II begins where the previous picture left off, with the scene in which Don Michael's lieutenants pay him homage as his father's rightful successor. Then the movie switches to a scene from the childhood of Michael's father, when young Vito's own father is murdered for defying the local Mafia don back in the Sicilian village where Vito was born. Vito's mother and older brother are also killed shortly afterward for attempting to take vengeance on the Mafia chief, and Vito, now an orphan, escapes to America.

In 1901, the child Vito goes through the immigration process at Ellis Island. The wide-eyed Vito Andolini cannot communicate with the American immigration official, so he stands by mutely as the officer mistakenly records his name as Vito Corleone, thereby naming him for his hometown of Corleone. The sallow, thin boy is diagnosed as having contracted smallpox and is therefore quarantined for three months on Ellis Island. The lad comes to America carrying another sickness as well, that of the vendetta. "This child will carry his vendetta-disease to the point of emerging as a Mafia don" and liquidating those who have harmed his family.[20]

Back in the present, the film focuses on another youngster, Michael's son Anthony, who is enjoying a big celebration in honor of his First Communion. The party is being held on his father's estate at Lake Tahoe, now the center of Michael's business operations. Michael, like his father before him, privately conducts his business affairs while the festivities are in full swing. "In the first *Godfather* there was a wedding scene in which the principal characters were introduced," Coppola says on the DVD. "Now the same thing happens at the First Communion ceremony in *Godfather II*."

While Michael is engaged in making Machiavellian deals in his shadowy study, he is "swallowed up in darkness; his face is often half-lit; his presence tends to recede into the darker parts of the frame," reflecting him as an enigma to those he is dealing with.[21] Michael bribes Nevada Senator Pat Geary with a large "donation," ostensibly for the state university but actually to buy Geary's support in securing a gambling license for one of the Corleone Las Vegas casinos.

The party scene demonstrates the participation by Mafia families in empty displays of religious belief—a Catholic wedding in *The Godfather* and a First Communion in *Godfather II*. But these participants steadfastly ignore the spiritual import of these time-honored religious rituals. The sacraments of Matrimony and of Holy Communion do not touch their lives in any meaningful way. Like Don Vito before him, Don Michael deploys Catholic ceremonies to legitimize his lifestyle.

The sacred First Communion ceremony is followed by a noisy, vulgar outdoor party that demonstrates just how far the Corleone family has drifted from its ethnic origins. "The Italian customs associated with the old country are no longer evident in the scenes set in the modern era," says Coppola. The hearty Italian street songs of the wedding reception in *The Godfather* have been replaced by suave-sounding dance numbers reminiscent of the big band era. Frankie Pantageli, who is from Vito's old neighborhood, asks the bandleader to play an Italian folk song—a Tarantella that had in fact been played at Connie's wedding in *The Godfather*—but "the hokey west coast musicians can only come up with 'Pop Goes the Weasel,'" Coppola notes in his commentary. This is followed by a cherubic boys' choir serenading Michael with a Tin Pan Alley number, "Mr. Wonderful."

The drunken Frankie, who disdains the music at the reception, also notices that Michael's guests are imbibing champagne cocktails rather than Italian vino, and he upbraids Michael for abandoning his roots. Frankie likewise excoriates him for doing business with "the despicable old Jew" Hyman Roth, whom Don Vito never trusted. Michael suggests to Frankie that his policy is to keep his friends close, but his enemies closer. Frankie, however, does not buy his explanation.

Throughout the party scene it becomes apparent that the family still hangs on to some vestiges of venerable Italian customs, such as a toast in Italian at dinner (e.g., "*Cent' anni*," which means, "hundred years," as in "Happiness for a hundred years"). Yet the in-laws who have been coming into the Corleone family lately are not of Italian origin and have no sense at all of the family traditions. Mama Corleone (Morgana King, repeating her role from *The Godfather*) expresses her displeasure at the fragmentation of the family and the diminishing of their ethnic identity. Fredo's wife Deanna, who is not Italian, is really a floozy and a drunk and crassly flirts with younger men at the reception. When Fredo futilely attempts to make her behave, she shouts at him that she resents how "these dagos" try to dominate their wives. "Never marry a wop!" she bellows for good measure.

Since Michael is head of the family, Connie goes through the motions of asking his permission to marry a WASP named Merle Johnson, whom Michael rightly infers is a fortune hunter. Connie has become a hardened, dissipated creature since the murder of her first husband, Carlo. Coppola comments on the DVD: "She has these fancy boyfriends. That's the only way she can rebel against her all-powerful brother, who killed her first husband."

Connie, who had a dream wedding in *The Godfather,* has taken to hooking up with playboy gigolos, and her frivolous marriage to one of them has recently ended in divorce. Now she is prepared to marry yet another one of the same ilk. Connie and Merle hold hands during their audience with Michael in a feeble display of solidarity, but this union is doomed to be short-lived. The wretched marriages of Fredo and of Connie reflect how "the family unity is really starting to break down in this period," concludes Coppola, referring to his pervasive theme about the role of family in modern society.[22]

After the First Communion reception, which is a major sequence in the film, the story shifts in due course to a key flashback in which we learn how the Old World criminal traditions imported to the New World add to the misery of struggling immigrants like Vito Corleone. The secret crime cartel known as the Black Hand, an early version of the Mafia in America, terrorized the Italian immigrants living in ethnic neighborhoods by extorting "protection money" from them. The term *Black Hand* referred to crude drawings of a shadowy hand that accompanied threats from these racketeers.

During the operetta performance Genco points out Fanucci, a Black Hand extortionist, to Vito and warns him that Fanucci extorts protection money from Italian immigrants. Fanucci's florid cape and curled moustache make him look like a villain from a nineteenth-century gaslight melodrama. When Fanucci subsequently attempts to terrorize Vito, his comrades, and their families, Vito finally assassinates him, thereby committing his first murder and, subsequently, committing himself irrevocably to a life of crime.

Throughout the picture Coppola makes it clear that the higher Michael rises in the hierarchy of Mafia chiefs, the lower he sinks into the depths of moral degradation. His wife Kay is appalled by what he has become and finally comes to the bitter conclusion that Michael will never change his ways and phase out his unlawful business interests, as he has promised her so often that he would. Indeed, it is far too late in the day for Michael to become a legitimate businessman, even if he wanted to. "He can never go back to the time before that moment in the restaurant when he shot his father's enemies," Pauline Kael writes. "Michael's act, which preserved his family's power," ruined his own life by setting him on the road to a life of crime.[23]

Michael is subpoenaed to testify before a Senate Committee investigating organized crime. The congressional hearing in the film is modeled on the televised hearings conducted by Senator Kefauver and Senator McClelland in the 1950s and 1960s (see chapter 4). Coppola thought that casting non-actors in bit parts in this scene might make it more real and convincing. He therefore hired real reporters and photojournalists to play the press corps in the sequence. He also cast two of his former mentors as senators: Roger Corman, producer of *Dementia 13,* and Phil Feldman, producer of *You're a Big Boy Now.*

Frankie Pantangeli, who has become completely alienated from the Corleone crime family, is the star witness against Michael. When Frankie takes the stand, he sees that Michael has imported Frankie's revered older brother Vincenzo from Sicily to witness his testimony. Acknowledging this old family tie, Frankie fakes an attack of "amnesia" and withdraws his charges against Michael.

Coppola created an air of authenticity in the scene by filming the testimony of Michael and other witnesses with a somewhat-less-than-polished photography and sound recording than he normally employed in the movie and thereby giving the sequence the genuine look and feel of a newsreel. Such craftsmanship on Coppola's part is all too often overlooked in critical assessments of his work.

Because Kay is now aware that Michael is a hardened criminal, she finally informs him that she is going to leave him and take their little boy and girl with her. At the climax of their dreadful quarrel, Kay reveals that the miscarriage she had told Michael she had suffered earlier was actually an abortion. She killed their unborn son, she explains, because she would not bring another child into the vicious Corleone world. Michael is shocked to learn of the loss of a second son, who would have helped to keep the Corleone name alive, and he angrily slaps his wife across the face. But it is Kay who has delivered the severest blow. Michael orders Kay to get out but to leave their children behind. "That Kay had deliberately aborted the baby was the suggestion of my sister Talia," says Coppola in his commentary. "Kay is appalled that Michael has gone scot-free after the Senate investigation." She tells him what she has done as her way of "resisting the terrible evil which is spreading out from the man she once loved. She had the abortion because she knew Michael would never forgive her, and she wanted out of her Mafia marriage."

The film continues to develop two separate story lines by showing both young Vito and Michael exacting revenge for earlier treachery. We watch Vito return briefly to the Sicily of his boyhood in order to stab to death Don Ciccio, the local Mafia chieftain responsible for the deaths of his parents and his brother decades before. Don Ciccio is an aging, decrepit man at this point, so Vito's gruesome vendetta-killing of the pathetic don, a crime committed with ruthless premeditation, illustrates the savage side of Vito's nature that lurks beneath the charming and civilized facade that he cultivates. In a parallel act of vengeance, Michael arranges for the assassination of rival mobster Hyman Roth, who had plotted to have Michael slain. Michael also has his weak and ineffectual older brother Fredo shot when he learns that Fredo, who all along had been jealous of his kid brother Michael for superseding him as head of the Corleone family, had cooperated with Roth's scheme to kill Michael.

Mario Puzo states in the documentary, "I didn't want Fredo killed, but Francis was adamant. So I said, 'Okay, but don't kill him until after his mother dies.' If Michael murdered his own brother while their mother was still alive, the audience would never forgive him, whereas they might forgive him if he did it afterwards." And so in the film Michael decides to spare Fredo while Mama Corleone is still matriarch of the family. At her mother's wake Connie, who is no longer the brazen hussy she was at the beginning of the movie, entreats Michael to forgive Fredo's treachery (in a scene that helped to win Talia Shire an Oscar nomination). While Michael hugs Fredo in a spurious gesture of fraternal affection, he glares at Al Neri, Michael's enforcer, thereby signaling to him that the time to take vengeance on Fredo is at hand.

The murder occurs when Fredo goes fishing just off the pier from Michael's Tahoe estate. Fredo says a "Hail Mary" to ensure that he will catch a fish. "When I was a boy of eight," Coppola recalls on the DVD, "I adored the Blessed Virgin Mary, who loves children. I believed that, if I said a 'Hail Mary' when we went fishing, I would catch a fish, and I did. So Fredo says a prayer to catch a fish just before Neri, who is in the boat with him, pulls the trigger."

Coppola shot the scene in which Neri liquidates Fredo in long shot in order to depict how it looked from Michael's point of view as he witnessed the killing through the Venetian blinds in his office. When Fredo is murdered, says William McDonald, the stony figure of Michael "stands gazing out of a window in the family compound." His transformation to monster now complete, "he has lost his soul as surely as Fredo's soul has departed."[24] In essence, Michael has lost his moral compass and may never find it again.

Once Michael has become permanently alienated from his wife, he is left a lonely, disconsolate man, living in virtual isolation in his heavily guarded compound at Lake Tahoe. Michael may have built the Corleone family into one of the strongest Mafia clans in America, but he has at the same time lost most of his own immediate family: he murdered his only remaining brother, his first wife was killed by his enemies, and his second wife has been banished.

Michael has always contended that the harsh measures he has taken were motivated by his determination to protect his family, and "the fortified compound" where they live is a grim, physical emblem of that commitment.[25] Yet by film's end the vile family business has invaded his home and all but destroyed it. As Talia Shire puts it, "Francis felt that he had to knock this family off" to show how their criminal activities destroyed the family.[26]

Even though Frankie Pantangeli has recanted his intention to testify against him, Michael is convinced that Frankie should pay for his initial willingness to do so. He sends Tom Hagen to visit Frankie, who is still in the FBI's witness protection program and is living at an army base. How a Mafia consigliere gained access to Frankie while he is sequestered in an army compound is never explained. In any case, Tom has a discussion with Frankie about how traitors were dealt with in the days of the Roman Empire, which is, after all, the structural model for the Mafia. "If they committed suicide, their families were taken care of by the Roman regime."[27] Coppola affirms that "Mario Puzo wrote this scene, based on the old Roman idea that a man's family would be spared if he did the right thing and opened his veins and bled to death in the bathtub." Frankie obliges, and his demise is "a Roman death."

The climactic sequence at the end of *Godfather II* in which Michael's principal enemies die in a series of brief vignettes recalls the similar montage at the conclusion of *The Godfather*. In quick succession Frankie Pantangeli slashes his wrists in the bathtub at the army base, Hyman Roth is assassinated at an airport as he is interviewed by reporters, and Fredo is shot in a rowboat while fishing on the Tahoe estate.

Says Coppola, "There's no doubt that by the end of this picture Michael Corleone, having beaten everyone, is sitting alone, a living corpse." The final image of Michael, sitting in a thronelike chair, brooding over the loss of so many of his family, recalls the shot in the film's first flashback in which the sickly young Vito Corleone sits in an enormous chair in a lonely hospital room at Ellis Island right after his arrival in the New World. The lad, we know, came to America because of a vendetta against his family in his own country, and he will grow up to wreak vengeance on the man who slaughtered his loved ones back home.

Years later his son Michael will in turn take it upon himself to avenge the murderous attack on his father's life. By so doing, he will inevitably become an integral part of the ongoing pattern of vengeance that began with the massacre of his ancestors long before he was ever born. Hence, there is a direct connection between the frail little boy sitting alone in the oversized chair early in the movie and his grown son sitting alone in a majestic chair late in the movie. Coppola articulates that connection in his remarks that in *Godfather II* his purpose was "to show how two men, father and son, were . . . corrupted by this Sicilian waltz of vengeance."[28]

The last major flashback takes place at the outbreak of World War II, December 7, 1941, just after the Japanese attack on Pearl Harbor. The Corleone family, including Michael, Sonny, Fredo, Connie, and Tom are waiting for Don Vito to come home for a surprise birthday party in his honor. Coppola had negotiated with Marlon Brando to make a cameo appearance in this scene as Don Vito, just as James Caan was willing to appear as Sonny. But Brando vacillated right up to the day that the scene was shot: "he was mad at Paramount for gypping him on the payment he received for *Godfather I*," Coppola explains in his DVD commentary. When Brando finally failed to show up to shoot the scene, Coppola improvised a variation on the scene as written—keeping Vito offscreen while everyone waits for him in the dining room.

Michael takes this occasion to announce that he has enlisted in the Marines. The scene as originally written is in the second draft of the script, dated September 24, 1973, which is in the Paramount Script Repository. In it Vito chides his son for risking his life for strangers, adding "I have hopes for you." In the revised version of the scene as it appears in the published version of the screenplay Vito is not present, so the volatile Sonny is given Vito's line about risking his life for strangers, while Tom says, on Vito's behalf, "Your father has plans for you."[29]

In retrospect, Coppola is convinced that the scene plays better without Brando. Vito is "a ghost that haunts the entire picture. It might have thrown the whole thing out of whack, had Brando been in the final flashback. So maybe God took care of me."[30] In any event, the flashback concludes as the family runs out of the room to greet Vito—except for Michael, who is left sitting alone at the dining room table. That he sticks to his decision to join the Marines indicates that he is already a loner, a willful, self-reliant individual who will live his life his own way.

In the movie's last shot of Michael, he is ironically still wearing his wedding ring. It is an empty symbol of his pose as a family man, for he is as pensive and alone at this moment as young Vito was in the quarantine cell on Ellis Island. In contemplating Michael at film's end, one recalls Robert Warshow's remark in "The Gangster as Tragic Hero," his seminal essay on the gangster film: "We are always conscious that the whole meaning of this kind of career is a drive for success; the typical gangster film presents a steady upward progress followed by a very precipitous fall."[31] One might say that the happy ending of a gangster picture is in the middle of the movie, when the racketeer is enjoying the fruits of his nefarious endeavors before his appalling and tragic descent at the end.

In *Godfather II,* Coppola tells me, he wished to show Michael "damning himself" because, at the final fade-out, he is just a lonely man, "sitting with these horrible ghosts inside his head." Elsewhere Coppola has added, "He's prematurely old," like the hero of *The Picture of Dorian Gray.*[32]

As already mentioned, Coppola had to trim the rough cut drastically to bring the final cut of the movie down to two hundred minutes. For my money, the only deleted scene that should have been retained was that in which Michael tracks down Fabrizio, his treacherous bodyguard from *The Godfather* who was responsible for Michael's first wife Appolonia being killed in a car explosion. Michael discovers that Fabrizio is now known as Fred Vincent and runs a pizzeria in Buffalo. One night Fred shuts up shop, gets into his car and it blows up, just as Appolonia's did. Had this brief episode been retained, it would have constituted another link between father and son: Michael's identifying and catching up with his wife's killer after more than a decade recalls his father's unerring ability to track down and murder, after more than fifteen years, Don Ciccio, who slaughtered his immediate family. As Coppola comments on the DVD, "Mario says in the novel that the Corleones believe that revenge is a dish best served cold." The Fred Vincent episode is included in the group of deleted scenes in a special section of the DVD of *Godfather II.*

"When *Godfather II* came out it did not get many good reviews," Coppola recalls in the documentary. "When it won all those Oscars, I was astonished that people liked a picture when I thought they didn't." Some of the early notices were nothing short of devastating, with one reviewer going so far as to say that *Godfather II* was a Frankenstein's monster stitched together from leftover parts of *The Godfather.* Leading the group of critics enthusiastic about the movie was Pauline Kael. "The daring of *Part II* is that it enlarges the scope and deepens the meaning of the first film," she cheers. "[T]he sensibility at work here is that of a major artist. . . . How many screen artists have been able to seize the power to compose a modern American epic?"[33]

As time went on, Coppola was hailed for having the courage to make an expensive mainstream motion picture that did not pursue a simple narrative line but constructed a contrapuntal movement of two generations of the same family—with many of the flashbacks (one-third of the entire picture) having Sicilian dialogue with English subtitles. Furthermore, Coppola was complimented for making a movie that, overall, was vigorously acted and sharply edited. *Godfather II* was a box-office hit, grossing $46 million domestically, but it was far behind the box-office bonanza that was *The Godfather,* one of the biggest moneymakers of all time.

On Oscar night Coppola became one of the few filmmakers in cinema history to win the triple crown: he received Academy Awards for directing *Godfather II,* for coauthoring the screenplay, and for producing the best picture of the year. Coppola also became the only filmmaker to be nominated for two best picture and two best screenplay Oscars in the same year, for he received nominations in both categories for *The Conversation* as well as *Godfather II.* He therefore was competing with himself, and he won both awards for *Godfather II.* Moreover, *Godfather II* is the first sequel ever to win best picture.

Robert De Niro won an Academy Award for his supporting role—in which he delivered nearly all of his lines in Sicilian, a language he did not understand. In addition, Nino Rota and Carmine Coppola won Oscars for the musical score. When his father's name was announced at the Oscar ceremonies, Coppola whistled excitedly through his fingers, and when he accepted the Academy Award for best picture, he added, "thanks for giving my dad an Oscar." Later he explained that he was gratified that he had finally provided his father with the big break he had always wanted as a composer. Ironically, Pacino did not win an Oscar, although he was nominated. Yet Michael Corleone is still considered Pacino's greatest role, "because Michael is one of the few movie characters to achieve an authentically tragic dimension."[34]

In mid-November 1977, NBC-TV broadcast, on four successive nights, "The Godfather Saga," a mini-series that was a seven-hour compilation of *The Godfather* and *Godfather II.* Coppola asked Barry Malkin to reassemble the footage of the two movies into chronological order. The mini-series, says Malkin, began with the "early 1900s scenes from *Godfather-II* and continued with *Godfather-I* in the middle, ending with the more contemporary stuff from *Godfather-II.*"[35] Coppola points out in his DVD commentary on *Godfather II* that when the film was edited for TV in straight chronology, according to his specific instructions, the story of young Vito and the story of Michael were not as compelling alone as when they were intercut in the original movie. This is because, as previously described, there are significant parallels between the father's life and the son's life, and these parallels are lost when the story is presented in chronological order.

For example, in the course of *Godfather II* Coppola switches between a family scene in Vito's young manhood to a family scene in Michael's time to illustrate how the warmth and radiance of young Vito's family is no longer discernible in Michael's chilly, bleak family setting. Vito sits on the front stoop, saying to his baby son, "Michael, your father loves you very much." This scene from the past gives way to the adult Michael returning to a frigid home, his son's toy car abandoned in the snowy yard, while inside his mother sits isolated and forlorn by the fire, a relic of the older generation of the Corleone family. It is the juxtaposition of scenes like these that caused Coppola to decide to "keep the parallel structure in *Godfather II* ever since, even now when the three films make one saga."

With the critical and popular success of the first two *Godfather* films—which won Coppola a total of five Oscars—he was riding high. He was regarded, because of his phenomenal success while still a director in his thirties, as a beacon to the younger generation of filmmakers.

It would be sixteen years before Coppola made the third and final installment of the *Godfather* trilogy. In the intervening years, while he busied himself with other projects, he steadfastly resisted all efforts on the part of successive regimes at Paramount to cajole him into making another sequel. "I couldn't see doing a third *Godfather* film," Coppola explains in his DVD commentary on *Godfather Part III*, "because Michael has damned himself in the second movie. He has lost his family and everything that he values. When I finished that film, with Michael in the hell he had created for himself, I thought I was done with *The Godfather*. There seemed to be nothing further to be said." Over the years Paramount sent him a variety of scenarios for a third film, churned out by different scriptwriters. None of these scripts focused on Michael, Coppola states in the documentary. "I thought it was crazy to make a third film without him being at the center of it." The scripts in question invariably wandered too far from the original plot line and went off on tangents involving Latin American drug cartels, South American dictators, and even the assassination of President Kennedy.

By 1989 the first two *Godfather* films had grossed over $800 million. At that point, Frank Mancuso, Paramount's chief executive, came to Coppola and said with some desperation, "Francis, we offer you *Godfather-III*; do it any way you want." Total creative control over the picture was "the magic word," Coppola concludes. "I felt that, if they gave me *carte blanche* to do *Godfather-III*, I might have an opportunity to do something artistic."[36] Indeed, Coppola wanted to link the final act of Michael's story to the tragic grandeur of Shakespearean tragedy. He refers to Michael's affinity with King Lear—the tormented, aging man whose empire is slipping from his grasp—as a source of inspiration for the film.

"The studio's blandishments became more honeyed": in addition to artistic control of the movie, Paramount offered Coppola $4 million to direct and coauthor the screenplay for the film.[37] In short, they "made him an offer he couldn't refuse," to cite a line from *The Godfather* that has become part of our language. Finally, Coppola took on the project, committing himself to making a third film that was worthy to stand beside the first two *Godfather* movies.[38]

The Godfather Part III (1990)

Coppola would again be collaborating with Mario Puzo on the screenplay of *Godfather III*. As in the case of *Godfather II,* Puzo had already worked on a preliminary draft of the script before Coppola came on board. Mancuso had enlisted Talia Shire to present Puzo's screenplay to her brother early on. At the time, Coppola took one look at it and tossed it into the fireplace. He was favorably impressed by one element in the discarded script, however: Puzo had introduced Sonny Corleone's illegitimate son Vincent, who, in *The Godfather,* had been conceived at Connie's wedding reception during Sonny's sexual encounter with bridesmaid Lucy Mancini. Since Michael was now in his middle sixties—the same age as Don Vito in *The Godfather*—Vincent would replace Michael as the young male lead in the picture, the role that Michael himself had filled in the previous two *Godfather* films. Nevertheless, Michael would continue to be a pivotal character in the present film, for in Coppola's mind Michael is the tragic figure of the drama.

While casting about for story ideas, Coppola began to read press accounts of the Vatican Bank scandal, in which the Mafia figured, and he thought he could work that into the story line somehow. "I felt I had a fertile story context," says Coppola, "one that wasn't just going to be about Venezuelan drug lords and machine guns."[39] He created the character of Archbishop Gliday—based on Bishop Marcinkus, an American bishop stationed in Rome who was implicated in some questionable Vatican financial transactions. (The real bishop happened to hail from Cicero, Illinois, Al Capone's old stamping grounds.) Archbishop Gliday is a highly fictionalized version of Bishop Marcinkus—for example, in the film Gliday is assassinated, while his real-life counterpart was relegated to forced retirement in Arizona by the Vatican after the Vatican Bank scandal broke. He was never officially charged with any financial improprieties.

"On *Godfather-III*, I worked more closely with Francis than on the other two scripts," Puzo remarks in the documentary. They checked into the Peppermill Hotel Casino in Reno, where they batted out a preliminary outline of the scenario. Then they moved on to New York where they continued their collaboration. Like the two previous *Godfather* films, this one was slated to be a Christmas release. That meant that they had to produce the first draft of the script in a brisk six weeks so that shooting could begin in late 1989, with the premiere in December 1990.

Coppola enjoyed devising the screenplay without studio interference. "It's a lot easier to write a script of this sort when you have freedom from the studio, rather than having to write a custom job," he explains. He and Puzo found themselves "involved in some extremely rich research into contemporary history," e.g., the Vatican Bank scandal. Then they placed their existing characters into a fictionalized version of these events.[40] They followed their customary procedure of writing separately and then revising each other's work. Coppola composed the first half, Puzo the second half, and then they "nailed them together." The script went through twelve revisions between April and November of 1989. Later, when the press reported that Coppola engaged in "endless rewrites" during production, he replied that, given the short time he and Puzo had to write the original draft of the script, it was inevitable that he had to revise the screenplay further, even during shooting.

The final shooting script of the third film is set twenty years after the end of the second film, when Michael is at long last endeavoring to make all of the Corleone family's investments legitimate—something he promised Kay when he married her.

In order to ensure continuity between the third film of the trilogy and its predecessors, Coppola reassembled most of the members of his production crew. This team of regulars included cinematographer Gordon Willis, production designer Dean Tavoularis, composer Carmine Coppola, and film editor Walter Murch, who had previously been sound engineer for Coppola. Furthermore, some of the key actors were once more on deck, including Al Pacino, Diane Keaton, and Talia Shire. Working closely with each of his creative collaborators unquestionably enabled Coppola to place on all three films, not the stamp of the studio, but the unmistakable stamp of his own directorial style—which is one of the hallmarks of an auteur.

The one major cast member from the first two films who did not return this time around was Robert Duvall. He found the salary he was offered to be unacceptable and was likewise dissatisfied with the size of his part. The actor felt that Tom Hagen simply did not play the vital role in

Godfather III that he did in the previous two films. "Not having Duvall in *Godfather III*," Coppola notes in his DVD commentary, "was a profound loss to me and to this movie."

Duvall was replaced by George Hamilton, in the role of B. J. Harrison, an unctuous corporate attorney. But Harrison, Michael's slick WASP lawyer, is not a member of the family, as was Tom, Don Vito's adopted son. So Harrison would not be Michael's confidante and ally in the manner that Tom had been. Coppola passed that function on to Connie, making her the first female member of the Corleone clan to have a say in family decisions.

Another new member of the cast besides Hamilton was Andy Garcia as Vincent Mancini, Sonny's bastard son. Garcia says that Coppola gave him valuable advice on how to play the part. "He said that Vinnie had the temper of Sonny, the smarts and ruthlessness of young Vito, the kind of calculation and coolness of Michael, and the warmth of Fredo." During filming he and Coppola adopted a sort of shorthand. Coppola would say, "This is a Sonny scene; this is a young-Vito scene; this one is a Michael scene; this one is a Fredo scene."[41] In short, Garcia became a repository for different aspects of the Italian family's complete male personas. "Vinnie is an outsider," says Garcia, and Michael Corleone takes him in. "The closer he comes to Michael, the more Vinnie becomes like him." Indeed, Garcia comes across in the movie like the young Al Pacino of *The Godfather*—very intense, very serious, and somewhat dangerous.

"The thing that is different about *Godfather III*," Coppola recalls in the documentary, "is that Michael is different." The third film begins twenty years after the close of the second film. Michael is getting ready for death, and he wants to rehabilitate himself. "So I wanted him to be a man who was older and concerned with redemption," Coppola continued. "Michael Corleone realized that he had paid very dearly for being a cold-blooded murderer, and was a man now who wanted to make peace with God." In brief, Michael is aware that his final reckoning is drawing near.

Coppola saw *Godfather III* as the epilogue of the story because Michael is asking, "what have I done with my life, what have I done with my family?"[42] "The screenplay deals with the themes of redemption and reconciliation close to Coppola's heart."[43] *Godfather III* depicts Michael as "a Mafia boss yearning to achieve respectability and craving forgiveness from the Church for his manifold sins." To the dismay of other Mafiosi, Michael is determined to sell off his casinos and other Mafia-related enterprises and to assume the role of a respectable international financier.

The movie's opening sequence accordingly depicts Michael, dressed in a medieval cape, receiving a papal honor: he is named a Knight of the

Order of St. Sebastian, in return for a handsome donation from the "Vito Corleone Foundation." The solemnity of the elaborate ritual is effectively undercut by the cynical implication that a gangster like Michael Corleone can buy himself "such a majestic honor."[44] What's more, Michael's apparent generosity to the church is not as altruistic as it might at first appear: "Michael intends, not so much to relinquish his ill-gotten gains, but rather to launder them."[45] Michael therefore becomes implicated in a crafty scheme to launder the Corleone funds by filtering large sums of cash through the Vatican Bank in exchange for saving the Vatican Bank from bankruptcy.

Furthermore, Michael's partnership with the Vatican enables him to purchase a controlling interest in Immobilare, a shadowy European conglomerate that is a real estate–holding corporation of the Vatican. Actually, Immobilare is a consortium of investors and politicians who are as corrupt as any of the lower-class Mafiosi whom Michael consorted with in New York City or Las Vegas. By getting the Corleone family entangled with these upper-class European crooks, Michael remarks wryly, "We're back with the Borgias!" He realizes that he has once more been drawn into conniving with unsavory characters in some dirty business deals, just when he had hopes of going completely legitimate. He moans, "Just when I thought I was out, they pull me back in!" The hypocrisy of this group of financial conspirators is underscored by the fact that they regularly begin their deliberations with a prayer.

"Originally we were going to begin the film with the sly Archbishop Gliday (Donnal Donnelly) coming to Michael, pleading that he bail the Vatican Bank out of its financial difficulties," Coppola states in his commentary. But Walter Murch, who had moved from sound specialist on *The Godfather* and *Godfather II* to one of the principal film editors on this film, "thought it better to stress the family side of the picture before we got into the business side of the movie. So we decided to begin with the ceremony in which Michael is honored by the Vatican for his charitable gifts to the Church." Therefore, the third film opens with an elaborate family celebration that recalls the wedding at the beginning of *The Godfather* and the First Communion at the beginning of *Godfather II*.

The reception for Michael serves as a family reunion, once more introducing Kay, who has married a second time; Connie, who is divorced again; and Michael's grown children Anthony (Franc D'Ambrosio) and Mary (Sofia Coppola, the director's daughter). Michael wants to revive his ties with his ex-wife and children in order to win back their trust. So it is obvious that family values continue to influence Michael's behavior in the last years of his life. Even in a world ruled by the Mafia's deadly code, family ties are still respected. Given the recurring emphasis on family in the trilogy, it is pellucidly clear that the concept of family is an important influence on the cinema of Francis Coppola.

Commenting on the DVD about the Vatican's willingness to make an unholy alliance with a Mafia chieftain like Michael Corleone, Coppola points out that history has shown the Vatican to be not only a spiritual community of the faithful but also a secular institution. "I respectfully submit that everything I put into the movie about the Vatican as a business organization being venal and mercenary because of its involvement in financial improprieties is true."

"At one point," he goes on, Immobilare, a Vatican-held company, "owned a controlling interest in Paramount Pictures. While I was making *Godfather I*, I sometimes went up in the elevator to visit Charlie Bludhorn in the Gulf and Western building in New York with some mysterious men who played a role in the enormous Vatican Bank scandal later on." One of the shady individuals whom Coppola refers to is very likely Michele Sindona, a notorious Sicilian financier with Mafia ties, who was associated with both the Vatican Bank and Immobilare. In 1972, through Sindona's machinations, Immobilare purchased a substantial interest in Paramount Pictures, thereby providing the studio with much-needed capital.

Suffice it to say that there is no little irony in the fact that *The Godfather* was financed by Paramount Pictures with at least some funds made available through the auspices of the infamous Mafia-connected financier Michele Sindona. As a matter of fact, Sindona had "deplored Paramount's decision to make *The Godfather*, which he felt betrayed the inner workings of the Mafia," according to Bernard Dick, who has provided the best account in English of Sindona's involvement with Paramount, Immobilare, and the Vatican Bank.[46]

As the 1970s wore on, however, Sindona's financial empire, erected on financial irregularities and fraud, began to crumble, precipitating the Vatican Bank scandal. Since Sindona was involved with both Immobilare and the Vatican Bank, Immobilare stocks plummeted and the Vatican Bank lost about $30 million. In 1986, when Sindona's links to the Mafia surfaced, he was extradited to Italy, where he was convicted of fraud and other crimes and sentenced to life imprisonment. Two days after the verdict, he unwittingly drank coffee laced with cyanide in his jail cell. He was apparently poisoned by the Sicilian Mafia to prevent him from divulging any information about their underworld activities. Cyanide poisoning is a common method employed by the Mafia to silence convicts who know too much.

Bludhorn told Coppola about the Vatican Bank's covert negotiations with Immobilare, which he had learned about through his dealings with Sindona in the early 1970s. Coppola accordingly incorporated this material in a fictionalized form into *Godfather III*. In sum, the package deals negotiated with the Vatican in the movie recall the Sindona affair. In the closing credits, Coppola dedicated *Godfather III* to Bludhorn because he "inspired" the film.

In the scene that portrays the high-level meeting in which Michael engineers his takeover of Immobilare, Coppola points out that "there is a sinister gentleman present who is based on another one of the mysterious men I saw in the elevator in the Gulf and Western building." In the scene in question Helmut Berger plays Frederick Keinszik, a financier with a shady reputation whom Coppola modeled on Roberto Calvi, who was ironically known as "God's banker" because of his involvement with the Vatican Bank. Coppola makes the Calvi character Swiss instead of Italian, in order not to identify him too closely with his real-life counterpart. In the film Keinszik, whom Vinnie refers to contemptuously as "the Swiss banker fuck," instigates an elaborate swindle to bilk Michael out of a substantial amount of the profits from his dealings with Immobilare.

Coppola balances the portrayal of the sly, oily Archbishop Gliday, who represents the Roman Catholic Church as secular institution, with the depiction of the pious, sincere Cardinal Lamberto (Raf Valone), who represents the Church as spiritual community. Lamberto is patently more interested in the state of Michael's soul than in the business proposition Michael brings to him. In fact, Michael achieves some solace from making a sacramental Confession to the cardinal, admitting the heinous sin of fratricide he committed when he had Fredo killed. When Lamberto soon after becomes Pope John Paul I, he vows to do some moral housecleaning in the Vatican Bank, but his untimely death prevents him from carrying out his reforms.

Principal photography commenced on November 27, 1989, at Cinecittà Studios in Rome where there would also be extensive location work around the city. The Sicilian village of Taormina, which served for the village of Corleone in the first two films, appears again in *Godfather III*. The Teatro Massimo in Palermo, Sicily, was selected for the opera house where Michael's son Anthony makes his opera debut in *Cavalleria Rusticana* at the climax of the movie.

When shooting in Europe was completed, the production moved to New York for more location work. Michael's receiving of the Order of St. Sebastian was filmed in the old St. Patrick's Cathedral, a neo-Gothic Church on Mott Street in Little Italy—the same church where the baptism of

Connie's son was filmed for *The Godfather*. Racketeer Joey Zasa (Joe Mantegna), one of Michael's most ambitious and dangerous adversaries, is in attendance. Joey Zasa, whose character was derived from Mafia hood Joey Gallo, is impeccably dressed for the occasion. He marches down the aisle and cavalierly hands his hat to his bodyguard before genuflecting to the altar. "Even before God, the Mafia preserves distinctions of rank," writes Barbara Harrison. "[I]t is the kind of detail only a director of Coppola's background and acuity would know to include."[47]

Before shooting began, Coppola had an artist make storyboards for all of the scenes. He then recorded them on videotape, with extras reading the dialogue for each scene. "If I got bored looking at the storyboards" for a particular scene, he notes, "I knew I should work on that part."[48] He used his customary method of encouraging the cast to improvise during rehearsals in order to improve a scene that was not working well. Andy Garcia testifies that he for one flourished in the spontaneous working atmosphere Coppola fostered on the set. "A good director like Francis will do takes where he is very specific," Garcia explains, and then he will say, "Okay, this is a free one; say whatever you want. I don't have to use it, but then again you might say one line that I can use."[49]

Coppola would sometimes experience periods of discouragement in the stressful atmosphere of shooting a major commercial picture on a tight schedule. Eleanor Coppola records in her notes on the making of the film that on March 6, 1990, while Coppola was still filming at Cinecittà, she discovered her husband "sitting on a sofa in Michael Corleone's living room, very depressed." He spoke of "how he hated that he was doing the same material he had done nearly twenty years ago" and how he hated the great amount of time it took to make a movie.[50] Shooting wore on until May 25. Eleanor Coppola records that the wrap party was rather subdued: the cast and crew that had been together for 125 shooting days were sorry to see it all end, even if Coppola was not.

The director then had to supervise the ending of the film for its premiere on December 20. He had only six months to whittle a mountain of footage down to a final cut of just under three hours running time. The pressure on Coppola increased as he worked around the clock to meet Paramount's deadline. He collaborated with principal editors Walter Murch, Barry Malkin, and Lisa Fruchtman and also supervised a battery of assistant editors who were brought in to expedite the finishing of the final edit on schedule. For the record, Coppola met the studio-imposed deadline, and the film opened on Christmas Day, 1990.

Press reports circulated that the production had gone out of control and had been plagued by "spiraling budgets." He responded that, admittedly, the original budget, $44 million, had finally swelled to $55 million, but a substantial part of the overage was due to finishing the film for the Christmas opening, which involved hiring additional editors. "Working with an army of editors," he said, meant that "we're paying maybe fifty times what it would cost if we could just mix with one editor." As usual, he concluded, certain journalists were determined to make him look like a crackpot and "inflate his troubles for a good story."[51]

The movie begins with the celebration of Michael's papal knighthood, which is Michael's bid for respectability. During the course of the reception Connie is at pains to pay lip service to the traditional ethnic customs of the Corleone clan. She sings with the band an Italian folk song, the same Tarantella that was played at her own wedding in *The Godfather,* and which Frankie Pentangeli had failed to get the orchestra to play at the First Communion party in *Godfather II.*

During the reception it seems likely that Vinnie will be Michael's heir apparent as head of the Corleone crime family. (Peter Cowie mistakenly refers to Vinnie in his Coppola book as the illegitimate son of Michael, rather than of his brother Sonny.) As the film unreels it becomes increasingly clear that Vinnie is the black sheep of the Corleone clan. He cleverly insinuates himself into the family business by systematically eliminating members of rival Mafia clans who are plotting against Michael and by seducing Michael's daughter Mary.

One of the Mafiosi that Vinnie liquidates is the truculent Joey Zasa, who envies the Corleones' wealth and power. Connie endorses Vinnie's assassination of Zasa because he is a threat to the family. "Connie emerges as a strong figure in this film," Coppola says in his DVD commentary. Now far removed from the victimized wife she was in *The Godfather,* she has evolved into "a combination of Lady Macbeth and Lucrezia Borgia."

Connie, a malevolent figure wrapped in a black shawl, is out for blood. She schemes to control and murder the Corleones' enemies with the pitiless efficiency once displayed by her brother Michael and by her father Vito. She sees Vinnie as her ally. The hotheaded Vinnie is like a young colt, and she views him as the only one of Michael's henchmen who possesses the muscle and drive to protect the family from rival gangs. With Connie as Vinnie's sponsor, it is not surprising that Michael eventually recognizes him as a surrogate son, made clear when Michael officially changes Vinnie's surname from Mancini to Corleone.

Some of Michael's underworld enemies conspire to thwart his negotiations with Immobilare and the Vatican Bank. There is, for example, the elderly Don Altobello (Eli Wallach), who, like the aging Hyman Roth in *Godfather II*, pretends to be Michael's friend but is really his arch enemy. His partner in crime is a cut-throat Italian politician named Lucchesi, whom Coppola based on a powerful Italian political figure. In addition, Archbishop Gliday has sold Michael out to his opponents. The unscrupulous Don Altobello, however, is the most evil and dangerous of Michael's enemies. He wants Michael dead and hires an assassin to gun Michael down while he is attending his son's debut in *Cavalleria Rusticana*.

For his part, Vinnie arranges to have his minions slaughter the Corleone's enemies while the family attends the opera performance. The film's finale, then, takes place during a majestic performance in Palermo of Mascagni's opera, which, appropriately enough, is about a vendetta in a Sicilian village. The melodramatic events onstage parallel the violent events offstage.

Connie takes it upon herself to personally exterminate Don Altobello. "Connie is almost satanic in this film," Coppola observes, "so ruthless has she become." She gives Altobello a box of poisoned cannoli to eat during the opera. Cannoli, Coppola reminds us, "was associated with murder in *Godfather I*." ("Leave the gun. Take the cannoli," Clemenza said to the hit man who murdered Paulie.) Moreover, Connie's poisoning Altobello was suggested to Coppola by the poisoning of Sindona in the wake of the original Vatican-Immobilare scandal.

The intercutting of the opera performance with the baroque orgy of murder Vinnie has orchestrated recalls the montage of violence and death that climaxes *The Godfather* and *Godfather II*. In quick succession we once again see a series of murders.

Keinszik, the Swiss embezzler, is smothered with a pillow by Vinnie's hoodlums, and his corpse is discovered hanging from a bridge in Rome (though his real-life counterpart, Roberto Calvi, was actually found suspended from Blackfrier's Bridge in London). Lucchesi is killed by Carlo, who was Michael's bodyguard during his sojourn in Sicily in *The Godfather* (again played by Franco Citti). Carlo smashes Lucchesi's thick glasses and rips open his aorta with a jagged piece of glass, as the blood gushes out. "This is a classic bit of carnage, served with gore sauce."[52] Archbishop Gliday is shot on the grand staircase of his episcopal mansion by Al Neri. He falls toward the camera and lands on the floor far below.

As the opera continues, Connie watches through her opera glasses as Altobello slumps over dead in his private box. Viewing the murder from a distance allows her to distance herself from her crime. Meanwhile, Altobello's hired gun attempts unsuccessfully to murder Michael in the course of the performance. That the murderer is disguised as a priest implicitly gives a diabolical cast to his character.

The febrile and ferocious assassin makes his second desperate effort to kill Michael outside the opera house after the performance. Tragically, Mary stops the bullet aimed at Michael and dies in the arms of her anguished father. With dreadful irony Michael unwittingly brings about "the last act of this tragedy of family power and ruin": the death of Michael's daughter on the steps of an opera house—cut down by the bullet that was meant for him.[53] The scene brings to mind Michael's observation, made earlier in the film, that "the only wealth in this world is children, more than all of the money and power on earth." As Michael crumples on the steps of the opera house, his mouth gapes open in a silent scream of agony and despair. "Walter Murch removed Michael's scream from the sound track, making it seem so much more agonizing," says Coppola. The movie's vigorous final thirty minutes is inspired moviemaking as a panoply of deaths both inside and outside the opera house coincides with Mascagni's brutal revenge drama.

In the original script Michael, and not Mary, was supposed to be struck down by the assassin's bullet, Coppola confides on the DVD. He was able to be ambushed by a gunman while leaving church on Easter Sunday. "But I decided that just to kill him at the end wasn't enough," given his record of bloodshed. "I finally came up with an ending which was worse for Michael than just dying"—he is left to live with the horrors of his life. In the ruined face of Michael Corleone, *Godfather III* locates an emotional gravity that is rare in American film. The movie is a slow fuse with a big bang— it ends with the tragedy of a man "aching for things past and loved ones lost."[54]

Godfather III premiered with a strong box office, despite mixed reviews. Surprisingly, the film earned $67 million in domestic rentals, $20 million more than *Godfather II*. One recurring source of criticism for the film was the casting of Coppola's daughter Sofia as Mary, Michael's daughter. Coppola chose her while she was visiting the set in Rome during the Christmas holidays. "I only put her in the role because the day before we were to shoot a scene with Winona Ryder as Mary, Winona dropped out," Coppola explains on the DVD. Ryder was diagnosed as suffering from exhaustion, the result of making two movies back-to-back without a break and then going on to *Godfather III*.

"The studio sent me a list of possible replacements," including Madonna and Julia Roberts, but they were all too old for the role. "I wanted an eighteen-year-old girl for the part. Granted Sofia was not an experienced actress, but it was Sofia that I had in mind when I created the character of Mary, the apple of her father's eye," a girl who is "sweet and kind."

Admittedly, Sofia Coppola was a movie actress who lacked the credentials for such a key role in an important picture. Still Coppola did not want to endure the costly delay involved in waiting for the studio to send over a replacement for Winona Ryder from Hollywood. He had been promised autonomy over the production, including casting, "so I exercised my rights and decided on Sofia. My decision was vilified by some critics, but I never regretted it. I was thrilled to have her play the part . . . because I saw her as just like the vulnerable kid Mary was supposed to be." Eleanor Coppola adds that her husband believed that the criticism leveled at Sofia "was meant for him, and that Sofia received the criticism the way Mary Corleone got the bullet intended for Michael."[55]

Talia Shire defended her brother's decision to cast her niece as Mary. "Had Sofia not jumped in, the picture would have been closed down," at least for a couple of weeks, which would have hurt the budget and the schedule. "I was concerned because I didn't want to see her get trashed by the critics, which is what happened. . . . Sofia was kind of heroic."[56]

My own judgment is that Sofia Coppola is certainly adequate as the young, awkward daughter of a powerful man. At times she is touching, as in her love scenes with Andy Garcia, who is quite tender with her. The release prints of the film run 161 minutes, while the version available on videocassette and DVD is 170 minutes. The additional nine minutes are accounted for by scenes that mostly feature Sofia Coppola. Apparently Francis Coppola wanted to restore scenes with Sofia that he had been prevailed upon to delete from the original version. For example, there is a scene reinstated on cassette and DVD in which Mary asks her father to reassure her that the Vito Corleone Foundation is genuinely legitimate. Michael assures her that it is not the money-laundering operation it is rumored to be, while he comforts her with the patronizing affection one would give a small child. While not a crucial addition to the picture, this scene does demonstrate that Michael is as adept at manipulating others, even those closest to him, as he always was.

Harlan Lebo quotes Michael Wilmington's balanced assessment of *Godfather III*. Wilmington grants that the movie has "grand moments to match either of its predecessors," but adds, "the complex financial conspiracy that underlies the story never becomes clear. . . . And yet, it is a wonderful movie."[57] To say that *Godfather III* is not in a class with masterpieces like its two predecessors is merely to recognize that it suffers only by comparison with the standard Coppola had set for himself by his previous achievements.

It is indeed a richly textured movie that proved to be the solid follow-up to its predecessors that Coppola hoped it would be. Despite the brittle elegance of the settings and the formality of some of the language, *Godfather III* is a film of deep feeling. The action sequences are directed in an appropriately hard-hitting style. Furthermore, Andy Garcia brings an angry intensity to his part as the implacable and indestructible Vinnie, who wreaks vengeance on the Corleones' enemies at film's end. As a matter of fact, the movie seems, in its detached way, to be trying to get at the quintessence of revenge films.

Moreover, the three *Godfather* films, taken together, qualify as one of the truly great epic sagas in all cinema and have earned $1 billion worldwide and still counting. Yet Coppola seems unimpressed by his achievement. He concedes that he enjoyed portraying his Italian heritage on screen, "but I always sort of resented that the trilogy took up so much of my life, and that it's about shooting people."[58]

On the contrary, the trilogy covers a span of some seventy years, from the childhood of Vito Corleone to the adult life of his son Michael, and explores large American themes—family, personal achievement, immigration. In sum, the *Godfather* trilogy, in its scope and majesty, stands as an enduring colossus of American cinema. Indeed, *Sight and Sound*'s international poll of film directors and film critics in 2002 rated *The Godfather* and *The Godfather Part II* among the ten greatest films of all time.

Although the *Godfather* films were productions originated by Paramount Pictures, Coppola continued to maintain his own independent production company, American Zoetrope, through which he initiated projects that he arranged to finance, shoot, and release in cooperation with various major studios. After finishing the first two *Godfather* films, he decided to turn to a project that had been on the back burner at Zoetrope since the late 1960s, a film about the Vietnam War entitled *Apocalypse Now*. If Coppola had reinvented the genre of the gangster film with *The Godfather* and *Godfather II*, he was now about to reinvent the genre of the war movie with *Apocalypse Now*.

6

The Unknown Soldiers

Apocalypse Now, Apocalypse Now Redux, and Gardens of Stone

Nothing comes free. One way or another, you pay for what you are.

—John Garfield as Paul Boray
in the film *Humoresque*

Life is a trail you follow in an unknown jungle. There is always uncharted territory ahead.

—Francis Ford Coppola

Apocalypse Now was originally conceived by George Lucas and John Milius as a film about the Vietnam War when Francis Coppola was just starting American Zoetrope. In early 1970 Coppola presented to Warner Brothers a package of seven projects that Zoetrope had in the works, among them a proposal for *Apocalypse Now*. Several months later, in November 1970, Warners summarily rejected six of the seven projects—Lucas's *THX 1138* was the only one that Warners produced—and the rest were shelved (see chapter 3).

After Coppola repaid Warners for the development money the studio had spent on the other six proposals, he owned the rights to all of these Zoetrope projects. *The Conversation,* one of the projects, was, as we know, directed by Coppola as a Paramount release. It was not until Coppola finished making *Godfather II,* however, that he decided to revive *Apocalypse Now.*

Lucas and Milius had begun discussing the possibility of a Vietnam War movie in 1968, while they were still film students at USC. Milius had heard numerous harrowing stories from friends who had been in Vietnam, which he planned to string together in the scenario. He wanted to call the movie *Apocalypse Now* "because of all those hippies at the time who had these buttons that said, 'Nirvana Now,'" which was a drug-related slogan of the hippy peace movement. "I loved the idea of a guy having a button with a mushroom cloud on it that said, 'Apocalypse Now,'" suggesting the idea of dropping the bomb and ending the war.[1]

Lucas and Milius collaborated on a preliminary treatment about Captain Willard, an American CIA intelligence officer, who must track down Colonel Kurtz, a rogue Green Beret Special Services commander operating along the Cambodian border who has "gone native," and liquidate him. Lucas suggested that they frame the story as a boat ride upriver, as the intelligence officer seeks out the Green Beret commander.

After they completed the prose treatment, Milius was to turn it into a screenplay. In discussing the script with Milius, Coppola recalled Joseph Conrad's 1899 novella, "Heart of Darkness," about a European ivory trader who disappears into the Congo jungle. He suggested that Milius use the search for a mysterious ivory trader named Kurtz, which provides the fundamental structure of "Heart of Darkness," as the basis of the screenplay. Milius agreed that "it would be interesting to transplant Conrad's 'Heart of Darkness' to Vietnam," and he proceeded to write a screenplay loosely based on Conrad's novella. While Milius was working on the script, news reports began to circulate about the case of Col. Robert Rheault, commanding officer of the U.S. Army Special Forces in Vietnam. Rheault was courtmartialed in 1969 for the murder of a Vietnamese guide he suspected of being a double agent. The international press called the investigation "the Green Beret murder case." The news coverage pointed out that the Green Berets were involved in guerrilla warfare and espionage activities involving links to the CIA—facts that were not previously known by the general public. Rheault's lawyer contended that liquidating enemy agents was standard procedure in wartime and that Rheault's suspicions were well-founded. The charges against Rheault were finally dropped, but his career was in ruins. Unquestionably, Rheault was the inspiration for Colonel Kurtz in Milius's scenario, for Kurtz is accused of executing no less than four alleged enemy agents in *Apocalypse Now.*

Milius transcribed material about the Rheault case into his screenplay directly from the newspaper headlines of the day. "I remember in 1969 when the story came out about Rheault," he says. "[T]he idea was that the U.S. troops were out there committing their own foreign policy." Indeed, Kurtz is described by an officer as operating well beyond official military policy for the conduct of the war. Moreover, Rheault's killing of the suspected Vietcong agent was described in official documents as "termination with extreme prejudice"—a phrase that would find its way into Milius's script and into the finished film.[2] Milius's script went through six drafts, with the final one dated December 5, 1969.

After finishing *American Graffiti* in 1973, Lucas proceeded with *Apocalypse Now* as his next film. He was convinced that it could be made cheaply by filming it in black and white in the style of a documentary (with 16 mm cameras) in the Philippines, employing a cast of unknowns and integrating newsreel footage with the fictional material. The original plan was that Lucas would direct and Coppola would produce.

In the summer of 1974 Lucas went to Coppola, who owned the rights to Milius's script, which had been rejected by Warners in 1970. Coppola proposed to produce the film for a greater share of the profits than Lucas would receive for directing it. Lucas turned Coppola down and turned his attention to making *Star Wars.* With that, Lucas ended his five-year partnership with Coppola in American Zoetrope. He says that "it was as if we were married and we got divorced. It's as close a relationship as I've had with anybody."[3] Coppola offered Milius the same financial arrangement to direct the movie, and Milius likewise rejected it. Moreover, Milius was incensed when he learned that Coppola planned to rewrite his screenplay and then direct it himself. He later referred to Coppola as "the Bay Area Mussolini."[4]

The press made much of Coppola's falling out with his "protégé" George Lucas over *Apocalypse Now,* but Coppola insists that they parted amicably. "There was no falling out between George Lucas and myself over *Apocalypse Now,*" he says. "I had financed it and owned the script, but George was busy with *Star Wars,* and John Milius was also busy; and so it fell to me to direct the project."[5] Coppola managed to slip a reference to Lucas into the film as a private joke: Harrison Ford has a cameo in the movie as Colonel G. Lucas.

As for Milius, he later conceded that, in retrospect, he appreciated how Coppola had subsidized him while he wrote the original draft of the script and recalled that Coppola's Zoetrope had given a boost to many budding filmmakers (see chapter 3). Furthermore, Milius said that he admired Coppola as a director, concluding, "There was no doubt, from the moment he stepped in to direct it, that he would make a much better picture than either George or I would have."[6]

Apocalypse Now (1979)

In the fall of 1975, when Coppola undertook to make the film, he substantially reshaped Milius's screenplay according to his own conception of the story. After examining Milius's first-draft script for *Apocalypse Now*, film scholar Brooks Riley points out that Coppola stuck very close to Milius's original scenario when he revised it for production six years later. If the revised script "strayed from the first draft," she writes, it was not so much away from Milius's conception of the plot "as toward Milius's source, the Conrad novella."[7] At one point Coppola had seriously considered changing the film's title to that of the novella, so "Heart of Darkness" is the spine of *Apocalypse Now*.

In the novella Charles Marlow, the narrator, is charged with the task of tracking down Kurtz, an ivory trader who has disappeared into the interior of the African jungle. Marlow in due course discovers that when Kurtz first went to the Congo he saw himself as a kind of missionary who wanted to civilize the natives he dealt with at his trading post in the jungle. In essence, the jungle is depicted in "Heart of Darkness" as a metaphor for the heart of darkness in each of us, that is, the inclination to evil that lurks within each of us. In Kurtz's case, once he was on his own in the jungle, he gradually became a ruthless, greedy despot who exploited the natives shamelessly.

In rewriting the screenplay, Coppola planned "to take John Milius's script and mate it with 'Heart of Darkness.' Consequently, my script is based on 'Heart of Darkness' to an even greater extent than the original screenplay."[8] Thus Coppola derived the character of the flipped-out freelance photojournalist in his screenplay from the young Russian sailor who is a disciple of Kurtz in "Heart of Darkness." Coppola even gives the photographer some of the Russian's dialogue verbatim from the book. For example, the photojournalist says to Willard, the Marlow character in the film, that Kurtz "has enlarged my mind; you don't judge him as you would an ordinary man." In brief, Coppola made the photojournalist "the equivalent of the harlequin Russian sailor . . . from Conrad."[9]

Brooks Riley notes two major alterations Coppola made in Milius's version of the script that are particularly significant. One change concerned the very beginning of the script. Milius begins his script, which is in the Research Library at UCLA, with a scene set in Kurtz's stronghold in the jungle, from which his rebel band makes its forays into "the deep tangled jungle" against the Vietcong, and in this scene there is a glimpse of Kurtz himself, exhorting his disciples.[10] By contrast, Coppola chose to follow Conrad in this matter by withholding our first sight of Kurtz until Willard finally tracks him down late in the film. Kurtz's absence from the film throughout most of its running time steadily builds suspense in the viewer, who continually wonders what this strange and mysterious individual will really be like once he finally makes his appearance. "To have shown Kurtz first, only to have abandoned him for the next two-thirds of the film," would have proved to be "a dilution of the film's carefully planned unveiling of the man."[11]

The other crucial revision Coppola made in Milius's screenplay concerned the film's conclusion. In Milius's conception of the film's finale, Willard is so mesmerized by the overpowering personality of Colonel Kurtz that he succumbs to the corrupting influence of this barbarous warlord. That is, Willard decides to join the native Cambodian tribesmen and the runaway American soldiers who make up Kurtz's army. Shortly afterward, the Vietcong attack Kurtz's compound, and Kurtz and Willard fight side by side until Kurtz is killed in battle. American helicopters, which are coming to rescue Willard, then appear in the sky over the compound, and Willard shoots wildly at them, as the film comes to an end.

Coppola was thoroughly dissatisfied with Milius's ending for the film. As Coppola describes this ending, Kurtz, "a battle-mad commander," wearing two bands of machine gun bullets across his chest, takes Willard by the hand and leads him into battle against the North Vietnamese.[12] Elsewhere he adds that, thus, "Willard converts to Kurtz's side; in the end he's firing up at the helicopters that are coming to get him, crying out crazily." Coppola dismissed Milius's ending as too macho and gung-ho, a "political comic strip."[13]

Needless to say, this finale of the film, as conceived by Milius, departs to a greater degree from Conrad's ending to the story than Coppola's ending for the film does. In Coppola's film Willard recoils from Kurtz's savage practices in the same manner that Marlow does in the book. Hence neither Marlow nor the film's Willard fall under Kurtz's sway as does Milius's Willard, who becomes another Kurtz.

For the record, "Heart of Darkness" does not appear in the screen credits of *Apocalypse Now* as the literary source of the film. As a matter of fact, a reference to Conrad's novella was originally listed in the screen credits, but Milius complained to the Screen Writers' Guild, and the reference to the book was removed. I asked Coppola if Milius vetoed the presence of Conrad's novella in the film's credits because he felt that citing Conrad's book as the source of the movie would minimize the importance of the material contributed to the screenplay by the scriptwriters, and Coppola declined to answer.

At any rate, years later Milius felt differently about the matter. He freely conceded that "Heart of Darkness" is indeed the source story for the film. "It was my favorite Conrad book," he said, and hence he wanted very much to bring it to the screen.[14] Significantly, the Academy Award nomination for the film's screenplay was in the category of best screenplay based on material from another medium—the only official acknowledgment that "Heart of Darkness" was the movie's literary source.

On the surface it seems that Conrad's novella is very different from Coppola's film. For instance, Conrad's story takes place in the Belgian Congo in the 1890s and focuses on Charles Marlow, a British sailor employed by a European trading firm as a captain of one of their steamboats. By contract, Coppola's film is set in Southeast Asia in the 1960s and centers on Benjamin Willard, an American Army officer. Yet, as film scholar Linda Cahir points out, although the settings and backgrounds of novella and film are quite different, the manner in which the story is narrated in each instance is "splendidly similar." For example, "each tale-proper begins with the protagonist's explanation of how he got the appointment which necessitated his excursion up river," Cahir points out. Marlow is dispatched to steam up the Congo in order to find Mr. Kurtz, an ivory trader who disappeared into the interior and never returned. Willard is mandated to journey up the Mekong River in a navy patrol boat to find Colonel Kurtz, who has recruited his own renegade army to fight the Vietcong. In addition, while Marlow and Willard each travel up a primeval river to fulfill their respective assignments, each speculates about the character of the man he is seeking, with the help of the information each has pieced together about him. Furthermore, the last stop for both Marlow and Willard, concludes Cahir, "is the soul-altering confrontation with the mysterious Kurtz."[15]

Moreover, one of the elements of Coppola's film that serves to bring it closer to the original story is the employment of Willard as the narrator of the film, just as Marlow is the narrator of the novella. Hence, the screenplay of *Apocalypse Now* remains most faithful to its source in its attempt to depict the action through flashback, with the narrator's comments on the action heard as voice-over on the sound track. Willard gives his personal reactions to his own experiences as he narrates them over the sound track.

Coppola's screenplay, dated December 3, 1975, is preserved in the Research Library at the University of California at Los Angeles. It begins and ends with scenes of Willard sitting on the deck of a cabin cruiser in the harbor at Marina del Ray, a beach town in Southern California. He is the bodyguard of the wealthy man who is hosting a party for his friends on deck. These scenes, which were never filmed, introduce Willard as narrator of the story. One of the guests in the first scene asks him to tell some stories about Vietnam, but he declines. "There's no way I can tell them to these people," he reflects in a voice-over. They wouldn't grasp what he had to say about the horrors of war.[16] Then the scene shifts to Saigon in 1968. The Marina del Ray scenes were to provide a framing device for the film. Consequently, in the final scene in the screenplay we return to Willard on the deck of the cabin cruiser, silently pondering all that has happened to him. There is no such framing device in the finished film.

Another scene in the script that Coppola did not film dramatizes how Willard returns to the United States and visits Kurtz's widow and son in a "scrubbed-clean California neighborhood."[17] Willard gently speaks of Kurtz's demise without suggesting that he killed Kurtz. When Mrs. Kurtz asks him what her husband's last words were, Willard cannot bring himself to inform her that Kurtz's final utterance was "the horror, the horror." He rather tells her that Kurtz died speaking her name. Willard, after all, does not wish to destroy her fond memories of her deceased husband, which are all she has left of him.

Eleanor Coppola mentions in *Notes,* her diary of the making of *Apocalypse Now,* that during postproduction Coppola still talked of "shooting one last scene," where Willard talks with Kurtz's widow and son, because he did not want the movie to end on a note of violence (i.e., with Willard's slaying of Kurtz). Coppola abandoned the idea on October 29, 1978.[18] Presumably Coppola discarded both the scenes with Kurtz's family, as well as the scenes aboard the cabin cruiser, because the expense of filming them did not justify their inclusion in a film that was going over length and over budget.

Coppola decided to shoot *Apocalypse Now* almost entirely on location in the Philippines because of the similarity of the terrain to Vietnam and because building and labor costs were in general lower there than in Hollywood. When Coppola approached the Pentagon in May 1975 for its cooperation in making the film there, he pointed out that Milius's initial script still needed considerable revision. Nevertheless, Army officials took one look at the screenplay and refused to cooperate with the film. They pointed to several objectionable passages, starting with the film's springboard incident, which has Captain Willard sent to assassinate the crazed, power-mad Colonel Kurtz. Coppola made no effort whatever to revise his screenplay according to Army specifications and dropped the matter. Once he began shooting the picture in the Philippines, Coppola arranged with the regime of President Ferdinand Marcos to rent American-made surplus helicopters and vital military equipment for the production.

In order to ensure that he would be relatively free of studio interference while shooting the movie, Coppola decided to finance the production, insofar as possible, with his earnings from the first two *Godfather* films. He started by investing $2 million of his own capital in the movie and then obtained $7 million in exchange for American distribution rights. But Coppola insisted on retaining control over the film as an independent production made by American Zoetrope. The other backers agreed, so long as he was held responsible for any overruns on the budget, which at that point he fixed as $12 million.

Coppola had difficulty in casting the picture, because several actors, including Al Pacino, whom he wanted to play Willard, were not willing to spend several months filming in the jungle. He became so frustrated about his casting problems that he furiously hurled his Academy Awards out of the window of his San Francisco home. Eleanor picked up the pieces and had them repaired. For the role of Willard he finally settled on Harvey Keitel (*Taxi Driver*). Three veterans of earlier Coppola movies signed on: Marlon Brando as Kurtz; Robert Duvall as Lieutenant Colonel William Kilgore (whose real-life counterpart, Colonel John Stockton, had inspired Milius to write *Apocalypse Now* in the first place); and G. D. Spradlin as General Corman, named after Coppola's early mentor, Roger Corman. Some other veterans of previous Coppola films were also on hand: production designer Dean Tavoularis; supervising editor Richard Marks; sound specialist Walter Murch, who would double as a film editor as well; and composer Carmine Coppola. New to the team was Italian cinematographer Vittorio Storaro (*The Spider's Stratagem*).

On March 1, 1976, Coppola embarked with his family for the Philippine Islands, where he rented a house in Manila, the capital of Luzon, the chief island, and set up a production office. Eleanor not only kept a diary, which she later published with Francis's approval, but also, at his suggestion, planned to make a promotional film for the United Artists Publicity Department. The promo film was eventually abandoned, and she subsequently turned over the footage to Fax Bahr and George Hickenlooper for their feature-length documentary, *Hearts of Darkness: A Filmmaker's Apocalypse* (1991).

Principal photography began on March 20, with a scene of Willard and the crew of his river patrol boat (called a PBR in military parlance, rather than an RPB). As shooting progressed, Coppola began to feel that

Keitel was miscast. Willard is really "an observer" of events early in the movie, "an introspective character," and Keitel found it difficult to play him as a "passive onlooker," Coppola explains. Keitel was playing Willard too aggressively, "too feverishly." Coppola huddled with his production team on April 16 and decided to replace Keitel with Martin Sheen, whom Coppola was confident could play Willard as the impassive individual the script called for.[19] Sheen took over the role on April 26.

Apocalypse Now is the only one of his films in which Coppola makes a cameo appearance. As Willard stands on the beach during a battle scene, Coppola, in the role of a TV newsreel director, shouts at him, "Don't look at the camera! Just go by like you're fighting!"

Replacing the male lead, of course, had put the film behind schedule. On May 25, while the unit was shooting at Iba, a village near Subic Bay, a much worse calamity took place. Typhoon Olga struck with its full fury and demolished the sets. The resulting damage was estimated at $1.32 million. On June 8 Coppola announced that he was suspending production for six weeks. So most of the cast and crew returned to the United States, while Tavoularis built new sets from scratch in a different location on higher ground to prevent further flooding.

Coppola spent some of the time afforded by the hiatus making further revisions in the script in consultation with Murch at his home in the Napa Valley outside San Francisco. One incident he devised came neither from Milius's script nor from Conrad's novella. It was incorporated into the script on pages dated June 29, 1976. Willard's PBR intercepts a sampan manned by North Vietnamese refugees. His crew suspects, quite gratuitously, that the occupants are really civilian Vietcong resistance fighters and massacres them all. An innocent woman lies dying, and the skipper of the PBR urges Willard to take her to a nearby field hospital. But Willard instead shoots the hapless peasant point blank in the chest, putting her out of her misery. He cannot risk jeopardizing his secret mission by taking her to a hospital. His action is remorseless because he realizes that he must press on with his mission, which overshadows any human concerns. Incidentally, this episode also foreshadows Willard as capable of exterminating Kurtz when the time comes.

The production log, which was included in the souvenir program for the movie, records that on July 27 the film unit returned to the Philippines and relocated at Pagsanjan, a two-hour drive from Manila. Because of major setbacks the production was now six weeks behind schedule and $3 million over budget, which UA agreed to put up.

Assistant Director Jerry Ziesmer, in his memoirs, gives a detailed account of the filming of *Apocalypse Now.* Ziesmer describes in great detail how the director encouraged Martin Sheen to get really drunk while shooting a scene early in the film. This scene was shot silently, so that Coppola talked Sheen through it as they improvised together. In the scene in question, Willard, who has already been missioned to assassinate various enemy agents in the field, is on a binge while awaiting his next assignment. "Francis wanted to see Willard come out of Martin Sheen, for Marty to reveal the assassin inside Willard," Ziesmer explains. At one point Sheen glares at himself in a mirror in his hotel room, and then he drunkenly smashes his own image with his fist and bloodies his hand. Sheen says in the documentary *Hearts of Darkness* that "Francis wanted to stop filming, but I said, 'No, let it go.' Willard was looking for the killer inside himself." That would explain how he could commit another assassination.[20] Ziesmer sagely adds a thought-provoking comment on the proceedings: "Should we have pushed and prodded Marty to the extent we did for a performance in a motion picture? Did the end justify the means?"[21]

Coppola's predilection for improvisation is well known, and he allowed Dennis Hopper in particular to improvise during his scenes. Coppola cast Hopper as the weird, mercurial photojournalist, an amusing figure inspired in part by Sean Flynn (the son of swashbuckling superstar Errol Flynn), who was a marijuana-smoking photographer during the Vietnam War. It seems that Hopper, who had been on a downhill slide throughout the mid-1970s, was deep into drugs and had been in and out of rehabilitation centers. He himself comments laconically in the documentary, "I was not at the time in the greatest shape." It was an open secret that Hopper was smoking grass while he was on location, and so he found it easy to play the photojournalist as a spacey, eccentric individual who goes around babbling mindlessly that Kurtz is a great man.[22]

Coppola beefed up Hopper's part during shooting with some additional dialogue. "Francis would come in with a small, white piece of paper, typed from top to bottom with suggested dialogue," which he would give to Hopper a couple of days in advance of shooting the scene he had just revised. Hopper's key scene is the one in which the photographer welcomes Willard to Kurtz's fortress and rambles on about Kurtz's exploits with his renegade band of warriors. At this juncture Hopper seemed incapable of remembering his lines, and Coppola was irritated when Hopper kept wandering too far from the dialogue as written. "For God's sake," he roared, "we've done thirty-seven takes, and you've done them all your way! Would you do just one for me, Hopper?" Hopper replied, "Alright. I'll do one for you!" and stuck essentially to Coppola's dialogue for once.[23]

A local tribe of 264 primitive Ifugao Philippine aborigines arrived in late August 1976 to play Kurtz's Montagnard followers, headhunters whom Kurtz has trained as part of his rebel army. Coppola thought that, rather than dress up Filipino extras as aborigines, it would be better to recruit authentic tribesmen. In the documentary Eleanor Coppola says that they actually lived on the Kurtz temple compound set while they worked in the film. The sacrifice of a *carabao,* which takes place during the Kurtz episode, was "a real ritual slaughter performed by the Ifugaos." As a result, *Apocalypse Now* is one of the few mainstream Hollywood films not to carry a statement in the closing credits that no animal was harmed during the making of the picture. When some filmgoers subsequently complained about the butchering of this water buffalo, Coppola answered that, as with the horse's head scene in *The Godfather,* some people were once again more outraged by the killing of animals than of people in the film.

On September 3, Marlon Brando arrived to play Kurtz for $1 million a week for three weeks. Brando showed up overweight and unprepared. "He was already heavy when I hired him," says Coppola in the documentary *Hearts of Darkness,* but by now he had ballooned to 250 pounds. "He had promised me he was going to get into shape, but he didn't. So he left me in a tough spot," because Kurtz is supposed to be wasting away from malaria. Coppola therefore had cinematographer Vittorio Storaro shoot Brando immersed in the cavernous darkness of his murky quarters, where Brando's girth would not be obvious. Actually, Storaro thought it dramatically right to photograph Brando as a disembodied voice so that Kurtz materialized out of the black void. "The Marlon Brando character represents the dark side of civilization," he explains. "[H]e had to appear as something of a pagan idol." As a result, Storaro filmed Brando "in the shadows or partially lit" and that gave him an air of mystery.[24]

Brando had also promised Coppola that he would read Conrad's "Heart of Darkness," but he admitted frankly that he had failed to do so. When Coppola remonstrated, "But you said you read it," Brando answered, "I lied." Coppola would work out a scene with Brando by improvising during rehearsals, then he would type up the dialogue in final form and shoot the scene the following day. When he attempted to steer the material back toward Conrad, "Brando resisted my doing so, saying it would never work."[25]

One day, when the improvisations with the temperamental Brando were going nowhere, Coppola lamented, "This is like opening night; the curtain goes up and there's no show." Coppola finally prevailed upon Brando to read "Heart of Darkness." The next morning Brando announced that the role of Kurtz was now "perfectly clear" to him and that he would play Kurtz closer to the way Conrad had written the character—which is what Coppola had been angling for all along.[26]

In the wake of the other woes that had dogged the production, Coppola suffered another unforeseen misfortune when his leading man suffered a severe heart attack on March 1, 1977. Sheen, like Pacino during the shooting of *Godfather II,* had collapsed because of the strain of carrying a demanding role during a strenuous shoot. Moreover, Sheen was working in isolated locations and in stifling heat. In addition, Sheen confessed that he was "smoking and drinking too much," and that had exacerbated his heart condition.[27]

Because of his serious condition, Sheen, an Irish Catholic, received the Last Rites from a Filipino Catholic priest, who did not speak English. A rumor quickly spread that Sheen was about to meet his Maker. The documentary *Hearts of Darkness* contains an excerpt from a taped phone conversation in which Coppola discusses the crisis with one of his staff. (The director of *The Conversation,* a film about wiretapping, had once more bugged himself.) Coppola is absolutely livid that his production assistant, Melissa Mathison, made an unauthorized statement to Barry Hirsch (Coppola's attorney back in Los Angeles) about the precarious state of Sheen's health, which could lead to rumors spreading all over Hollywood like wildfire. "Fucking gossip can ruin us!" he exclaims. Coppola informs his subordinate that he plans to announce that Sheen has been admitted to a Manila hospital suffering from "heat exhaustion." In order to squelch the spread of further gossip that Sheen is near death, Coppola blurts out, "Marty is not dead . . . until I say so!"

Some commentators on the documentary have said that Coppola's last remark seems callous. He responds that his purpose was to avoid the panic that would ensue if rumors that Sheen could not finish the picture reached United Artists officials. They might just pull the plug on the production by pressuring Coppola into cutting the film, together with the footage that he had shot up to that point, which was not enough to make a coherent narrative. "The idea was not to tell anyone that the situation was more serious than it was," he says. "If you view my statement out of context, it seems I didn't care about Marty."[28]

In actual fact, Eleanor Coppola explains in the documentary, Francis was able to shoot around Sheen by filming master shots with Sheen's brother Joseph as a double, shooting over the double's shoulder. Then, when Sheen came back, Coppola shot the close-ups of him, which could be woven into the scenes. Sheen did return to work, groomed and rested, on April 19.

Ziesmer explains how the shooting period of *Apocalypse Now* lasted an unprecedented 238 days, spread over fifteen months. He is quite candid in detailing how the shooting schedule and the budget of the film steadily got more and more out of hand: "All of us were at fault. First of all, there were too many of us in the Philippines making the movie. All of us worked to please Francis Coppola, the world's most respected film director. If he asked for a hundred explosives, we prepared five hundred. . . . To please him we felt we could never tell him 'No,' and in order not to do that we all bought more, hired more, rented more. We got the bigger, the newer, the best." For example, George Nelson, the Oscar-winning set decorator (*The Godfather*), rented some very expensive antiques for the colonial house in the French plantation sequence, which had to be imported from Paris. Ziesmer concludes ruefully, "No one told Francis about the cost."[29]

When John Milius was not invited to visit the set, he joked that Coppola feared a coup. Actually, the worried UA executives had sent a delegation to check out Coppola's progress at one point, and he feared that UA might yet lobby to have Milius, himself a writer-director, replace him. Admittedly, some of the budget overages were not Coppola's fault, such as natural disasters and the outrageous fees President Marcos was assessing for the use of the Philippine Air Force helicopters. Be that as it may, the budget eventually soared to $31 million, and Coppola was responsible for $14 million in overruns when he film was completed. Just when the press had christened the movie "Apocalypse Never," Coppola decided to drop some minor scenes from the shooting schedule, and the production wrapped.

The last shooting day was May 21, 1977. According to the production log, Coppola addressed the cast and crew at day's end: "I've never in my life seen so many people so happy to be unemployed."[30] Shortly after, Coppola and company pulled up stakes and went home. Coppola still required an additional $10 million for postproduction. UA, which had by this time sunk $25 million into the production, was reluctant to invest any more. So he had to sink his personal assets into the film, which included mortgaging his home on Pacific Heights in San Francisco, to bring the picture to completion.

One journalist quipped that Coppola had virtually pawned his wedding ring just to finish his picture. Coppola was not amused. He recalls that he was crushed at the time when the press ridiculed *Apocalypse Now* because it seemed to be an out-of-control "financial boondoggle." Why was it a crime, he wondered, for him to spend his own money on a serious war picture, when the studios were willing to bankroll movies "about a big gorilla (*King Kong*) or a jerk who flies across the sky (*Superman*)?"[31]

Press reports about the turbulent shooting period continued to circulate long after the film wrapped. One dispatch concerned corpses of North

Vietnamese regulars killed by Kurtz's renegade army, which are strewn around the grounds of his temple compound. It was alleged that there were some real cadavers mixed in with the dummy corpses on the Kurtz compound set. The film's press office vigorously denied this news story. More precisely, Dean Tavoularis points out that he had obtained a lot of bones from a restaurant, which he piled up in Kurtz's courtyard. When the crew noticed the stench and the rats crawling over the bones, one of them surmised that they were human remains, which was decidedly not the case. (There is a close-up in the documentary of a pile of these bones with flies buzzing around them that is not in the finished film.)

The temple set was modeled on Angkor Wat, an ancient temple still preserved in Angkor, Cambodia. Tavoularis explains that Kurtz's macabre compound, complete with its decaying temple, was meant to reflect Kurtz's descent into madness and barbarism—and Conrad's vision of the depths of human depravity: there are altars covered with plastic skulls as well as heaps of bones scattered around the set, and an eerie mist that envelops the compound. "I was living in the house of death that I was making," Tavoularis remembers, and growing depressed because of the grotesque atmosphere as time went on. The whole picture, he concluded, "was a nightmare."[32]

A much more unsettling report in the press about the production stated that Coppola had had a nervous breakdown late in the shooting period. This news dispatch had been given some credence when Coppola himself introduced *Apocalypse Now* in a press conference at the Cannes International Film Festival in May 1979, which I was present to hear. He made the following declaration, which was widely quoted thereafter: "*Apocalypse Now* is not about Vietnam; it is Vietnam. And the way we made it was very much like the way the Americans were in Vietnam. We were in the jungle, had access to too much money, too much equipment; and little by little we went insane. After a while, I was a little frightened, because I was getting deeper in debt and no longer recognized the kind of movie I was making. The film was making itself, or the jungle was making it for me." He seemed to be saying that the film had been made in just the kind of muddle that had doomed the U.S. Army in Vietnam.

Eleanor Coppola in her diary confirms the serious bout of depression Coppola experienced during filming. She records on March 14, 1977—almost a year to the day after principal photography had begun—that Coppola suffered what she termed "a sort of nervous breakdown."[33] He was rehearsing a scene on the set, when suddenly he sank to his knees and began to weep. Then he suffered an "epileptic seizure, thrashing about on the floor and foaming at the mouth." He was delirious and was afraid he was going to die. His final request was that George Lucas should finish *Apocalypse Now*.[34] Two days later he was back on the set, as if nothing had happened.

In discussing this incident, Coppola states emphatically, "I am an epileptic," and the seizure he suffered on the set of *Apocalypse Now* was genuine.[35] He also admits that he pretended to have a fit while he argued with the studio brass about casting Brando in *The Godfather*. But that was a gag, he says, and the Paramount executives present knew it.

More recently, David Thomson has written that Coppola "ran into a 'Heart of Darkness' of his own while making the picture: He was out of control.... began to use drugs," and became involved with another woman. Thomson quotes Brando as stating that during shooting Coppola was "alternately depressed, nervous, and frantic."[36]

In addressing himself to Thomson's remarks, Coppola states, "To say I began using drugs" during production "is a great overstatement." He confesses that he had begun chain-smoking cigarettes, which he had never done before. "At the worst I began smoking marijuana" during filming and postproduction, "but that was the extent of it."[37] In short, he never developed the sort of drug addiction that plagued Dennis Hopper in the mid-1970s.

He was exhausted from the endless shoot, he explains, and worried about going further and further over budget and over schedule, not to mention the crises precipitated by Sheen's heart attack and the typhoon. Admittedly, smoking cigarettes and grass was making him weird at times, he concludes. In the documentary *Hearts of Darkness* Coppola remarks in a taped conversation with his wife during shooting, "This film is a $20 million disaster. Why won't anyone believe me? I'm thinking of shooting myself." He is then shown holding a prop revolver to his head—a melodramatic gesture that he hardly meant to be taken literally. Yet William Phillips, in his essay on the documentary, takes Coppola at his word when he writes, "So anguished did he become that he was considering . . . how he could commit suicide."[38]

During postproduction, in the fall of 1977, Coppola was diagnosed by a psychiatrist as having manic-depressive tendencies, for which lithium, a tranquilizer, was prescribed. Because Coppola did not want it bandied about Hollywood that he was taking medication, he arranged to have the prescription written under the name of Kurtz. "Lithium made me nauseous," he explains, so he ultimately decided that he could arrive at some sort of emotional stability without it, "and I just stopped."[39] At all events, Coppola contends that the idea that he suffered a "so-called breakdown" during shooting is "exaggerated; it was much more your basic, old-fashioned mid-life crisis."[40]

Coppola's mid-life crisis also involved his renewing his personal relationship with Melissa Mathison, who served as his production assistant on *Apocalypse Now,* as she had done on *Godfather II* (see chapter 5). Eleanor Coppola gives an anguished account in her diary of the whole affair. She writes that on April 13, 1978, she found a loving card from Mathison and confronted her husband about it. Coppola's mother Italia commented afterward, "I love that Ellie; she's a saint. Even when Francie was with that Other Woman, he loved Ellie; and when that Other Woman wanted him to leave Ellie, he wouldn't. Ellie—she stayed; and she gained."[41] (Mathison later married one of the cast of *Apocalypse Now,* Harrison Ford.)

When Coppola returned to San Francisco, he was faced with one million feet of film (about 250 hours) to edit into a feature. He began working with supervising editor Richard Marks and coeditors Walter Murch, Gerald Greenberg, Lisa Fruchtman, and Barry Malkin, plus a bevy of assistant editors. They were using the state-of-the-art editing facilities at American Zoetrope in Coppola's Sentinel Building, as well as an annex that had been installed across the street.

Coppola transferred all of the footage to videotape, which was much easier to work with than cumbersome reels of 35 mm film. Once a scene had been edited, it would be transferred to celluloid. Gerald Greenberg states that Coppola parceled out specific sequences for each editor to work on: "it behooved us to break the film up, so we could each concentrate on just these sequences."[42] Greenberg's superb editing of Kilgore's helicopter attack became a benchmark for the other editors. Since Coppola was determined to give a definite shape to *Apocalypse Now,* he sometimes would stay up most of the night to do a preliminary edit of a crucial scene and then turn it over to the editing team the next morning.

Furthermore, he shot some additional footage on his Napa Valley estate near San Francisco and in the surrounding countryside in order to plug up some holes in the narrative. The shots of Willard reading Kurtz's dossier and commenting on it as he journeys upriver were done at this time. Willard is impressed with Kurtz's heroism in the days before he went off the deep end. "What balls!" he exclaims in reading of Kurtz's valiant exploits.

The first rough cut, which was finished in the late summer of 1977, ran seven hours, remembers Richard Marks. It ultimately took two years to create the final cut. "I'll probably never work on anything that monumental again."[43]

Walter Murch doubled as sound specialist as well as a film editor. He emphasizes that *Apocalypse Now* was the first stereo film he ever worked on. "There are two channels of sound in both the back and the front of the movie theater," he explains, "so, with stereo, you give the audience a sense of being surrounded by sound."

When Murch began mixing the sound track in the fall of 1977, he noted that the original narration in the Milius screenplay had long since been abandoned. "I felt that there was so much turbulence in the storytelling," he recalls, "that the only way of clarifying the plot was to re-place the narration. It seemed necessary, because Willard is such an inac-tive, inarticulate character—the only way to get inside his head is to have him relate to us through the medium of narration."[44] Richard Marks agreed: At the beginning of the film, "there is Willard, a soldier and a CIA opera-tive, who is given a mission. You're asking the audience to identify with a hired killer and to follow him up the river." But they would not identify with him, "unless they could understand his pain" by way of his voice-over narration.[45]

Coppola concurred with Murch and Marks and eventually brought in Michael Herr to compose a new narration in the spring of 1978. A former war correspondent in Vietnam, Herr had published a series of articles on the war in *Esquire* magazine, and they were subsequently collected in a book, *Dispatches* (1977), which is generally considered to be the best reportage by any correspondent to come out of the war. As a matter of fact, Herr's ar-ticles in *Esquire* had been the source of some of the incidents that Milius had woven into his original script.

Herr found that the narration written by John Milius was too gung ho and too tinged with machismo and, as such, "totally useless. So, over a period of a year, I wrote various segments of narration. Francis gave me very close guidelines."[46] At the point Herr first viewed the rough cut, in February 1978, it was five hours—two hours shorter than the first cut of August 1977. Major excisions had been made, particularly in the Kurtz com-pound sequence, removing much of Brando's improvisations (which sur-vive in fragments as voice-overs in the completed film) as Marks and his editing team pared down and simplified Brando's remarks.

Herr's hardboiled narration fleshes out Willard's character with sig-nificant details—something Milius's narration failed to accomplish. When Willard is given his mission to assassinate Kurtz, a rogue officer who has committed unspeakable atrocities, Willard muses over the sound track, "Everyone gets what they want. I wanted a mission; and for my sins, that's what I got." As two officers come to his hotel room to summon him, he continues, "They brought it up to me like room service—a real choice mis-sion, and when it was over, I'd never want another." Willard's remarks echo

Conrad's narrator in "Heart of Darkness," when Marlow says he was given the mission to find Kurtz in order to pay for his sins. Furthermore, through Willard's narration we learn of his cynical attitude toward the top brass and their conduct of the war: "They were four-star clowns, who were going to end up giving the whole circus away." He never expresses himself that bluntly to others. In brief, the film is inconceivable without Herr's narration.

While Coppola continued toiling on the rough cut, he opted to have some test screenings in the spring of 1978. In fact, he is credited with "beginning the Hollywood vogue of test-screening movies," declares Michele Wallens. "I was, and probably still am, a theater director," says Coppola. Out-of-town tryouts are "part of a long-standing tradition in the theater, and I was looking for a modern way of accomplishing it" for a film.[47]

Filmgoers were given a letter from Coppola at the test screenings, inviting them "to help me finalize the film." After one test screening in New York City in May 1978, he addressed a memo to himself in the wee hours in his hotel room. He was distraught when some preview cards said that the final section of the movie in Kurtz's compound failed to jell. Moreover, he was disappointed that several filmgoers thought the Kilgore helicopter attack, which he considered a run-of-the-mill action sequence, was the highpoint of the whole movie. "The film reaches its height level during the fucking helicopter battle," he moaned. "My nerves are shot, and my heart is broken."[48] The premiere, which had been delayed from Christmas 1978 to Easter 1979, was now postponed until August 1979, much to the displeasure of the feisty young Andreas Albeck, the new president of UA. United Artists was on the verge of financial collapse, and the studio needed a blockbuster to save it. Albeck was desperately hoping that *Apocalypse Now* would help.

Across the street from the Sentinel Building was the skyscraper that housed the headquarters of Transamerica Corporation, a conglomerate that owned an insurance company and many other diverse business interests. It was also the parent company of UA, which it had acquired in 1967. James Harvey, executive vice president of Transamerica and chairman of UA, became increasingly worried about *Apocalypse Now*, as UA continued to pump additional funds into the film's postproduction phase. Coppola gave Harvey a telescope with a note, saying, "So that you can keep an eye on me," by training the telescope on Coppola's office across the street.[49] As in the case of Charles Bludhorn, head of the parent company of Paramount while Coppola made the first two *Godfather* movies, the filmmaker thought it wise to be on good terms with the big boss. Still, the fate of *Apocalypse Now* was shrouded in the San Francisco fog.

Already displeased with Coppola, the UA brass were chagrined by his decision to go for broke and unveil what he termed "a work in progress" at the Cannes International Film Festival on May 13, 1979. One official stated that Coppola's decision constituted "momentary insanity born of arrogance."[50] Coppola saw it as the most public "sneak preview" in cinema history—a chance for him to obtain worldwide publicity for his beleaguered movie. He did that and more: *Apocalypse Now* won one of the two Grand Prizes awarded at the Festival that year, and Coppola became the only director ever to win the *Palm d'Or* (Golden Palm) at Cannes twice (the first time was for *The Conversation*). Coppola's gamble had paid off. Consequently, the top executives at UA and Transamerica were reassured by this turn of events. I personally observed that after the award ceremony on May 24, when Coppola was being interviewed by a swarm of journalists on the front steps of the *Palais des Festivals*, the director of *Apocalypse Now* was being hailed as the top auteur filmmaker of his generation.

The one sour note struck at Cannes was that the film's ambiguous ending was thoroughly disliked by many members of the international press corps. As a matter of fact, Coppola had experimented with more than one ending for the picture during postproduction. He said at the time that "working on the ending is like trying to crawl up glass by your fingernails."[51]

The first ending Coppola considered came right from his version of the screenplay: Willard orders what he calls a "purgative air strike" on Kurtz's temple compound over the shortwave radio, before making his getaway downriver in his PBR. Shortly afterward, according to the script, "The air strike hits with all its force. Balls of fire sweep down on the temple; it is the biggest fireworks show in history."[52]

As it happened, Coppola had to destroy the Kurtz compound set when he decamped from the Philippines, so he blew it up and had his camera crew record the multiple explosions with several cameras. He was therefore able to insert this footage of strobe-lit flames into the film to portray the bomber attack on Kurtz's fortress. But Coppola rejected as too violent this ending in which Kurtz and his army of barbarous ex-soldiers and savage natives, all wearing war paint, are annihilated.

In the second ending he devised, the one shown in Cannes, Willard assassinates Kurtz with a machete, then stands frozen on the temple steps, aware that when Kurtz's people genuflect before him in homage they expect him to replace Kurtz as their godlike leader. At the final fade-out, Willard is still on the steps, unable to decide what direction he should take. "The film thus ends with a moral choice," says Coppola. "Will Willard become another Kurtz? Or will he learn from his experience" and decline to be their new master? "The audience didn't like the ending shown in Cannes," he continues—nor did his staff.[53] The audience experienced the frustration that comes from witnessing an unresolved dilemma. So Coppola jettisoned that ending and chose a third ending, one in which Willard definitely refuses to become the incarnation of Kurtz, since he is unwilling to embrace Kurtz's warped, malevolent philosophy. Instead, he leaves Kurtz's kingdom behind and boards his PBR, which will take him back to civilization. "So many people preferred this ending, because it gives a sense of finality, that I am using it," he said at the time. "I mean, I'm making this film for people, so the hell with it!"[54]

The movie premiered in August 1979 in a few large cities in 70 mm, for reserved-seat performances at which programs were distributed in lieu of screen credits. This version did not include the air assault on Kurtz's compound, which Coppola had rejected earlier. "People are not interested in just seeing helicopters fly by or in seeing explosions," he explains. "[T]hey want a story and character interaction."[55]

The foreign distributors, who had partially financed the movie, urged Coppola to end the film with the aerial attack that would reduce Kurtz's domain to pebbles. Coppola thought of a way to mollify the foreign distributors. It was not feasible to provide programs for the film when it went into wide general release in conventional 35 mm prints in most cities throughout the country. So he decided to attach the end credits to the regular 35 mm prints and to superimpose them over the infrared, phosphorescent footage of the explosions taken from the movie's first ending, so that the movie ended with a violent finale. Most critics around the country who saw this ending assumed Willard called in the bombing raid that destroys Kurtz's realm. When items began to appear in the trade press stating that the film had two endings, one for the 70 mm prints (without the air strike) and one for the 35 mm prints (showing the air strike), Coppola regretted reinstating the bombing of Kurtz's kingdom in the 35 mm prints.

He responded to the press by declaring flatly that the infrared footage was not intended to change the film's ending because it was "clearly background for the credits." As he told Tony Chiu, "The explosions are purely a graphic device, not a story point." Yet he subsequently reversed his position and admitted to Gene Siskel that the multiple explosions under the closing credits in the 35 mm prints quite understandably led most critics who saw it to believe that this footage did in fact portray the air strike ordered by Willard. Therefore, Coppola concludes, it was a mistake to attach the footage of the explosions to the 35 mm prints of the movie.[56]

He further states that he had become increasingly convinced, while editing the film, that it should not conclude with a warlike, apocalyptic finale portraying the volcanic eruption of the air assault on Kurtz's temple compound in which Kurtz's whole army perished. That is why he rejected the first ending he had concocted for the rough cut, which graphically portrayed the air strike. This decision was in keeping with his inclination to evade violence rather than exploit it in his films. Citing T. S. Eliot's "Waste Land," he told me, "I wanted the film to end, not with a bang but a whimper." Indeed, he had the photojournalist recite this line from Eliot's poem while talking to Willard.

Coppola now feels that the bombing attack was contrary to the essential meaning he ultimately wanted to express, which was that Willard was journeying toward a postwar world that would be at peace. Indeed, even Kilgore says, "Some day this war's gonna end"—one of the last statements Kilgore makes in the movie and one that is later repeated by Willard. So it is that in the videocassette and DVD prints of the film the closing credits are superimposed on a neutral black background, without the explosions.

Nevertheless, although the aerial assault is not shown in the videocassette and DVD versions of the film, there are references to it. When Willard has started downriver in his PBR after killing Kurtz, GHQ contacts him on the shortwave radio and asks if he had any further instructions about the air strike. He switches off the radio, thereby refusing to cancel the order given earlier for the air assault. Furthermore, the last shot of Willard's face in close-up at the end of the movie is accompanied by a helicopter flying across the screen, above a conflagration in the forest below. Since Willard did not call off the bombing, this image implicitly foreshadows the aerial attack on Kurtz's kingdom. So we may assume—even without the bombing attack on Kurtz's fortress actually being shown—that Willard let the bombing proceed. When I showed Coppola an earlier draft of this chapter, I asked him if that was a reasonable assumption, and he did not take issue with it. He is apparently content to allow the viewer to infer that the air strike took place "off-stage" if they choose.

After all, in Kurtz's camp, chaos has long since replaced military professionalism as the order of the day. Torture and bloody executions are the main activities. They seem to occur randomly "and attest to the insanity of Kurtz's army of mercenaries."[57] For Willard to order the air assault on the compound and rain down fire from heaven on Kurtz's rebel band of crazed deserters and headhunters—who, after all, have already committed untold atrocities and continue to be a menace to the war effort—seems as morally justified as the assassination of Kurtz.

In the last analysis, the two endings (one with the air strike shown, the other with it implied) are not radically different. In any case, Howard Hampton contends that "it is difficult to accept an unambiguous resolution for the film," and Coppola in interviews over the years has never been able to provide one.[58]

Ultimately, Coppola eliminated the explicit portrayal of the aerial assault because he was determined to end the film on a positive note, which is why he had originally planned to film Willard's visit with Kurtz's widow and son. At any rate, Coppola chose to focus at the end on Willard returning to the PBR, just as a cleansing rain washes over his body, and he sails downriver to salvation, a sadder but wiser man.

Apocalypse Now, as released in 1979, opens with a riveting scene, a hypnotic montage of a phantom helicopter flying through the jungle amid smoke and napalm flames, accompanied by the whirling of a chopper's rotary blades. Jim Morrison and the Doors sing the phantasmagoric "The End" on the sound track, an ironic choice to have at the beginning of the film. The image dissolves to Willard, a burnt-out intelligence officer lying drunk and nearly naked on a rumpled, sweat-soaked bed in a Saigon hotel, while a ceiling fan slowly revolves above him. He is groggily awakening from a nightmare about the war, which was prompted by the thump of the ceiling fan sounding like a helicopter. A full-time Green Beret and a part-time CIA assassin, Willard is awaiting a secret assignment.

Captain Benjamin Willard is mandated by General Corman to penetrate into the interior of the jungle and track down Colonel Walter E. Kurtz, a renegade officer who has raised an army composed of deserters like himself and of native tribesmen in order to fight the war on his own terms. When he locates Kurtz, Willard is to "terminate his command with extreme prejudice," which is military jargon meaning that Willard should assassinate Kurtz. Kurtz, it seems, has taken to employing brutal tactics to attain his military objectives. Indeed, some of his extreme measures have sickened the members of the Army intelligence staff who have succeeded in obtaining information about him. "Every man has got a breaking point— you have and I have," Corman tells Willard. "Walt Kurtz has reached his. He has gone insane. He's out there operating without any decent restraint, totally beyond the pale of acceptable human conduct, and he is still commanding troops in the field."

Willard's first reaction to his mission is that liquidating someone for killing people in wartime seems like "handing out speeding tickets at the Indianapolis 500." Besides, even though Willard has been ordered to eliminate no less than six other "undesirables" in the recent past, this is the first time his target has been an American and an officer. He therefore decides to withhold judgment about Kurtz until he meets up with him personally.

Near the beginning of the trip Willard and the crew of his small craft witness an air assault in which an officer, who is aptly named Kilgore, systematically wipes out a strongly fortified enemy village from the air. (He is named Kharnage in Milius's script.) His bravado and bombast recall the title character from the Coppola-scripted *Patton*. Like Patton, Kilgore sports pearl-handled revolvers (see chapter 1). Kilgore, all decked out with a Stetson and gold neckerchief, looks as if he should be leading a cavalry charge rather than a helicopter attack. He even has a bugler with an old-fashioned cavalry bugle to sound the call to arms like a cavalry charge. Kilgore's fleet of helicopters is equipped with loudspeakers that blare forth Wagner's thunderous "Ride of the Valkyries" as the choppers fly over the target area. "Wagner scares the hell out of them," Kilgore tells Willard, who is observing the operation as a passenger in Kilgore's copter. As a napalm strike wreaks havoc and destruction on the village below, Kilgore exults, "I love the smell of napalm in the morning. It has the smell of victory."

Kilgore, a fanatic filled with delusions of grandeur who dominates his men and decimates an occupied coastal village with maniacal glee, prefigures Kurtz. "If that's how Kilgore fought the war," Willard muses, "I began to wonder what they had against Kurtz." To give Milius his due, the Kilgore episode was incorporated into the shooting script just as he wrote it, including the stunning use of "The Ride of the Valkyries."

As Willard chugs up the Mekong River into uncharted territory in search of Kurtz, his journey becomes a symbolic voyage backward in time toward the primitive roots of civilization. The air attack on a North Vietnamese village carried out by Kilgore utilizes all the facilities of modern mechanized warfare, from helicopters and rockets to radar-directed machine guns. By the time Willard's boat reaches Kurtz's compound in the heart of the dark jungle, the modern weaponry associated with the helicopter attack earlier in the movie has been replaced by the weapons of primitive man, as Kurtz's native followers attack the small vessel with arrows and spears. In entering Kurtz's godforsaken outpost in the wilderness, Willard has equivalently stepped back into a lawless, prehistoric age where barbarism holds sway.

In fact, the severed heads that lie scattered about the grounds mutely testify to the depths of pagan savagery to which Kurtz has sunk during his sojourn in the jungle. Furthermore, it is painfully clear to Willard that, despite the fact that Kurtz's native followers revere him as a god-man, Kurtz is incurably insane.

Willard also discovers, when he at last meets Kurtz, that Kurtz is slowly dying of malaria. Hence his physical illness is symbolic of his moral sickness. When Kurtz takes Willard into custody, he is aware of the object of Willard's mission. "You are an errand boy," Kurtz scoffs, "sent by grocery clerks to collect the bill."

Malaria-ridden and delirious, Kurtz spends hours haranguing Willard about his theories of war and politics, which he maintains lie behind his becoming a rebel chieftain. Kurtz does this because he wants a brother officer to hear his side of the story. He desires to pass on to Willard the baton of his beliefs. Moreover, Kurtz ultimately wants Willard to explain to his son his father's reasons for acting as he has. Significantly, even in the depths of his madness, Kurtz has not lost sight of the preciousness of family attachments—a reflection of Coppola's perennial theme of the importance of family.

By contrast, Willard is aware in the opening scene that his wife is divorcing him and that he has lost his family. The loss of home and family, "of conventional belonging and attachment, is the context for Willard's drunken *danse macabre* in the opening scene."[59] Willard regrets the loss of family. Captain Colby, one of the deserters who has joined Kurtz, totally repudiates his family—he sends a bulletin to his wife, "Sell the house! Sell the car! Sell the kids! I'm never coming back!"

In Kurtz's own mind, the ruthless tactics he has employed to prosecute the war represent, in essence, his unshakable conviction that the only way to conquer a cruel and inhuman enemy is to become as cruel and inhuman as the enemy and to crush him by his own hideous methods.

By now Willard has definitely made up his mind to carry out his orders to kill Kurtz, and Kurtz, who has sensed from the beginning the reason Willard was sent to find him, makes no effort to stop him. As Willard reflects in his voice-over commentary on the sound track, Kurtz wants to die bravely, like a soldier, at the hands of another soldier and not to be ignominiously butchered as a wretched renegade. Indeed, in order to die like a soldier, Kurtz dons his Green Beret uniform while he is waiting for Willard to come and assassinate him.

Coppola adapted Willard's ritual slaying of Kurtz from what he calls "the classic myth of the murderer who goes up the river, kills the king, and then himself becomes the king," according to the old adage, "the king is dead; long live the king." The director unearthed this "granddaddy of all myths" in James Frazer's study of primitive tribes, *The Golden Bough: A Study of Magic and Religion* (1922), an edition of which is visible in Kurtz's quarters in the film. According to Frazer, certain primitive peoples believed that the mystic tribal leader must be killed by his successor when he becomes too feeble to continue to rule.[60]

Willard accordingly enters Kurtz's smoky lair and assassinates him with a scimitar. At the suggestion of Vittorio Storaro, who viewed the rough cut, Willard's killing of Kurtz is intercut with shots of the Cambodian tribe that is part of Kurtz's army slaughtering a sacrificial water buffalo, a scene that suggests that Willard implicitly sees his "execution" of the diabolical Kurtz for his hideous war crimes as a kind of ritual slaying.

After Willard has slain Kurtz, he pauses at Kurtz's desk and notices a typescript lying on it. We see in close-up that scrawled in red across one page is the statement, "Drop the Bomb. Exterminate them all!" This is Kurtz's manner of indicating his way of ending the Vietnam War: he would like to have seen all of the North Vietnamese soldiers and non-combatants alike destroyed from the air. Kurtz's cold-blooded statement recalls a similar passage in the novella in which Marlow peruses a report that Kurtz had prepared for the International Society for the Suppression of Savage Customs. The report ends with a postscript, presumably added much later: "Exterminate the brutes."[61] As mentioned, there remains in the film the lingering implication that Willard turns Kurtz's declaration against Kurtz's own savage army and has the bombers destroy "the brutes," although the aerial bombing is never shown.

As Willard leaves Kurtz's quarters, Kurtz's worshipful tribesmen submissively lay their weapons on the ground before him as he passes among them. Clearly, they believe that the mantle of authority has passed from their deceased leader to the man he allowed to slay him. But Willard has no desire to become Kurtz's successor. Willard, his mission accomplished, walks out of the compound and proceeds to the riverbank, where his patrol boat awaits him. As the boat pulls away from the shore, Willard hears the voice of Kurtz uttering the same phrase he had spoken just before he met his Maker: "The horror, the horror." At the end Kurtz was apparently vouchsafed a moment of lucidity in which he realized what a depraved brute he had become. To Willard the phrase represents his own revulsion at the vicious inclination to evil he had seen revealed in Kurtz—a tendency that Kurtz had allowed to overpower his better nature and render him more savage by far than the enemy he was so intent on exterminating.

Hence the theme of the movie is the same as that of Conrad's novella. "In *Apocalypse Now* just as in 'Heart of Darkness,' the central journey is both a literal and a metaphoric one," writes Joy Boyum. It is fundamentally "a voyage of discovery into the dark heart of man, and an encounter with his capacity for evil."[62] In harmony with this observation, Coppola tells me that he too "sees Willard's journey upriver as a metaphor for the voyage of life, during the course of which each of us must choose between good and evil."

Although some critics found those scenes in which Kurtz theorizes about the motivation for his unspeakable behavior wordy and overlong, most agreed that the movie contains some of the most extraordinary combat footage ever filmed. Spectacular scenes like Kilgore's helicopter attack have prompted some commentators to declare that *Apocalypse Now* towers above any war picture ever made.

Many critics show great appreciation for the cinematography. Indeed, Coppola worked out with Storaro an effective visual scheme for the movie. The scenes of the PBR going upriver, en route to Kurtz's compound, demonstrate that color photography need not be a postcardlike mimicking of natural, realistic color. The pale yellow light of a dawn or the dusky blue of a twilight represent pure visual poetry. The images have an allure all their own, and the tribal rites in Kurtz's temple compound achieve an off-kilter sort of beauty. Indeed, Storaro states in his 2003 memoir, *Writing with Light,* that he had an almost intuitive understanding of the dramatic interplay between light and dark in the film.

Besides the Grand Prize at Cannes, the picture won two Academy Awards: Vittorio Storaro won an Oscar for cinematography, and Walter Murch won for sound design. Coppola himself won a Golden Globe Award from the International Press Association in Hollywood and a British Academy Award as best director. Robert Duvall likewise won a Golden Globe and a British Academy Award as best supporting actor. Furthermore, by the late 1990s the movie had grossed nearly $200 million worldwide, exclusive of its theatrical release in an expanded version, *Apocalypse Now Redux,* in 2001.

Apocalypse Now Redux (2001)

Coppola explains in his "Director's Statement," issued when *Apocalypse Now Redux* was released, that he limited *Apocalypse Now* to two and a half hours for its original release in 1979 because he feared that the movie would otherwise be "too long and too strange" for the mass audience. "[W]e shaped the film that we thought would work for a mainstream audience of its day, making it as much a genre 'war' film as possible."[63]

In the intervening years since its original release *Apocalypse Now* had become an established American classic. When the American Film Institute picked the best one hundred American films made during the first century of cinema, *Apocalypse Now* was among them, along with *The Godfather* and *The Godfather Part II.* In releasing an expanded version of *Apocalypse Now,* Coppola banked on the fact that audiences would welcome an extended version of a picture that had enjoyed such enormous critical and popular success over the years. So Coppola and Walter Murch resurrected fifty-three minutes of original footage that had been cut from the film the first time around and dispersed it throughout *Apocalypse Now Redux,* which was appropriately unveiled at Cannes in May 2001. Although the film was not in competition this time, it was still generally regarded as one of the best films on display at the festival that year.

In *Redux* there is more of Kilgore, the obsessed martinet, since the battle scenes in which he figures are expanded in this new version. Ziesmer explains why Coppola included a shot of a Catholic chaplain celebrating Mass on a makeshift altar near a bombed-out chapel in the midst of one of the battle sequences, while helicopters are flying overhead. Coppola, recalls Ziesmer, was inspired by an image in Fellini's *La Dolce Vita* (1960) in which a chopper flies over the churches of Rome.

There is also an added scene with the Playboy bunnies on a USO tour of the battlefront, who give a show for the troops in the original cut of the film. Richard Blake, among other film historians, erroneously assumed that the second scene with the bunnies was scripted but never shot—but it was indeed filmed and then deleted from the film at the editing table, and it is restored in *Redux.*

Actually, the exteriors for the second bunny scene were shot during the torrential rains that caused the production to be shut down in 1976. Willard and his crew encounter the bunnies, sometime after the USO show, at a Medevac Camp (a medical evacuation station) in a downpour. They are stranded in their grounded chopper because it has run out of gas. Willard offers to supply them with two drums of diesel fuel in exchange for their "servicing" his men, much to the disapproval of Chief (Albert Hall), the straight-arrow pilot of Willard's PBR. "You're giving away our fuel for this playmate of the month," he chides Willard. "No, the playmate of the year!" Willard retorts with sardonic humor. On a more serious note, Coppola observes that the playmates, like Willard and his men, are in Vietnam on a mission that will degrade them, "except the girls are being exploited in sexual ways."[64]

There is one additional scene with Kurtz: Willard is listening to Kurtz scoffing at a report from *Time* magazine about how well the war is supposedly going. It is the only time we see Kurtz in daylight—for once he is not hidden in darkness, and the sunlight exposes him as the raging demon that he is.

The most substantial addition to the film is the French plantation sequence. Milius had devoted eleven pages to this episode in his script, and Coppola had extended it to twice that length in his revised screenplay. It runs close to half an hour in *Redux*. As Sheen describes it in the documentary *Hearts of Darkness*, "Willard and his team come ashore at a French rubber plantation" that is guarded by French soldiers who emerge like ghosts from the fog.

At this fog-enshrouded outpost in the jungle Willard and his men find a fractious colonial French family. Hubert DeMarais (Christian Marquand) and Roxanne Sarrault (Aurore Clément), his widowed daughter-in-law, invite them for a formal dinner in their house, a relic of the French colonial past. "They had been fighting the Vietcong long before we did, and they weren't letting go," says Sheen in the documentary.

The dinner scene, as included in the documentary, is accompanied by a voice-over that inexplicably is not in the scene as it appears in *Redux*. In his narration, Willard says, "It was like having dinner with a family of ghosts. They were trying to convince themselves that it was still 1950. They weren't French anymore; they would never be Vietnamese. They were floating loose in history without a country. They were hanging on by their fingernails, but so were we."

The ethereal Roxanne seduces Willard with opium as she murmurs to him, "There are two of you, don't you see? One who kills and one who loves." The bedroom scene is filmed in autumnal tones verging on sepia, and it dissolves to a misty dawn, when Willard and his crew must continue on their way.

That *Apocalypse Now Redux* is a unique film is borne out by the fact that only one major Hollywood film has since treated the French conflict with the Vietnamese: Phillip Noyce's *The Quiet American* (2002). Set in 1952, the movie depicts the final French defeat and withdrawal from Indochina. In the course of *The Quiet American*, Thomas Fowler, a British war correspondent, asks Alden Pyle, an American associated with the U.S. legation in Vietnam, why the United States continues to meddle in Southeast Asian affairs. Significantly, Fowler seems to be echoing Humbert DeMarais's words to Willard in Coppola's film: "Why don't you Americans learn from our mistakes?" Willard has no ready answer to offer DeMarais, just as Pyle cannot reply to Fowler in the later film.

Coppola was dissatisfied with this whole sequence when he shot it. In *Hearts of Darkness* he addresses the cast and crew on the set when the sequence is finished: "I was very unhappy with the scene on every count. Everybody forget that we ever shot it. It no longer exists." He further comments in the documentary that he was incensed because the sequence was time-consuming and costly to shoot, as Ziesmer mentions above. "I was angry at the French sequence, so I cut it out," says Coppola. During postproduction he stuck to his decision because he was convinced that he could not afford to insert a sequence that added twenty-five minutes to the film's running time.

But when he and Murch were putting together *Redux*, he wanted to include it because the journey upriver is "a journey going backward in time; and Willard and his men pass through the 1950s" at the French plantation before reaching "primordial, prehistoric times" at Kurtz's camp.[65]

Milius was gratified that both the "Medevac scene" with the bunnies and the French plantation sequence were rescued from the cutting room floor, since they both originated in his script. Unquestionably, the restored scenes in *Redux* add extra richness and complexity to the characterizations. Reviewers of *Redux* almost unanimously concur that, with the restored version of *Apocalypse Now*, Coppola had overhauled a movie that, by turns, was first thought of as Coppola's folly, then was dubbed an outstanding war movie. It now stands confirmed as a mind-blowing masterwork. Several critics included *Apocalypse Now Redux* on their year-end list of the best films of 2001, although *Apocalypse Now* was actually a 1979 release. They agreed that, by using Conrad's "Heart of Darkness" as the focus on the film, Coppola proved with *Apocalypse Now/Apocalypse Now Redux* that an auteur can, with his own personal vision, transform a literary source into a monumental motion picture.

After the excesses that marked the making of *Apocalypse Now*, Coppola, after finishing the film in 1979, said, "Sometimes I think, why don't I just make my wine" (he owns a vineyard near his Napa estate) "and do some dumbbell movie every two years?"[66] But Coppola continued making movies that mattered to him. In between *Apocalypse Now* and *Apocalypse Now Redux* he made another film about the Vietnam War, *Gardens of Stone*. It has no stunning battle sequence, since it takes place stateside. In contrast to a king-sized war epic like *Apocalypse Now*, *Gardens of Stone* tells what Coppola calls a more intimate, personal story. While *Apocalypse Now* depicts the Vietnam War itself, *Gardens of Stone*, its companion piece, is concerned with the home front during the same period.

Gardens of Stone (1987)

In the spring of 1985 Victor Kaufman, chief executive of Tri-Star Pictures, invited Coppola to a luncheon meeting at which he offered him the chance to direct *Gardens of Stone,* which Ronald Bass had adapted from the novel by Nicholas Proffitt. The novelist had served three years in the Old Guard, the venerable army unit that oversees military burials at Arlington National Cemetery near Washington, D.C. Subsequently, he was a war correspondent for *Newsweek* in Vietnam. Proffitt's novel centers on the Old Guard, and Coppola was initially attracted to the project because he had been fascinated by the splendor of army ritual since his days at a military academy as a teenager. Furthermore, Coppola, whose recent movies had not been financially successful, frankly needed money.

The plot of the novel shows how a world-weary member of the Old Guard, Sergeant Clell Hazard, is rejuvenated by his relationship with a young, idealistic cadet, Jackie Willow. Although Proffitt's book is clearly an anti-war novel, it portrays both enlisted men and officers in a much more sympathetic light than did *Apocalypse Now.* Proffitt's stance toward the military, which Bass brought over into the script, appealed to Coppola. He liked the idea of depicting the army in a more positive light than he had in his previous Vietnam film. "The whole of the army as an old institution with lots of powerful traditions that are handed down, particularly in its code of honor—I liked that part of it, and I tried to depict it."[67]

Gardens of Stone presents the benign image of the army as a large family and shows how the elders in the family endeavor to give the younger members the benefit of their experience—only to lose some of them in battle. The message Coppola extracted from the story was that "we are sworn to protect our children" and yet we keep putting them in circumstances that make that impossible, so that "you end up burying them, all dressed up in military ritual."[68]

Coppola, we remember, had had a falling out with the Pentagon over the script for *Apocalypse Now,* and he had therefore been denied the army's cooperation in making the movie. He ruefully remembers that, as a result, he was forced to rent helicopters and other military equipment from President Marcos's regime in the Philippines for exorbitant fees.[69]

In the present instance, Coppola literally could not afford to alienate the Pentagon a second time, since *Gardens of Stone* simply could not be made without access to Arlington National Cemetery and the military training base at Fort Myer that figures prominently in the story, not to mention the equipment and personnel that the army could make available.

Aware that the army had not liked *Apocalypse Now,* producer Michael Levy tactfully told a high-ranking general, "You know, Francis also wrote *Patton.*" The general responded, "That's one of my favorite pictures" and added that he was favorably impressed with the present film's scenario.[70]

Above: After serving his apprenticeship under independent producer Roger Corman, Coppola wrote and directed his first feature, *Dementia 13,* which Corman produced. The film featured Mary Mitchel and William Campbell (Museum of Modern Art/Film Stills Archive). *Below:* In the psychological thriller *Dementia 13,* the lives of newlyweds Kane (Mary Mitchel) and Richard (William Campbell), a sculptor, are threatened by a serial killer (Museum of Modern Art/Film Stills Archive).

Coppola wrote the screenplay for Jack Clayton's film of F. Scott Fitzgerald's *The Great Gatsby*, starring Mia Farrow and Robert Redford. This is the only script Coppola wrote for another director after becoming a director himself (Author's Collection).

Elizabeth Hartman and Peter Kastner in *You're a Big Boy Now,* which Coppola submitted as his master's thesis at UCLA (Ohlinger's Movie Material Store).

Fred Astaire in *Finian's Rainbow,* one of the last big Hollywood musicals (Ohlinger's Movie Material Store).

Shirley Knight as a distraught housewife in *The Rain People*. This film is considered one of the first feminist films to come out of Hollywood (Ohlinger's Movie Material Store).

James Caan as the mentally retarded hero of *The Rain People*, which won the Grand Prize at the Cannes International Film Festival (Ohlinger's Movie Material Store).

Right: Gene Hackman as Harry Caul in *The Conversation,* which won the Grand Prize at the Cannes International Film Festival (Ohlinger's Movie Material Store). *Below:* Harry Caul (Gene Hackman, far left) in *The Conversation* (Ohlinger's Movie Material Store).

Marlon Brando in the title role of *The Godfather,* which earned Academy Awards for both Francis Coppola and Brando (Museum of Modern Art/Film Stills Archive).

Above: Robert Duvall as Tom Hagen and Marlon Brando as Vito Corleone at a summit meeting of Mafia chiefs in *The Godfather* (Museum of Modern Art/Film Stills Archive). *Right:* Don Vito Corleone (Marlon Brando, right) names his son Michael (Al Pacino) as his successor in *The Godfather* (Ohlinger's Movie Material Store).

Lawyer Tom Hagen (Robert Duvall), Kay Corleone (Diane Keaton), and Michael Corleone (Al Pacino) at a Senate investigation of the Mafia in *Godfather II* (Museum of Modern Art/Film Stills Archive).

Robert De Niro won an Academy Award for playing the young Vito Corleone in the flashback sequences of *Godfather II.* Coppola received Oscars for directing the film, coauthoring the screenplay, and producing the best picture of the year.

In *Godfather II*, Michael Corleone (Al Pacino) ostensibly forgives his brother Fredo (John Cazale) for betraying him, all the while planning to have him murdered (Museum of Modern Art/Film Stills Archive).

Francis Ford Coppola (center) directs Joe Mantegna (left) and Al Pacino (right) on the set of *Godfather III* (Museum of Modern Art/Film Stills Archive).

In *Apocalypse Now*, Colonel Kurtz (Marlon Brando) is a renegade American officer who has sunk into madness during the Vietnam War (Museum of Modern Art/Film Stills Archive).

Above: Captain Willard (Martin Sheen) is captured by natives in *Apocalypse Now* (Museum of Modern Art/Film Stills Archive). *Below:* Colonel Kurtz (Marlon Brando) harangues Captain Willard (Martin Sheen) in *Apocalypse Now* (Museum of Modern Art/Film Stills Archive).

A Catholic chaplain offers Mass (center) in the extended battle scene in *Apocalypse Now Redux,* the expanded version of Coppola's film (Cinemabilia).

Jackie Willow (D. B. Sweeney), a young recruit, with officers Clell Hazard (James Caan) and Goody Nelson (James Earl Jones) in *Gardens of Stone,* Coppola's follow-up to his earlier Vietnam film, *Apocalypse Now* (Ohlinger's Movie Material Store).

Above: Frederic Forrest as Hank and Nastassia Kinski as Leila in *One from the Heart* (Ohlinger's Movie Material Store). *Below:* Teri Garr as Frannie in *One from the Heart,* Coppola's least successful film (Ohlinger's Movie Material Store).

Dallas (Matt Dillon), Ponyboy (C. Thomas Howell), and Johnny (Ralph Macchio) are buddies in *The Outsiders* (Ohlinger's Movie Material Store).

Ponyboy (C. Thomas Howell) is comforted by his brothers Sodapop (Rob Lowe) and Darrel (Patrick Swayze) after he is injured in a street fight in *The Outsiders* (Ohlinger's Movie Material Store).

Above: Mickey Rourke as Motorcycle Boy in *Rumble Fish,* Coppola's follow-up to *The Outsiders* (Ohlinger's Movie Material Store). *Below:* Patterson (William Smith), Rusty-James (Matt Dillon), and Motorcycle Boy (Mickey Rourke) in front of the clock without hands in *Rumble Fish* (Ohlinger's Movie Material Store).

Above: Richard Gere as Dixie Dwyer and James Remar as notorious gangster Dutch Schultz in *The Cotton Club* (Ohlinger's Movie Material Store). *Below:* From *The Cotton Club,* Maurice Hines as Clay Williams and Gregory Hines as Sandman Williams at the legendary Harlem nightclub of the film's title (Ohlinger's Movie Material Store).

Above: Kathleen Turner in the title role of *Peggy Sue Got Married* (Author's Collection). *Below:* Peggy Sue (Kathleen Turner) as a teenager, with her boyfriend and future husband Charlie Bodell (Nicolas Cage), in *Peggy Sue Got Married* (Ohlinger's Movie Material Store).

Francis Coppola directing *Tucker: The Man and His Dream* on location (Larry Edmond's Cinema Bookshop). Jeff Bridges in the title role of *Tucker: The Man and His Dream*, with one of his Tucker autos (Ohlinger's Movie Material Store).

Mina (Winona Ryder) is seduced by Dracula (Gary Oldman) in *Bram Stoker's Dracula* (Ohlinger's Movie Material Store).

Above: Jonathan Harker (Keanu Reeves) and Mina (Winona Ryder) in *Bram Stoker's Dracula* (Ohlinger's Movie Material Store). *Below:* Lord Arthur Holmwood (Cary Elwes), Dr. Jack Seward (Richard E. Grant), and Abraham Van Helsing (Anthony Hopkins) prepare to confront Dracula (Ohlinger's Movie Material Store).

Francis Coppola directing *Jack* (Ohlinger's Movie
Material Store).

On the set of *Jack*, Francis Coppola (immediately right of center) directs Jennifer Lopez and Robin Williams (both left) (Ohlinger's Movie Material Store).

Robin Williams discusses a scene with Coppola (Ohlinger's Movie Material Store).

Above: Coppola discusses a scene with Claire Danes (center) and Matt Damon (right) on the set of *The Rainmaker* (Museum of Modern Art/Film Stills Archive). *Below:* Matt Damon as Rudy Baylor, an idealistic young lawyer in *The Rainmaker* (Courtesy of the Academy of Motion Picture Arts and Sciences).

Deck (Danny DeVito) and Rudy (Matt Damon) discuss an insurance fraud case in *The Rainmaker* (Ohlinger's Movie Material Store).

The U.S. Army promised full cooperation with the production so long as certain adjustments were made in the script, such as limiting the amount of foul language spoken by the officers and men. Also, two brief scenes were to be excised from the screenplay. One had to do with an incident that Proffitt had himself witnessed while he was in the Old Guard: a young widow drunkenly spit on her deceased husband's grave, bellowing, "At least now I know where you are spending your nights." Another scene depicted an irritated sergeant smacking a serviceman around for failing a routine barracks inspection.

When Coppola revised the script in tandem with Bass, he complied with the army's demands. For example, Coppola altered the barracks scene so that when the sergeant raises his hand to strike the recruit Jackie intervenes and stops him. In return, Lieutenant Colonel John Meyers, who was appointed principal military adviser on the movie, provided access to Arlington National Cemetery, as well as Fort Myer in Virginia. He also supplied the U.S. Army Marching Band, six hundred enlisted men to serve as extras, plus several helicopters and other military equipment—all for reasonable fees. One journalist joked that the Army had provided Coppola with sufficient troops and material to invade a small country. Coppola freely admits that he had to compromise in order to get army cooperation on the film. Filmmaking is the art of compromise, he explains: obviously *Gardens of Stone* is more conservative in tone than *Apocalypse Now* because it was made in collaboration with the army, whereas *Apocalypse Now* was not.

While reworking the script, Coppola points out, "I was trying to be faithful to the book. I didn't want to juice the film up with superfluous plot and conflict." That explains the absence of battle scenes in the film, even when Jackie, the young hero, is shipped overseas to the front. The war is depicted solely by a series of newsreel clips shown on television back home: close-ups of the anguished faces of suffering soldiers, shots of the wounded being stowed aboard helicopters by their comrades at arms. In not foregrounding the war, Coppola admits, "you lose the benefits which such violent turbulence will give you." He was relying instead on character development rather than gratuitous excitement to involve the audience.

When he is reminded of the violent battle scenes in *Apocalypse Now,* Coppola responds that *Apocalypse Now* was *set* in Vietnam. "It was about the spectacle of destruction, of warfare, of men on the brink," soldiers in the war zone who were "out of control."[71] By contrast, *Gardens of Stone* is *about* the Vietnam War, but it is not *set* in Vietnam. He wanted to show the decent, human side of the military this time around, not the violent side.

As usual, Coppola enlisted crew members from his previous pictures, including production designer Dean Tavoularis, editor Barry Malkin, and composer Carmine Coppola, who scored the music for the military band. Gian-Carlo "Gio" Coppola, the older of Coppola's two sons, was again in charge of videotaping rehearsals so that the director could discuss various scenes with the actors. He was assisted by his buddy Griffin O'Neal, the troubled son of actor Ryan O'Neal, who had just finished a year in a drug rehabilitation program.

Once again Coppola called on actors who had appeared in his other films. James Caan, cast as an old-timer, Sergeant Clell Hazard, was emerging from a five-year hiatus from films, during which he had successfully controlled his substance abuse (something O'Neal had so far failed to do, as we shall shortly see). Yet no studio would hire Caan because he was branded as a cocaine addict, until Coppola loyally insisted on casting his old college chum in *Gardens of Stone.* "Francis—God bless him—fought very hard for me," says Caan.[72]

Sam Bottoms and Larry Fishburne, veterans of *Apocalypse Now,* were again playing Vietnam vets in the present film. Additional cast members included D. B. Sweeney as Jackie Willow and Mary Stuart Masterson as Jackie's fiancée Rachel. As a matter of fact, the young actress's parents in the film were played by her real father and mother, Peter Masterson and Carlin Glynn. Rounding out the cast was Anjelica Huston as an antiwar activist who is also a reporter for the *Washington Post.* Huston said she took her role because "it's very important to have a woman's point of view in a movie about Vietnam. We've seen all these movies that have to do with the boys going over and getting killed; but women have also suffered terribly because of the war." Echoing Coppola's remarks on the subject, she continues, "Women conceive and bear children, and then these children are sent off to be mutilated and killed. It's tragic."[73]

Before shooting started in May 1986, Coppola followed his customary procedure of putting his ensemble of players through two weeks of rehearsals, during which, Coppola explains, they engaged in improvisations as a means of developing their characters "and filling in any gaps in the script." The actors rehearsed the scenes in sequence, as if the script were a theatrical play, and the rehearsals were videotaped by Gio Coppola and his video crew. The scenes were then assembled into a full-length, preliminary version of the film, as if it were an "animated storyboard." This is what Coppola terms "the off-Broadway version of the movie," which affords the director and the cast a preview of the finished film.

Once filming began, Coppola had each scene recorded on videotape as it was shot so that he could have an instant replay of each take and make necessary adjustments before doing another take. "I use it as a kind of sketchpad," he says.[74]

Early in the shooting period, while the unit was on location in the Washington area, the production closed down to celebrate Memorial Day on May 26. Gio Coppola and Griffin O'Neal took a fourteen-foot speedboat for a spin on the South River on Chesapeake Bay, with O'Neal at the wheel. They had had wine at lunch and beer on board, so that O'Neal, whose alcohol consumption was well above the legal drinking limit, was in no condition to be steering the motorboat. He attempted to pass between two large craft, failing to notice that there was a taut towline linking them. When he slammed into the towline, Gio Coppola hit the deck hard and sustained massive cranial injuries. Gio, age twenty-three, was declared dead on arrival at Anne Arundel County General Hospital. His fiancée, Jacqueline de la Fontaine, was three months pregnant when Gio died, and she eventually gave birth to Francis Coppola's first grandchild, named Gian-Carla Coppola. O'Neal, who sustained only minor bruises, was subsequently convicted of reckless endangerment and gross negligence (not manslaughter, as some news reports said). He was sentenced to 416 hours of community service, eighteen months of probation, and a paltry two-hundred-dollar fine.

Two days after Gio's death, a memorial service took place in the military chapel at Fort Myer, where Coppola was filming. This writer was among the countless people in the film world who sent him their condolences at the time. Coppola announced that shooting would resume. He was confident that Gio would have wished that he finish the picture, "since he had worked with me. God gave me Gio and God has taken him away."[75] Nevertheless, Coppola collapsed on the set shortly after the resumption of filming, and his physician ordered him to rest for five days, after which he proceeded with the shoot. Roman Coppola, Gio's younger brother, took over Gio's responsibility for videotaping the scenes as they were shot.

Coppola kept his grief in check by working steadily. Only three weeks after Gio's demise, Coppola was back filming scenes in the same chapel where his son's funeral had taken place. The director mused afterward that he has often found that the movies he makes reflect a good deal of what is happening in his own life at the time. Still, he never dreamed that the making of *Gardens of Stone* would affect his own life so profoundly. "I had to do a movie about the burial of young men," and suddenly he found that "my own boy would die right in the midst of it, and the funeral ceremony would be in the same chapel where we shot a similar scene in *Gardens of Stone*."[76] In his journal he later recorded, "My son Gio is gone, but his memory is not. His laughter lives on in his daughter Gia. It is amazing how much she is like him."[77]

The eight-week shoot wrapped on August 5, 1986, right on schedule and just slightly over the $13.5 million budget. After completing a number of movies, Coppola says, he understands how prolific directors like John Ford (*Stagecoach*) turned out so many high-quality movies in the old days. "As you get more experienced," he observes, "I think you work faster."[78]

When Coppola moved into postproduction, he collaborated closely with editor Barry Malkin, who had worked on *Apocalypse Now*. Malkin agreed with Coppola that the film "was an elegy of sorts, since it was about death. . . . It's brooding, purposely so. In my first cut I constructed certain sequences to exactly document the way the honor guard did their ceremonies" when burying their fallen comrades. This is because "it was impressed on me that in the end the army . . . would look at the cuts and make sure we had done them properly. So the first time I put the sequences together, I followed the ceremonial rites to a tee."[79]

In filming these burial rites, Coppola had been at pains to capture the grandeur and pace of the ritual, but preview audiences found these scenes tedious. "A young audience—and young audiences are pretty much what you get in these previews—saw these scenes" as just a lot of marching, he explains, "so we had to modulate these drills."[80] In the end, adds Malkin, "we were allowed" by the military advisers "to skip over parts of the ceremonies because they took too long."[81]

Gardens of Stone opens with Lieutenant Jackie Willow's military funeral at Arlington National Cemetery, near the Tomb of the Unknown Soldier, complete with a twenty-one-gun salute. The American flag is removed from the casket, folded, and presented to Rachel, Jackie's young widow, who is flanked by her parents. Jackie reads his last letter home, voice-over on the sound track. It is addressed to Clell Hazard. "This may be my last letter," he says. "You tried to tell me how it was, but I was too young." Jackie speaks with the detached perspective of the dead. This is one of the few instances in cinema history in which a film opens with a character talking from beyond the grave. Billy Wilder's *Sunset Boulevard* (1950) is another salient example.

In this fashion Jackie introduces the extended flashback that covers the events leading up to his funeral, and it is to his funeral that the movie returns at the film's conclusion. Hence, Jackie's obsequies serve as the narrative frame for the entire picture. The story proper begins in flashback a year earlier, with Jackie arriving at Fort Myer as a trainee. He soon encounters Sergeant Clell Hazard, a combat veteran who has become increasingly demoralized as he observes the Army futilely waging a war in Vietnam he is convinced is unwinnable. "I care about the U.S. Army," he says to a friend.

"That's my family. The only one I got. And I don't like it when my family is in trouble." It is clear that Hazard has always defined his self-image in terms of his membership in the armed forces.

After four years in Vietnam, Hazard is now a member of the Old Guard, a special unit that serves as the honor guard for the burials at Arlington National Cemetery (the gardens of stone) of servicemen killed in Vietnam. In practice this can involve participation in as many as fifteen funerals a day. Hazard is convinced that the experience he has gained from his tours of duty, both in Korea and in Vietnam, is being squandered. He would much prefer to train cadets for combat so that his expertise could well save some lives.

Depressed by the continuing loss of so many young lives, Hazard sardonically tells Jackie Willow, a young recruit in the Old Guard, that burying is their business and business has never been better. Bright-eyed, impetuous Jackie insists that the war is not lost and that the right kind of soldier could make a difference. Hazard, on the other hand, thinks Jackie far too idealistic nd tells him so repeatedly. Nonetheless, the rambunctious lad is itching to plunge into the fray in order to do whatever he can to help win the war.

Since Jackie is the son of an old comrade of Hazard's in Korea, Hazard nurtures paternal solicitude for the young man and discourages him from volunteering for combat. To no avail. Jackie in due course is shipped overseas, where he is killed in action just a few weeks before he completes his tour of duty. During the ceremonies at graveside for Jackie, we can hear a couple of the younger members of the Old Guard muttering their favorite jingle: "Ashes to ashes and dust to dust; / Let's get this over and get back in the bus." Jackie no doubt recited this same impish little ditty when he was part of the ceremonial guard.

Hazard is divorced and has lost custody of his son to his ex-wife. It is not surprising, then, that Jackie had become a surrogate son for Hazard during their time together in the Old Guard. So he feels as if he has indeed lost a son when Jackie is killed. The aging soldier remembers that Jackie had dreamed of winning the Combat Infantry Badge while he was in Vietnam but did not live long enough to receive one. Hence Hazard places his own C.I.B. on Jackie's coffin before the interment, equivalent to a gift from father to son. Hazard also decides, in the wake of Jackie's death, to return to the battleground in Vietnam in the hope that he can teach other young fighting men everything he knows about how to survive under fire, since he never got the chance to help Jackie in this way.

Coppola explains that he ultimately decided to make this muted, elegiac film about the special ceremonial unit of the army because it is consistent with the theme that frequently appears in his films, the significance of family. To be precise, he valued the opportunity to present an in-depth portrayal of servicemen as a sort of family whose members are bound together by a traditional code of honor and by mutual loyalty and affection. In short, his goal in making the film was to limn military men, not as conventional movie stereotypes, but as complicated human beings. He accomplished this task quite satisfactorily, as reflected in the solid characterizations of Clell Hazard and Jackie Willow and in the subtle father-son relationship that gradually develops between them. Coppola portrays very warmly the fatherly relationship of the tough old sergeant and the enthusiastic young rookie so that we cannot help but care about them.

Critical reaction to *Gardens of Stone* was very reserved indeed, with most reviewers praising individual aspects of the film, but not the whole show. For example, Jordan Cronenweth's cinematography was lauded for giving the movie a mellow, autumnal look with its muted, pastel tints. (More than one critic pointed out that the melancholy tone of the picture could be attributed to some extent to the personal tragedy that had intervened in Coppola's life while he was making the movie. Coppola once again demonstrated his skill in drawing the best from his actors, as with Caan's sturdy performance as the grizzled veteran, matched by Sweeney's smart, alert portrayal of a recruit.

But the film as a whole was thought to rely too much on character and mood and not enough on dynamic storytelling. Coppola himself confessed that he was aware of this problem from the get-go: "I was trying to orchestrate a piece that didn't have a strong narrative," and it showed.[82] It seemed that Coppola strained too hard to wring pathos out of the melancholy tale. For example, Jackie's funeral, which frames the picture, appeared to be designed to squeeze every last tear from the tragedy. In the end, *Gardens of Stone* was judged to be no more than workmanlike moviemaking.

Inevitably *Gardens of Stone* was compared to *Apocalypse Now*, much to the later film's disadvantage. Referring to Jackie's funeral, Richard Blake asked, "Why did Coppola, whose own strong *Apocalypse Now* presented a searing portrait of Vietnam and its corrosive effects on human values, turn to sentimentality in *Gardens of Stone*?[83] The film's somber vision was to some degree responsible for its dismal performance at the box office. Coppola consoled himself with a "Certificate of Appreciation for Patriotic Civilian Service" from the Army, which endorsed the film as displaying the devotion to duty and strong leadership that characterizes the United States Army.

Coppola concedes that he probably would not have chosen to make *Gardens of Stone* had it not been for the fact that the film production studio he had launched in the early 1980s had collapsed into bankruptcy. In order to pay his debts, he was compelled to become a "hired gun," working non-stop on a variety of projects to pay his bills. The next section of this study will examine how Coppola's dream of owning and operating his own studio as a haven for independent filmmakers turned into a nightmare.

Part Three

Artist in
an Industry

7

Exiled in Eden

One from the Heart

There is no point in hating Hollywood. That would be like hating the Sphinx. It's just there, and it will go on being there, whether you like it or not.

—Ken Russell, film director

Hollywood is still held together by palm trees, telephone wires, and hope.

—John Schlesinger, film director

Although both of the *Godfather* films were productions originated by Paramount Pictures, Coppola continued to maintain his own independent production company through which he initiated projects, such as *Apocalypse Now,* that he arranged to finance, shoot, and release in cooperation with various major studios. He initially named this operation, which he established in San Francisco in 1969, American Zoetrope, after the primitive mechanism that was a forerunner of the motion picture projector.

In 1980 he purchased the old Hollywood General Studios in the heart of the film colony, which had all the elaborate technical facilities necessary for shooting a motion picture that his San Francisco setup did not have. He christened his new acquisition Zoetrope Studios and envisioned it as similar to a repertory theater company where a group of artists and technicians would collaborate in making movies together.

He had passed the studio every day as a high school student during the period when the family lived in Los Angeles, and now it was his. Since *One from the Heart* was to be the first film Coppola directed at his own studio, it is important to outline the inauguration of Zoetrope Studios at this point before discussing the film itself.

Zoetrope Studios

Hollywoodites talked about Coppola's empire-building with tolerant chuckles, and one industry insider quoted the old adage about directors who started their own studios: "The lunatics are taking over the asylum." Even George Lucas criticized his former mentor for buying a studio in Hollywood. "I thought Francis was betraying all of us in San Francisco who had been struggling to make this community a viable film alternative," he said at the time.[1] For his part, Lucas had set up Lucasfilm, his independent film company, in Mill Valley in the Bay area, a good distance from Hollywood. Coppola replied that his office complex at the Sentinel Building in San Francisco would continue to be the principal base of operations for his independent film unit, though shooting would be done at Zoetrope Studios in Hollywood.

Coppola envisioned his high-tech studio in Hollywood as a paradise for creative production specialists, who would function independent of the suffocating Hollywood establishment. "This feeling of being a part of a family, this closeness would be stimulating to professionals," he said.[2] Among the "family members" would be Zoetrope regulars like production designer Dean Tavoularis and sound specialist Walter Murch.

Coppola officially purchased the ten-acre movie lot on the corner of Santa Monica Boulevard at Las Palmas Avenue on March 25, 1980. He embarked on his daring enterprise by putting up $7.6 million for the studio by means of some cash and several mortgages on his assets. The studio housed nine sound stages, several office suites, thirty-four editing rooms, and a special-effects shop, plus ample rehearsal space. He also used his personal fortune, which was largely derived from his share in the profits of the first two *Godfather* films, to renovate the studio. Built in 1919, Hollywood General was one of the oldest studios in town. It had fallen into disrepair in recent years since its glory days, when silent screen comedian Harold Lloyd made *Grandma's Boy* there in 1922 and British director Michael Powell directed *The Thief of Bagdad* there in 1939. Coppola borrowed an additional $3 million to modernize the facility with the latest technical equipment. He hired 184 employees, including office staff and film technicians.

The purchase of Hollywood General Studios implicitly represented an endeavor on Coppola's part to put the auteur theory into practice in a significant manner by making and releasing his own pictures. The purpose of owning his own studio, Coppola explains, "was simply to own the rights to my movies."[3] He took over the bungalow on the lot that was once used by Lloyd and was still named for him.

Robert Spiotta, a fellow Hofstra alumnus with business experience as an executive of Mobil Oil, was named president of Zoetrope Studios. Lucy Fisher, a former vice president at Twentieth Century-Fox, was named vice president. Mona Skager, who had been with American Zoetrope from the beginning, continued as a production executive, and Coppola appointed himself artistic director.

The fact remained that Coppola simply could not afford to produce and distribute a film without the financial backing of one of the major studios. "He understood that his (and his studio's) future still depended on industry financing," says Jon Lewis in a book-length study of Coppola's studio. He would also need to negotiate "bank loans secured against his own future film revenues."[4] The first film on the production docket that he planned to direct himself was *One from the Heart,* a romantic comedy with songs set in Las Vegas.

Coppola was determined to run Zoetrope Studios more efficiently than he had run American Zoetrope in its early days in the 1970s (see chapter 3). Indeed, back in the spring of 1977, he had addressed a memorandum to the staff of American Zoetrope expressing his displeasure at the lack of organization in the operation of the film unit at the headquarters in the Sentinel Building in San Francisco.

Some Coppola commentators describe the memo as paranoid. Yet it begins with a tactful introduction that hardly smacks of paranoia: "I realize that . . . it must be difficult for people who are working with me to understand exactly what I expect of them." He goes on to establish the point that "we will maintain these facilities in order to better realize my own projects" exclusively. In the future, "we will not be in the service business." His point was that when he founded American Zoetrope in 1969 as an independent production unit he planned to have a number of young directors making films there. That meant that the resources of the facility were eventually stretched thin. Furthermore, some of the aspiring filmmakers whom Coppola had taken under his wing were not experienced enough in their craft to handle expensive equipment properly, and some equipment was damaged or lost.

He added that "it is very important for me to dispel the seven-year ambience of a happy hangout around the old American Zoetrope." Coppola thought that the atmosphere sometimes seemed to be that of a frat house rather than of a film organization: "I expect people to dress and behave as they would for any other company." He was not, after all, running a film school for wanna-be moviemakers or sponsoring other filmmakers' work. "The era of American Zoetrope being a Haven for young filmmakers . . . to find a home is really no longer in the cards." In short, Coppola's dream of American Zoetrope as a community of film directors had proved impractical and had finally evaporated. Gone were the days when, as George Lucas puts it, Coppola would hand a camera to any zealous young filmmaker who showed up at the front door (see chapter 3).

Occasionally, he added, he would allow an established director to make a film for American Zoetrope. Indeed, he planned to have German director Wim Wenders direct *Hammett* for American Zoetrope. Nevertheless, American Zoetrope would continue to be fundamentally a one-client organization, "and the sooner we are able to gear ourselves to that fact, the better the company will run."

In reference to the criticism he had received in the press for the budget overruns on *Apocalypse Now,* he declared, "I know that the amounts of money I deal in seem unreal to most people—they do to me as well. But please always remember that I work with these amounts because I am willing to risk everything for my own creative work. . . . I am cavalier about money because I have to be, in order not to be terrified every time I make an artistic decision." The memo concludes: "I have heard that success is as difficult to deal with as failure—perhaps more so. Euripides, the Greek playwright, said thousands of years ago: 'Whom God wishes to destroy, he first makes successful in show business.'"[5] (What Euripides really said was, "Whom Jupiter wishes to destroy, he makes crazy.")

The memo was unfortunately leaked by a disgruntled employee to the *San Francisco Chronicle* and was subsequently reprinted in full in *Esquire* magazine. Asked about this memorandum, Coppola explains that he composed it because he was unhappy about "the infighting among the staff at American Zoetrope. I wanted to organize American Zoetrope more efficiently, and wrote this memo to make my position clear. Then it was published and a lot of people in the industry ridiculed me, because I sounded like a desperate guy trying to hold onto his company." If he seems paranoid, he concludes, it was because he "was scared"—frightened that he might indeed lose control of his independent film company. In actual fact, Coppola had every reason to spell out his priorities for his staff. It was even more imperative that his independent film unit run efficiently now that he had his own studio and was about to put *One from the Heart* into production.

One from the Heart (1982)

Armyan Bernstein's screenplay for *One from the Heart* was set in Chicago, but Coppola decided to move the story to Las Vegas. He viewed Las Vegas as a fabulous town that would provide a more romantic atmosphere for a love story than a midwestern metropolis like Chicago. He also decided to add songs to the film to lend the love story a more lyrical quality.

Coppola was familiar with legendary Las Vegas as an interesting setting for a film from making the first two *Godfather* films in which the Corleones move to Las Vegas to exploit the lucrative business enterprises available to them there. Unlike the Corleones, the central characters in *One from the Heart* are average middle-class types who have come to Las Vegas with more modest aspirations.

It somehow seems appropriate that a director who was willing to risk the future of his studio on an expensive production like *One from the Heart* should set the film in Las Vegas, the gambling capital of America. Still, Coppola was known for bringing in dark horses as winners in the past, as he had done with unpromising projects like the *Godfather* films and *Apocalypse Now*.

Coppola decided to shoot *One from the Heart* at Zoetrope Studios rather than on location in Las Vegas. Slogging through the mud in the Philippine jungles while making *Apocalypse Now*, "I realized I wanted to make films in a studio again," he explained. He described the picture as a modest effort, like "a student film on a studio scale."[6] Coppola commissioned Tom Waits to write nine jazzy/bluesy songs for his "fable with music," as Coppola called it. The songs, which would be sung on the sound track by the composer and country balladeer Crystal Gayle, were meant to comment on what was happening to the characters. Coppola brought in legendary movie hoofer Gene Kelly (*Singin' in the Rain*) to supervise the dance numbers, which were to be choreographed by Kenny Ortega, Kelly's protégé. Vittorio Storaro, ace cinematographer on *Apocalypse Now*, agreed to shoot *One from the Heart*.

Since Coppola was committed to shooting *One from the Heart* on the sound stages at Zoetrope Studios, Dean Tavoularis got going on constructing a number of mammoth sets. He employed 350 union construction workers, including 200 carpenters, to build a residential neighborhood, a section of McCarran Airport, and a desert motel. The most fabulous set that Tavoularis created was the mind-boggling replica of the Vegas Strip of casinos along Fremont Street. It encompassed miles of neon lights and a paved intersection (the neon lights alone on the expensive set cost $1 million). Tavoularis also had a detailed scale model of Las Vegas made for use in long shots. The sets covered nine sound stages in all. Without a doubt, Tavoularis's cityscape added a touch of gloss to the movie. The overall budget of the movie, including the costumes for the Vegas nightclub shows that figure in the film, was computed to be $15 million. So much for Coppola's "student film" on a studio scale.

Everyone agreed that the sets were spectacular. Mona Skager, associate producer on the film, explained that Coppola wanted *One from the Heart* to be filled with elaborate sets and costumes so as to be a glamorous feast for the eye. Still, some of the staff wondered if a lightweight love story needed to be staged in such grandiose terms.

Mindful of the spiraling budget, Coppola decided to avoid paying superstars astronomical salaries—he had not forgotten Brando's hefty salary for *Apocalypse Now*. Hence Coppola hired relative unknowns in the leads: Teri Garr (*The Conversation*) was cast as Frannie; Frederic Forrest (*Apocalypse Now*) as Hank, her live-in lover; Raul Julia as Ray, a lounge waiter that Frannie is enamored with; and Nastassia Kinski as Leila, a high-wire artist who has run away from the circus, to whom Hank is attracted. Nevertheless, some Zoetrope staffers were concerned that the film's principal actors might not have enough marquee value to draw the mass audience to the picture.

The simple plot of the film turns on Hank, a tough guy with a soft center, and Frannie, his tart-tongued lover, who have grown bored with one another. The story takes place on Independence Day weekend, and both seem to want to be independent of each other. Frannie, who is employed in a travel agency, fantasizes about going off to the tropics with a handsome male. Hank, who runs an auto repair shop and junkyard, daydreams about a romantic adventure with a gorgeous girl. Everyone collides, sexually and emotionally, in the course of the film, and Hank and Frannie seek to clean up the mess they have made of their relationship at the fade-out.

Coppola describes *One from the Heart* as a "musical parable about a couple being together, breaking apart, each having an affair, and getting back together again." One of the reasons he was attracted to the scenario was that it dealt with the temporary breakup of a long-term relationship. He had lived through a similar experience during the making of *Apocalypse Now*, as we know, and it was still fresh in his mind (see chapter 6). To that extent, making the movie was a form of "therapy" for him.[7]

Coppola planned the production with great care. He began by having storyboard sketches made for the individual shots, amounting to five hundred drawings. Then he had the storyboards photographed on videotape and recorded actors reading the lines for each scene. In this way, the storyboards seemed to come to life. This technique gave Coppola a rough draft of the final film. The next step was to transport the cast to Las Vegas, where they spent two days doing a walk-through of the script in authentic locations. This run-through was also videotaped. Viewing the videotape afterward gave Coppola the opportunity to fix a scene that was not working satisfactorily before he actually shot it in the studio. He termed the videotaped storyboards and the videotaped run-through the "previsualization process" of the movie. He likened the technique to the dress rehearsal of a play in the theater, thereby reminding us once again that he started out at Hofstra University as a theater major.

When shooting commenced on February 2, 1981, Coppola had a silver Airstream trailer, which he christened the "Silverfish," stationed near the set. It was filled with high-definition TV monitors, control boards, and microphones. "I'm rarely in the van during an actual take," he explained to Lillian Ross when she visited the set, "but in the van afterward I can review each shot and know right away whether I want to . . . make a change in a scene.[8] The system, which he dubbed "electronic cinema," allowed Coppola to make a preliminary edit of each scene when it was filmed.

For the record, Scott Haller, who also visited the set, observed that Coppola all too often directed scenes from inside the Silverfish—more often than he had led Ross to believe. In directing a scene from the trailer, according to Haller, Coppola's disembodied voice issued directions, which were relayed to cast members on the set "via a loud speaker, for everyone to hear."[9] Teri Garr told me (during a brief interview when she was working on another film) that some of the actors complained that they found it disturbing that the director was sequestered in an off-stage control booth. His voice was amplified over a public address system, as if he were Jupiter on Mount Olympus or the Wizard of Oz. Garr herself felt somewhat uneasy with a "remote-control" director: "We couldn't talk back to him. We just listened and took direction. We felt like puppets."

Coppola later countered that he was on the set to rehearse the actors before a scene was filmed and only retreated to the Silverfish when they were ready to do a take so he could watch it on the monitor. Be that as it may, as shooting progressed, this method of directing generated so much tension on the set that some of the cast whispered that "Big Brother is watching you." Consequently, Coppola gradually tapered off from using this technique toward the end of filming.

Another departure from the conventional way of shooting a film—besides "previsualization" and "electronic cinema"—that Coppola employed was to shoot many unbroken takes, lasting up to ten minutes apiece. Coppola, collaborating with Storaro, kept the camera on the go during these extended takes, as it unobtrusively glided from one character to another, closing in at times to capture a key gesture or remark then falling back for a medium or long shot as the action and dialogue continued. In this fashion, the camera would draw the filmgoer into the scene and explore the action at close range and not simply remain a remote observer watching the action from a distance like a spectator at a stage play.

Coppola was convinced that an extended take, uninterrupted by the customary cuts to other angles, enabled his actors to give a sustained performance throughout a scene and thus build it steadily to a dramatic climax. One thinks, for example, of the quarrel scene early in the movie that peaks with Frannie walking out on Hank, which was done as a long take.

In order to capture the ambiance of Las Vegas during a festive Fourth of July celebration, Coppola and Storaro gave the film a bright look, often using saturated colors—pulsating magentas and gaudy oranges. Indeed, the film is sumptuously shot, and Coppola's virtuosity and visual flair are never in doubt.

As filming continued, friction developed on the set between Coppola and Gene Kelly, who was lending Kenny Ortega a hand in staging the dance numbers. Kelly was distraught when Coppola called for an assortment of extras to mill around the Vegas street set during a production number. Coppola maintained that the extras added color to the scene, whereas Kelly contended that they merely got in the way of the dance chorus.

Their tempers really erupted when Coppola ordered Kelly to choreograph a dance routine for Nastassia Kinski, which was to be shot the following day. Kelly stubbornly maintained that it would take him several days to work out the number and rehearse Kinski adequately. When Coppola stuck to his guns and demanded that the number be ready the next day, Kelly stormed off the set. In fairness to Coppola, it should be noted that Tommy Tune, a dancer in *Hello Dolly!* (1969), the last musical Kelly himself directed, told me that Kelly gave him several weeks to learn a dance routine that he could have mastered in an afternoon. At any rate, Kelly subsequently dissociated himself from *One from the Heart* and eventually issued a statement that declared, "In no way does *One from the Heart* represent any of my choreography.[10] (One recalls that Coppola had a falling out with choreographer Hermes Pan on his earlier musical, *Finian's Rainbow,* which likewise ended with director and choreographer parting company.)

In early February 1981, Paramount had agreed to distribute the film. They offered an advertising budget and promised prints to theaters across the country on February 10, 1982. Armed with the Paramount distribution deal, Coppola obtained a loan from Chase Manhattan Bank to finance production. According to Lillian Ross—who charts the financing and marketing of *One from the Heart* with mind-numbing documentation—Chase Manhattan Bank loaned Zoetrope Studios a total of $19 million. "Then we borrowed $3 million from Jack Singer, a Canadian investor, who is primarily in the real estate business," Robert Spiotta told Ross, "and we put up the studio as collateral." That was enough financial backing to put the picture on forward drive.

As the production period wore on, however, the costly sets and costumes, plus the endless rehearsal necessary for blocking out the complicated lengthy takes, added up to one inescapable fact: the picture was falling way behind schedule and going over budget in a way that recalled the dog days on *Apocalypse Now*. Assistant director Jerry Ziesmer, we remember, observed that no one wanted to say "No" to Coppola, even when the production costs of *Apocalypse Now* skyrocketed. Similarly, Mona Skager, associate producer of *One from the Heart*, states that Coppola had gathered around him a group of "yes men" who never questioned his decisions or procedures.

One day, however, Skager confronted Coppola, pointing out that "*One from the Heart* started at $15 million; and the way it is going, I don't think it's $15 million; I think it's $23 million." She adds, "He really got upset with me."[11] "I was running a movie studio that had no money," Coppola explains. "As we went along in shooting *One from the Heart*, we were always short of money." As a result, "everybody at Zoetrope took a big pay cut; they were wonderful."[12] Because of the cash-flow crisis, studio employees accepted half pay. What's more, at a critical moment, when Coppola failed to meet the weekly payroll, he held a meeting at which he explained his financial predicament and asked the employees if he could defer paying their wages for a couple of weeks. Studio workers voted against the wishes of their unions that they walk off the picture and shut down production. Someone shouted, "We're with you!" This display of loyalty reduced Coppola to tears. It seems that the studio employees were impressed that Coppola was willing to invest his own money and personal property in the movie. It was around this time that they started sporting buttons proclaiming the credo, "I Believe in Francis C." Coppola emphasized that "all these people were paid in full eventually," but their attitude at the time was quite generous.[13]

The actual filming, which began on February 2, 1981, stopped on

March 31. But then Coppola began to rethink and redesign certain key scenes and resumed filming after three weeks, adding thirty-two days to the shooting schedule. Filming was finally finished on June 29. The making of *One from the Heart* involved seventy-nine days of rehearsals and seventy-two days of shooting.

"After that the film went into postproduction." In all, two hundred thousand feet of film had been shot, which Coppola had to pare down during postproduction to ten thousand feet for a final cut. "We were over budget by $4 million," notes Spiotta. Consequently, "Chase Manhattan had to provide further funds in the form of personal loans guaranteed by Mr. Coppola, . . . utilizing as collateral just about everything he has," including his 1,700-acre estate in the Napa Valley."[14] Because Coppola had over the years sunk most of his funds into real estate, he had little ready cash—an accountant would say that he had a shortage of liquid funds. "My home telephone has been shut off," he declared, "because I haven't been able to pay my bill."[15] The first time that happened was when he was an impoverished graduate student at UCLA two decades before.

When he was asked why he did not turn to George Lucas, his erstwhile protégé, for financial backing, Coppola replied, "My friendship with George is such that . . . he would help me in other ways. George is a friend, not in a money-lending way, but more in the way of giving me a lift to the airport when I needed it." Lucas, who was made rich by *Star Wars,* responded that, "if Francis needed help, he only had to ask for it. He never did," even when Lucas offered him an "interest-free loan."[16] Possibly Coppola did not want to trade on his friendship with Lucas.

Veteran editor Rudi Fehr worked on the film during postproduction. When Coppola made *Finian's Rainbow* and *The Rain People* for Warners, Fehr was in charge of postproduction there, "and Mr. Coppola and I hit it off very well."[17] After Fehr retired from Warners, Coppola asked him to supervise the edit of *One from the Heart,* working with two other editors in order to meet the deadline for finishing postproduction.

Coppola decided to take a print of the still-unfinished film to Seattle for a sneak preview in the spring of 1981. Fehr strongly advised him against previewing the film when optical effects like dissolves and fades had yet to be achieved and some of the songs were still missing from the sound track. He pointed out that Jack Warner believed that a picture should not be previewed "until you can put your best foot forward, when you have everything ready. If you and I don't know what's wrong with the picture, . . . you can't ask an amateur audience to tell you what's wrong with it."[18]

But Coppola was adamant about the preview since he wanted some

preliminary feedback from an audience. He chose Seattle for the sneak because he wished to avoid previewing the film in the Los Angeles area, where
a local newspaper critic might see it and write a premature review in a
major metropolitan daily (something that had happened when he test-
screened *Apocalypse Now* in Los Angeles, much to Coppola's chagrin at the
time). As it happened, Richard Jameson, a local Seattle critic, caught the
sneak preview of the movie and wrote a review for *Film Comment,* a film
journal, but at least his remarks were not published in a big L.A. daily.

Before the Seattle screening Coppola asked the audience to make al-
lowances for the fact that the film still needed some finishing touches. Then
he invited them "to participate in a revolutionary experience—to play an
actual part in the making of a major motion picture" by giving him their
comments on preview cards.

Jameson's own remarks in *Film Comment* foreshadowed the critical
reaction to the picture at the time of its official release: that Coppola was
unduly interested in the technical side of filmmaking, that the elaborate
long takes, large-scale sets and fancy costumes dwarfed the small-scale love
story. The film's title is ironic, wrote Jameson, since Coppola has "heart
trouble." "The heart this movie proceeds from is cold" in that "the film
suggests very little caring about the real-life dilemmas of its amorous search-
ers."[19] Moreover, Jameson reported, lobby comments on the part of some
of the filmgoers afterward coincided with his own reaction to the picture.
The lukewarm reaction to the test screening of the film unquestionably
influenced Coppola's decision, mentioned already, to resume shooting in
April.

When Coppola was finishing postproduction on New Year's Eve, 1981,
he decided to hold a final public screening of the movie at Manhattan's
cavernous Radio City Music Hall, known as "the showplace of the nation."
He wanted to draw attention to the film and had employed a similar tactic
when he showed *Apocalypse Now* in Cannes. As was the case with *Apocalypse Now,* he was worried that *One from the Heart* was being prejudged in
the press, that reports about escalating budgets and extended shooting
schedules might hurt the picture. "I just wanted a chance to show *One from
the Heart* clean to an audience one time before it went into the funnel" of
distribution, he said.[20] Nevertheless, Paramount was dismayed by Coppola's
snap decision to personally schedule a public preview of the movie without
even consulting them—just as United Artists had been against the Cannes
screening of *Apocalypse Now* (see chapter 6). Furthermore, Paramount was
already annoyed with Coppola because of the multiple delays in delivering
the picture to them.

Coppola scheduled two evening screenings of the picture on January 14, 1982, which were attended by six thousand people who were anxious to see what Coppola had wrought. After the first screening Coppola held a press conference in a backstage rehearsal studio, attended by major movie critics and journalists from several cities. Coppola "took the first question square in the face and bled as if it had been a brick." A radio reporter said that he had not interviewed anyone after the screening who had liked the picture. Coppola replied that "there weren't many walkouts" and that "a lot of people who spoke to me told me it was an unusual and beautiful picture." And so it went. He concluded the press conference with an exhortation to the press to support filmmakers in their efforts to make quality pictures. "Why don't we all *cheer the filmmakers on?*"[21] Coppola reflected after the press conference that, given the negative tone of some of the questions, it was evident that many of the journalists present "had already formulated their opinion, even before we had the preview."[22]

Paramount, as mentioned, was no longer on good terms with Coppola, and he announced at the press conference that he had terminated his distribution agreement with the studio. On January 29, he declared that Columbia Pictures would distribute *One from the Heart.* Columbia took over the advertising campaign for the picture and agreed to supply twenty-five prints of the film, which would be booked into forty-one theaters in eight major cities, including New York, Chicago, and Los Angeles. It would open on schedule on February 10, 1982.

After a brief release on videotape in 1983, the film disappeared. *One from the Heart* was not available on TV or home video for two decades, until it was released on DVD in 2004. Since the movie was out of circulation for so long, it is appropriate to summarize the scenario in some detail. The picture opens with a blue theater curtain parting—a stage convention that suggests that the film goes all out for artifice. A paper moon is seen floating in the sky with the film's title superimposed on it. The opening credits are presented most inventively; they appear on the neon signs outside the Vegas casinos.

We soon meet Frannie, a plain Jane who works in the Paradise Travel Agency and fantasizes about going to Tahiti. Hank, her equally unattractive live-in lover, runs an auto repair shop and junkyard called Reality Wreckers and dreams of making a success of the business. It is the eve of the anniversary of their meeting on the Fourth of July weekend five years before.

In one of the extended takes that Coppola employs throughout the film, Storaro's camera starts out at a high angle above a residential street, then gradually cranes downward to follow Frannie from her car to the shabby bungalow she inhabits with Hank. Along the way the groceries she is carrying fall out of the bags onto the sidewalk. The camera then tracks behind her as she trudges through the messy dining room and kitchen, while Crystal Gayle sings on the sound track, "I'm sick and tired of picking up after you." Hank arrives home shortly afterward.

They begin to bicker, as Frannie complains that Hank has gained weight, and Hank retorts that she no longer shaves her legs—they both have neglected their physical appearance. Clearly, they take each other for granted and their life together has grown stale. "Life has to be more than this," Frannie says laconically, "if this is it, it's not enough."

As they continue to exchange mutual recriminations, Frannie finally says that she is going to leave Hank. He replies disconsolately, "My folks were always fighting, but they knew they loved each other, and they were together. But nowadays you just move on. Ain't nobody committed to nothing but having a good time." Hank and Frannie represent the sort of touching losers and dreamers who live on the fringe of any big city. They are the typical outsiders who yearn to be insiders but lack the talent and initiative to realize their dreams. Hence they remain on the outside looking in, jealous of the big-time spenders they see in downtown Las Vegas and dissatisfied with a monotonous existence they have grown tired of. For them the American Dream is tarnished.

Their domestic argument ends with Frannie stomping out of the house to stay overnight with her friend Maggie (Lainie Kazan), while Hank spends the night in the flat of his friend Moe (Harry Dean Stanton). While Moe commiserates with Hank in Moe's living room, the wall behind them is suddenly revealed to be a gauze scrim. It becomes transparent as the lights come up on Frannie and Maggie, who become visible through the scrim as they discuss her breakup with Hank. Coppola utilized the scrim effect in order to glide smoothly from a scene with Hank to a scene with Frannie, but some critics complained that the device calls attention to itself, rather than to the characters.

The following evening Frannie and Hank are back home, dressing to go out on a date—but not with each other. The gloomy atmosphere of the scene is underscored by Tom Waits vocalizing on the sound track, "I'm just a scarecrow without you / Baby please don't disappear." Frannie has an assignation with Ray (Raul Julia), a suave Latino who is a singing waiter in a piano bar, while Hank plans to pair up with Leila (Nastassia Kinski), a glamorous circus acrobat. Ray dances with Frannie and sings her a sultry ballad in the Tropical Club where he works, then they dance a tango down the glittering, sizzling Vegas strip, with passersby joining in as a dance chorus. This is, of course, the film's big production number. Meanwhile, Hank takes Leila to his junkyard, where she performs for him. She begins her specialty number by tap dancing atop the hood of his convertible and then soars above him as she does her highwire act.

At sunrise Leila vanishes "like spit on a griddle," as she puts it. He realizes that he misses Frannie and, accordingly, rousts her out of Ray's motel room. As he drags her back to the bungalow, she tells him that she is drawn to Ray because he sings to her instead of yelling at her as Hank does. "If I could sing for you, I would," Hank answers sheepishly.

Frannie decides to use two airline tickets to Bora Bora, which she had purchased to celebrate her fifth anniversary with Hank, to have Ray accompany her on the trip. She and Ray head for McCarran Airport, where Hank catches up with them at the departure gate. Desperate, Hank plaintively sings "You Are My Sunshine" to Frannie in a broken, off-key voice, which comes straight from the heart. But Frannie stubbornly boards the plane with Ray anyway.

Back home, Hank sits sullenly in the dimly lit living room and melts into tears, mirroring the downpour outside (perhaps an implicit reference to *The Rain People,* in which a character says, "people made of rain cry themselves away.") But "Hank is forgetting that the sun follows the storm." Assuming that Frannie will never come back to him, he begins burning her belongings.[23] A cab stops outside. Frannie has returned. Suddenly the whole house is aglow with light, as if by magic. Frannie and Hank wait on their balcony for the dawn, which promises a new day and a fresh start for them. After each of them has experienced a brief fling with a fantasy lover, they are convinced that they belong together. Sometimes, the film implies, a couple must break up before they can truly come together.

Coppola's point, writes Richard Corliss, is that "Hank and Frannie, prosaic souls in a neon paradise, may be seduced by their surroundings into a one-night stand with advertised ecstasy, but that real life must proceed in equal doses of pleasure and accommodation."[24] Hopefully, in harmony with Coppola's theme, they will regain the family-like sense of community they had lost. At any rate, the paper moon reappears in the night sky and the blue theater curtain swings across the scene to end the movie.

Some of the notices that followed the unveiling of the film at Radio City Music Hall echoed Jameson's judgment from the Seattle sneak preview: Coppola was more preoccupied with style than with substance in the picture. Consequently, the personal saga of Hank and Frannie was overwhelmed by the razzle-dazzle of the Vegas setting and the stunning cinematic techniques already described. As a result, these critics believe that by film's end the filmgoer has been treated to such a visual display of impressive cinematic techniques that that is all they can remember. In essence, the picture seemed an elaborate frame surrounding an empty canvas. In other words, the lackluster script did not justify a production with a $27 million price tag. As Pauline Kael writes, "This movie isn't from the heart; it's from the lab. It's all tricked out with dissolves and scrim effects. . . . In interviews Coppola talked about directing the movie from inside a trailer while watching the set on video equipment. This movie feels like something directed from a trailer. It's cold and mechanized; it is a remove from the action."[25]

The minority report was filed by critics who found the movie funny and tuneful and engaging. They paid court to the extraordinary achievements of Tavoularis's production design and Storaro's eye-filling lensing. Jerome Ozer cites Sheila Benson's rave review in the *Los Angeles Times*, which called the movie "a work of constant astonishment. . . . It's easy to love *One from the Heart*; you just let yourself relax and float away with it." She did not even mind the "silhouette-thinness" of the characters. Musicals have been far more bereft of emotion than this one, she remarked, "and very few have dared this greatly." A few critics saw the film as a pleasant, old-fashioned romance, set in a richly colored Las Vegas wrapped in neon, palm trees, and bungalow courts and punctuated with torchy barroom ballads on the sound track.[26] Nevertheless, there were not enough positive reviews to save the picture.

Admittedly, *One from the Heart* is more noteworthy for its sophisticated cinematography and elegant sets than for its routine story line. But even an off-form Coppola film deserves to be seen, and it is a great pity that *One from the Heart* was out of circulation for twenty years. (I saw the film when it opened in Chicago in 1982 and later viewed a tape of the picture owned by a private collector of Coppola memorabilia, but the DVD release in 2004 came too late for me to see it again in preparation for this book.) After all, the cast performs credibly, and Waits's songs are amiable, even if they do not always illuminate story or character to any great degree. Seen today, now that the fuss and fury have long since died down, it is a charming comedy, poetic and funny; and that is all it ever was. The apotheosis of the film would come in July 2003, when the Academy of Motion Picture Arts and Sciences would sponsor a screening of the film with Coppola present to lead a discussion. But that was far in the future.

At all events, the picture opened on February 11, 1982, on forty-one screens just in time for Valentine's Day, because Coppola thought of the picture as a musical Valentine. By April 1, it was still playing in only one theater, the tiny Guild Theater next door to Radio City Music Hall, the site of its gala preview showing months before. The next day Columbia withdrew the picture from distribution with Coppola's consent. "I must admit that when *One from the Heart* was removed from release, I was very hurt. I thought I had done good work," says Coppola. "With the benefit of hindsight, I realize that having unknown actors in a film that was so unusual was a handicap."[27] He also felt, in retrospect, that the movie was overshadowed in the minds of the public by press coverage of the money troubles that plagued the production, as he had feared it would be. During its release, the film earned a meager $1.2 million in gross box-office receipts. Coppola could see the handwriting on the wall and decided to sell the studio.

On April 20, 1982, Coppola announced that Zoetrope Studios (the actual property) was up for auction since he was committed to paying back the loans he had secured from Chase Manhattan Bank, Jack Singer, and others to renovate the studio and to make *One from the Heart*. Spiotta in due course resigned as president of Zoetrope Studios, and Coppola resumed full control of American Zoetrope. Negotiations for the sale of the studio to potential buyers dragged on for two years. It became obvious that Jack Singer was the only individual willing to make a serious bid for the property. Coppola's creditors threatened foreclosure on Zoetrope Studios, so on February 10, 1984, Coppola sold the studio to Singer for $12.3 million—a bid considerably below Coppola's asking price of $17 million, the appraised value of the property—in order to pay some of his debts.

Coppola returned his entire operation to the American Zoetrope offices in the Sentinel Building in San Francisco, which he continued to run as an independent production unit, producing films in partnership with major Hollywood studios. But he no longer owned his own studio. Not surprisingly, Singer changed the name of the studio in Hollywood to Singer Studios, and he rented its facilities to independent producers to make films there—but he produced no films of his own.

Wim Wenders's *Hammett* (1983)

The other picture that hastened the demise of Zoetrope Studios was *Hammett,* a Zoetrope production directed by the respected German filmmaker Wim Wenders. It was originally slated to be Zoetrope Studio's first release, but, as things turned out, it was not released until after *One from the Heart.* The script was based on a novel set in 1928 in which Dashiell Hammett, the famed author of hardboiled detective fiction like *The Maltese Falcon,* solves a real-life mystery involving a missing Chinese prostitute.

Wenders collaborated on the script with a string of screenwriters, who complained that he insisted on departing substantially from the original story line. Finally Coppola ordered him to stop the multiple rewrites of the script and to commence principal photography. On February 4, 1980, Wenders began filming, with Frederic Forrest in the title role. But Wenders continued revising the script nonstop throughout the production period. Coppola ultimately decided that Wenders had reworked the screenplay to the point where it involved an impenetrable mystery that was not adequately solved at the end. Wenders had not been shooting the approved screenplay, Coppola explains, "and I could not dissuade Wim from this path. . . . So I stopped production" and postponed the remainder of filming indefinitely.[28]

During the hiatus Coppola had the screenplay totally overhauled by still another scriptwriter, who attempted to steer the story back to the original plotline and provide a coherent ending. The new script entailed the reshooting of eighty percent of the picture. Michael Powell, whom Coppola had appointed Senior Director in Residence, urged him to shelve the picture rather than throw good money after bad. Coppola summoned Wenders back to finish the shoot in the fall of 1981, after Coppola had himself completed the filming of One from the Heart. Wenders finished filming in a record twenty-three days. Coppola monitored the reshoot by regularly viewing the retakes done by Wenders and offering him suggestions. But Coppola did not reshoot any scenes himself, as Leonard Maltin mistakenly asserts.[29]

Recalling the troubled production period of Hammett, Gregory Solmon observes, "Just ask Wim Wenders, who worked for Coppola, the executive producer on Hammett, how little the latter values a director's artistic freedom—unless he happens to be the director."[30] This statement is severely unfair to Coppola when one considers that he had to scrap much of what Wenders originally shot because it departed significantly from the official script—at a considerable financial loss to Coppola. In the end Hammett wound up costing $10 million, considerably over schedule and over budget.

Hammett, which was to be distributed by Warner Brothers, had its world premiere at the Cannes Film Festival on June 6, 1982, where it received a poor press. Many of the press corps complained that Hammett's convoluted plot yielded only a murky solution to the mystery about the missing Chinese call girl. She turned out to be embroiled in a complex conspiracy to blackmail some corrupt city officials, which was never adequately explained. In sum, the film was dismissed as an undistinguished detective yarn, mere "private eye-wash." Warners accordingly gave the film a token release and then shelved the picture.

Seeing the film on videocassette today, one notices an effective performance by Forrest as Dashiell Hammett. And the picture is further enhanced by Philip Lathrop's mood cinematography. With all its shortcomings, *Hammett* is a treat for mystery fans.

During the time that shooting on *Hammett* was suspended, Wenders returned to Europe and made *The State of Things* (1983), a movie about a hapless German director named Friedrich (clearly modeled on Wenders), who is making a picture for an eccentric American producer who is short of funds. Gordon, the producer, who is played by Allen Garfield (*The Conversation, One from the Heart*), seems to be based on Coppola. Adding credence to this theory that is widely held in film circles is the fact that, like Coppola, Garfield has a stocky build. In addition, there are parallels between the movie that Friedrich is making for Gordon and *Hammett*, the picture that Wenders was making for Coppola. When Friedrich's film goes over budget, Gordon shuts down the production. "I never thought Gordon had it in him to leave us stranded," Friedrich moans.

Friedrich confronts Gordon about abandoning the production in the producer's mobile home, which obviously recalls Coppola's Airstream trailer, the Silverfish. While arguing with Friedrich, Gordon exclaims in exasperation, "I never thought I'd see the day when I'd be working with a German director!" He then explains that the investors would not put up more funds to keep the picture afloat because the script was too muddled—precisely Coppola's complaint about Wenders's much-rewritten screenplay for *Hammett*.

Wenders maintains that the producer in *The State of Things* "is really not Francis Coppola. I don't think you can find any traces of *Hammett* or Coppola in *The State of Things*."[31] On the contrary, given the many references in *The State of Things* to Coppola's dealings with Wenders on *Hammett*, enumerated above, it seems slightly disingenuous for Wenders to maintain that he did not have Coppola in mind when he created the character of Gordon. After all, when Wenders made *The State of Things* Coppola had suspended filming on *Hammett*, and Wenders had no guarantee that it would ever be finished.

In any case, Zoetrope Studios collapsed into bankruptcy under the combined failures of *One from the Heart* and *Hammett*. Coppola's debt was estimated to be between $40 and $50 million. "That was a kamikaze attack," he says. "I went down in flames by myself."[32] Still, he never regretted gambling on running his own studio. "Why was it so bad that I wanted a little studio to turn out films?" he mused.[33] "If you don't bet," he told me, "you don't have a chance to win. You can't be an artist and play it safe."

History has a way of repeating itself in Hollywood. Coppola's experience with Zoetrope Studios recalls that of silent filmmaker D. W. Griffith (*The Birth of a Nation*), who opened his own studio at Mamaroneck, New York, in the early 1920s. As an independent producer, Griffith had to handle the overhead expenses of maintaining the Mamaroneck facility, which included meeting the weekly payroll. Unfortunately, Griffith was no more of a businessman than Coppola proved to be. He lacked the business acumen to budget a production in a way that would make possible a reasonable return on the financial investment that had been made in the picture. Similarly, Coppola lacked the know-how to manage a motion picture studio on a profit-making basis. When Griffith's movies did not make money, he inevitably lost his studio, just as Coppola did half-a-century later. In conversation with Griffith's second wife, Evelyn Griffith Kuze, it became clear to me that Griffith's decline was ultimately the result of his failure to reckon with the fact that the movie business was just that—a business. That was a lesson Coppola likewise had to learn. After Zoetrope Studios closed down, Coppola became what he termed "a cinematic hired gun," steadily directing pictures to shore up his faltering bank account and pay his debts.[34]

In fact, by the time *One from the Heart* and *Hammett* had tanked, he was totally immersed in the production of *The Outsiders,* a movie about juvenile delinquents to be shot entirely on location in Tulsa, Oklahoma. "I decided I would work continuously until I paid off my debt," Coppola stated stoically. "I sure put in the hours."[35] The *Los Angeles Times* declared at the time that, despite all the guff Coppola had taken for the failure of Zoetrope Studios, "Francis Coppola is, without question, one of the giants of the American cinema."[36] Coppola's efforts to operate his own studio added to his image as a Hollywood maverick in the minds of younger filmmakers. They respected him for risking his own capital on *One from the Heart.* He was not reckless with other people's money. Moreover, if Coppola could produce a flop like *One from the Heart,* George Lucas, his contemporary, was just as capable of producing a turkey like *More American Graffiti* (1979). As a matter of fact, *The Outsiders* would prove a box-office bonanza for Coppola, which would put him on the road to financial recovery.

8

Growing Pains

The Outsiders and *Rumble Fish*

You learned too much in those days before you came of age.
This savage knowledge ought to come slowly, the gradual fruit
of experience.

—Graham Greene

You should be prepared for experience, knowledge, knowing:
not bludgeoned unaware in the dark as by a highwayman or a
footpad.

—William Faulkner

In the fall of 1980 Coppola received a joint letter from the librarian of
Lone Star High School in Fresno, California, Ellen Misakian, writing on
behalf of several of the students who also signed the letter. After the release of *Apocalypse Now* Coppola had served as executive producer on
The Black Stallion (1980), which was made under the banner of American Zoetrope in San Francisco and directed by Carroll Ballard, who had
attended film school with him at UCLA. *The Black Stallion*, a touching
story of a boy and his beloved horse, became a hit with the youth market.
The librarian accordingly urged Coppola to bring another teenage story,
The Outsiders, to the screen. "I feel our students are representative of the
youth of America," she wrote. "Everyone who has read the book, regard-

less of ethnic or economic background, has enthusiastically endorsed the project."[1]

Coppola was struck by the fact that the novel had been turned into a bestseller by its devoted teenage readers. The book, which was required reading in some high schools, had sold four million copies since its publication in 1970. The novel's huge teenage following guaranteed a pre-sold audience for the movie, and Coppola saw the project shaping up to be the box-office success he needed to keep up his payments to his creditors in the wake of the demise of Zoetrope Studios in Hollywood (see chapter 7).

The author of *The Outsiders,* S. E. (Susan Eloise) Hinton, was only sixteen when she wrote the book. She had disguised the fact that the novel was written by a girl by using a pen name, because she feared that her young readers might question the authenticity of her books about teenage boys if they were aware that the author was a female. As a matter of fact, her readership never guessed that the author was a girl, probably because when she was growing up most of Susie Hinton's close friends were the group of boys that she regularly hung out with.

Coppola was convinced that *The Outsiders* was written with the authentic voice of a youngster, as she told the story of three brothers who endeavor to maintain themselves as a family after both their parents have died in an auto accident. "As I was reading the book, I realized that I wanted to make a film about young people, and about belonging," says Coppola, "belonging to a peer group with whom one can identify and for whom one feels real love. Even though the boys are poor and to a certain extent insignificant, the story gives them a kind of beauty and nobility."[2]

Furthermore, the novel made him feel nostalgic for his own youth when he was growing up in Queens and saw youth-oriented movies like *Beach Blanket Bingo.* Moreover, Coppola belonged to a street gang known as the Bay Rats when he was fifteen and going to high school on Long Island. He decided not only to produce the movie but to direct it himself and to dedicate it to the librarian and students of Lone Star School in a citation in the film's end credits because they had inspired the film.

The Outsiders (1983)

Making *The Outsiders* appealed to Coppola for a variety of reasons. He was aware, in the wake of *Apocalypse Now* and *One from the Heart,* that he was no longer viewed by studio executives as a director who could be counted on to deliver a picture on time and on budget. Coppola realized that he could easily design a film about teenagers on a much smaller scale than the big-budget movies he had made during the previous decade. He could thus prove to the money men that he was still quite capable of making a picture quickly and for a reasonable budget. After all, there would be no million-dollar sets for the movie, since *The Outsiders* would be shot on location in Tulsa, Oklahoma, Hinton's hometown, where the story is set. In addition, he would cast promising young actors in the picture who did not yet command big salaries.

He thus hoped to put behind him the imbroglio that surrounded the production and release of *One from the Heart*—which he referred to ruefully as "chaos incorporated"—while he was working in Tulsa. Rather than hang around Hollywood and "be whipped for having committed the sin of making a film that I wanted to make," he explains, "I escaped with a lot of young people to Tulsa." He adds, "I used to be a great camp counselor, and the idea of being with half-a-dozen kids making a movie seemed like being a camp counselor again. It would be a breath of fresh air."[3]

American Zoetrope was so strapped for capital that Coppola could offer Hinton a measly five hundred dollars to option her novel, plus a percentage of the profits. The young novelist accepted the offer. Kathleen Rowell, another young writer, was commissioned to adapt the book for film. The story involves the ongoing feud between two gangs of teenage boys living in Tulsa in the 1960s. One group is made up of underprivileged lads known as greasers, who are from the shabby north side of the city. The other group is made up of upper-class youngsters known as socs (*soc* rhymes with *gauche* and is short for *socialite*), who live on the prosperous south side of town. "All of the greasers were orphans, all outsiders," says Coppola, "but together they formed a family." Hence, the film touches on the common theme of family in Coppola's work.[4]

Coppola was disappointed in Rowell's adaptations of the novel. The two drafts of the screenplay she had done had meandered further and further away from the book. Conscious that Hinton's readers would resent a movie that diverged too much from the novel, Coppola decided to do a wholesale rewrite of her screenplay, sticking as closely as possible to the literary source. He respected Hinton as a serious writer.

"When I met Susie," Coppola says, "it was confirmed to me that she was not just a young people's novelist, but a real American novelist. For me the primary thing about her books is that the characters come across as very real. Her dialogue is memorable, and her prose is striking. Often a paragraph of her descriptive prose sums up something essential and stays with you."[5]

Lillian Ross, in her exhaustive essay on Coppola, reports that he was busy rewriting the script for *The Outsiders* in the early spring of 1982, just three weeks before shooting was scheduled to begin in March. His own version of the script went through several drafts until he finished the final shooting script, dated March 1, 1982, which is on file in the Script Repository at Warner Brothers, the film's distributor.

When one examines the script, it is evident that Coppola's version is extremely faithful to the source material, even incorporating actual dialogue from the book at times. What's more, Coppola continued to revise the final shooting script before filming began at the end of March, and these additional rewrites were incorporated into the screenplay on pages dated March 12 through March 19. (Additional pages of last-minute revisions that are inserted into a shooting script are customarily dated in order to indicate that they supersede earlier versions of the same material.)

Because of the substantial work he did in completely overhauling the script, Coppola petitioned the Screen Writers Guild to award him an official screen credit as sole author of the screenplay for *The Outsiders.* Normally, a claimant submits a scene-by-scene analysis of the script to the Guild in order to demonstrate that they composed the bulk of the script in question (i.e., more than 50 percent). But Coppola was so confident that he had right on his side that he merely sent the Guild a copy of the script with a short letter, stating that he understood the need for arbitration in these matters, "but this script is totally my writing."[6]

Because he supplied no detailed analysis of the screenplay to support his petition, the Guild awarded sole screen credit to Katherine Rowell, who had done two drafts of the script before he took over. It is worth noting that the screen credit Rowell received for *The Outsiders* did not serve to advance her career as a screenwriter, since she was never listed as author of a major motion picture again.

Coppola claims that he lost the arbitration battle because of the Writers Guild's "antiquated procedures." The Guild's decisions, he explains, always weigh heavily in favor of the first writer to do an adaptation of a literary work for film because they establish the characters and the basic plot for the screenplay, "even if it isn't a particularly effective or do-able script." The burden of proof lies with the writer who revises the original script. He concluded, "Even though I sat down and wrote the script that I used, the Guild gave her *all* the credit. Yet that woman simply did not write the script of the film that I made."[7]

Coppola brought together a number of production associates he was accustomed to working with, including composer Carmine Coppola and production designer Dean Tavoularis. Tavoularis chose abandoned, deserted areas of Tulsa for location sites in order to convey the greasers' sense of being outcasts. "The book was a kind of *Gone with the Wind* for kids, an epic classic struggle between the greasers and the socs, i.e., the poor and the rich, during the 1960s," Coppola explains. Indeed, the dog-eared paperback copy of *Gone with the Wind* that the young hero carries around with him almost amounts to a talisman. "*The Outsiders* takes place in an enchanted moment in time in the lives of all these boys. I wanted to catch that moment; I wanted to take these street rats and give them heroic proportions."[8]

Coppola told his father, Carmine Coppola, that, since *The Outsiders* was a *Gone with the Wind* for teens, he wanted "a kind of schmaltzy classical score," similar to the one Max Steiner had written for the 1939 movie of *Gone with the Wind*. The score is the key to *The Outsiders,* Coppola explains. That is to say, the fact that the music is composed in a romantic style "indicates that I wanted a movie told in sumptuous terms, very honestly and carefully taken from the book without changing it a lot." Hence, he envisioned the movie to be like *Gone with the Wind,* not so much in content as in style. He was "putting the emphasis on that kind of *Gone with the Wind* lyricism which was so important to Susie Hinton when she wrote it. . . . It appealed to me that kids could see *Outsiders* as a lavish, big-feeling epic about kids."[9]

For a cinematographer Coppola turned to a fellow alumnus of UCLA's film school, Steven Burum, who had done second unit photography for *Apocalypse Now. The Outsiders* would be filmed in widescreen and color in order to recreate the world of romantic melodrama characteristic of films about juvenile delinquency from the 1950s, such as the James Dean vehicle, *Rebel without a Cause* (1955).

For his part, Coppola shrewdly chose what one observer termed an honor roll of hot young actors, including Tom Cruise, Emilio Estevez, Rob Lowe, Ralph Macchio, and Patrick Swayze. Coppola thereby launched a whole generation of young film actors with this picture. The seven-week shoot was budgeted at $10 million. Coppola brought with him to Tulsa the technical equipment that he had already bought and implemented on *One from the Heart,* including the Silverfish trailer, with all of its electronic facilities. So, since the equipment was already in place, there was no need to charge a considerable amount of expensive electronic equipment against the budget of the present film.

Coppola had not yet secured a distributor for *The Outsiders* by the time he set up shop in Tulsa. Before leaving Hollywood for the Tulsa shoot, he had gone from studio to studio with the script under his arm, hawking what he considered to be a bankable property: the screen adaptation of a popular adolescent novel, to be made on the cheap and on the double—but he found no takers. Once he arrived in Tulsa, however, he at last succeeded in getting Warner Brothers to distribute the film and to provide some front money for production.

Warners' decision came as a big surprise to Hollywood insiders, since in the late 1960s that studio had turned down a package of film projects Coppola had presented to them. They even demanded that he reimburse them for the development funds the studio had spent on these projects (see chapter 3). But, as film historian Jon Lewis opines, in Hollywood it seems best to have a short memory. The studio administration apparently chose to forget that Coppola's parting shot on that occasion was to state that he was an artist, while the suits that ran Warners were Philistines. Be that as it may, Coppola's distribution deal with Warners enabled him to obtain further financing from Chemical Bank.

Aware of how Coppola had gone way over schedule on *Apocalypse Now* and *One from the Heart,* Warners kept him on a short leash. He was committed to sticking to the stipulated timetable for shooting and for postproduction in order to have the movie ready for release in the fall of 1982. Coppola assembled his cast and began rehearsing with them in early March, employing the "previsualization" method he had used for *One from the Heart.* He converted the gym of an abandoned schoolhouse into a rehearsal hall, where he videotaped the rehearsals in order to aid the young actors in developing their characterizations. Tom Cruise remembered these "workshop" rehearsals as very beneficial to the cast, helping them not only to build up their roles but also to "learn more about acting."[10]

Coppola ultimately videotaped a dress rehearsal, with the actors in front of a blank screen. Then he superimposed images from the dress rehearsal tape onto stills of the exterior location sites in Tulsa and on shots of Tavoularis's interior sets. By the time principal photography began, Coppola had a clear concept of how each scene would look when filmed.

Shooting started on March 29, 1982. Coppola utilized his "electronic cinema" procedure during filming, but he placed his video monitor near the set. He was therefore on the set with the actors during each take, not locked away in the Silverfish van as he had often been while filming *One from the Heart.* He would watch an instant-video replay of each take after it was photographed in order to ascertain if he wanted to make any adjustments in how the scene was being played. He would later review each scene, once it was in the can, on the monitor in the trailer, noting down suggestions for film editor Ann Goursaud, who was doing a preliminary edit of the movie back in Hollywood while it was being shot.

Because of his esteem for Hinton as a novelist, Coppola involved her in the shoot. "Once I sold the book," she observes, "I expected to be asked to drop off the face of the earth. But that didn't happen. I know that I had extremely rare experiences for a writer. Usually the director does not say, 'Boys, these are important lines, so you've got to know them word for word,' which is what Francis said to the actors." In addition to monitoring the script, Miss Hinton was on the set every day, supervising haircuts and wardrobe. "The boys depended on me a lot," she says. "I was kind of a greaser den mother, and they were always consulting me."[11]

Coppola got along famously with the young actors during filming because he treated them like adults. Thus he occasionally encouraged them to improvise a line of dialogue, and they made a considerable contribution to the movie because they spoke the same language as the characters they were playing. Emilio Estevez (the oldest son of Martin Sheen, using his father's real surname), helped to bring his character to life as one of the greasers by devising his own ducktail hairdo, a style quite popular with teenage boys in the 1960s.

The shooting period went smoothly and was nearly disaster-free. The only serious mishap occurred when Coppola was filming the scene when the greasers rescue some kindergarten kids from a fire in an abandoned country church. Coppola's thirst for realism went a little too far during his staging of the scene on location in an abandoned church in a country pasture. "More fire!" he shouted to his technicians, who stoked the blaze and accidentally sent the church steeple up in flames.[12] Just as the local fire department, which was standing by, was ready to intervene, a downpour suddenly started, as if on cue, and doused the fire.

Shooting wrapped on May 15, as planned. Estevez, who had visited his father on the set of *Apocalypse Now,* commented that Coppola "is getting his credibility back as a director who can deliver on schedule."[13]

Coppola invited Hinton to confer with him on the editing of the film during the summer of 1982, utilizing American Zoetrope's postproduction facilities in San Francisco. The Warners brass were dissatisfied with the rough cut, however, insisting that young people would not sit still for a teen picture that clocked in at two hours of screen time. The studio decreed that Coppola should shorten *The Outsiders* to ninety minutes and postponed the film's release from the fall of 1982 to the following spring. Coppola sought to oblige the studio, and some weeks later he presented the Warner executives with a cut that ran ninety-one minutes. He followed his customary practice of scheduling a test screening of the picture, and the largely teenage audience was wowed by the movie. Warners accordingly slated the film to open on March 23, 1983, with a saturation booking of 829 screens across the country.

"I feel *The Outsiders* suffered a little bit from the chaos of everybody at Warners turning yellow when they saw the rough cut of it, and that influenced it being cut shorter and shorter," Coppola commented later. He did not understand Warners' lack of faith in the film, since "I thought it was very much like the book," and the novel was a bestseller.[14] He regretted that in condensing the film he was forced to delete some of the scenes devoted to character development in favor of keeping mostly the plot-driven scenes.

The movie starts with a pre-credit sequence, in which Ponyboy Curtis (C. Thomas Howell), the film's narrator, opens a composition book and writes *The Outsiders* on the first page as he begins to write a composition for his teacher about some recent events in which he has figured. We hear him recount what happened, voice-over on the sound track, as the plot unfolds. The screenplay, as noted, is very faithful to its literary source, even down to having the movie begin with Ponyboy reciting the first lines of his composition while he is writing them down—lines that come straight from the novel: "When I stepped out into the bright sunlight from the darkness of the movie house. . . ." Ponyboy then starts to tell the story, in which he figures both as participant and witness.

Ponyboy is the youngest of the three recently orphaned Curtis boys. Darrel, the oldest (Patrick Swayze), works hard to support his two younger brothers, and argues with Ponyboy, the youngest brother, about his belonging to a street gang. Sodapop, the middle brother (Rob Lowe), plays the role of conciliator between his two brothers. Ponyboy belongs to the greasers, most of whom are orphans like himself, boys who have consequently formed a surrogate family of their own. The gang member Ponyboy looks up to as a father-figure is Dallas Winston (Matt Dillon), a street-wise young fellow who has just gotten out of jail.

One night Ponyboy and his other chum, Johnny Cade (Ralph Macchio), are accosted by some members of the rival gang who are drunk. When the other boys attack Ponyboy, Johnny panics and pulls a knife, stabbing one of them to death. At this very moment the color red suffuses the screen, pouring downward from the top of the frame to the bottom, in much the same way as the crimson blood runs down the mortally wounded boy's shirt. Burum's camera then looks down from above on the chilling sight of the corpse of the dead lad, face-down, in death.

Johnny and Ponyboy run to Dallas for help, and he advises them to hide out in an abandoned country church for the time being. The film has no shortage of visual imagery, as is evident from the scene just described. In addition, when Ponyboy and Johnny move into the ramshackle church, Coppola cuts to two bunny rabbits huddled underneath the porch—a metaphor for the two fugitive lads hiding out together. This is shortly followed by the image of two spiders crawling up a web, implying the entanglement of the two youngsters in a web of circumstances from which they find it hard to extricate themselves.

Despite the trouble the boys are in, they experience a charmed interlude alone together. The country church becomes their sanctuary. Coppola employs shots of some incandescently beautiful sunsets in this bucolic sequence to symbolize the brevity of youth. "When you watch the sun set, you realize it is already dying," he explains. "The same applies to youth. When youth reaches its highest level of perfection, you can already sense the forces that will destroy it."[15] Coppola's remark becomes still more meaningful when one relates the golden sunsets pictured in the movie to a poem by Robert Frost that Ponyboy recites to Johnny in which the poet likens the innocence of childhood to gold. Johnny picks up on the poem's theme by offering his pal this advice: "Stay gold, Ponyboy, stay gold." This is Johnny's way of encouraging Ponyboy not to lose the fundamental wholesomeness of youth as he grows older and is forced to face more and more of the grim realities of the adult world.

Although these two adolescent males bear visible masculine traits (reflected in "the outward trappings of fist fights and interest in athletics"), Johnny and Ponyboy repeatedly express affection for one another.[16] Their comradeship, says Richard Corliss, is not only familial but "unselfconsciously homoerotic. Left to their better selves, they can easily go all moony over sunsets, quote great swatches of Robert Frost's verse, or fall innocently asleep in each other's arms. Their ideal world is . . . a locker room; no women need apply to this dreamy brotherhood." Another critic hazarded that the boys' leather jackets, coupled with their male camaraderie, betoken a homosexual undertone in the film that recalls the homosexual-biker picture, *Scorpio Rising* (1964).[17]

Those critics who have inferred a hint of homosexuality in this film misconstrue the value that Coppola places on male companionship in his movies (one thinks of the solders' camaraderie in his two Vietnam movies). In the present instance, Ponyboy and Johnny have not yet experienced a deep relationship in their lives. Consequently, they are experiencing in their friendship a relationship that is fulfilling for them on an emotional level that has nothing to do with sex. Coppola suggests that adolescent boys must first know what true male companionship can be before they can go on to experience a meaningful relationship with a member of the opposite sex. By the same token, Dallas's protective feelings toward Ponyboy and toward Johnny in particular imply a fatherly solicitude similar to that Darrel feels toward his two younger brothers, whom Darrel obviously sees as surrogate sons.

Dallas comes to the hideout of Johnny and Ponyboy later on to tell them that Cherry (Diane Lane), a witness to the fatal stabbing, is willing to testify in their behalf, and they decide to give themselves up. Before they can start back to town, however, a fire breaks out in the dilapidated church, and the trio are suddenly called upon to save the lives of some children who happen to be in the old building when the blaze starts. Tragically, Johnny is severely burned during the course of the courageous rescue effort.

Friction between the greasers and the socs finally erupts into an all-out rumble in a vacant lot at night. Coppola stages the rumble with a real flair. The flames of the bonfire in the center of the field reflect the mutual animosity of the combatants, which has been ignited by the battle. Smoke from the fire obscures the figures of the opponents as they grapple with each other, and when a storm breaks, the boys' movements become increasingly more savage as they struggle in the mud. Dallas's battle cry is, "Let's win one for Johnny!" Two-Bit Matthews (Emilio Estevez) and Steve Randall (Tom Cruise) are in the forefront of the greasers' brigade. The greasers, with Dallas leading them, triumph over the socs.

But the victory is undercut by the remark of one of the socs to Ponyboy: "It doesn't matter that you whip us. You'll still be where you were before, at the bottom, and we'll still be the lucky ones, at the top with all the breaks. Greasers will still be greasers, and socs will still be socs." Similarly, when Johnny hears about the battle while in the hospital, he comments that gang wars are futile: "It's useless. Fighting don't do no good."

Just before he dies, Johnny "utters his lament for doomed youth."[18] He says stoically, "Sixteen years ain't long enough. Hell! There are too damned many things that I have not yet seen or done" in this brief life. When Johnny expires, Dallas cries out bitterly, "This is what you get for helping other people!"

Later on, Dallas, the ex-convict, lapses into his old ways, attempts to hold up a store, and is killed in a reckless scuffle with the police. He dies with Johnny's name on his lips. Reflecting on the loss of his two best friends, Ponyboy hopes to come to terms with this double tragedy by writing down what happened in a composition for his teachers. After all, one of his brothers tells him, "Your life isn't over because you lose someone."

We see on one half of the widescreen Ponyboy pick up his well-thumbed copy of *Gone with the Wind,* in which he finds a note that Johnny left for him. At that moment, Johnny materializes as an apparition on the other half of the screen, assuring Ponyboy that life is worth living. "There's still lots of good in the world," says Johnny before his image fades. This touching fantasy sequence, dated March 12, 1982, in the script, was a last-minute addition Coppola made to the shooting script, which is itself dated March 1.[19] And so the movie ends where it began, with Ponyboy writing the essay that forms the content of the film's spoken narration.

As Coppola describes the final scene in the screenplay, "Ponyboy sits at his desk, folds back the cover of his theme book, and looks at the sunset, remembering. . . . He takes up his pen and starts to write, 'When I stepped out into the bright sunlight from the darkness of the movie house. . . .'"[20] Thus the movie has come full circle by repeating the opening lines.

Among the scenes Coppola had to jettison from *The Outsiders* in order to edit the movie to the length stipulated by Warners, the one that would have really enhanced the picture by its inclusion comes near film's end. There is a rap session in which the Curtis brothers, Ponyboy, Sodapop, and Darrel, reflect frankly on the life lessons they have learned from their recent shared experiences. They renew their closeness as a family as Sodapop says, "If we don't have each other, we don't have anything. If you don't have anything, you end up like Dallas," who was an unhappy loner. This scene underscores the film's affirmation of the young people's deep need to belong, and as such might well have been included in the movie.[21]

The Outsiders was a bona fide blockbuster, despite the fact that some critics dismissed the movie as a minor melodrama unworthy of Coppola's directorial talents. On the contrary, the picture deserves a respected place in the Coppola canon for various reasons. On the technical side, Burum's camerawork is superb. The widescreen, color photography lavishes mellow softness on burnished visuals, which are hazy with summer heat in the sequence of Johnny and Ponyboy's sojourn in the country. There are shots of the pair silhouetted against a blood-red sunset, reminiscent of similar images in *Gone with the Wind,* Ponyboy's favorite film. Moreover, Coppola stages some of the scenes featuring the greasers in a manner that recalls earlier films about teenage street gangs. "The greasers, with their sleek muscles. . . . display a leonine athleticism as they make their way towards a rumble, moving through vacant lots or doing a graceful, two-handed vault over a chain-link fence."[22] They thus summon images of the agile movements of the street gangs in *Rebel without a Cause.* Furthermore, Carmine Coppola's highly romantic score is reminiscent of Leonard Rosenman's music for the same film. The score for *The Outsiders* is imposing and yet is still basted with a little schmaltz, as Francis Coppola had requested.

The film segues seamlessly from documentary-like portrayals of the youngsters' shabby lives in a dead-end, poverty-trap slum to the dramatic tragedy in which Dallas, who has freaked out after Johnny's death, becomes a dazed, ruined presence. Coppola is adept at depicting the alienation so characteristic of the youth subculture. *The Outsiders* in the last analysis is a downbeat, unpatronizing tale about brutalized teens, marked by inspired naturalism of both dialogue and performance.

Not the least of the movie's virtues is the host of consistently excellent performances that Coppola drew from his appealing young cast, who graduated into starring roles in a number of youth-oriented pictures: Tom Cruise (*Risky Business*), Patrick Swayze (*Dirty Dancing*), Emilio Estevez (*The Breakfast Club*), Matt Dillon (*Drugstore Cowboy*), C. Thomas Howell (*Red Dawn*), and Ralph Macchio (*The Karate Kid*).

After the overwhelming problems Coppola encountered in financing and marketing *One from the Heart,* some critics found it refreshing to encounter a Coppola film that, bless it, was only a conventional genre picture about teenage rebellion. What's more, the youth audience took the picture to their hearts. The film earned $12 million in its first two weeks in release and eventually reaped $100 million in profits, which helped to put some cash in the coffers at Zoetrope. *The Outsiders* generated just enough money "to help me at a time when I needed some big bucks," says Coppola.[23]

The Outsiders subsequently spawned a TV miniseries in the spring of 1991. It premiered with a ninety-minute pilot that picked up where the 1983 movie left off. The pilot opens with footage from Coppola's movie of Dallas being shot by the police, followed by Dallas's funeral. Afterward, a welfare worker warns Ponyboy (Jay Ferguson) and Sodapop (Rodney Harvey) that if they participate in any more rumbles between the greasers and the socs they will be taken away from the custody of their older brother Darrel and placed in foster homes. The pilot was followed by seven weekly installments. Coppola supervised the series, but he did not direct any of the episodes.

After finishing the feature film of *The Outsiders,* Coppola followed it immediately with the screen adaptation of another Hinton novel. While he was shooting *The Outsiders* in Tulsa, Coppola got the idea that he would like to employ the same crew and locations for a second teen movie. As Hinton tells it, "Halfway through *The Outsiders,* Francis looked up at me one day and said, 'Susie, we get along great. Have you written anything else I can film?' I told him about *Rumble Fish,* and he read the book and loved it.

He said, 'I know what we can do. On our Sundays off, let's write a screenplay, and then as soon as we can wrap *The Outsiders,* we'll take a two-week break and start filming *Rumble Fish.*' I said 'Sure, Francis, we're working 16 hours a day, and you want to spend Sundays writing another screenplay?' But that's what we did."[24]

In the novel, Rusty-James, a disadvantaged teenager from a broken home, looks up to his older brother, who is known only as Motorcycle Boy, the leader of a local gang. The relationship of the two brothers struck a chord in Coppola. His brother August, who is five years his senior, included young Francis in his activities and provided a strong role model for him when they were growing up. August Coppola "was my idol," Francis Coppola says, "just took me everywhere when he went out with the guys because he was the leader of the gang," which was called the Wild Deuces. "He always looked out for me."[25] A dedication to August Coppola, who eventually became a college professor, appears in the end credits of *Rumble Fish*: "To August Coppola, my first and best teacher." As it happened, Coppola hired August's son Nicolas to play a gang member named Smokey in *Rumble Fish,* but Nicolas Coppola took the professional name of Nicolas Cage in order to obscure the family connection with the director of the film. Still, in the movie Nicolas Cage wore a copy of his father's own jacket from high school days, with Wild Deuces displayed on the back.

Coppola planned to go from one film right into the other. The piggy-backed production of the two Hinton movie adaptations recalled the circumstances of his shooting *Dementia 13* twenty years before. After Roger Corman finished shooting *The Young Racers* in Europe, Coppola convinced Corman to let him make *Dementia 13* back-to-back with the racing picture, since the expenses involved in transporting the crew and technical equipment to Europe had already been accounted for (see chapter 1). Similarly, Coppola reasoned that he could make *Rumble Fish* with the same production team and equipment he had assembled in Tulsa for *The Outsiders.*

Rumble Fish (1983)

Never one to repeat himself, Coppola took a radically different approach to *Rumble Fish* than he had employed on *The Outsiders.* The latter film was romantic melodrama along the lines of *The Godfather,* while he envisioned *Rumble Fish* as an art film, designed more in the direction of *Apocalypse Now.* Susie Hinton wrote the book five years after *The Outsiders,* when she was more mature, and, consequently, "it had tremendously impressive vision and dialogue and characters," says Coppola.[26] Stephen Farber records,

"Coppola actually co-wrote the screenplay. Mr. Coppola concentrated on structure and visual imagery, while Miss Hinton wrote all the dialogue. She found to her surprise that she had certain talents for screenwriting."[27]

Hinton begins the novel in the present and then has Rusty-James narrate the story in flashback, a device she had likewise utilized in *The Outsiders*. Coppola rejected the flashback structure—which he had employed in his film of *The Outsiders*—for the movie version of *Rumble Fish,* presumably because he wanted to take a different approach to the material than he had taken in his previous Hinton film. Otherwise, the shooting script for *Rumble Fish* follows the novel quite faithfully. The screenplay, which is on file in the Script Repository of Universal Studios, the distributor of the film, is dated May 4, 1982.

Hinton mentions that every time she got a letter from a youngster who said *Rumble Fish* was his favorite novel the return address was invariably a reformatory. This is understandable, since the novel portrays youthful angst and rebellion even more frankly than *The Outsiders. Rumble Fish* has a darker, grittier quality than *The Outsiders.* Hence, Coppola chose to shoot it in black-and-white.

In concert with production designer Dean Tavoularis, Coppola chose location sites in Tulsa that were grimmer and grimier than those used in *The Outsiders.* He wanted locations marked by dampness and humidity in order to create the ambience of a desolate wasteland sweltering in the heat of high summer. Coppola asked Tavoularis, in his designing of the sets, to adapt at times the techniques of Expressionism from the Golden Age of German silent cinema. It is not my purpose to dwell in detail on the influence of expressionism on *Rumble Fish,* but the following observations are in order.

Expressionism sets itself against naturalism, with its mania for recording reality exactly as it is. Instead, the expressionistic artist seeks the symbolic meaning that underlies the facts. Foster Hirsch describes expressionism in film in the following terms: "German Expressionistic films were set in claustrophobic studio-created environments, where physical reality was distorted." To be precise, expressionism exaggerated surface reality in order to make a symbolic point.[28] Coppola employed one of the techniques of the old-time German expressionistic filmmakers by having Tavoularis paint forbidding shadows on the walls of the dark alleys in the tawdry slums in order to make them look more menacing. Thus, this is a tortured, moody motion picture, filled with fog and shadows.

Cinematographer Burum, working in concert with Coppola, made full use in *Rumble Fish* of expressionistic lighting, which lends itself so readily to the moody atmosphere. Thus a sinister atmosphere was created in certain interiors by infusing them with menacing shadows looming on walls and ceilings, which gave a Gothic quality to faces. All in all, the black-and-white cinematography, with its night-shrouded streets and alleys, ominous corridors, and dark archways, gave this modestly budgeted feature a rich texture.

Nonetheless, Coppola insisted that expressionism be employed in the picture in only a few key scenes. After all, excessive use of expressionistic techniques in a commercial Hollywood movie would have seemed heavy-handed.

Motorcycle Boy, Rusty-James's burned-out older brother, is color-blind, due to the brain damage he has suffered in numerous fist fights and rumbles. His color-blindness is also a symbol of the disillusioned young man's view of the somber world in which he lives. This confirms Coppola's decision to shoot the movie in black-and-white, with a few judiciously chosen color overlays, as in the shots of the Siamese fighting fish that give the film its title. The rumble fish therefore serve as a metaphor for Motorcycle Boy, a colorful individual who is caught in drab, black-and-white surroundings.

Motorcycle Boy's vision of life permeates the film, and that clearly justifies the black-and-white photography. The contrast between the color cinematography of *The Outsiders* and the black-and-white photography of *Rumble Fish* brings into relief how different Coppola intended his two teen gang movies to be in style and concept. It was crucial for him, he declares, to draw a clear distinction between the two films since he was employing the same production crew and same location for both movies. *The Outsiders* was a blueprint in color of a story about juvenile delinquents, while *Rumble Fish* was its negative in stark black-and-white, a film about deeply disaffected and alienated youngsters.

Although the production team included Coppola regulars like Tavoularis and editor Barry Malkin, Francis Coppola did not call once more upon Carmine Coppola to compose the score for the present film. The director instead opted to have a background score that relied heavily on percussion and so commissioned Stewart Copeland, the American drummer for the British rock band the Police, to provide the score. Copeland did principally use percussion for the background music for the film, but he also recorded Tulsa street sounds—such as traffic noises, police and ambulance sirens—and wove them into his score, which included not only drums but a piano and a xylophone. Coppola believes that percussion instruments are exciting in themselves, so he encouraged Copeland to use percussion alone in certain scenes. The rumble at the beginning of the movie seemed to be a perfect place for a percussion solo, which, in the context of the scene, sounds very sinister and ominous. Copeland's spare percussive score was as far removed as it could be from the saccharinity that sometimes marked Carmine Coppola's music for *The Outsiders*.

After demonstrating that he could make a mainstream Hollywood commercial film like *The Outsiders*, Coppola set out to confirm his status as a Hollywood maverick by conceiving *Rumble Fish* as a picture that audaciously departed from the conventions of a routine genre picture. Shooting the film in grainy black-and-white, with an avant-garde score, set *Rumble Fish* apart from the usual Hollywood output.

Two of the lead actors in *The Outsiders* reappear in *Rumble Fish:* Matt Dillon was signed to play Rusty-Jones and Diane Lane (who played Cherry, the girl with whom the Matt Dillon character had a brief flirtation in *The Outsiders)* would be Patty, Rusty-James's girl in *Rumble Fish*. Mickey Rourke, who had auditioned for *The Outsiders*, was selected to play Motorcycle Boy. From *Apocalypse Now*, Coppola re-called Dennis Hopper as the drunken father of Rusty-James and Motorcycle Boy and Larry Fishburne as a member of a rival gang, called Midget because he is so tall. Finally, Vincent Spano took the part of Steve, Rusty-James's naive but likeable sidekick. The swarthy actor peroxided his hair in order to lose the darkly handsome look he had as a teenage heartthrob in previous teen films.

Coppola spent two weeks videotaping rehearsals for *Rumble Fish* in the school gym where he had rehearsed the cast of *The Outsiders*. He encouraged the young actors at times to improvise dialogue containing the profanity that lower-class boys ordinarily employed. Once again he taped a final run-through of the whole script, which served as a "previsualization" of the film. He then screened it for the cast and crew to get their reactions.

Principal photography could not begin until Coppola had secured a distributor who would put up some front money for *Rumble Fish*. Warner Brothers bowed out because they were not interested in releasing a second youth picture on the heels of *The Outsiders* that might compete with it. By the end of June, Coppola had cut a distribution deal with Universal, with release set for the fall of 1983. Filming accordingly started on July 12, 1982, only a few weeks after the production phase of *The Outsiders* was finished.

Steven Burum, in consultation with Coppola, often employed flat, harsh lighting to give the movie a stark and brutal look. He photographed some scenes with an unsteady hand-held camera: "We wanted," he said, "to give people a feeling of uneasiness," that there is something off-kilter in the unstable world in which the kids live.[29]

What's more, Tavoularis's seedy sets encompassed thick coats of dust, peeling paint, cracks in the walls, and creaking stairways in the slum dwellings where the gang members live. As the camera explores the cramped living quarters Rusty-James shares with his father and brother, the viewer gets a sense of the confinement the boys who live there must endure.

During filming Hinton was herself impressed with her ability to rewrite material under the gun. "Working with Francis," she recalls, "I could never tell when he was going to turn to me and say, 'Susie, we'll need a new scene here to make this play.' I could have it for him in three minutes, and it was pretty good, too."[30] This sort of emergency writing on the set yielded some memorable bits of dialogue. Some of the nifty lines one hears spoken from the screen are not in the final shooting script and, therefore, must have been supplied by Hinton on the set, perhaps with the help of the cast during improvisations. For example, Motorcycle Boy expresses his fatherly concern for his troubled younger brother in terms that remind one of Darrel dealing with his surrogate son Ponyboy in *The Outsiders*. (As a matter of fact, Motorcycle Boy has one confab with Rusty-James in the same Rexall drugstore in Tulsa that Dallas robbed in *The Outsiders*. Coppola thereby makes a subtle cross-reference from one film to the other.)

In one conversation Motorcycle Boy asks Rusty-James why he is so messed up, and Rusty-James replies laconically, "I'm alright." But big brother is not to be put off with a dodge. "Talk to me," he insists. "Why are you fucked up all the time one way or another, huh?" Rusty-James can only grunt, "I don't know," in reply. Motorcycle Boy's crude language belies the genuine caring he nurtures for the welfare of Rusty-James, for whom he subconsciously feels something of a father-figure. In short, Motorcycle Boy does not want his brother to follow him down the road to ruin.

During shooting Dennis Hopper saw the advantage of Coppola replaying each scene on the TV monitor in the Silverfish in order to make modifications in each scene as it was filmed and to make notes to pass on to editor Barry Malkin. "Francis's genius is really in his technology," says Hopper.[31]

The filming of *Rumble Fish* went off as efficiently as the shooting of *The Outsiders*, and production finished in October. Once more Coppola was on schedule and on budget. The endless shooting schedules and exorbitant budgets of *Apocalypse Now* and *One from the Heart* seemed at this point to belong to the distant past.

Coppola collaborated closely with Barry Malkin on the edit of the movie. Malkin particularly enjoyed cutting together the rumble scene that occurs near the beginning of the movie when Rusty-James takes on the leader of an opposing gang. The fight comprised eighty-one shots in two minutes of screen time. "It's generally easier to cut . . . a flashy, razzle-dazzle action sequence," explains Malkin, "than it is to edit a dialogue sequence with a lot of characters sitting around a table," which can seem quite static and boring to the viewer.[32]

After postproduction was completed, the premiere of *Rumble Fish* was delayed until the fall of 1983 so that the release of *Rumble Fish* did not follow too closely on the first-run showings of *The Outsiders,* which came out in the spring of 1983. Since *Rumble Fish* was thought to be an art film, it was considered too sophisticated to attract the same wide, youth audience that saw *The Outsiders.* So Coppola decided to premiere the movie at the New York Film Festival on October 7, 1983, in order to bring it to the attention of a more mature audience. The critics who saw the picture at the Festival screening, however, were by and large unresponsive to the movie, just as the reviewers had been to *One from the Heart* when it premiered at Radio City Music Hall. Coppola tells me that the snobbish New York critics had been lining up against him since *Godfather II.* "They won't even throw me a bone," he laments.

Rumble Fish begins with clouds hurtling across a darkening sky (by means of Burum's speeded-up photography). The swiftly moving clouds, coupled with the frequent images of clocks—including one huge clock without hands—are meant to express a feeling of urgency, of the unstoppable passage of time—a fact of life Coppola says young people find hard to grasp. He particularly wished to heighten the effect of time running out for the disenchanted and self-destructive Motorcycle Boy, whose hour of doom may be approaching.

There is a sign spray-painted on a brick wall, "The Motorcycle Boy Reigns." It reminds Rusty-James how much he misses his older brother, Motorcycle Boy, who had been the leader of the street gang Rusty-James belongs to until he left town a couple of months earlier. Rusty-James is challenged to fight with Biff Wilcox, the leader of another gang. Members of both gangs show up for the rumble. The fight takes place near a freight yard in a steaming, wet alley, which almost makes the summer heat palpable.

"It is a dance of violence"—designed by choreographer Michael Smuin of the San Francisco Ballet—in which "the gangs form a male corps de ballet," with the movements of the fighters "lit by flashes from the windows of a passing train."[33] The balletic movements of the youths recall the staging of the rumble in the musical *West Side Story* (1961). During the slugfest, Biff, who is high on drugs, pulls a knife on his opponent. Rusty-James, in turn, swings from a waterpipe to avoid being cut, and the waterpipe bursts. Then he hurls Biff through the window of a deserted building.

Suddenly Motorcycle Boy appears out of nowhere, astride his bike. Rusty-James is momentarily distracted by his brother's unexpected appearance, and Biff slashes Rusty-James with a jagged piece of glass from the broken window. The blood gushing from Rusty-James's wound has been prefigured by the water rushing from the waterpipe. Motorcycle Boy retaliates by unleashing his riderless bike at full throttle on Biff, who is totally flattened by it. The image of Motorcycle Boy astride his cycle, which recurs in the film, evokes Marlon Brando as the biker in *The Wild One* (1954). Motorcycle Boy is likewise a bored and aimless nonconformist, "the quintessential teen anti-hero," determined to beat the system or die trying.[34]

On the way back to the tenement the boys inhabit with their father, Motorcycle Boy tells Rusty-James that during his sojourn in California he located their mother, who had deserted them in childhood. She is living in Los Angeles with a movie producer. Their father is glad to see the return of the prodigal son. The squalor in which the family lives is reflected in the messy tenement flat, while the empty booze bottles in the dirty sink symbolize the disorder of their dad's life, especially the manner in which he neglects his sons. Coppola sometimes photographs the father, who lives in an alcoholic haze, from a tilted angle, indicating that he is unsteady, off-balance.

Because he is color-blind, Motorcycle Boy says that he perceives the universe as if he were watching a black-and-white television set. He cannot "see what is over the rainbow." Significantly, the only color in his world he can see is that of the crimson rumble fish, which he shows to Rusty-Jones in a pet shop. In order to convey that Motorcycle Boy is color-blind, Coppola felt that Motorcycle Boy should occasionally see color for a few seconds, and then the color would disappear. Then it occurred to Coppola that "only the fish themselves—which serve as a metaphor for the story—would be in color."[35]

Motorcycle Boy calls the Siamese fighting fish "rumble fish" because they possess a fighting instinct that drives them to attack each other. Indeed, Motorcycle Boy says that if one holds a mirror up to the glass of the fish tank the rumble fish will even attack their own reflection. Motorcycle Boy senses a kinship between these hostile creatures and the rival gangs, who have rumbles to fight with each other.

In essence, Motorcycle Boy himself represents the young urban toughs who inhabit the crooked streets and shadowy alleys of their sleazy world, for he is at odds with society and refuses to conform to its norms. He is revered by his youthful peers for his stubborn attitude, which is antiestablishment and antiauthority. Motorcycle Boy's basic flaw, says Coppola, "is his inability to compromise, and that's why I made him color-blind. He interprets life in black-and-white."[36]

Rusty-James, an inarticulate, confused young man, is discouraged because the other gang members, who unabashedly admire his brother, constantly remind him that he is no match for Motorcycle Boy. "He's like royalty in exile," one of them opines. But Motorcycle Boy no longer has any such delusions of grandeur about himself. It is a bit of a burden to be Robin Hood, Jesse James, and the Pied Piper, he confesses to Rusty-James. He sees himself as little more than "the Neighborhood novelty."

Motorcycle Boy comes across a tattered photograph of the two brothers in childhood in which he holds his baby brother in a protective embrace. "You follow me around like a lost puppy," he later says to Rusty-James as they watch the rumble fish in the pet shop. "I wish I had been the big brother you always wanted." He has the nagging feeling that he has let his younger brother down, both as a role model and as a gang leader. "If you're gonna lead people, you've gotta have somewhere to go," he reflects. He implicitly realizes that he is a lost cause. Coppola pictures Motorcycle Boy as a kind of rat who cannot find his way out of a maze. Furthermore, more than once the brothers are photographed through a fence or the metal bars of a fire escape, suggesting that they are imprisoned together in a cruel and indifferent world and must stick together for survival.

One night Motorcycle Boy takes Rusty along with him as he breaks into the pet shop. He opens all the cages and releases the animals. This scene recalls Killer Kilgannon's similar action in *The Rain People*, which Hinton says she saw before she wrote *Rumble Fish* (see chapter 3). Motorcycle Boy then grabs the fishbowl containing the rumble fish, his "aquatic brothers," and tells Rusty-James that he intends to set them free in the nearby river. "They really belong in the river," he tells Rusty-James; "I don't think they'd rumble if they were in the river."

When the police arrive, Officer Patterson (William Smith), who has been convinced all along that Motorcycle Boy is a menace to society, goes after Motorcycle Boy. Patterson functions as the Angel of Death in the movie, for he has metaphorically hovered above Motorcycle Boy's head, waiting for him to step out of line. He seizes the opportunity afforded by the pet shop break-in to shoot Motorcycle Boy dead. The lad had hoped to escape the corrosive atmosphere of the big city by flight to a more wholesome environment, but for Motorcycle Boy, brutalized by life on the street, it is already too late. He is gunned down at the climax of *Rumble Fish*, just as Dallas was shot in cold blood in *The Outsiders*, in both instances by trigger-happy cops. Society has no place for rebellious loners like Dallas and Motorcycle Boy.

Patterson throws Rusty-James up against a police car and frisks him, and Rusty-James sees his own reflection in the car window in color—the only color image in the film besides that of the rumble fish. He smashes the window in anguish and frustration. His action of hitting his own reflection parallels a rumble fish attacking its own reflection in a mirror held up to the fish tank. Since the rumble fish are a symbol of "self-destructive teenagers trapped in urban poverty," they represent Rusty-James's determination to escape the narrow existence in which he feels entrapped.[37]

Coppola, who had used long takes extensively in *One from the Heart*, employs some extended takes impressively in this movie. At this point, for example, the camera tracks slowly from Motorcycle Boy's corpse, past the curious onlookers to Steve, Rusty-James's loyal friend who shares his grief. Then it passes on to the brothers' fuddled father, who turns away from his son's dead body, downs a swig of whiskey, and stumbles away from the tragic scene. This panning shot is much more effective than a series of quick cuts to various bystanders would have been, since the solemn, slow pan underlines the funereal sadness of the occasion.

The shooting script ends much differently than the film. The last scene as described in the shooting script concludes with Motorcycle Boy lying dead on the ground, "with the rumble fish flapping and dying around him, still too far from the river, . . . as the police car drives off with Rusty-James."[38] In the movie as released, Rusty James silently carries the fishbowl to the nearby river bank, then he fulfills his brother's last wish by throwing the rumble fish into the river. Remembering his deceased brother's advice that he should get out of town and follow the river clear to the sea, Rusty-James mounts his brother's motorcycle and roars off into the night.

There follows a brief epilogue that is also not in the shooting script and, therefore, like the wordless actions of Rusty James just described, must have been invented by Coppola during filming, since Hinton attests that it was he who contributed the visual imagery to the film. The movie concludes with Rusty-James in silhouette, astride the cycle on a California beach, silently watching the seagulls flit over the Pacific Ocean. He has indeed reached the sea. Moreover, he is now liberated from his hero worship of his brother and is no longer living under Motorcycle Boy's shadow. He is now prepared to get a fresh start in life—alone.

Coppola thought that throughout the film the underappreciated younger brother was certainly the more promising of the pair. In the end, says Coppola, Rusty-James has ceased to worship his brother as a false idol and grasped the fact that it is he who has survived, not his older brother. He has realized that "he, not his brother, is the one who is blessed."[39] Clearly,

Coppola's altered ending to the film gives it a more positive conclusion than the one in the screenplay, which concludes with Rusty-James being arrested and the rumble fish floundering on the ground.

It is generally believed that the negative reaction to the film at the New York Film Festival sabotaged the movie's chances to succeed with the public. If the movie failed on its original release, it is to some degree because *Rumble Fish* is an austere picture that is not easy to love. Several reviewers across the country subsequently condemned the movie as hopelessly obscure and pretentious. They pointed to the fantasy sequence in which Rusty-James passes out after he and his buddy Steve are pummeled by muggers. Rusty-James has a rapturous "out-of-body experience," in which he believes he is dead. As he floats above the city, he sees his comatose body stretched out on the ground below. He even imagines his own wake in a pool hall, as his grieving friends offer a toast "to Rusty-James, a real cool dude."

This fantasy sequence is surely relevant to the film, since it patently reflects a pathetic wish fulfillment on Rusty-James's part: he pictures himself being esteemed by his old buddies as a legend like his older brother, which is sadly not the case. David Ehrenstein calls this "wonderfully wacky moment" just the kind of element in a Coppola film that his critics dismiss as mere "visual trickery." One critic grudgingly complimented the movie for possessing a feverishly, partially redeeming grandeur, as evidenced in the fantasy sequence just noted. Another reviewer went so far as to state that this whimsical sequence reminds one that Coppola can be one of the most powerful filmmakers of our time. He summed up the picture by saying that Coppola has created a bleak, oppressive world, a simmering limbo of pool parlors, bars, and teen hangouts—clearly the work of an artist who refuses to surrender. Yet another critic observed that it seems that Coppola, still the maverick, simply will not behave. Prodded by the suits who run the studios to turn out another crowd-pleaser like *The Outsiders,* he instead followed up that picture that had captured the youth market with a baroque film, more likely to appeal to the much smaller art house set.[40] A small group of Coppola well-wishers endorsed his sophisticated handling of his material in *Rumble Fish,* calling it a brave film from a director who stands apart from the "flavor-of-the-month" mentality in Hollywood, whereby producers try to cater to the changes in public taste.

Rumble Fish has gained a following over the years. It is now seen as a highly inventive film that maintains an abrasive edge. The plot moves gamely along to the climax, where Motorcycle Boy's fate is sealed. While some reviewers saw the grim, forbidding movie as an addled, disjointed tale of young drifters, it is really a thought-provoking slice of street life about some losers who are being deprived of the little they have left to lose. The austere lighting and black-and-white photography help to give the movie genuine intensity, as the camera lingers on scenes of dereliction, finding artistic beauty in foggy railroad yards and smoky cafes. In fact, Dean Tavoularis's stark production design and Steven Burum's black-and-white cinematography deserved more credit than they got at the time of release for the shadowy, atmospheric netherworld they helped Coppola to create.

Coppola complained with some justification that the critics who reviewed the picture from the New York Film Festival did not even bother to acknowledge the performances in the film. Matt Dillon gives a much more shaded depiction of the misfit Rusty-James in *Rumble Fish* than he did in his rather perfunctory portrayal of Dallas Winston in *The Outsiders*. Mickey Rourke gives the performance of his career in his understated reading of Motorcycle Boy, and Vincent Spano gives an immaculate portrayal of Steve, Rusty-James's good-hearted best friend, who has the same sort of dogged devotion for Rusty-James that Rusty-James himself has for Motorcycle Boy. All three young actors effectively project the inner turmoil of modern young people.

Nevertheless, the movie did not find an audience at the time of its initial release and was pulled from distribution after only seven weeks, with a mere $1 million in earnings. By contrast, *The Outsiders* racked up a $12 million gross while it was playing first run. Still, *Rumble Fish*, like *One from the Heart*, attracted a larger audience in Europe than it did in the United States.

The Outsiders and *Rumble Fish* are linked and not only because they are both based on youth-oriented novels by S. E. Hinton that examine ritual gang violence. They are further connected by Coppla's consistent theme of family, which is quite visible in both movies. The Matt Dillon characters in *The Outsiders* and in *Rumble Fish* derive a sense of family from fellow gang members. Dallas Winston's dysfunctional family is all but nonexistent in *The Outsiders* and he has no contact with them to speak of. If he cares about anyone, it is Johnny and Ponyboy. Rusty-James's family in *Rumble Fish* collapsed when his mother took off for California, his father took to drink, and his brother became a restless vagabond. Rusty-James attempts to reestablish a family-like bond with Motorcycle Boy when the latter returns from California, but they never really reconnect. If anyone truly cares about Rusty-James, it is Steve, even when Rusty-James takes his friendship for granted.

Coppola's faith in *Rumble Fish* as a significant film has been vindicated, to the extent that it has over the years achieved the status of a cult film, and it is often shown in college film courses. Furthermore, film historians acknowledge in retrospect Coppola's artistic courage in making an unrelentingly pessimistic picture about modern youth, which transcends the simplistic presentation of youngsters in more innocuous, safe teen flicks. "That film has gained some sort of underground status," says Barry Malkin. "The black-and-white photography with splashes of color, the painted shadows of the German expressionistic cinema," and Stewart Copeland's music "have garnered a following."[41] Summing up Coppola's two youth movies, Bergan perhaps says it all when he declares that "both films proved that Coppola was not content to make genre movies in a conventional way" but, instead, breathed new life into the old formulas.[42]

Since *Rumble Fish* failed to find an audience at the time of its original release, however, Coppola found it difficult at the time to mount another production. Quite unexpectedly he was brought in at the eleventh hour to help salvage a picture entitled *The Cotton Club* by none other than his old nemesis from *The Godfather* days, Robert Evans.

9

Night Life

The Cotton Club

I don't like crap games with barons and earls;
Don't go to Harlem in ermine and pearls
. . . .
That's why the lady is a tramp.

> —Words and music by Lorenz Hart and Richard Rodgers

Very often performers were court jesters or troubadours for the
gangsters, whether they liked it or not, because the gangsters
owned the place. That's part of the world they were in.

> —Martin Scorsese

Robert Evans, who was production chief at Paramount when Francis
Ford Coppola filmed *The Godfather* there, in due course left his position to become an independent producer, releasing films through Paramount. After producing successful movies like *Chinatown* (1974), Evans
subsequently turned out some flops. To make matters worse, he was
convicted of cocaine possession. By the early 1980s, Evans's career was
in dire straits, and he hoped to get back on top by making *The Cotton
Club*.

In 1982 Evans optioned James Haskins's *The Cotton Club*, a coffee-
table book that was a nonfiction picture-history of the famous Harlem

nightclub that enjoyed its heyday in the Roaring Twenties, a cabaret where the drinks were cold and the jazz was hot.

The Cotton Club was designed as a musical about the famed Harlem nightspot that flourished in the Prohibition Era, where the entertainers were black and the customers were white. Because the club was run by racketeers, the plot at times takes on the dimensions of a gangster picture, thereby recalling Coppola's *Godfather* films. The concept of blending the format of the movie musical with that of the gangster movie—the two most popular film genres during the period of the early talkies—seemed like a dandy idea in theory, but it proved difficult to work out in practice.

Evans planned to finance the picture through private investors so that all the rights to the picture would belong to him. In his familiar fashion of expressing himself in crudities, he touted the film project to prospective investors as filled with gangsters, music, and "pussy galore," a reference to the temptress with that name in one of the James Bond movies.[1] He eventually made a deal with Ed and Fred Doumani, owners of the Tropicana and El Morocco casinos in Las Vegas. The brothers were reputed to have links to the Mafia in Vegas, but Evans believed that their checkbooks were as good as anyone else's. The Doumanis committed themselves to investing in the film, which Evans budgeted at $20 million.

One of the project's drawing cards was that Evans had signed superstar Richard Gere (*An Officer and a Gentleman*) to appear in the movie. Gere would play one of the rare white musicians who appeared at the Cotton Club. Evans also obtained Gregory Hines, the popular black actor-hoofer whose own grandmother had danced at the Cotton Club, to play a featured role.

Since the present film was to some extent a gangster picture, Evans commissioned Mario Puzo—who by this time had co-written the screenplays of *The Godfather* and *Godfather II*—to do the first draft of the script. But Evans was dissatisfied with the screenplay Puzo submitted in the summer of 1982. Since all Puzo had to work with was Haskins's nonfiction account of the Cotton Club, he had to weave a plotline virtually out of whole cloth, and his scenario simply did not hold together.

Orion Pictures was willing to distribute the picture, provided that Evans could present them with a viable script. It occurred to Evans that he should corral Francis Coppola, the experienced script doctor who had saved *Patton* and other screenplays over the years, to do a rewrite of Puzo's draft.

The producer was aware that Coppola had creditors snapping at his heels in the wake of the collapse of Zoetrope Studios in Los Angeles (see chapter 7). Indeed, Coppola was still living under the shadow of bankruptcy, and the bill collectors were already getting into his wife's jewelry box. Al-though Evans and Coppola had had multiple clashes during the filming of *The Godfather,* Evans was confident that Coppola would be glad to make a fast buck revising Puzo's *Cotton Club* screenplay.

In March 1983 he phoned Coppola and begged him to rescue the script: "Francis, my baby is sick and needs a doctor." He added for good measure that the trio responsible for *The Godfather*—Evans, Puzo, and Coppola—would then all be involved in *The Cotton Club.* Evans was convinced that the new picture would be "*The Godfather* with music," and would prove to be another winner.[2] Coppola remembers that Evans called him "in des-peration with some hokey metaphor that his baby was sick and needed a doctor. I said I'd be happy to help him for a week or so, no charge."[3] That week eventually stretched into a commitment on Coppola's part that lasted well over a year, as he ultimately not only rewrote the script but directed the film as well.

The Cotton Club (1984)

Coppola was frankly appalled by the Puzo screenplay, which turned out to be an undigested mishmash of hoods and jazz. It was, in brief, a shallow gangster story devoid of any zest. So he accepted Evans's offer of five hun-dred thousand dollars to do a full-fledged reworking of the script. Coppola invited Evans, Gere, and Hines to his estate in the Napa Valley, where he held a week-long script conference. He even mapped out on a blackboard his concept of the script as a gangster musical. Each day concluded with Coppola cooking a huge Italian dinner for his collaborators.

He then flew to New York City, where he engaged in background re-search on the scenario before attacking the screenplay. Coppola burrowed through countless volumes on Harlem, racketeers, and jazz while listening to Duke Ellington recordings.

Coppola's first musical, *Finian's Rainbow,* had dealt in some degree with the black community, and now he wanted *The Cotton Club* to do the same (see chapter 2). In the light of his voluminous research, Coppola de-cided to soft-pedal the gangster elements of the plot and focus more on the Harlem Renaissance, when Afro-American culture flourished in literature, music, and dance in New York's black community in the Roaring Twenties.

The Harlem Renaissance was epitomized by the Cotton Club, located on the corner of 142nd Street and Lenox Avenue in Harlem, where top black entertainers performed between 1923 and 1935. Duke Ellington's or-chestra was the house band from 1927 to 1930, when Ellington was replaced by Cab Calloway. The bands accompanied singers like Lena Horne and Ethel Waters and dancers like Bill "Bojangles" Robinson. The chorus girls were ballyhooed as tall, tan, and terrific, and the club was elaborately decorated like an old-fashioned Southern plantation. But, according to club policy, only well-heeled white patrons were welcome at the Cotton Club. Indeed, it was fashionable for upscale white clientele to go slumming at the Harlem club to drink bootleg liquor from drinking glasses disguised as tin cans and listen to jazz.

Club policy was dictated by Owney Madden, a gangster who ran the club as a front for his racketeering, with financing from a syndicate of white criminals. So entertainment and crime were inextricably linked in the operation of the Cotton Club, as Martin Scorsese states in an epigraph for this chapter.

"In reading some of the research," Coppola explains, he discovered that the Jazz Age was "a very rich and very stimulating period. So I ultimately took a shot at the script. . . . I sort of fell in love with the Cotton Club. It's an epic, it's a story of the times": it tells the story of the black entertainers, of the white gangsters, "everything of those times."[4]

On April 5, 1983, Coppola finished his first rewrite of the Puzo script in which he emphasized the cultural achievements of the Harlem Renaissance. Evans was severely disappointed with Coppola's draft, since Coppola had considerably reduced Richard Gere's role in the film in order to foreground the black performers at the Club. The producer fumed that Coppola's script departed drastically from the scenario that he had outlined at Napa. Evans maintained that it read like a grant proposal for a documentary about the Harlem Renaissance—it even included readings by black poets. With Gere's strong support, Evans insisted that Coppola build up the white superstar's role in the picture. Coppola thus felt that Evans was selling him down the river and ruefully suspected that the script was not going to turn out to be the tribute to black popular culture he had envisioned it to be.

The Doumanis demanded that Evans show them Coppola's first version of the screenplay, the one Evans himself was not satisfied with. He diffidently submitted it to them, along with a bogus note, to which he had forged Coppola's initial "F" as a signature, stating: "Well, after twenty-two days, here is the blueprint. Now let's get down to writing the script."[5] The counterfeit note was meant to assure the Doumanis that Coppola was committed to a complete rewrite of the script, but they were not taken in. They still threatened to snap their purses shut if a better script was not in the offing.

Evans panicked and frantically cast about for other investors. He got to hear about Elaine Jacobs (a.k.a., Karen Jacobs-Greenberger), a rich, blonde divorcée from Texas who was interested in getting into the film business. She was in fact involved in dubious dealings with the underworld and had ties to a Colombian drug cartel. But Evans at this juncture felt that beggars couldn't be choosers and agreed to let Jacobs put him in touch with Roy Radin, a sleazy variety show promoter from New York. Radin arranged a multimillion-dollar loan from some of his disreputable financial sources in order to provide Evans with additional backing for *The Cotton Club*. Hearing about Evans's negotiations with Jacobs and Radin, one trade paper commented that Evans was willing to make deals with individuals whom most reputable producers would hesitate to shake hands with.

Shortly afterward Radin had a major falling out with Jacobs, who discovered that he had surreptitiously possessed himself of two hundred kilos of cocaine from her private stash. Radin was last seen on May 13, 1983, getting into Jacobs's limo, on his way to a dinner meeting with her at La Scala at which they were presumably going to bury the hatchet. As a matter of fact, the hatchet, so to speak was buried in Radin: his decomposed corpse turned up a month later in a remote canyon on the outskirts of Los Angeles. He had been shot several times through the head, and a stick of dynamite had been shoved into his mouth and the fuse lit. Evans, aware that the drug dealings between Radin and Jacobs had gone sour, went ballistic. A detective on the case later testified that Evans confided to the Doumanis, "That bitch killed Radin; and I'm next"—though there was no evidence that Jacobs was a threat to Evans.[6]

Still, Evans was inevitably dragged into the case as a material witness, and so Jacobs's trial was dubbed by the tabloids the *Cotton Club* murder case. He was eventually exonerated of any involvement in Radin's death, while Jacobs was convicted of the kidnapping and killing of Radin in retaliation for the theft of the cocaine. Evans rewarded the Los Angeles homicide squad with autographed copies of the script for *Chinatown*. Needless to say, the loan Radin had engineered for Evans never materialized. Brett Morgen and Nanette Burstein's documentary *The Kid Stays in the Picture*, based on Evans's autobiography of the same title, is riveting in its coverage of the *Cotton Club* murder case. It includes newsreel footage of the murder scene and of Jacobs's trial.

Meanwhile Coppola, who staunchly contends that he was completely ignorant of Evans's negotiations with Jacobs and Radin, soldiered on with the screenplay, with Evans, Gere, and Hines kibitzing over his shoulder. He decided that the only way to make more room for the white gangster plot in the scenario was to have the story of the Cotton Club's black entertainers simply provide a backdrop for the melodrama about the white mobsters. Evans, along with Gere and Hines, bought the concept.

Because Coppola as screenwriter seemed to be so cooperative, Evans broached to him the possibility of directing the movie. In June 1983 Coppola agreed to helm *The Cotton Club*: "I knew that *The Cotton Club* material was so rich," he says, "that, if I had control, there was no reason why I couldn't make a beautiful film out of it."[7]

The Doumanis reaffirmed their role as investors in the film in the light of the new script and recruited Denver oilman Victor Sayyah as a co-investor. Like the Doumanis, Sayyah was known to be a tough customer and to drive a hard bargain. The trio advised Evans that Coppola must not overspend on this picture as he had on his previous musical, *One from the Heart*. "Don't worry, I can control Francis," Evans reassured them. He assumed that Coppola had been chastened by the recent commercial failure of *Rumble Fish* and would be more open to listening to an experienced producer like Evans.[8] By the time Coppola signed on to direct the movie, however, the project was plagued with a variety of production problems. Coppola did his best to improve matters, which to him basically meant ignoring Evans, who had been mismanaging the production.

The producer had rented the Astoria Studios in Queens to shoot the picture, and a host of highly paid technicians had already been working there for six months with minimal supervision from Evans. Preproduction costs were running to $140,000 a week and had risen alarmingly to $13 million before Coppola took over the direction of the movie. For example, production designer Richard Sylbert, whom Evans had engaged before Coppola came on the picture, had recreated a lavish replica of the Cotton Club. The set's authentic detail amazed former employees of the original club who inspected it, but the Cotton Club set alone cost $5 million.

Coppola demanded total creative control of the production from this point onward, since he was no longer just the scriptwriter. As writer alone he was willing to defer to Evans on the script, but as director he reserved the right not only to final cut but to further revise the script during production. In negotiating with Evans, he was very clear on this point, he remembers, "because Bob Evans is a known back-seat driver, a man who is prone to tinker with other people's work from his office or apartment."[9]

Coppola decided that the screenplay was not up to par and called in Pulitzer prize-winning novelist William Kennedy, who had written a trilogy of novels about the Roaring Twenties, including one about racketeer "Legs" Diamond. He wanted Kennedy to ensure period accuracy in the script and to provide some terse, pungent dialogue. Evans balked at bringing in yet another expensive writer, but Coppola insisted. Coppola and Kennedy began their collaboration in the same suite at the historic Astoria Studios in which the Marx Brothers had held forth while filming *The Cocoanuts* there in 1929. The pair worked round the clock in a feverish, pressured atmosphere that Kennedy likened to that of the city room of a large metropolitan newspaper.

One of the major obstacles they met in rewriting the script, according to Kennedy, was the "perpetual task of enhancing Richard Gere's role."[10] Since Gere as Dixie Dwyer, the lone white musician at the Cotton Club, was the male lead, he had to be central to the study. So Dixie became an employee of the infamous Dutch Schultz (James Remar), a sadistic real-life mobster who frequented the club. For the record, Dutch Schultz was born Arthur Flegenheimer. He took his pseudonym from a hoodlum named Dutch Schultz, who had flourished in the 1890s. Good-natured musician Dixie Dwyer comes off as a foil to racketeer Dutch Schultz, whom Coppola and Kennedy frankly found a far more intriguing character to develop than Dixie. The screenwriters produced what they called a "rehearsal script," which had already gone through several drafts, just in time for the cast to use it during the rehearsal period that would precede principal photography.

In addition to Richard Gere and Gregory Hines (as Delbert "Sandman" Williams), the cast now included Bob Hoskins as Owney Madden; Diane Lane, who had appeared in two previous Coppola films, as Vera Cicero, Dixie's inamorata; and Leonette McKee as Leila Rose Oliver, Hines's love interest. Gregory Hines's own brother, Maurice, played Delbert's brother Clayton Williams. Julian Beck, co-founder of New York's Living Theater, was cast as Sol Weinstein, Dutch Schultz's grizzled, world-weary enforcer—this was a casting coup similar to Coppola's snagging the Actors Studio's Lee Strasberg to appear in *Godfather II*. Fabled Broadway musical comedy queen Gwen Verdon took the part of the Dwyer boys' mother. Nicolas Cage was given a meatier role than he had had in *Rumble Fish*, that of Gere's tough younger brother, Vincent "Mad Dog" Dwyer. Larry Fishburne, by now a Coppola regular, played "Bumpy" Rhodes, a black hood.

Evans and Coppola squabbled over casting decisions on this film, just as they had on *The Godfather*. Evans in particular contested Coppola's wish to hire Fred Gwynne, known primarily as a comic strip actor; Coppola wished to cast Gwynne against type as hangdog Frenchy DeMange, Madden's chief henchman. Since Evans had disputed several of Coppola's earlier decisions, such as the hiring of William Kennedy, Coppola finally lost patience with the producer and issued an ultimatum to him. Declaring, "I'm fed up with you. Tired of your second guessing,"[11] Coppola threatened to quit and take the next plane for San Francisco if Evans did not cease challenging his casting choices. Evans gave in and cast Gwynne, but he referred to Coppola afterward sardonically as Prince Machiavelli.

Although Evans had earlier assured the Doumanis that he alone could control Coppola, he failed to realize that Coppola, still the Hollywood maverick, insisted on doing things his own way and would not be dictated to by producers. He understandably was determined to hold on tenaciously to the artistic control of the production that Evans had promised him.

The three-week rehearsal period commenced on July 25, 1983. Once more Coppola videotaped the rehearsals, allowing the cast to improvise bits of dialogue within certain limits. He would incorporate any of the improved dialogue he thought had worked particularly well into the script at the end of each day. He wound up the rehearsal period by employing his "previsualization" technique. He taped a complete run-through of the screenplay with the actors in front of a blue screen. Then he replaced the blue background with suitable shots of Harlem in the Roaring Twenties, inspired by Haskins's book of photos.

Evans had personally selected the technical crew before Coppola came in, and Coppola did not want a crew made up of Evans's partisans who were already prone to criticize his directorial decisions. On a day known ever after as "Black Sunday," a reference to the title of one of Evans's flops, Coppola summarily fired several technicians, as well as choreographer Dyson Lovell. (For the record, Coppola had now parted company with the original choreographer on all three of his musicals.) He dismissed Lovell, he explains, because the routines Lovell had designed up to that point were not vintage Cotton Club numbers. They rather suggested a glitzy *Ice Capades* salute to Duke Ellington. For Lovell, Coppola substituted Michael Smuin, who had choreographed the fight scenes in *Rumble Fish,* and mollified Lovell with a credit as executive producer.

Coppola likewise dismissed the director of photography, John Alcott, because he had to work too closely with the cinematographer to go with an Evans pick. He approached Gordon Willis (*Godfather* and *Godfather II*), but Willis stated flatly that he did not believe in directors "sitting in trailers and talking to people over loudspeakers," a practice Coppola had instituted after the two *Godfather* films.[12] As we know, Coppola had learned by painful experience on *One from the Heart* that he had to be on the sound stage to set up each shot. He would continue the practice he had established on *The Outsiders* and *Rumble Fish,* however, of reviewing each take on a monitor close to the set and only retreat to the Silverfish trailer to view each completed scene before he passed it on to editor Barry Malkin, a veteran of several Coppola films. In any case, Coppola finally replaced Alcott with British cinematographer Stephen Goldblatt (*The Hunger*).

Coppola and Kennedy, as said before, had continued to revise the screenplay during the rehearsal period. The final shooting script, dated August 22, 1983, was circulated to cast and crew just days before principal photography officially began on August 28. On the first day of filming Richard Gere was nowhere to be found. Coppola was advised by an intermediary that the star was unhappy with the way Coppola was handling the production. Gere was accustomed to learning his lines and shooting the script as written. To him Coppola's flexibility about changing the script seemed haphazard. The screenplay, he believed, was becoming more and more elusive. Gere was also dissatisfied with his financial arrangement on the picture. This led Coppola to surmise that Gere's refusal to come to the set was mostly to get himself a bigger piece of the pie.

Coppola shot around Gere for the first week, commenting wryly, "I specialize in being a ringmaster of a circus that's inventing itself."[13] When Evans boosted Gere's income for the picture, Gere showed up for work at the beginning of the second week of shooting, thus confirming the suspicion of Coppola, who saw Gere's making trouble at the outset of filming as thoroughly unprofessional. The incident created bad blood between director and star, and their relationship was strained throughout the production experience. At one point Coppola snapped at Gere, after a disagreement over a scene, that Gere obviously did not like him—he assured Gere that the feeling was mutual.

Coppola was further incensed when he had been directing the movie for a month without receiving a penny of his salary. He was so strapped for ready cash because of his precarious financial status that American Express canceled his credit card. So Coppola threatened to walk off the picture if his salary was not immediately forthcoming. Evans paid up.

Another financial crisis arose when the cast and crew missed a paycheck, and the unions simply ordered the union employees to go on strike until they were paid. (Gone were the days when studio employees would work for deferred wages, as they did on *One from the Heart*.) Coppola sprinted into the center of the soundstage and guaranteed that he would pay everyone out of his own pocket before the shoot was over, if need be. As it happened, an armored car drove onto the lot later in the day with the checks, but Coppola's rather operatic gesture was generally appreciated nonetheless—even though he obviously could never have hoped to make good his grand promise.

Recalling Evans's constant interference during the shooting of *The Godfather,* when Evans was studio boss at Paramount, Coppola took the precaution of barring him from the set of *The Cotton Club.* He was able to make this stricture stick by once more threatening to quit: "Who needs this?! You need me, I don't need you," he stormed at Evans. "You stay; I leave."[14] Evans was conscious that Orion had more confidence in Coppola, who had directed the recent blockbuster, *The Outsiders,* than in Evans himself, who could not boast of a hit in living memory. Therefore, in order to acquire $15 million from Orion to cover mounting bills, Evans reluctantly relinquished total control of the production to Coppola and agreed to stay off the set. When asked by film historian Peter Biskind about his reaction to Coppola's interdict, Evans answered bitterly, "I wanted to pick him up and throw the fat fuck out of the window."[15] "It was like giving up your kid, but I had no choice," Evans laments in his memoirs. "I was quarantined to what was commonly called 'the crisis center,'" a Manhattan town house that served as his home and office during production.[16] He finally faced the fact that if Coppola was calling the shots there was no point in his being around the set anyway.

Since Coppola found it helpful to have his co-scripter Susie Hinton on the set of *Rumble Fish* for last-minute rewrites, he decided to keep Kennedy on salary while *The Cotton Club* was in production. Gregory Hines remembers, "Francis at times would come on the set and say, 'We don't have a scene here,'" and begin reworking it with the cast. "Then you'd see the scene come together." Afterward, Coppola and Kennedy would put the scene in final form in the script.[17]

When Gere and some of the other actors complained about the ever-evolving script, Coppola emphatically pointed out that some of the key alterations in the script were made at the behest of the principal investors, the Doumani brothers and Sayyah. "They kept asking me to figure out ways to rewrite, to lower the budget," by eliminating from the script some of the locations and some of the sets, Coppola explains.[18] Hence Coppola would try to figure out ways to stage more scenes in the Cotton Club in order to trim the number of settings needed for the film and to make more use of Sylbert's multimillion-dollar Cotton Club set.

Still the endless script revisions caused delays in shooting. After all, substantially reworking a scene with the actors prior to shooting was time-consuming—as Gordon Willis complained vociferously while photographing *The Godfather.* As a result, filming fell increasingly behind schedule. Thus actors would show up on the set in make-up and costume to do a scheduled scene, only to find by the end of the day that Coppola would not get to that scene until the next day at the earliest. This situation was repeated throughout the shoot with some regularity. Bob Hoskins's scenes were delayed so often that he really got bored sitting around his dressing room day after day, "waiting for something to happen." Eventually, he says, "you forgot what you do for a living."[19] Diane Lane adds, "This went on for months. We never knew when we were going to shoot."

Nicolas Cage became so frustrated by the delays that one day he angrily trashed his dressing room. "I was slated for three weeks' work," he explains. "I was there for six months, in costume, in makeup, on the set" in case Coppola got around to doing a scene in which Cage was scheduled to appear.[20] Francis Coppola tactfully explained his nephew's behavior by saying that Cage's fit of rage was meant to help him in preparing to play the ruthless "Mad Dog" Dwyer in the picture, a character based on the real gangster "Mad Dog" Coll.

The trio of investors constantly pressured Coppola to cut expenses, but, as Coppola periodically reminded them, the production had been running full speed ahead for six months before he came on board, and "the Tiffany concept" of the production had already been firmly established. The shooting period for *The Cotton Club* eventually ran to eighty-seven days, spread over twenty-two months. By the end of shooting, the budget had skyrocketed to $48 million, nearly double the original figure.

Toward the end of filming, the Doumanis realized that the Christmas season was coming, and, if principal photography continued during the Christmas holidays, the overtime paid to the union crew members would be prohibitively expensive. The Doumanis and Sayyah, who had no previous experience in the picture business and who had had no luck in dealing with Coppola, were finally fed up. In fact, Sayyah got so infuriated during a cost-accounting conference with associate producer Melissa Prophet, Coppola's liaison with the investors, that he went berserk and hurled her through a plate glass window.[21] A wag quipped that a Prophet is not known in her own country. With that, Sayyah sheepishly repaired to Vegas.

The brothers brought in a hoodlum from Las Vegas named Joey Cusumano, who was known to be associated with the Vegas Mafia, to scare Coppola into finishing the film before Christmas and gave him a coproducer screen credit on the film for his trouble. Cusumano, whom Ed Doumani complimented for his "street savvy," did threaten Coppola during a production meeting. He pointed to the Silverfish trailer and said ominously, "You see this Silverfish! If we go past December 23, this is going into the ocean with the rest of the fishes."[22] Coppola (who had gotten along with the Mafiosi who showed up on the location sites of *The Godfather* when he was shooting in Italian neighborhoods in New York) knew how to patronize a mobster. (Cusumano would subsequently be jailed for racketeering in Las Vegas after his chores on the film were finished.)

Coppola announced posthaste that he was going to draw on his early experience working on Roger Corman's low-budget flicks (see chapter 1). He would abandon any further rewrites and shoot the remaining scenes with maximum efficiency. Three days in a row he did a dozen camera setups per day, whereas he had previously been averaging two to three setups a day. On December 22, Coppola took the unit to Grand Central Station to film the final scene, which he and Kennedy had not had time to script. Coppola kept the cameras rolling for nearly twenty hours and wrapped the picture at 6:00 AM on December 23, 1983, Cusumano's zero hour.

When filming was completed, Evans sued Coppola because he wanted to be consulted on the editing of the film. When Evans contended in court that the budget had ballooned to over $40 million with Coppola running the show, Barrie Osborne, Orion's official representative on the picture, responded that the studio believed that $40 million was "a normal figure for the scope of the picture," especially "when you have a director of Coppola's stature."[23]

Coppola won the case, retaining control of the film's editing process. So Evans was banished from the editing room just as he had been barred from the set. He took some consolation in the $500,000 cash settlement with the Doumanis, which he received in exchange for relinquishing all of his rights over the film. He also retained the official screen credit as principal producer of the film, since he had personally originated and developed the project.

Evans declared in a press interview at the time that he was satisfied with the outcome of his lawsuit since he no longer had to play David, doing battle with Goliath (Coppola). He also repeated his claim in the interview that Coppola was mostly to blame for the overages on the production. Evans states that Coppola was so incensed at these remarks that he bashed his fist on his desk several times in anger and had to be taken to a hospital emergency room for treatment. More recently, when asked about his volatile relationship with Evans, Coppola coolly observed, "For years Evans has put out a stream of nonsense about me, and I have pretty much ignored it. I only wish him well."[24]

During postproduction Coppola was faced with a half-million feet of film, which he had to edit into a movie with roughly a two-hour running time. In order to release the film at Christmas 1984, Coppola employed a battery of eighteen editors during postproduction, with Barry Malkin and Robert Lovett as supervising editors.

Coppola had learned his lesson with *One from the Heart* when it came to having premature test screenings of a film (see chapter 7). In the late spring of 1984 he had a private screening of a 140-minute rough cut for an invited audience that included no film critics and no industry executives. The reaction was mildly favorable, but several of the viewers thought the film overlength. Accordingly, Coppola decided that the movie should be edited down close to two hours. One way of shortening the film was to condense the songs and dances performed by the black entertainers at the Cotton Club and leave the main plot about the white mobsters pretty much intact.

Barry Malkin, for one, was not in harmony with this decision, though it was endorsed by Orion. "*The Cotton Club* was a film that got compressed to its detriment," he contends. "Right from the very beginning, there's a dance piece involving the Cotton Club girls, and it's intercut with the titles." Originally this dance routine, shot in smoky color, was a self-contained sequence, and some of it was lost when it was combined with the opening credits, which are in black-and-white. This number displayed the sassy, high-kicking chorines as they paraded across the screen, accompanied by the original recording of Duke Ellington's band playing "The Mooche," all wailing clarinets and sultry strings. "I preferred it when it was . . . a separate sequence," Malkin concludes. In sum, Malkin thought *The Cotton Club* "would have been more successful in a longer version."[25]

In the fall of 1984 Orion sponsored sneak previews of the picture in Boston, Seattle, and San Diego. Evans saw the sneak in San Diego as a paying customer—"Though I wasn't invited, I was there," he remembers—and he was severely disappointed with the picture. He went back to his hotel and stayed up all night composing a thirty-one-page memo to Coppola. Evans told him in effect that "there's a great picture there, but it's not on the screen—it's on the cutting room floor."[26] Ed Doumani personally delivered Evans's memo to Coppola in Napa. He reported to Evans that Coppola commented that "he would not implement any of that prick's suggestions."[27] Actually, Coppola was miffed at Evans's insistence that he lengthen the film's running time, since Coppola had shorn much of the background material about the Cotton Club and the Harlem Renaissance at the script stage at the behest of Evans and the Doumanis. The maestro, concludes Evans, purposely ignored his every written word.

Malkin was not aware that he was in full accord with Evans on wanting a longer final cut. He said afterward that he worked eighteen months on the picture and never once laid eyes on Bob Evans. In any event, there was no indication in the preview cards from these advance screenings that the audience wanted more of the performers at the Cotton Club. On the contrary, the younger members of the preview audiences consistently complained that there was too much tap dancing. As a result, the dance routines were further truncated as one of the ways of bringing the film in at two hours. In retrospect, Coppola acknowledges that "we eliminated about twenty minutes or so" of the musical numbers "that probably should not have been cut out."[28] "The response of the test audiences is paramount," adds Malkin—"it becomes the bottom line; the tail wags the dog."[29] Orion allowed Coppola to restore nine minutes of material to plug up some holes in the plot, if not to lengthen any of the dance numbers. So the film was finally released at 128 minutes.

The plot of *The Cotton Club* as released revolves around the lives of two pairs of brothers, and their stories are told in parallel fashion. The white brothers are Dixie and Vincent Dwyer. Dixie Dwyer, a cornet player, is the token white musician at the Cotton Club and is allowed to sit in with the band. He is also a minion of beer baron Dutch Schultz and secretly falls for Dutch's teenaged gun moll, Vera Cicero. His younger brother Vinnie is an inexperienced hood who hopes to gain the Dutchman's favor by becoming Dutch's bodyguard. The two black brothers are Delbert "Sandman" Williams and Clayton Williams, a dance team at the Cotton Club. Sandman longs to make it big as a solo act in order to impress Lila Rose Oliver, a satiny torch singer at the club. Clay is hurt when Sandman goes off on his own, but they eventually are reconciled.

Since the story of the white characters eclipses that of the black characters in the picture, a fair amount of screen time is spent in portraying how Dixie uses his association with Dutch Schultz to snag the title role in a Hollywood gangster picture called *Mob Boss*, in which he imitates his erstwhile boss Dutch Schultz. To that extent Dixie is based on George Raft, a dancer in New York nightclubs who, by his own admission, got help from top underworld figures in his struggle to make it in pictures. He gained overnight success as a coin-flipping gangster in *Scarface* (1932). Gere even had his hair brushed back flat with brilliantine just to look more like Raft. (Dixie's parlaying his mob connections into a screen career recalls the episode in *The Godfather* when Vito Corleone fostered the movie career of Johnny Fontane, who, as we know, was modeled in some ways on Frank Sinatra.) Dixie "turns his back on the world of violent crime in order to mock it in the movies."[30]

At one point Dixie and Vera actually get to do a complete musical number, when he accompanies her on his cornet as she warbles, "Am I Blue?" Their song is not shortened, possibly because of its significance in presaging that they eventually will be united in a real-life duet, after he makes it big in Tinsel Town.

One way Coppola bolstered the gangster plot in the picture was by interpolating into the story some historical events from the gangster wars of the Roaring Twenties. Vincent "Mad Dog" Dwyer was inspired by Vincent "Mad Dog" Coll, as was mentioned earlier. Like his namesake, Vinnie Dwyer is a reckless, unpredictable hoodlum who quickly makes a number of enemies in the underworld. As Owney Madden says in exasperation, "What do you do with a mad dog in the street?" Madden arranges for Vinnie to be riddled with bullets in a drugstore phone booth. This is precisely how Mad Dog Call met his death.

By the same token, the movie also incorporates the death of Dutch Schultz just as it happened in reality. Madden, who is described as a "class guy" when it comes to running the Cotton Club, is as ruthless as the rest of the gangsters in the picture when the occasion arises. He decides in consultation with real-life Mafia czar Charles "Lucky" Luciano (Joe Dallesandro) that the hotheaded Dutchman's violent, mercurial behavior is getting out of hand. Moreover, they fear that Dutch might panic and spill his guts to the new crime commissioner in New York, Thomas Dewey, who has amassed impressive evidence about Dutch's crimes. Coppola inserts a private joke in the dialogue at this point: one of Luciano's henchmen advises him that the Dutchman is not bullet proof, so they should treat him "like we treated Coppola," someone that the mob had rubbed out!

Madden and Luciano arrange to have Dutch Schultz mowed down in the Palace Chophouse and Tavern in Newark, New Jersey—an event that actually took place on October 23, 1935. Dutch's murder conjures up memories of Michael Corleone opening fire on two of the Corleones' enemies in a Bronx restaurant in *The Godfather*. In conceiving the scene depicting Dutchman's murder, Coppola recalls, "I started with the notion that tap dancing sounds like machine guns."[31] He then got the ingenious notion to intercut Gregory Hines's rapid-fire tap dancing at the Cotton Club with the machine gun bullets that slaughter Dutch Schultz in the Newark restaurant, so that the sound of the tap dancing melds with that of the machine gun fire on the sound track. At this point the gangster picture and the movie musical truly intersect. The Dutchman slumps over the table dead, as Sandman finishes his routine.

One critic indicated that *The Cotton Club* was not a satisfying film because, as producer David O. Selznick (*Gone with the Wind*) once said, blood and jokes do not mix. As a matter of fact, the film is not really a comedy with music but a drama with music. It is indeed a very dark film, with a high body count—many more characters bite the dust than I have detailed here. The only unalloyed optimism reflected in the movie is the reunion of the two couples, one white, the other black, in the finale. Otherwise, the picture is mainly serious melodrama.

At film's end Vera is now free of Dutch and can marry Dixie, and Sandman has likewise won the heart of Lila. Coppola accordingly stages a grand finale that cuts between Grand Central Station and a Grand Central set on the Cotton Club stage—a sequence that is not in the shooting script and, consequently, was created by Coppola during filming.

In this final production number montage, "the conclusion of the narrative is blended together with a Cotton Club production spectacular," and the delirious crosscutting between Grand Central Station and the Cotton Club stage makes it difficult to distinguish between the two locations: Sometimes it appears that the club chorus is dancing in Grand Central Station.[32] On stage, Clay Williams leads the Cotton Club company through a dance number set in the depot, and the action shifts to Sandman and Lila at Grand Central Station going off on their honeymoon, while Dixie is reunited with Vera on the depot platform. The two couples travel off on the Twentieth Century Limited toward marital bliss, to the tune of Duke Ellington's "Daybreak Express." Pianist-humorist Oscar Levant once described the movie musical as a series of catastrophes ending in a floor show. That description certainly fits *The Cotton Club*, which has its share of catastrophes and yet concludes with a dazzling production number.

The most noticeable flaw in the film is its lack of a solid story line, possibly due to the fact that the major source of the screenplay was Haskins's nonfiction pictorial history of the club. Consequently, Coppola was handicapped by the necessity of creating a coherent narrative of his own, something that had stymied Puzo. Moreover, the film was ostensibly structured to tell the stories of the two sets of brothers, whose lives are influenced by their association with the Cotton Club and the gangsters who run it. But the producers, as stated, mandated that the main plot be devoted to the Dwyer brothers, with the Williams brothers relegated to a subplot. As a result, "the parallel stories are not effectively intertwined—they simply pass in the night," the way that the two pairs of brothers pass each other on the street in one scene.[33]

Admittedly, Coppola made some concessions to Evans and the Doumanis at the script stage and to the Orion executives during the final edit, but the moguls' effort to control the irrepressible maverick Francis

Coppola met with only limited success. *The Cotton Club* turned out to be essentially a Francis Coppola film, certainly not a Robert Evans film. "Regardless of the input Coppola gets from others on a picture, it somehow always turns out fundamentally the way he wants it to," one industry insider, who spoke on condition of anonymity, told me. "I have never figured out how he does it." That makes Coppola a genuine auteur, the author of every film he has made. Indeed, the relationships of the two pairs of brothers reflect Coppola's constant theme about the dynamics of family and recall the complicated interactions of the Corleone brothers in the *Godfather* films. In short, that theme helps to tie his films together.

In fact, the parallels between *The Cotton Club* and the first two *Godfather* films led Pauline Kael to assert that *The Cotton Club* had fallen woefully short of the standard for the gangster picture that Coppola had established with those earlier films. Instead, she continues, the present film is "a composite of the old Warner Bros. gangster pictures and musicals of the 1930s." It seems that Coppola had skimmed the top off every 1930s movie he had ever seen, "added seltzer, stirred it with a swizzlestick, and called it a movie."[34]

Still Coppola's Jazz Age gangster musical had some fans among the critics. There were those who hailed it as a glorious celebration of a bygone era. Furthermore, Coppola shows himself once more in this picture to be a master of visual imagery. One dandy visual metaphor in the film is built around the barrier that separates the tarty Vera from Dixie as long as she is the Dutchman's property. Coppola visualizes the obstruction that this barrier initially places between them by photographing Dixie and Vera on different sides of symbolic barriers. For example, their exchange of good-byes as they part after one of their encounters occurs while they are on opposite sides of the fence that encloses the apartment building where Dutch Schultz has Vera ensconced. The image suggests that Dixie is barred from entering the world Vera at this point still inhabits with the Dutchman. As Vera and Dixie make love in a later scene, the shadows cast by the lace curtains on the windows make a netlike pattern on their naked bodies, implying that they are caught in a net from which they cannot at the moment get free.

At times the picture is like a three-ring circus, with nightclub sequences that are suitably noisy and flamboyant. The production numbers at the club are captured by Coppola's flexible and fluid camerawork. In general, Coppola directs throughout with a vigor that compensates for the derivative elements of the plot, which have been lifted from old musicals and gangster pictures.

The Cotton Club premiered in New York City on December 8, 1984, with an eye on an initial release during Christmas week in selected key cities. Despite the mixture of positive and negative notices, the movie performed well in the marketplace during its opening run. But Orion, which controlled the film's nationwide distribution, was disheartened by the downbeat reviews and mounted a half-hearted publicity campaign across the country. When exhibitors realized that Orion was not really behind the film, they backed off from booking it. If *The Cotton Club* lost money, film scholar Jon Lewis affirms, Orion must bear much of the blame because it botched the movie's general release.

Moreover, Evans had insisted from the start on a screenplay in which the story of a black cabaret during the Harlem Renaissance was overshadowed by the gangster story line. As a result, black audiences did not flock to see the movie. Thus, the fact that *The Cotton Club* only racked up $25 million in domestic rentals cannot be laid at Coppola's door.

The Cotton Club has its share of eye-filling musical numbers, featuring the celebrated dancer Gregory Hines, plus some exciting action sequences built around harrowing gangland shootouts between rival mobs of bootleggers. Nevertheless, despite Coppola's conscientious efforts to whip the movie into shape, *The Cotton Club* remains a hybrid, a mixture of two disparate screen genres that, in the last analysis, never quite coalesce into a unified work of art.

Be that as it may, it is well worth noting that when Gregory Hines died in August 2003, several obituaries singled out *The Cotton Club* as a major film for which he will be remembered. The *New York Times,* for example, wrote of his rare screen presence in *The Cotton Club* and recognized his graceful, self-assured performance in the film, whether he was acting the role of an ambitious hoofer or tap-dancing solo or with his brother Maurice. The vitality and comic intelligence of his stage performances, said the *Times,* easily translated to the screen in *The Cotton Club.*

Still *The Cotton Club* is a film worth watching, and it has attracted on videocassette and DVD some of the wider audience it deserves. Indeed, the sale of the ancillary rights to television and home video eventually accounted for the film's breaking even and ultimately realizing a modest profit. In any case, Coppola had much better luck with his next venture, *Peggy Sue Got Married,* when he was called in yet again to save a project that was foundering.

Part Four

The Vintage Years

10

The Past as Present

Peggy Sue Got Married and "Rip Van Winkle"

We may be through with the past, but the past is not through with us.

—Donnie Smith, a former Quiz Kid
in the film *Magnolia*

I've spent much of my life trying to outrun the past, and now it floods all over me.

—Ian McKellen as James Whale in
the film *Gods and Monsters*

At this juncture Francis Coppola still considered himself a hireling who was compelled to accept projects brought to him by the studios because he was not in a position to originate projects of his own. Still facing bankruptcy because of the demise of Zoetrope Studios in Los Angeles, he had arranged to pay off some of his debts at thirty cents on the dollar. But this accommodation depended on his making regular payments to his creditors.

Even the Sentinel Building, the headquarters of American Zoetrope in San Francisco, which continued to house his offices and editing facilities, was in danger of being lost to him if he could not ante up the $1.7 million he still owed on it. The *San Francisco Chronicle* reported that the Sentinel Building, which was topped with a blue-and-green cupola, would be put up for sale "unless, of course, the Seventh Cavalry arrives with the cash to save Coppola's cupola."[1]

The Seventh Cavalry did arrive, in the person of independent producer Ray Stark, for whom Coppola had labored as a screenwriter in the mid-1960s at Seven Arts (see chapter 1). Stark was planning *Peggy Sue Got Married*, a time-travel fantasy, as an independent production to be released by Tri-Star Pictures. TV director Penny Marshall had been set to make her feature debut with *Peggy Sue*, but she left the project in November 1984 after a dispute with the screenwriters.

The property languished in limbo until Stark finally approached Coppola and made him an offer he could not refuse: Stark agreed to pay Coppola $3 million to direct the picture. Because of his financial bind, Coppola committed himself to lensing *Peggy Sue Got Married*, and he immediately utilized more than one-third of his directorial fee to save the Sentinel Building, just hours before the deadline.

Coppola was still bitter about his experience with *The Cotton Club*. He had been called in to salvage a production that was already out of control when he took over, yet he was already being blamed in some quarters for the film's tepid critical reception. His financial straits resulting from *The Cotton Club* compelled him to direct the romantic fantasy film *Peggy Sue Got Married*, which was not exactly his cup of tea. "*Peggy Sue*, I must say, was not the kind of film that I normally would want to do," he explains. "At first I felt the script—although it was okay—was just like a routine television show." Nevertheless, "the project was ready to go and they wanted me," and he had so many debts that he simply had to keep working.[2]

Peggy Sue Got Married (1986)

In July 1983, Arlene Sarner and Jerry Leichtling, a husband-and-wife screenwriting team, had brought *Peggy Sue Got Married* to the attention of producer Paul Gurion, who in turn interested Ray Stark in making the picture for his independent film unit. The title of *Peggy Sue Got Married* was derived from a popular song by the late rock-and-roller Buddy Holly. The scenario portrays Peggy Sue as a middle-aged woman whose marriage to her husband Charlie is on the rocks. She is magically transported back to her senior year in high school and comes to terms with her past life. The screenwriters presented the first draft of the script to Gurion on December 2, 1984, and it was passed on to Coppola. Kathleen Turner (*Body Heat*) was picked to play the title role because she was halfway between the ages of the younger and the older Peggy Sue, whom she would be portraying in the movie.

Turner would not be available until she finished another picture, however, so shooting was postponed until August 1985. That gave Coppola time to tinker with the script, in collaboration with Sarner and Leichtling, during the preproduction phase. After all, Francis Coppola, the maverick, was not a director to be handed a script that he did not revise to suit his vision of the material.

One of the major inflections Coppola gave the script was to strengthen the emotional center of the film. His model was the last act of Thornton Wilder's play *Our Town*, "when the daughter goes back and sees her mother and her youth," he says. "I was looking for more of that small-town charm and emotion."[3] *Our Town* is a work steeped in Americana that depicts the day-to-day lives of ordinary citizens living in a whistle-stop. Like *Our Town*, *Peggy Sue Got Married* is a paean to those mundane details of life that we take for granted—and that pass away all too fleetingly. The kind of emotion Coppola helped to inject into the screenplay is evident in the scene where Peggy Sue encounters her mother for the first time in her dream of the past, after the hands of time have been turned back to her teen years. Peggy Sue is touched to see Evelyn, her mother, looking so young. She hugs Evelyn and blurts out, "Oh, Mom, I forgot that you were ever this young!" Peggy Sue is pleased to have her mother restored to her, but Evelyn wonders why her daughter is embracing her so warmly. This scene, more than any other in the movie, was inspired by a parallel scene in *Our Town*.

Later on, Peggy Sue becomes teary when she speaks on the phone with her grandmother, Elizabeth Alvorg, who has since died. Coppola indicates in the script that Peggy Sue be photographed in somber silhouette as she talks to her "dead" grandma, because Peggy Sue is "literally reviving the ghosts of memory." She knows what lies ahead: "death and decay for the family she once took for granted."[4]

Kathleen Turner observes, "I saw Francis, together with the original writers, take out gags that undercut the sentiment" of the story.[5] For example, Coppola deleted a farcical sequence marked by smatterings of piquant sex, in which a male student hypnotizes Peggy Sue to make her take off her blouse. In fact, the more Coppola worked on the script, the more he found it an endearing, bittersweet tale and the more he found himself getting involved in it.

Coppola was going for deeper characterization in the rewrites, so he developed the role of Charlie Bodell, Peggy Sue's wayward husband, in the revised screenplay. He shows how Charlie's failed career aspirations help to account for his unhappiness in his later life. Coppola also strengthened the role of Richard Norvik, who had a crush on Peggy Sue in high school. Richard, a science whiz kid, reminded Coppola very much of himself when he was in high school. Like Richard, young Francis was a technology fanatic—his nickname in high school was "Mr. Science," because he loved to experiment with electronic gadgets.

When it came to casting, Coppola conferred with Gurion much more harmoniously than he had with Robert Evans on either *The Godfather* or *The Cotton Club.* It was actually Gurion and not Coppola who chose Coppola's nephew, Nicolas Cage, to play Peggy Sue's unfaithful husband. Sofia Coppola, the director's daughter, would appear as Peggy Sue's kid sister Nancy. Many members of the supporting cast willingly took part in the film just to work with Coppola: Don Murray (*A Hatful of Rain*) and Barbara Harris (*Family Plot*) were cast as Peggy Sue's parents, Jack and Evelyn Kelcher; Maureen O'Sullivan (*Hannah and Her Sisters*) and Leon Ames (*Meet Me in St. Louis*) as Peggy Sue's grandparents, Elizabeth and Barney Alvorg; John Carradine (*The Grapes of Wrath*) appeared as an old friend of Barney's.

Two staples of Coppola's production crew were on hand, production designer Dean Tavoularis and editor Barry Malkin. The underscore was to be composed by John Barry (*Body Heat*), who was responsible for the background music in *The Cotton Club.* Coppola selected Jordan Cronenweth as director of photography, because he was impressed with Cronenweth's work on Ridley Scott's *Blade Runner.*

Because the picture is essentially an extended dream sequence, Coppola had Cronenweth suffuse the movie with bright, saturated colors to give it a nostalgic glow. "The basic approach," said Cronenweth, was to make *Peggy Sue Got Married* "a contemporary *Wizard of Oz,* painted with broad strokes."[6] After all, Peggy Sue is knocked into the middle of her high school years the way that Dorothy in *The Wizard of Oz* is knocked into the middle of next week. The present film is a fanciful picture of the past that is meant to crystallize for the viewer Peggy Sue's yearnings for her lost youth. Hence, the movie is bathed in a golden glow and amounts to a valentine for a vanished past.

As always Coppola prefaced the shooting period with a couple of weeks of videotaped rehearsals, ending with a taped run-through of the whole script. "It was like acting school, with all the improvisations," some of which resulted in rewrites of the dialogue, Turner remembers. "[P]eople were really getting involved in the process and it was working."[7]

Principal photography commenced near the end of August 1985 and involved location filming in Petaluma, California, which Coppola and Tavoularis had selected to serve as Santa Rosa, the small California town in which Peggy Sue grew up. Setting the film in Santa Rosa is perhaps an homage to Hitchcock's *Shadow of a Doubt* (1943), which was co-written by Thornton Wilder and which takes place in the same sleepy town of Santa Rosa. Coppola was partial to the town because it was only an hour away from his Napa estate.

The shooting phase lasted eight weeks, ending in late October, and it proceeded without any noticeable mishaps. Turner recalled that she got along famously with her director, once she made one thing perfectly clear. She had heard about Coppola's penchant in the past for monitoring a scene while it was being shot on the TV screens in his Silverfish trailer. So she told him that if he was inclined to watch a scene being filmed in *his* trailer she would perform the scene in *her* trailer. And that was that.

Coppola was absolutely determined to bring in the picture on schedule and on budget in order to wipe out the bad press he got for the overages on *The Cotton Club*. "We were under such pressure to finish it on schedule that we averaged close to an eighteen-hour day," says Turner.[8] Coppola even shot the last scene, the reconciliation of Peggy Sue and Charlie, between 1:00 AM and 4:00 AM on the last official day of the shoot. Coppola of course collaborated closely with editor Barry Malkin on the final cut, and postproduction went as smoothly as the shooting period had. The premiere was set for the fall of 1986, after the plethora of teen flicks released during the summer had played out.

The opening credits of *Peggy Sue Got Married* are accompanied by Buddy Holly's original recording of the title song. From the film's opening sequence onward, Coppola demonstrates that he is in total control of his material. The picture begins with a shot of a TV set on which Charlie can be seen doing a commercial for his hardware store. Coppola's camera pulls back to reveal Peggy Sue primping at her dressing table before departing for the high school anniversary party. Her back is to the television set, indicating that she has, at this juncture, turned her back on her philandering spouse.

Coppola pulled an adroit visual trick in the shot of Peggy Sue's reflection in her dressing table mirror in this scene. Because it is a large mirror, the camera would have been visible in the mirror if he placed it behind Turner as he photographed her image in the mirror. So he arranged to have Turner's double sitting at the dressing table with her back to the camera. There is, in fact, no mirror at all—only a frame—so that it is really Turner herself, and not her reflection, that is facing the camera.

Like Natalie Ravenna in *The Rain People*, Peggy Sue Bodell has walked out on her husband, for the time being at least. She is separated from Charlie, and their two children, Scott and Beth, live with her. She has become more successful in her business—running her own bakery—than Charlie has in running his hardware business, although Charlie was the once-promising class hotshot in high school. Peggy Sue is embarrassed by Charlie's goofy TV commercials as "Crazy" Charlie, the Appliance King, which her teenage daughter Beth, of course, thinks are terrific.

At any rate, Peggy Sue manages to pour herself into her glittery prom dress, which is described as a "blast from the past." As she struggles into the outfit, she implies that it must have shrunk while hanging in the closet all these years (!). But the gown is really an uncomfortable reminder that her figure is not as slim as it used to be and serves as an apt prelude to the woeful evening ahead in which she is forced again and again to acknowledge that she is neither as young nor as resilient as she once was. When she arrives at the party, which is being held in the school gym, she is chagrined to see an enormous blowup of a photograph picturing herself and Charlie as king and queen of the senior prom. The photo captures them at a moment in time when their relationship was happy and carefree rather than sad and careworn, which is what it eventually became. Some of the alumni regress to high school behavior, thus Walter Getz (Jim Carrey) begins behaving like the class clown he once was. He says that his motto in high school was, "When it comes to girls, what Walter wants, Walter gets!"

Visual metaphors abound in the movie. As a balloon floats upward toward the rafters of the gym, one of the alumni reaches for it, but it gets away. So too, many of the hopes and dreams that Peggy Sue and her classmates nurtured when they were young have eluded their grasp, driven off by the frustrations and disappointments of later life—epitomized, in her case, by her foundering marriage to Charlie. When Charlie himself makes his appearance at the reunion, he is at first barely visible in the shadowy doorway. He is but a dim figure from Peggy Sue's past, someone whom she will get to know all over again, as she relives the past and is thereby able to come to terms with the present. She is distressed at seeing Charlie again—she had hoped that her two-timing husband would have the decency not to show up at the reunion.

Peggy Sue in due course is crowned queen of the reunion. When an enormous cake, topped with sparkling candles, is wheeled in to celebrate the occasion, Peggy Sue faints dead away. She wakes up back at old Buchanan High in 1960, her senior year. Although Peggy Sue appears physically unchanged to the filmgoer, her friends and relatives in 1960 see her as seventeen.

The movie has its share of sly ironies that play on the audience's knowledge of the subsequent course of history. Since Peggy Sue is a visitor from the future, she makes a number of remarks that baffle those around her. She giggles when she discovers that her father has just bought the family a new car—an Edsel. Although her father is proud of this vehicle, Peggy Sue is already aware that the Edsel, with its gaudy grilles and tasteless chrome decorations, would become the Ford Motor Company's biggest commercial failure. At another point her parents are chagrined when Peggy Sue takes a couple of swigs from her dad's whiskey bottle as she announces "I am an adult! I want to have fun! I'm going to Liverpool to discover the Beatles!!!"

Peggy Sue has brought with her on her trip down memory lane her forty-two-year-old mind, and she thus views things from a more mature perspective than she possessed the first time around. So, when Peggy Sue tells her younger sister that she would like to get to know her better, she adds a perceptive remark that could only have come from her older self: "I have too many unresolved relationships."

One relationship she has failed to resolve in her later life is that with her estranged husband, Charlie Bodell, who, of course, is still a teenager when Peggy Sue meets him in the course of her return visit to her youth. She and Charlie married right after high school but have since split up because Peggy Sue discovered that he was cheating on her with a younger woman, whom she calls "Charlie's bimbo." Asked at the reunion why she has separated from Charlie, she answers laconically, "We just married too young, I guess, and ended up blaming each other for all the things we missed."

Charlie seems an uncouth, not to say callow, adolescent when Peggy Sue meets up with him as she revisits her past. Still, with adult hindsight, she regrets that his singing career as a member of a pop quartet fizzled and he had to settle for going into his father's hardware business. In one scene we see Charlie, decked out in his garish gold-lamé jacket, singing with the group. He is hoping to make a guest appearance on a TV show as a vocal sensation, but the nearest he will ever come to television, Peggy Sue knows, is his appearances in his silly TV commercials as "Crazy" Charlie the Appliance King.

Peggy Sue chats with Charlie just before he goes to audition for an agent, and after they part the viewer stays with Charlie as he gets the brush-off from the agent. Charlie, it seems, is dismissed as a "rebel without a cause." This scene represents the only serious failure in narrative logic in the entire movie. Since the audience is seeing every incident in the film from Peggy Sue's perspective, a scene at which Peggy Sue was not present has no place in her dream of the past. Nevertheless, Coppola slips this lapse of narrative logic by the filmgoer so adroitly that hardly anyone who sees the film notices it. Commenting on this scene between Charlie and the agent, Barry Malkin says that it was "an afterthought. We were trying to make Charlie's character more sympathetic." He feels that a filmmaker need not allow himself to be "boxed in" by the rules of narrative logic if it means missing out on a good scene—rules were made to be broken, he concludes.[9]

In the course of reliving her past, Peggy Sue wonders if she could have made a better match than Charlie. So she reconsiders the two lads who were attracted to her besides Charlie. There is the brainy science genius, Richard Norvik (Barry Miller), who is generally considered to be a creep by his peers. Walter Getz has dubbed Richard "Mr. Square Root," with the accent on *square*. Peggy Sue feels protective toward Richard. When the class bully torments him, she snaps, "You macho schmuck!" Little wonder that Richard acknowledges that she alone treats him with respect.

Peggy Sue feels sorry for Richard, but she realizes that pity should not be confused with love. Peggy Sue tells Richard that she is reexperiencing her adolescence, and he assures her that he believes in time travel. In fact, he shyly proposes to her, beseeching her to marry him instead of Charlie and thereby changing her destiny. But Peggy Sue gently turns him down.

The other chap who was interested in Peggy Sue during her high school days was Michael Fitzsimmons (Kevin J. O'Connor), a rebellious beatnik who is pictured at one point on a motorbike—recalling Motorcycle Boy from *Rumble Fish*. She is fascinated by this free spirit. Indeed, at the reunion she confesses to a friend that "Michael was the only boy in high school I wish I'd gone to bed with—besides Charlie." Accordingly, in the course of her foray into the past she allows Michael to make love to her in a bucolic field after they smoke marijuana together. But it is all too evident that Michael is not the marrying kind, and so their romantic fling never really gets off the ground.

Michael is an aspiring writer, a would-be Jack Kerouac, and Peggy Sue foretells his subsequent success as a novelist. She even encourages him to make their short-lived romance the basis of a novel. When she gives him the air, Michael smirks, "So are you going to marry Mr. Blue Impala and graze around with all the other sheep for the rest of your life?" "No," she retorts. "I already did that."

Peggy Sue ultimately decides that none of the young men in her life—Charlie, Richard, or Michael—are viable prospects for matrimony. Therefore, she decides not to marry anyone this time around. "Petty Sue *got* married—case closed!" she states emphatically. "I don't want to marry anyone!" When Peggy Sue tells her story about time travel to her grandfather, Barney Alvorg, she confides to him that she does not desire to continue living in the past—she wants to return to her adult life. He spirits her away to his Masonic lodge, where his fellow members are prone to dabble in the occult. The grand master (John Carradine) accordingly presides over a ritual calculated to catapult Peggy Sue back to the future. But before she leaves the past behind, she has one last crucial confrontation with young Charlie.

Early in the movie, during the reunion celebration and before being transported backward in time, Peggy Sue muses to herself, "If I knew then what I know now, I'd do a lot of things differently." But the question is, now that she appears to have the chance of a lifetime to change her destiny by altering her past, will she?

In Charlie's case, when he comes to court Peggy Sue in the course of her return trip to her adolescent years, her sour experiences with him in later life prompt her to break their engagement. "I'm not going to marry you a second time," she tells the uncomprehending Charlie, who cannot foresee the future as she can. Charlie woos Peggy Sue by producing a locket that her mother has given him, containing photos of him and Peggy Sue as babies. She realizes that the locket matches the one she carries—which she had showed her friends at the reunion—containing pictures of their two children, the fruit of their marriage. Their lovers' quarrel comes to an end when they kiss and make up and make love—this occasion turns out to be the time Charlie gets Peggy Sue pregnant, with the result that she does in fact decide once again to marry Charlie. In short, she winds up not doing things any differently the second time around after all, although she had promised herself she would!

Back in present time, Peggy Sue has been taken to the hospital in the wake of her fainting spell at the reunion. Charlie is at her bedside when she awakens and begs her to take him back. Their daughter is there too, and the three of them embrace. For Peggy Sue the high school reunion has proved to be the occasion of a family reunion as well. The reconciliation of Peggy Sue and her husband at the fade-out challenges the viewer with the notion that, as Gene Siskel puts it, "it is a generous and proper idea for us to accept the whole package, faults and all, of the people we care about." *Peggy Sue Got Married* thus reaffirms the need we all have to preserve strong family ties in life, a perennial Coppola theme. "I think what Francis brought to the movie that is distinctive," Turner observers, "is his great sense of family."[10]

Peggy Sue's one souvenir of her journey into the past is a novel by Michael Fitzsimmons, which was inspired by their brief encounter. He dedicated the book to her, and she has it with her in the hospital scene.

The concluding hospital scene did not satisfy Coppola when he examined it in the rough cut during postproduction. Because he had committed himself to finishing the film on schedule, he had shot the scene in
the wee hours of the morning on the last scheduled day of the shoot. In the
rough cut the cast looked exhausted and his direction appeared perfunctory. Ray Stark granted permission for Coppola to reshoot the scene—indeed, Coppola wanted to restage it so that the last shot of the film would
match the opening shot, thereby allowing the opening and closing images
of the film to serve as bookends for the movie.

Peggy Sue Got Married begins with a shot of Peggy Sue reflected in her
dressing table mirror. It concludes with a shot of Peggy Sue, Charlie, and
Beth appearing together in the mirror in her hospital room. Whereas Peggy
Sue was a solitary figure in her bedroom mirror at the outset, at film's end
she is surrounded in the hospital mirror by her husband and daughter.
"Coppola's last mirror shot frames Peggy Sue in a cheerful family context."[11]

Peggy Sue Got Married was selected to be screened on the closing night
of the New York Film Festival on October 5, 1986, and it was hailed as
Coppola's spectacular return to form. The critics' enthusiasm for the movie
went a long way toward eradicating the disastrous premiere of Rumble Fish
at the same festival three years before. Peggy Sue then opened on eight-
hundred screens across the country, in a saturation booking, five days later.
Given the commercial success of both The Outsiders and Peggy Sue, Coppola
was now able to make a sizeable dent in his outstanding debts. Peggy Sue
became his highest-grossing film of the decade. In its first three weeks of
general release the picture grossed nearly $22 million.

Jordan Cronenweth was the recipient of the American Society of
Cinematographer's first annual award for his work on the film, and he was
likewise singled out for praise in several of the notices. So was Kathleen
Turner, whose performance in a difficult role was universally acclaimed
and merited her an Oscar nomination.

Many reviewers were pleasantly surprised to find Coppola helming a
light-hearted, humorous film, his first comedy since One from the Heart.
One critic even suggested that Peggy Sue Got Married was the Coppola movie
that really should have been entitled One from the Heart. After all, Peggy
Sue is an anodyne recreation of small-town life in the 1960s and revels in
the atmosphere of a kinder, gentler age. It evokes the past as an innocent,
more wholesome time. In fact, it is more about preserving the past than
changing it, as the central character sets out to recapture the family values
of her youth.

Some critics faulted Nicolas Cage's performance as Charlie, but it was fundamentally a thankless role. *Variety* described Charlie Bodell as a "primping, self-centered, immature high school jerk who is really insecure deep down."[12] As a matter of fact, one can easily see how Charlie will grow into an obnoxious TV appliance pitchman later on. Consequently, Cage's ostentatious, mannered approach to the role seemed on target. Charlie, as both teenager and adult, can be endearing or exasperating, and Cage at various times portrays him as both.

Coppola had discovered several promising young actors in his earlier films, particularly *The Outsiders*. In the present movie, Jim Carrey, whom he chose to play happy-go-lucky Walter Gertz, would go on to become a superstar, as would Helen Hunt, who played Peggy Sue's daughter, Beth. Hunt subsequently won an Academy Award for *As Good as It Gets* (1997). Coppola never lost his canny eye for fresh talent. All in all, *Peggy Sue Got Married* is a remarkable fantasy that was warmly applauded by the critics and the general public. Coppola managed to turn out a touching film that ranks high on the list of his best movies.

When the starting date of *Peggy Sue* was postponed because of a prior commitment of Kathleen Turner's, Coppola found time to direct a fifty-minute film for Shelley Duvall's cable TV series, *Faerie Tale Theater*. Duvall, a veteran actress (*The Shining*) was executive producer and host of the series that featured TV adaptations of classic fairy tales. She offered Coppola "Rip Van Winkle," the last of the twenty-six episodes in the series. Coppola was drawn to the project because the stakes were low and the salary quite reasonable. The TV production would help him continue to pay off his debts, which is also precisely why he signed to direct *Peggy Sue*.

"Rip Van Winkle" (1985)

Coppola began collaborating on the teleplay of "Rip Van Winkle," based on the Washington Irving short story, with writers Mark Curtis and Rod Ash in late November 1984. Irving's tale, first published in his *Sketch Book* (1820), depicts how Rip Van Winkle woke up from a twenty-year nap to find that he had missed the American Revolution. The schedule called for a six-day shoot with a $650,000 budget. Coppola rehearsed the actors for a couple of days, starting on November 28, before shooting commenced. "We're breaking all records in Francis's career," stated coproducer Bridget Terry. "Not only is this the first television film he's ever directed, but it's the shortest schedule he's ever had."[13]

Coppla was not dismayed by the frugality of the production. He was revisiting the days when he was turning out "no-budget" pictures for poverty row producer Roger Corman (see chapter 1). "The bigger the budget, the less freedom you have," he explained. He pointed out that he had exercised considerable artistic freedom on movies like *The Rain People, The Conversation,* and *Rumble Fish* because they had relatively meager budgets. He thought that he was well suited "to a medium where the budgets are smaller and yet the imagination is bigger."[14]

Coppola cast Harry Dean Stanton (*One from the Heart*) in the title role; Talia Shire (the *Godfather* films) as Wilma, Rip's shrewish wife; and John P. Ryan, who played a gangster in *The Cotton Club,* as the ghost of the ancient mariner, Henry Hudson.

Coppola engaged Japanese production designer Eiko Ishioka to create stylized sets for the telefilm. Irving remarks that the Catskills are really enchanted mountains and appear at times to take on a life of their own: every change of weather produces some change in the hues and shapes of these mountains. This observation, which found its way into the script, inspired Eiko Ishioka to create a "living mountain" (a common technique of Japanese stagecraft) consisting of five people crouching under a sheet of canvas that alters in shape and color to suit the mood of a given scene. For example, when Rip's wife berates him for being a shiftless no-account, the mountain undulates ominously in the background to suggest her mood. Coppola instructed director of photography George Riesenberger to favor primary colors in shooting the picture: deep blue for nightfall, glowing scarlet for sunset, and an eerie green for the apparition of Henry Hudson and his ghostly crew.

As the telefilm opens, a pair of gnarled hands takes a book off a cobwebbed shelf, while the narrator intones, "This story takes place in the early Dutch settlement of New York, before this country was a country." We then meet Rip Van Winkle, an amiable Dutch loafer who is regularly scolded by his peevish wife for loitering at the local tavern and going hunting in the Catskills instead of toiling on their little farm. Talia Shire, decked out in a fearsome black wig, recalls Connie, the disgruntled wife she played in the *Godfather* films.

One evening Rip goes off hunting in the upper reaches of the Catskills to escape his nagging wife. As he wanders deeper into the woods, a ghost suddenly materializes from the murky green fog. "I am Commander Heinrich Hudson," the spectral figure declares to Rip. Hudson is dressed in a traditional Dutch naval captain's uniform, which is tattered with age. He then introduces to Rip his band of merry men as the crew of the good ship *Half Moon,* which foundered off the coast some one hundred and fifty years before. "We discovered this land at the time, and it is sacred to me," Hudson explains. "I return every twenty years to see if future generations are taking care of it."

Rip is appointed cupbearer to the crew. He is given a keg of a mysterious brew and told to keep their flagons filled as they engage in a spirited game of ninepins (bowling). Rip samples the tasty draught himself and eventually imbibes copiously from the keg. The revelers finally disappear, leaving Rip behind, sound asleep. As a matter of fact, the magic beverage causes Rip to sleep for twenty years. When he awakes, he is sporting a straggly white beard, and he finds the village much changed.

For one thing, the sign over the village inn, which once bore the likeness of King George III, has been replaced by one with the image of George Washington, thereby indicating to the viewer, if not yet to Rip, that the American Revolution has transpired while Rip slept. When he inquires at the tavern if anyone knows Rip Van Winkle, the customers point to Rip Van Winkle, Jr. (also played by Stanton). The young man is dozing on the porch (like father, like son). Young Rip informs his father that Wilma "broke a blood vessel screaming at a travelling salesman a couple of years ago and died."

Rip regales the group with the tale of his fantastic experience with Henry Hudson and the crew of the *Half Moon*. The narrator adds, voice-over on the sound track, "In time he became a legend in the village, and he never grew tired of telling the children his story." A shot of Rip and the village children freezes into a picture in the same book which the narrator was holding at the beginning of the film. He then closes the volume and replaces it on the shelf, and we see his face for the first time: it is Henry Hudson, grinning at us at the fade-out.

Since Coppola's episode of *Faerie Tale Theater* was slotted as the last segment of the series to be televised, it was first aired after *Peggy Sue Got Married* had opened. Some critics noted a link between the telefilm and the feature: In *Peggy Sue* the heroine is transplanted into the past—in "Rip Van Winkle" the hero is transported into the future. Moreover, "Rip Van Winkle," like *Peggy Sue*, got uniformly good notices, and deservedly so (although more than one critic stated that the telefilm's literary source was a novel, rather than a short story). Coppola's telemovie was described as a slightly fractured but never totally Grimm fairy tale.

In bringing Irving's storybook classic to life, Coppola tackles the material with antic glee and serves up engaging, warmhearted whimsy. His direction is spry and imaginative, and, though he is a stylist, it is evident that he cares about actors and performance—Harry Dean Stanton, Talia Shire, and John C. Ryan could not be better. "Rip Van Winkle," in short, is an unqualified artistic success. Happily, the *Faerie Tale Theater* TV series has not sunk without a trace, as so many television series do. The telefilms in the series were released on video and DVD in 2002. The most prominent filmmaker to direct a segment of the series is clearly Francis Ford Coppola.

With the box-office triumph of *Peggy Sue Got Married,* plus the well-received "Rip Van Winkle," Coppola was in a position to bargain with the studio moguls to do a film he had wished to make for several years. As early as 1975 he had mentioned in interviews that he wanted to film the life of the innovative automobile designer Preston Tucker, but he could not find the necessary financing. Finally, in 1986, an independent producer came forward and offered to back *Tucker: The Man and His Dream.* It was none other than Coppola's erstwhile protégé, George Lucas, whose professional relationship with Coppola dated back to the earliest days of American Zoetrope.

11

The Disenchanted

Tucker: The Man and His Dream and *New York Stories*

A good salesman could sell bubblegum in the lockjaw ward at Bellevue.

—Seth Davis, a stockbroker
in the film *Boiler Room*

Preston Tucker, the maverick automobile inventor who was the subject of Coppola's biographical film, first came to Coppola's attention when, as a child of eight, he saw the first Tucker automobile on display in 1948. He never forgot the experience and decided to make a movie about the flamboyant inventor many years later.

Preston Tucker was born in suburban Ypsilanti, Michigan, in 1903. He got his start in the auto industry by selling used cars. By 1935 he was entering racing cars in the Indianapolis 500, sponsored by none other than auto tycoon Henry Ford. During the Second World War, Tucker operated the Ypsilanti Machine and Tool Company, which had several profitable defense contracts. He designed an assault vehicle that had a cruising speed of 150 mph, but military officials nixed it as going too fast. The gun turret he designed for the combat car was utilized on bombers.

At the end of World War II, Tucker decided the time was right to produce the revolutionary auto he had had in mind for some years. In 1946 he organized the Tucker Corporation, with former executives from Chrysler, Ford, and General Motors on the governing board. Tucker mounted an advertising campaign to herald the Tucker automobile as "the car of tomorrow, today."

"Thanks to World War II," says Roger White, a specialist in the Smithsonian Institution's Division of Transportation, "no new cars had been made since 1941. So the Tucker car, with its rocket-ship styling, captured the imagination of the American public." Moreover, the safety features Tucker had developed "were an unusual and timely idea."[1] The Tucker car boasted an air-cooled, rear-mounted engine with a 160-horsepower motor and an automatic transmission. In addition, the safety features included a pop-out safety windshield made of shatter-proof glass, a padded dashboard, and a third "Cyclops" headlight that swiveled with the steering wheel, providing motorists with additional illumination on turns. Because of the car's sleek exterior, which resembled a rocket ship, it was christened the Tucker Torpedo.

In July 1946 Tucker leased a huge 457-acre factory at 7601 South Cicero, on Chicago's Southwest Side, a former Dodge plant that had turned out B-19 bomber engines during the war. He supervised his engineering team in designing a hand-built prototype. The prototype was unveiled at the Chicago plant in June 1947. When Tucker attempted to drive the prototype onstage, the car, which had been assembled from spare parts scavenged from junkyards, simply refused to start. His rag-tag mechanics hastily made some last-minute adjustments in the vehicle backstage. When the audience finally got a look at the first Tucker Torpedo, they were simply delighted.

Tucker took the prototype on a triumphant nationwide tour, and young Francis Coppola, age eight, was dazzled by it when his father took him to see it at an auto exhibition on Long Island. Coppola recalls in his commentary on the DVD of *Tucker,* "When I was a boy, my father conducted the orchestra for auto shows, and I traveled with him sometimes." Carmine Coppola had been enthusiastic about the Tucker car for some time and had shown Francis magazine stories about it. When Francis finally saw the Tucker prototype, "I thought it was a beautiful, gleaming car; it looked to me like a rocket ship." Carmine Coppola actually ordered a Tucker Torpedo," and I kept asking my father when our Tucker was going to come."[2] To finance the manufacturing of his car, Tucker sold stock in the corporation to small-time investors, from pharmacists to grocery store managers. Carmine Coppola invested five thousand dollars of his savings in Tucker stock.

While Tucker was on his nationwide tour with the prototype, some executives back at the plant in Chicago were resigning because the Tucker Corporation was desperately underfinanced and was running short of steel and other raw materials. "It was not an ideal time to be entering the field; the steel shortage was acute after the war. Tucker was taking on a major, maybe a staggering load," White explains. "To produce a reasonably priced mass-market car takes an enormous amount of capital and time—even under the most advantageous of circumstances."[3]

Furthermore, industry experts wondered if Tucker could mass-produce enough cars—even with the best of intentions—to make a decent profit. To make matters worse, rumors were flying that the Big Three in Detroit (Ford, Chrysler, and General Motors), were in cahoots with Senator Homer Ferguson of Michigan to sabotage Tucker's whole operation. Ferguson denounced Tucker to the Securities and Exchange Commission (SEC), allegedly to repay the campaign contributions of the Big Three. William Kirby, Tucker's lawyer, always maintained that the Big Three were afraid to compete with the Tucker Torpedo, and so engineered Tucker's downfall. "The SEC had more time to investigate Tucker than he did to build his car," Kirby contends.[4]

In January 1949, Otto Kerner, the U.S. Attorney in Chicago, presided over a grand jury investigation of the Tucker Corporation. In March, Tucker was indicted for violating SEC regulations and for mail fraud. More specifically, he was accused of employing the mails for fraudulent purposes, by conning investors into purchasing stock in an automobile he had no hope of ever manufacturing. Tucker was vilified in the press as a combination of circus showman P. T. Barnum and crooked New York Mayor Jimmy Walker. He was ridiculed as a charlatan with a taste for high living and a fashionable wardrobe.

Nevertheless, the jury acquitted Tucker of all charges. Tucker, they decided, was in good faith in endeavoring to manufacture a revolutionary automobile. By this time, however, Tucker was forced to file for bankruptcy because of the expensive trial, and his investors—including Carmine Coppola—lost every cent of their investments. Carmine broke the news to his son: "He told me that our Tucker was never going to come, because all the other auto companies thought it was too good; and they put him out of business. I thought that was an injustice."[5]

Withal, Tucker ultimately managed to produce fifty Tucker Torpedoes, which featured innovations that eventually became standard equipment on the American automobile. In 1956 he died of lung cancer at the age of fifty-three. Although he died in relative obscurity, he was at the time of his death working on various inventions, including a mini-refrigerator that people in the third world could afford.

Although Tucker was a controversial figure, even his enemies admitted that he was an inspiring leader and an almost messianic salesman. But even his friends had to concede that he was a disastrous business manager. He could be described, in the last analysis, as an honest man with a great idea but a bad business sense. Coppola gave this thumbnail sketch of Tucker in 1975:

> Tucker designed a car that could be built for a fraction of the kind of money the major companies were spending on their new models. It was a safe car, a revolutionary car in terms of engineering, and it was a beautiful car. In every way, it was a much better machine than the stuff the major companies were offering, the companies created by Ford and others. But Tucker was called a fraud and he was destroyed. If he were alive today, he'd be hired by one of the major car companies and his inventions would be . . . filtered out to the public as the company deemed economically prudent. Not to benefit the public but the company, and only the company.[6]

Still, Coppola had no illusions about Tucker. Elsewhere he describes Tucker as "a loveable American con man" (!). He continues, "I like him because he feels human." He is "the used car salesman with his heart in the right place. . . . He wore those brown-and-white pointy shoes; and he was handsome and good with the ladies. He talked fast." Coppola concludes, "I'm going to make a film of Tucker's story some day."[7] When he learned as a boy that Tucker was never allowed to manufacture his car, Coppola says in the documentary "Under the Hood" (2000), which accompanies the film on DVD, that it "instilled in me the wish to find out what happened."

Tucker: The Man and His Dream (1988)

Coppola toyed with the notion of making a movie about Preston Tucker as early as 1962, when he was a film student at UCLA. He dated a girl who took him to a museum where a Tucker Torpedo was on display, and that rekindled his interest in Tucker.

"Right from childhood I have always been stimulated by stories about great enterprises," Coppola told me. He states in his commentary on the

DVD that he saw Tucker at the time he first considered making a film about him as a larger-than-life figure like Charles Foster Kane, the newspaper magnate in Orson Welles's 1941 movie *Citizen Kane.* "I wanted my film about Tucker to be an exposé, stark and heavy, about the man and his company being destroyed by larger corporate interests."

In 1975 Coppola acquired the rights to film Tucker's life from the Tucker estate and purchased one of the surviving Tucker cars for good measure. He told the Tucker family about seeing a Tucker Torpedo as a boy, he says in the documentary, "and they were flattered that I had a personal connection to Tucker." The following year Coppola mentioned in a memo reporting on the status of American Zoetrope to his staff that "the sums spent on *Tucker*" to secure the rights to the story "will finally reach the cash box in two years from now."[8] So Coppola at that juncture was hoping to put *Tucker* into production after *Apocalypse Now,* an eventuality that never came to pass.

It seems that Coppola was drawn to tell Tucker's story on film because of the affinities between the film director and the automobile maker. Coppola shared Tucker's charisma as a talented, fast-talking entrepreneur, which enabled him to persuade industry officials to back projects he wanted to film. Moreover, like Tucker, Coppola became a celebrity by manipulating the media to promote his accomplishments, as when he showcased *Apocalypse Now* at the Cannes Film Festival and *Peggy Sue Got Married* at the New York Film Festival.

Furthermore, both men were gamblers whose most ambitious business ventures left them broke (as, in Coppola's case, when Zoetrope Studios in L.A. went belly up). The effusive Coppola candidly notes that he identified with Tucker, the rebel inventor, because Tucker was a tireless self-promoter. "When you tell people your dreams out of enthusiasm, somehow it makes them disgusted," he comments. "I think a lot of my problems would not have been as aggravated had I not in my enthusiasm irritated people." When a filmmaker goes around saying that he uses state-of-the-art technology that the studios do not possess, "it's taken as criticism, although that's not how it was intended."

In sum, Coppola obviously identified with Tucker's independent spirit. Both Tucker and Coppola could be called likeable mavericks. As one of Coppola's friends has put it, "Maybe Francis is the Tucker of our day."[9] "I see parallels between Tucker and Francis," George Lucas states in the documentary. "Both are flamboyant characters and are very creative; both like innovation—thus Francis likes interesting camera techniques."

By the late 1970s, Coppola's concept of the film had evolved. He now conceived it as a dark musical drama. He therefore enlisted Leonard Bernstein (*West Side Story*) to compose the music and Betty Comden and Adolph Greene (*Singin' in the Rain*) to write the lyrics. Coppola invited them to spend a week at his Napa estate, driving around the countryside in Coppola's Tucker while they planned the film. "Leonard Bernstein was impatient that I didn't have the project more worked out," Coppola says in his DVD commentary. "Well, Francis," chided Bernstein, "you can't rush into this like *Apocalypse Now*. We have to know what the approach is." Coppola then outlined the plot in detail for Bernstein and pointed out where the songs could fit into the story, "and Bernstein actually wrote one song," says Coppola. But the project was stopped dead with the disaster of *One from the Heart*, "and my studio was coming down around me."

After Coppola lost his shirt on Zoetrope Studios, the Tucker project, which he had originally planned to make there, fell through. He could not interest any major studio in backing his Tucker film. In the wake of the debacle of *One from the Heart*, he says, "people thought my projects were too grandiose."[10]

Gio, Coppola's elder son, was an auto buff, and he very much wanted his father to make the film. He was familiar with the Independence Day parade held each year in Calistoga, California, just north of Coppola's Napa estate. On July 4, 1985, Coppola states in his DVD commentary, Gio coaxed Francis into allowing him to drive his Tucker car in the parade, with Francis riding in the back seat. "Let's dust it off and drive it around," Gio urged. The spectators along the parade route cheered as Coppola and his Tucker passed by.

"George Lucas was there," Coppola continues, and he inquired, "What happened to your Tucker idea?" When Coppola told him that he had long since written it off, Lucas replied, "Why not make it anyway, but not as a musical?" Because it was Gio who really rejuvenated the project, Coppola concludes, "I dedicated the film to Gio—he loved cars so much."

Coppola confesses, "I have tended to make projects so big that I really couldn't pull them off." Consequently, he was anxious to collaborate with Lucas, who could see to it that Coppola made a film on a smaller scale than usual, one that could be potentially marketable. When he approached Lucas, who had helped Coppola inaugurate American Zoetrope in San Francisco in the late 1960s, Lucas agreed to produce the picture. Coppola, Lucas remembers, had wanted to make *Tucker* as long as he had known him. Over the years he had shown Lucas the Tucker Corporation's promo films for the car. "I thought it was the best project Francis had ever been involved with," says Lucas (who also owns a Tucker Torpedo), because it was the story of a little guy pursuing his dream and attempting to beat the system, something that audiences could identify with.[11]

Recalling how Coppola had helped him finance *American Graffiti,* Lucas wanted to return the favor by not only producing *Tucker* but also helping Coppola to finance the film through his independent production unit, Lucasfilm, which he had established with the profits from *Star Wars.* By late 1986 Paramount Pictures had agreed to help finance the film and to distribute it. The budget was set at $25 million. Richard Macksey compliments Coppola for his ability to obtain backers for a project he wants to make: "His perilous if uncanny power to enlist backers probably depends upon his temperamental inability to fold in a poker game; movie-making and risk-taking are synonymous to him."[12]

"It was a flip-flop," having George Lucas produce *Tucker*, says Coppola in the documentary short on the DVD entitled "Under the Hood." "Now he was the producer, while I had produced a couple of his films." He continues, "George and I have different talents and therefore they mesh. George's talent is in designing and editing a film," while Lucas maintains in the documentary that he got his storytelling ability from Coppola.

When Lucas opts to produce a picture, he is no mere figurehead. He offers input to the director all along the way. Thus he vetoed Coppola's concept of a down-beat musical, in favor of an up-beat, non-musical version of Tucker's life. After all, Coppola had never made a commercially successful musical, from *Finian's Rainbow* to *One from the Heart* to *The Cotton Club.* "Francis can get so esoteric, it can be hard for an audience to relate to him," Lucas declares. "He needs someone to hold him back. With *The Godfather* it was Mario Puzo; with *Tucker* it was me."[13]

Coppola and Lucas endeavored to think of a way to sugarcoat the story of a creative individual who does not accomplish his dream. It was finally Lucas who came up with the solution. As Lucas puts it, in the end Tucker may not have manufactured his car, "but he was not defeated as a creative person. They couldn't crush his spirit."[14] In "Under the Hood" Lucas states that the picture is about "the conflict between the bureaucratic–status quo mentality and the creative impulse that says, 'Let's do it differently!'" When the individual collides with the establishment, the establishment usually survives while the individual loses out in most cases. He thought a film about Tucker could examine the lasting impact of the individual, even when he loses. In short, "I wanted to make it an uplifting experience," Lucas concludes, "and Francis didn't resist."[15]

Asked what drives Coppola, Lucas responds, "What drives a tiger? He wants to be in control of a situation, which is obvious from his life. I can say no to him, . . . but it's hard to say no to Francis."[16] Yet Coppola willingly went along with Lucas's concept of the movie: "I knew George has a marketing sense of what people might want. He wanted to candy-apple it up a bit," says Coppola. Audiences loved the optimistic *Peggy Sue Got Married*. Hence, he decided, "If that's what they want from me, I'll give it to them."[17]

Lucas insisted that Coppola have a finished script before shooting began so that the ceaseless delays occasioned by the rewrites on films like *The Cotton Club* would not plague the filming of *Tucker*. Lucas suggested screenwriter Arnold Schulman (*Goodbye, Columbus*), and Coppola invited Schulman to stay with him in Napa for a couple of weeks for script conferences. Since the Tucker family had script approval, Schulman had to appease them as well as Coppola. When the Tuckers insisted that the script make no reference to Tucker's mistress, Coppola had no problem in deferring to them on this point. He wanted to emphasize Tucker the family man in the movie, in harmony with his ongoing theme about the importance of family relationships.

Since David Seidler is listed in the screen credits of the film as coauthor of the screenplay, Goodwin and Wise wrongly assume in their book on Coppola that Seidler and Schulman collaborated on the script. But Schulman affirms that he never even met Seidler. Schulman was initially to receive sole screen credit for the screenplay. As a matter of fact, the title page of the shooting script, dated March 9, 1987, which is in the Paramount Script Repository, lists only Arnold Schulman as the author of the script. Seidler, who had worked on an early draft of the script, got wind of this, however, and he claimed that he deserved to have his contribution to the film acknowledged with a coauthor screen credit.

When Seidler enlisted the Screen Writers Guild to arbitrate the matter, Schulman insisted that he made no use whatever of Seidler's draft, since it was a perfunctory recital of the facts of Tucker's life, totally lacking in dramatic substance. "His script started with Tucker at six years old and included every detail of the man's life until the day he died," Schulman contends. "Since it was a real-life story, obviously there were going to be incidents in it similar to those in my script. . . . If ten writers write ten different scripts about Abraham Lincoln, in all of them there's going to be a Civil War and Abe's going to get shot in the end."[18] Schulman had no better luck in fighting for a sole screen credit for *Tucker* than Coppola did in negotiating for a sole screen credit on *The Outsiders*. The Screen Writers Guild upheld Seidler's contention that he be named coauthor of *Tucker*.

Coppola did his best to round up a production crew of artists he had worked with before. Besides the ever-faithful production designer Dean

Tavoularis, he managed to corral costume designer Milena Canonero (*The Cotton Club*) and cinematographer Vittorio Storaro (*Apocalypse Now, One from the Heart*). Coppola and Storaro decided to photograph *Tucker* in ultrasaturated colors to give the film the lustrous, lacquered look of an auto industry promotional film.

Jeff Bridges, with his good looks and winning smile, won the title role, while Lloyd Bridges, his father, nabbed the part of Senator Homer Ferguson, Tucker's principal antagonist. Martin Landau was assigned to play Abe Karatz, Tucker's top financial officer and best friend. Coppola also reengaged some actors from his other films: Frederic Forrest (*Apocalypse Now, One from the Heart*) was picked for Eddie Dane, Tucker's chief mechanic; Joan Allen, who was one of Peggy Sue's close friends in *Peggy Sue Got Married,* was given the nod for Vera, Tucker's wife; and Dean Stockwell (*Gardens of Stone*) would impersonate millionaire inventor-industrialist Howard Hughes.

In early April 1987 Coppola assembled the cast on one of Lucasfilm's sound stages in San Rafael, north of San Francisco, for two weeks of rehearsals. The rehearsal period, Coppola contends, "lets the actors spend time together without being pressured or having to perform," and they could improvise to polish their characterizations.[19] Landau in particular found these rehearsals helpful. He envisaged Abe at the beginning of the movie as "a lonely New York Jewish guy with no family or friends, who sits in cafeterias and reads newspapers and lives for deals."[20] Landau adds in the documentary, "Tucker brings Abe to life. He gives him a sense of belonging, and Abe finds he can dream again. In the course of the film, because of his commitment to Tucker and his dream, Abe "grows into a warm, feeling, and caring human being."

The rehearsal period culminated, as usual, with a complete walk-through of the script, that was videotaped as a sort of home movie, thereby giving the director and the actors a preview of the film. Landau adds that the videotaped run-through especially helped him to grasp the evolution of his character during the story.

Tavoularis remembers *Tucker* as one of the most carefully designed movies that he ever worked on with Coppola. Long before the cameras turned, he joined Storaro at a bungalow on Coppola's estate, where the trio pored over the script for a week, discussing how each scene should be shot and sharing ideas about locations, set designs, and decor. During the shooting phase, says Tavoularis, "I think we shot about ninety percent of what we talked about at that cottage."[21] Coppola, after all, was committed to appease Lucas by bringing the film in on schedule and on budget.

Tavoularis and Coppola selected location sites in the Bay Area, in easy commuting distance from Coppola's Napa home. In Sonoma, in northern California, they found an enormous manor house that was subsequently turned into Tucker's home in Ypsilanti, Michigan. Tavoularis converted the ballroom of the senior citizens' hotel in Oakland into the courtroom where Tucker's trial for fraud took place. He built several of the sets in a huge abandoned factory, which had once been owned by the Ford Motor Company, on Harbor Way in Richmond, California. The ground floor became the Tucker plant, while the second floor housed the factory's offices.

Tucker's plant did not have an assembly line, because he was never able to arrange to mass-produce the Tucker Torpedo. But the old Ford plant used in the film to stand in for Tucker's factory did have an assembly line, and so in the movie the Tucker plant has an assembly line. In dramatizing Tucker's life on the screen, Anahid Nazarian, Coppola's chief research assistant, notes that certain liberties of this sort inevitably were taken with Tucker's life.

For example, on the one hand, all the evidence shows that Senator Ferguson was out to get Tucker. It is also known that competitive car manufacturers employed FBI agents to monitor the private tests of the Tucker Torpedo conducted on a speedway, in the hope of spying out flaws in the car's performance. On the other hand, Coppola admits in his commentary on the DVD, there is no documentation to support the suggestion that Ferguson was personally responsible for "the spy watching from the stands, as shown in the film," during the test runs. Coppola wanted to have a clear-cut villain to play the role of Tucker's nemesis, and Ferguson was elected. According to Nazarian, in the script Ferguson was made more of a villain than he was in real life in order to bring into relief the conspiracy between powerful industry executives and influential politicians aimed at ruining Tucker. She adds that "people who were there found a lot of what they call errors" in the movie and peppered the Zoetrope office with complaints. She responded that "we knew the facts, but to fit the spirit of the story into a film that is exciting and has characters you love and characters you hate—that made us change a lot of things."[22]

One thing that did not change was the screenplay, since, as mentioned, Lucas was adamant that Coppola follow the script as written once principal photography began. The shoot started on April 13, 1987. Schulman, who had been on hand for rehearsals, visited the set during filming and was gratified to learn that Coppola was faithfully following the shooting script as written: "An actor would ask, 'Can I try the line this way?'" Coppola would think for a moment and then reply, "Why don't you do it the way it's written?" When Schulman thanked Coppola for respecting his writing, Coppola answered, "A hundred hacks can rewrite another hack, and nobody will know the difference; but one good writer cannot rewrite another good writer," because their individual styles are different.[23]

Coppola favored long takes while shooting *Tucker*, as he had on some other films, notably *One from the Heart*. Thus, in a single, uninterrupted tracking shot, the camera would take in the action by dollying from one actor to another as each contributed dialogue to the scene. The complicated choreography of these scenes meant that the actors had to move with the same precision as the camera and be careful not to wander out of camera range. "I've never done a film this complicated as far as camera moves," Jeff Bridges said.[24] He got around the problem by marching like a robot through the first take, just concentrating on staying in the frame. He added emotion to his performance from the second take onward.

Jeff Bridges did enjoy doing scenes with his father, Lloyd Bridges, who played Homer Ferguson, the industry-backed senator. "It was fun to act with Dad," says Bridges. "He'd give me tips and I'd give him suggestions; he even took some of my advice."[25]

Working swiftly and efficiently, Coppola completed principal photography on July 17, after just thirteen weeks of shooting. During postproduction, George Lucas sat in, while Coppola and editor Priscilla Nedd shaped the footage Coppola had shot into a final cut. Coppola and Lucas had no serious disagreements en route. The postproduction stage went along smoothly, commented Coppola, since he had begun with a strong script. That made the editing phase relatively easy, as the edited material was forged into a compelling narrative.

Afterward Coppola opined in a published interview that he bought George Lucas's idea that giving the film a light touch would make it more palatable to the public, so he abandoned the notion of going with the darker vision of the material he had originally envisioned. "I think it's a good movie; it's eccentric like the Tucker car—but it's not the movie I would have made at the height of my power," when he owned his own studio.[26] Lucas wanted to dispel the notion that he had imposed his concept of the film on Coppola, so he issued a statement in response, saying, "The truth of it is, Francis and I worked on the movie together, and he made the movie he wanted to make. Who knows what it would have been if he'd have made it 'at the height of his power'?"[27]

Nevertheless, the trade press reported industry gossip of a rift between the "reckless" Coppola and the "less-assertive" Lucas, implying that Coppola bossed Lucas, not the other way round. Coppola emphasized in reply that he had not sought to overshadow the younger man. Indeed, Coppola scoffed at the notion that "George was in my shadow." Added Lucas, "The truth is, we've always worked together; it's always been a collaborative sort of thing" as they kibitzed on each other's scripts and shared ideas over the years.[28] "I don't think my relationship with Francis has changed much," Lucas comments in the documentary. "We're like family, and there's an energy and an emotional exuberance that comes out of that— sometimes it's conflict, sometimes devotion."

Eleanor Coppola endorsed Lucas's remarks: "I think it's a remarkable collaboration. Francis has suffered from not having a producer he can believe in," she states. He has often been at odds with studio executives while making a movie because "they haven't understood him or made funds available in the areas where he needed them. He therefore felt relieved to have George Lucas as his producer," since Lucas is a fellow filmmaker. "Both men have become established in their own realm, and now they are reunited as equals. Francis listened to George's opinions and ideas with respect."[29]

The film's opening credits are superimposed on Coppola's facsimile of a promotional short made by the Public Relations Department of the Tucker Corporation. It has a cheerful voice-over narration, snappy 1940s Big Band music, and snapshots from the Tucker family album. "It's like a promo film of the 1940s," says Coppola. "The sort of thing that Detroit manufacturers used to show their dealers."[30] (The *Tucker* DVD includes an authentic 1948 promo film made by the Tucker Corporation, entitled, "Tucker: The Man and the Car.")

Coppola's version of a Tucker promo film recounts Tucker's life through World War II, telling how Tucker invented a high-speed, bullet-proof assault vehicle with a machine gun turret. The narrator states that the army found the combat car impractical, "but the gun turret was immediately pressed into service" on bombers. "The turrets were built in the barn next to Tucker's home in Michigan," says the narrator, as the promo (and the credit sequence) comes to an end.

The credit sequence sets the tone for the film to follow, Coppola explains on the DVD: "I had the desire to make the movie in the style of a 1940s promo film that had been produced by Tucker's Public Affairs office—with a great deal of showmanship. After all, this was a kind of Horatio Alger story." Coppola, in concert with Tavoularis, Storaro, and his other collaborators, gave the entire movie the brash, peppy flavor of a promotional documentary, with sunny exteriors and glowing interiors, plus warm, earthy colors in the costumes.

The film proper begins in 1945 at Tucker's Ypsilanti homestead. The story gets rolling as Tucker convinces Abe Karatz, the seedy promoter who becomes Tucker's financial adviser, that his concept of the "car of tomorrow, today" is a workable one. Abe, who happens to be named after "Honest Abe" Lincoln, pledges Tucker that he will do his best to get the project jump-started. He tells Tucker frankly, "I don't have connections in the auto industry, but I have connections who have connections."

Abe, in due course, negotiates with the United States government to grant Tucker a lease on a former Dodge factory in Chicago that recently, during the war, has been utilized as a defense plant. But Tucker has to commit himself to producing fifty Tucker Torpedoes within the next three months, and so Abe hires a former Detroit auto executive, Robert Bennington, as chairman of the board, in order to give the company some credibility with Washington.

Tucker addresses a government committee at a luncheon in Washington in order to clinch the deal for the Chicago factory. He shows slides of traffic accidents, declaring melodramatically, "The tycoons in Detroit don't give a damn about people—all they care about is profits. The Big Three should be convicted of criminal negligence" because their cars lack the safety features of the Tucker Torpedo. The slides of the gory traffic accidents are intercut with shots of the committee members being served rare, bloody roast beef—something they find hard to swallow under the circumstances.

It is clear in viewing Coppola's "auto" biography, *Tucker: The Man and His Dream,* that, as he himself says, his cinematic imagination was inspired by creating a film centering on an automaker's technical ingenuity. In essence, since Tucker's car was a mechanical miracle, he wanted his film to some extent also to be a mechanical marvel—a movie that emphasizes a variety of technical effects, from crane shots to split screens (where the frame is divided between two parallel scenes, shown on the screen side by side.) "I always like my movie's style to reflect the subject matter," he states on the DVD.

There is, for example, a tricky split-screen shot when Tucker phones his wife back home from his hotel after the Washington luncheon. The camera glides from Tucker in his Washington hotel on the left to include the Tucker living room on the right, so that the two settings virtually melt into each other. We see separate shots of Tucker and Vera juxtaposed on the screen simultaneously as they converse. Their juxtaposition implies their closeness—the bond between them—as if they were together in the same room. Coppola comments on the DVD, "Here is a basic use of a theatrical scene transition, which we experimented with in *One from the Heart*. We pan from one set to the one built right next to it. So in this case, you go from the husband to the wife." Coppola "never ceased to experiment with eye-catching compositions and off-beat storytelling techniques, such as the use of the fake publicity film in *Tucker*" and the split-screen effect that "connects Tucker with his wife as they talk on the phone."[31] (As Tucker walks away from the phone, incidentally, a sign on the wall comes into view that reads appropriately, "Where there's a will there's a way.")

Another cinematic effect, inspired by a sequence in *Citizen Kane*, occurs in a later scene. In Welles's film Charles Kane, the publisher of the *Enquirer*, lures the top reporters from a rival newspaper to work for him. A still photograph of the new additions to the *Enquirer* staff seems to come to life, as the photo dissolves into a shot of the men posing for the picture at Kane's party, welcoming them to the *Enquirer*. In a similar manner Coppola has a photo of the newly constituted board of directors of the Tucker Corporation dissolve to a shot of the board members having a conference. "This transition was stolen from *Citizen Kane*," says Coppola in his DVD commentary. "My father always said, 'Steal from the best.'"

Coppola proves himself a master of visual metaphors once again when Tucker's dedicated crew, led by Eddie Dane, are renovating the old Chicago plant to produce the Tucker Torpedo. Tucker mutters to himself, "I may have a ringside seat at my own crucifixion," if the local premiere of the prototype does not come off on schedule. Tucker then watches as the "T" in Tucker is hoisted into place on the sign over the factory. Coppola observes in his DVD commentary that the "T" looks like a cross and subtly foreshadows that Tucker will subsequently be crucified by the power structure in Detroit.

The film includes a short sequence in which Tucker has a private meeting with rebel inventor-industrialist Howard Hughes. Coppola describes Hughes in his DVD commentary as "Tucker a thousand times over. He liked to set his sights on things that were out of reach." The scene is based on the recollection of one of Tucker's sons who accompanied his father to meet Hughes in a hanger in Long Beach. This is where Hughes housed history's largest aircraft, nicknamed the Spruce Goose, which was so enormous that it proved impractical for manufacture. "We used the real plane in the scene," says Coppola in his commentary. The Spruce Goose looms behind Hughes and Tucker as they converse—two iconoclastic legends on the fringe of American capitalism. Hughes gestures toward the plane, laconically, commenting, "They say it can't fly; but that's not the point." He implies that the goal of an invention is not marketability but the satisfaction of creating something unique. Tucker nods in agreement. After all, Tucker is not in the business of building empires. He is in the business of building dreams, as the film's subtitle implies.[32] Hughes ends their conversation by urging Tucker to continue battering at the big auto manufacturers.

One of the scenes that is central to the film has Tucker unveiling his prototype auto to the press and his investors. Coppola injects humor into the proceedings by turning it into a comedy of errors in which Tucker's crew of mechanics backstage are hastily putting the finishing touches on the Tucker Torpedo. He intercuts what is going on in front of the curtain and behind it with panache and style: Tucker stalls for time by bringing on stage some shapely dancing girls he calls the Tuckerettes and then introducing his family. Meanwhile, his mechanics are frantically fixing an oil leak and dousing a fire on the underside of the vehicle. Coppola actually based this scene on photos of the real event. He uses an impressive high-angle shot, with the camera craning up over Tucker's head as he finally introduces the Tucker Torpedo to the impatient audience. Then the camera sweeps over to the dazzling car itself, surrounded by the Tuckerettes as it revolves on a turntable.

The Tucker car scores a big hit on its first public appearance, and Tucker soon after tours the country in a chartered plane, showing off the Tucker Torpedo at auto exhibits. But storm clouds are gathering over Tucker's corporation back in Chicago. Senator Ferguson and his cohorts mount a campaign to have the SEC charge Tucker with fraud and questionable business practices. The investigators uncover the fact that "Honest Abe" Karatz had once served time for bank fraud. When Tucker returns home, Abe goes to the factory and tenders his resignation to Tucker, lest his sullied reputation be used against Tucker. "Captains go down with their ship," Abe remarks to Tucker, "not businessmen."

Abe then makes a statement that in actual fact echoes the words of Carmine Coppola to young Francis when Carmine told his son that their Tucker was never going to arrive. Abe says forlornly to Tucker, "You made the car too good." The cocky Tucker responds, "That's the whole idea, isn't it? To build a better mousetrap." Abe answers ruefully, "Not if you're the mouse." He adds, "My mother said, 'If you get too close to people, you catch their dreams.'" As Abe concludes, the lights in the factory are shut off for the night, and the Tucker plant dwindles into darkness, symbolizing that there are dark days ahead.

Although Tucker was not permitted to speak in his own behalf at the trial, Coppola gave him a summation speech in the film. "A trial is a kind of drama," he explains on the DVD, and so he wanted the lead character to have his day in court and make a final plea. But Tucker's courtroom speech is fiction. Tucker addresses the jury, explaining how the establishment wants to maintain the status quo and so squashes the little fellow with fresh ideas: "If Ben Franklin were alive today, he'd be arrested for flying a kite without a license."

He declares in his peroration, "If big business closes the door on the little guy with a new idea, we're not only closing the door on progress, but we're sabotaging everything that we fought for during the war. Everything that this country stands for." Coppola comments in his DVD commentary that he had Storaro dim the lights in the courtroom during Tucker's final speech to create a bleak, shadowy atmosphere, "In order to stay with the somber mood of the scene."

Tucker is acquitted by the jury, and he accordingly ushers them outside the courthouse and gives them all a ride around the square in the fleet of Tuckers that are parked outside. He has, after all is said and done, managed to manufacture fifty Torpedoes, and he comments grandly, "Fifty cars or fifty million—it's the idea that counts—and the dream." He implies that it is not winning that counts, but how you play the game. Storaro photographs the big parade of Tuckers in the final scene in bright sunshine, in sharp contrast to the dark courtroom scene preceding it.

Coppola was able to commandeer twenty-one of the forty-six surviving Tuckers for the movie's grand finale, but a couple of them were temporarily out of service. "They had to be chained together," says a Tucker owner whose vehicle participated in the scene. "One that ran was hooked to one that didn't." It was difficult to keep a car that didn't run from running into the one just ahead of it while the parade was in progress.[33]

One of the few additions Coppola made to the script occurs during the parade. In the screenplay, Tucker simply says to Vera, "The car is great."[34] In the film, as Tucker rides in a Tucker Torpedo, he muses out loud about his next invention, "a portable kerosene refrigerator that people in poor countries can afford." This additional bit of dialogue shows more clearly that Tucker's spirit was not broken. Rather, he was already looking to the future and his next project. Coppola reflects in his DVD commentary, "He was already designing a cheap fridge so that poor kids could have cold milk and not die of rickets in South America." He continues, "Tucker won his case. He was found not guilty of misappropriating money from investors," but by then he was already bankrupt. "A special commission led by Senator Homer Ferguson saw to it that the Tucker Corporation was evicted from its factory. The establishment takes away from you what isn't under their control. The people at the top don't want change lest they lose their privileged position." Spoken like a true maverick.

Withal, Coppola insisted on ending the movie on a note of affirmation. He affixed a printed epilogue to the film, also not in the script, that reads, "Although only fifty Tucker cars were ever produced, forty-six of them are still road worthy and in use today. Tucker's innovations were slowly adopted by Detroit and are found on the cars you are driving now."

Roger Ebert points out that automotive history would not have been substantially different if Tucker had put his dream car into mass production. The Tucker probably would have thrived in the late 1940s, "and then joined the long, slow parade of the Hudson, the Kaiser, the Nash, the Studebaker, the Packard" and all of the other cars that came and went after the war.[35] Nevertheless, as Jay Scott emphasizes, the film is really not about the car—it is about the man. The movie "extols the value of vision, even if the vision is unrealized. The theme of the movie is that it is the quality of the vision itself that counts."[36]

Tucker's family cooperated with the making of the film wholeheartedly and provided Jeff Bridges in particular with a wealth of information. Bridges admits that one of the few times his characterization of Tucker deviated from Tucker's true personality was in the scene in which Tucker is given disappointing news by his chief mechanic. He is told that they do not have time to incorporate all of the new safety features into the prototype before the deadline set for the public exhibition. Tucker picks up the phone from his desk and hurls it against the wall in anger. "He'd never do that," says Bridges. "If he did have negative feelings, he'd never show them." From watching the Tucker family's home movies and from talking to his children, Bridges learned that Tucker "didn't want to waste energy by nurturing hostile feelings within himself. He would look at obstacles as challenges."[37] Little wonder that Tucker often bursts out in a chorus of "Hold that Tiger," which characterizes his get-up-and-go spirit during the movie. That little ditty certainly fits Bridges's overall interpretation of Tucker. Throughout the movie Bridges steadfastly wears a confident grin that mirrors the gregarious charm and pep of a man who simply declines to acknowledge defeat.

Tucker reflects a common theme in the Coppola canon, an appreciation of the binding strength of the family unit. For important public occasions—from the unveiling of the Tucker prototype to the courtroom trial—the family conspicuously stands by Tucker. Moreover, there is the scene in which Tucker's oldest son (Christian Slater) turns down the chance to attend Notre Dame in order to help his father build the first Tucker Torpedo. Similarly, Coppola's elder son Gio asked his father to allow him to leave school when he was sixteen in order to work with his father in the movies—another parallel between Tucker's life and Coppola's.

In August 1988 *Tucker* was released on 720 screens across the nation. It started strong, taking in nearly $4 million on its first weekend, thereby being numbered among the top ten moneymakers in the country. But the picture soon slipped out of the top ten. It eventually racked up a mere $19 million in domestic rentals. Foreign distribution, plus the sale of ancillary rights to TV and home video, would improve the movie's profit picture, of course.

The early, unenthusiastic notices in the daily papers acknowledged that Coppola had a vivid imagination, but decried the many disconcerting shifts in tone caused by the tension between the essentially bleak story and its sunny treatment. Thus Coppola's enthusiasm for visual flourishes and quirky characterizations undermined the atmosphere of tension he had managed to create in the dramatic scenes dealing with the forces arrayed against Tucker. Some of the subsequent reviews, appearing in weekly and monthly magazines, voiced the opinion that the picture had been vastly underappreciated by the newspaper reviewers and endorsed the movie's rousing high spirits and razzle-dazzle showmanship. A few critics even believed that the film marked the comeback of a major auteur, who was fighting his way back from disappointing pictures like *Gardens of Stone* and *The Cotton Club* to significant, workmanlike filmmaking. Coppola's faith in the film has ultimately been vindicated in that *Tucker* has become enormously popular on TV, given the number of times it is shown annually.

It is not surprising that a movie maker named Francis *Ford* Coppola, who was born in Detroit, should be fascinated by someone associated with the automotive industry. Tucker developed plans for a car that was way ahead of its time in terms of engineering, yet the auto industry at large stubbornly resisted his innovative ideas. Unfortunately, Coppola told me, creative people do not always get a chance to exercise their creativity, whether it be in Detroit or Hollywood. Putting it another way, it was appropriate that a maverick filmmaker would film the life of a maverick inventor. "I grew up as a kind of outsider, someone who didn't fit in anyplace," he says; "and I think I'm hooked very strongly toward making movies about what it's like trying to go your own way." *Tucker* is about the construction of a dream automobile. "Overall I seem to be tracking the through-line of the odd man out."[38]

After finishing *Tucker,* Coppola went on to contribute a segment to an anthology film entitled *New York Stories.* This omnibus movie was the brainchild of Woody Allen, who proposed to fellow filmmakers Martin Scorsese and Francis Coppola that they each create a self-contained urban story, about a half-hour in duration, which could be filmed in a month.

The only cord linking the three short films together would be the common New York City setting. Naturally Coppola jumped at the chance to be associated with a film that involved two other important directors. Furthermore, Coppola had shot films like *You're a Big Boy Now, The Godfather,* and *The Cotton Club* in New York and was to that extent identified with the city. Given the trio of distinguished directors, Allen and producer Robert Greenhut easily found the $15 million needed to back the movie and enlisted Touchstone Pictures, a subsidiary of Walt Disney Pictures, to distribute the picture.

After casting around for a subject, Coppola came up with the idea of doing his segment along the lines of writer-vocalist Kay Thompson's children's books. Thompson had penned four books in the 1950s about Eloise, a precocious child who lives in the Plaza Hotel in New York, and Coppola wanted to deal with a similar little girl in his short film. Writing a script about a youngster gave him the chance to collaborate with his seventeen-year-old daughter Sofia on the screenplay. The scenario was about an eleven-year-old child named Zoe, who lives at the exclusive Sherry-Netherlands Hotel on Fifth Avenue, dines at the posh Russian Tea Room, and has her own credit cards. It would be entitled "Life without Zoe."

New York Stories: "Life without Zoe" (1989)

"Dad took me to Las Vegas and he got a suite," Sofia remembers. "[H]e ordered room service and we worked away, writing every day." It was like a writing workshop for her.[39] Coppola chose Vegas to work on the screenplay because he loved to labor on a script in Vegas or Reno, where he could work long hours and then go to the casinos for relaxation. In fact, he and Mario Puzo collaborated on the *Godfather* scripts at times in Reno.

The short film developed into a family project: Sofia not only co-wrote the screenplay with her father, but she also designed the costumes. Her aunt, Talia Shire (from the *Godfather* films) would have a featured role, and her grandfather, Carmine, composed the score. In addition, some old hands from other Coppola films were recruited: production designer Dean Tavoularis, editor Barry Malkin, and cinematographer Vittorio Storaro. The director of photography, in tandem with Coppola, chose a luscious color palette to approximate the world of luxury the film depicts.

Zoe (Heather McComb) points out, "My parents named me Zoe because Zoe means life in Greek." Zoe, of course, was associated in Coppola's mind with the name of his independent film unit, American Zoetrope, since

Zoetrope means in Greek "the movement of life," a reference to primitive motion pictures.

Zoe's father, Claudio Montez (Giancarlo Giannini) is a renowned flautist, who frequently goes on concert tours around the world and is seldom home. Claudio is separated from Zoe's mother, Charlotte (Talia Shire), a fashion photographer who likewise travels a lot. Zoe, who is sophisticated beyond her years, lives at the Sherry-Netherlands hotel where Hector, the family butler (Don Novello), pampers her in her parents' absence. Zoe attends an exclusive private school, but complains that she has no friends her own age, since she is surrounded by adults most of the time. She yearns to see her parents reunited so that they can form a family once more (another reference to Coppola's constant theme).

In June 1988 Coppola transported the Silverfish trailer, complete with its TV monitors and other audio-visual accessories, to New York, where he would film "Life without Zoe" on location in Manhattan. The ritzy Apthorp apartment building on the Upper West Side was employed for some scenes. Coppola tended to stay unobtrusively on the sidelines in the Silverfish, out of the way of the crew, while they set up each shot according to his detailed advance instructions. He watched the preparations on a TV screen in the trailer and occasionally gave additional directions to the crew by telephoning to the set. When all was in readiness, Coppola went on the set where he occupied a high-backed canvas chair near the camera and viewed each take with one eye on a small TV monitor perched on his knee.

During shooting Coppola worried that the mass audience would not find a "poor little rich girl" an appealing heroine. He did not want Zoe to come across as a smug, spoiled brat belonging to the privileged class. He rather wished the story to suggest that material prosperity is no substitute for a loving family. Consequently, he did not intend *Zoe* merely to celebrate a world of status and wealth.

Zoe at one point meets a mysterious, beautiful Arab princess, the wife of a wealthy sheik, who had given one of her priceless earrings to Claudio as a token of her esteem for his musical virtuosity. On second thought she fears that her jealous husband might suspect that she is romantically involved with Claudio, so she wants to get the earring back. Because Claudio is away, the princess hopes Zoe can retrieve the jewel from the hotel safe where Claudio has placed it for safekeeping. Zoe thus becomes involved in a bogus robbery of the safe when some of the princess's retainers "steal" the earring, which Zoe then smuggles back to the princess.

When her father returns from his travels, Zoe proudly explains what she has done. She obviously wants to impress her dad favorably. He is indeed relieved that the precious earring has been returned to the princess—since Charlotte might have otherwise thought that the gift of the earring betokened that there was something between Claudio and the princess. "This is the wrong time for a misunderstanding between your mother and me," he tells Zoe, who he knows wants her parents to reconcile. "Little Miss Fixit" eventually decides to cement the reconciliation between her parents by arranging to fly to Greece with Charlotte to attend Claudio's concert at the Acropolis in Athens. So the little film ends with a family reunion.

Editor Barry Malkin characterizes "Life without Zoe" as a "contemporary fairy tale," a kind of fable out of the Arabian Nights, in which the Arab princess is a damsel in distress saved by the timely intervention of an imaginative young girl. But Malkin was dissatisfied with the way the segment turned out. At the behest of the Disney organization, the parent company of Touchstone, "we abbreviated the episode and removed some material from the film. I feel we rendered the story less faithfully and hurt it," he maintains. "I was sorry that a number of things wound up on the cutting room floor. And I know Francis feels that way too."[40]

Indeed he does. Coppola emphasizes that the script had more character development, especially in terms of Zoe's relationship with her father. She finds it burdensome to cope with a famous father who is emotionally unavailable to her. The Disney executives liked the "Eloise at the Plaza" dimension of the story, he says, but during editing the studio asked that some of the material about Zoe's troubled relationship with her father be jettisoned. Disney wanted the episode to be a lightweight anecdote, not a character study about a little girl trying to relate to a remote father who pretty much ignores her. "In an attempt to make the story delightful and charming," Coppola concludes, this material was largely eliminated.[41]

It is not surprising, therefore, that when *New York Stories* was released on February 26, 1989, some reviewers found "Life without Zoe" woefully rushed and bursting with loose ends and unfulfilled promises. The episode admittedly teeters on the brink of mawkishness in the sentimental family reconciliation. Yet it is still a visually arresting, engaging rite-of-passage comedy, particularly since Don Novello brings some snap to the role of Hector, the benevolent butler who caters to Zoe when her parents are on the road.

Looking back on Coppola's career in the 1980s, one can say that he made two features (*The Outsiders* and *Peggy Sue Got Married*) and one short film ("Rip Van Winkle") that were hugely successful. But he also made resounding flops like *Tucker* and "Life without Zoe." He once told me that he tends to see the movies he has directed in the past as providing him with the sort of experience that would help him to make better films in the future. "So the only thing a filmmaker can do," he concludes, "is just to keep going." Down the road he would regain the favor of the critics and of the public when he reached back to the nineteenth century to film Bram Stoker's classic horror novel, *Dracula.*

12

Fright Night

Bram Stoker's Dracula

A man digs his own grave and should, presumably, lie in it.

—F. Scott Fitzgerald

For me the past is forever.

—F. Scott Fitzgerald

Because Winona Ryder had had to bow out of *Godfather III* because of illness, she was anxious to work with Coppola in another film. When she read James Hart's screen adaptation of *Dracula,* based on Bram Stoker's 1897 novel, she not only wanted to play the heroine in the film, but she also asked Coppola to direct it. She passed the script on to him, and Coppola was immediately interested. What especially impressed him about Hart's screenplay was that it followed the novel so closely, for all of the previous movie adaptations had tossed out large sections of the book.

Abraham Stoker (1847–1912) was born in Dublin, but he eventually moved to London, where he managed the Lyceum Theater for the famed actor Sir Henry Irving. But he still found time to write novels. There was a vogue in England at the time for the stories of Edgar Allan Poe, and a number of Gothic horror novels enjoyed great popularity. So Stoker decided to cash in on the craze for Gothic fiction and composed *Dracula.* Although a few horror novels about legendary vampires had already been published in the nineteenth century, Stoker was the first to give his tale a historical foundation by grounding his main character in the bloodthirsty fifteenth-century prince Vlad Tepes, who was born in Transylvania, a province of Romania. The manner in which Stoker merges authentic history with folklore distinguishes his *Dracula* from the stories about vampires that preceded it, writes literary historian Leonard Wolf. Moreover, says Wolf, "Stoker's achievement is that he created an adventure story whose chief image—an undead creature who drinks the blood of attractive young women—shimmers with erotic meaning." Dracula, as Stoker conceived him, at first seems to be elderly and therefore an embodiment of ancient evil. Then, as he is nourished by his victims' blood, he is transformed into a dashing young seducer.

In addition to eroticism, Wolf continues, Stoker's novel possesses a religious component, for the vampire, after all, has lost his soul. In turn, "the vampire, taking the blood of his victim," is a threat to the soul of the victim, who may likewise become one of the undead. The story, as Stoker tells it, therefore takes on "the larger meaning of a fight between the cohorts of God and those of Satan."[1] That is why the vampire hunters, who are on the side of the angels, employ as defenses against the fiendish vampires such sacramental objects of Catholic ritual as crucifixes and blessed holy water. Since Stoker was a Dublin-born Irishman, it was not surprising that his novel would be infused with elements of his Catholic religion. In brief, Stoker's novel is a tale for the ages, portraying the struggle between the forces of good and evil, light and darkness, day and night. Indeed, Dracula represents the dark side of our own natures—which is why we want to see him vanquished.

Stoker cast the novel in the epistolary format, a narrative form dating back to Samuel Richardson's *Pamela* (1741). In *Dracula,* the narrator, an English gentleman, employs letters and diary entries as documentation in order to lend credibility to his bizarre account of preternatural horror.

The great German filmmaker F. W. Murnau made the first film adaptation of Stoker's book in 1922, ten years after the novelist's death. Murnau had been denied permission to film *Dracula* by the Stoker estate because Stoker's widow deemed the silent cinema a primitive art form, less dignified than the theater. Undeterred, Murnau went ahead with the film. He changed the title of the movie to *Nosferatu,* an archaic Slavonic term used in the novel to refer to the undead. In addition, he altered Dracula's name to Count Orlok and transferred the setting from Dracula's native Transylvania to Bremen, Germany. Moreover, Murnau omitted some incidents from the book and added others. Thus, in the film the vampire (Max

Schreck), a cadaverous creature with a batlike visage, unleashes a plague of rodents on Bremen, an episode not in the book. "It's a free retelling of the story," says Coppola, "with many plot elements that differ from the novel."[2] Nevertheless, despite the various departures from the novel, the film was recognizable as an adaptation of Stoker's book, and the Stoker estate sued the film's producers for making an unauthorized film of the book. The estate's legal action limited the movie's initial release, but it eventually became widely available in the 1990s.

Stoker's widow approved a stage dramatization by Hamilton Deane, since she respected the theater as a legitimate art form. Deane simplified the action by eliminating the historical prologue involving Vlad Tepes and the closing scene in Dracula's castle in Transylvania in which Dracula is confronted by the vampire hunters. He kept only the central section of the novel, which is set in London, where Dracula pursues fresh victims. The play opened in February 1927 in London and was successful enough to warrant a New York production. John Balderston reworked Deane's play for the Broadway premiere, which took place in October. The New York production ran for thirty-three weeks and made a star of Hungarian actor Bela Lugosi (who was actually born in Transylvania). Unlike Max Schreck's grotesque vampire in *Nosferatu,* Lugosi came across as suave and cultured, impeccably attired in evening clothes, a tuxedo, and cape. He thus conveyed the fatal attraction of evil. Lugosi was asked by Universal Pictures to repeat the role in Tod Browning's 1931 film version.

It is important to note that Browning's film was derived for the most part from the Deane-Balderston play and not directly from Stoker's novel. The same can be said of the subsequent movie versions of Stoker's story. Indeed, one of the things in Hart's screenplay that most appealed to Coppola was the fact that Hart had gone back to the original novel as the source of his script and did not use the stage play. Indeed, Coppola noted approvingly that Hart had even worked into the screenplay the collection of letters and journal entries by which the story is told in the book.

Coppola had been a fan of horror movies since childhood, and he had enjoyed going to horror flicks with his older brother August when he was a youngster. "When I was a boy, *Dracula* was one of my favorite scary movies," he remarks. He was enthralled by this weird creature who sucked his victim's blood. "Because I was so obsessed with how scary Dracula was, I looked him up in the *Encyclopedia Britannica* that our family had, and I was very struck that Dracula was based on a real person, that he once lived, an historical figure: Vlad Tepes, the champion of the Romanians against the invasion of the infidel Turks."

Although Vlad Tepes was born in Transylvania, a region in Romania, he actually reigned in southern Romania, in the principality of Wallachia on the banks of the Danube. Nevertheless, Stoker consistently referred to Dracula as a native of Transylvania, and to this day it is Transylvania that is associated with the Dracula legend. This fierce leader of the Romanian crusaders protected Romania, which was the gateway to Christian Europe, against the invasion of the Turkish sultan's Muslim hordes. He earned the epithet Vlad the Impaler from impaling slaughtered enemy warriors on stakes and displaying them in full view of the advancing Turkish army. Even in that barbarous era, Vlad the Impaler's blood lust was thought to be excessive. His enemies called him Vlad *Dracul*—which means "devil."

Still, young Francis Coppola was fascinated by Vlad: "I was maybe twelve when I read about him, but I remember that Vlad had impaled a lot of people on stakes and the invading Turks saw this and just turned around and left rather than tangle with this guy." He still thinks that historians have judged Vlad too harshly. As a ruler, Coppola explains, "Vlad Dracula was an enlightened despot." He was evenhanded in the way he meted out justice: "he impaled and tortured even some of his own people, regardless of their standing in the community." Stoker employed the real historical figure of Vlad Dracula in his novel, "and then invented the idea of this person becoming a vampire."

Dracula's first wife was Princess Elisabeta, who, because of a Turkish ruse, was falsely informed that Vlad had been killed in battle. The grief-stricken young woman jumped off the tower of Castle Dracula and drowned in the river below. "So the seeds of the story of the beloved woman, Dracula's long-lost love, also lie in actual history," Coppola points out. And Stoker worked her into the novel as well.[3]

For the record, the historical Vlad Dracula was slain in battle outside the city of Bucharest some years later, in 1476, at the age of forty-five. He was decapitated and his head was sent by his Turkish foes to the sultan in Constantinople as evidence that the ferocious Vlad Dracula had finally bitten the dust. It was Stoker's genius to turn this historical figure into a vampire.

In the novel, however, Dracula renounces God and embraces Satan in the wake of his wife's suicide. He becomes Dracula the vampire, and, as one of the undead, he searches through the centuries for his beloved Elisabeta. She turns up four hundred years later, reincarnated as Mina, an English girl, and he vows to make Mina his vampire bride.

Coppola was first exposed to Stoker's novel when he was in his teens. "When I was thirteen or fourteen," he recalls, "I was a drama counselor at a camp in upstate New York; I would read aloud to the kids at night, and one summer we read the entire original version of Bram Stoker's *Dracula*." The boys found it a chilling experience. It was around this time that Coppola saw the Browning version of the Stoker story with Bela Lugosi: "I loved Lugosi," he recalls, but he was disappointed that the Lugosi picture, like all of the other previous adaptations of Stoker's story that depended on the stage play, were so different from the original book.[4]

"I was amazed how much they held back from what was written in Stoker's novel," he recalls in his production journal. The whole last section of the novel, "when the vampire killers pursue Dracula back to his castle in Transylvania, and the whole thing climaxes in an enormous John Ford shoot-out—no one had ever portrayed that" in a Dracula movie.[5] "I knew enough about the authentic *Dracula* to realize that it had never been made as a movie," he concludes.[6]

With *Dracula*, Coppola returned to the horror genre for the first time since *Dementia 13*, his very first feature. Soon after Coppola examined James Hart's screenplay, he issued a press release, announcing that he would film *Dracula* for American Zoetrope, his independent production unit, and that the picture would be financed and distributed by Columbia Pictures. Coppola had pitched the property to Columbia not only as a horror flick but as "an erotic dream" in which he planned to star several attractive young actors. He thereby convinced Columbia that the project was marketable, and they gave it the go-ahead.

Bram Stoker's Dracula (1992)

In November 1990 Hart was invited to meet with Coppola at his home in the Napa Valley, the original Inglenook estate near the original Inglenook winery, which Coppola now operated as the Niebaum-Coppola winery. On the estate grounds is a bungalow where Coppola holds conferences during the preproduction phase of a film—the same cottage where he met with Dean Tavoularis and Vittorio Storaro when they were planning *Tucker*. Although Hart had composed the original draft of his script, which had been entitled *Dracula: The Untold Story*, as early as 1977, he found discussing the revised screenplay with Coppola a revelation.

Coppola smiled at him over his glasses like a mischievous professor, Hart remembers. Then he opened the screenplay, "a conductor about to commence a symphony. For the next two-and-a-half hours I sat at the Master's feet as he went through my screenplay page by page, mesmerizing me, telling me with images 'the erotic fever dream of a movie' he would turn those words into."[7]

Coppola was intent on giving *Bram Stoker's Dracula* the look of a sumptuous horror film along the lines of Stanley Kubrick's *The Shining* (1980) and still stay within the stipulated budget of $40 million—which was modest for a top-level costume picture. He hit upon the idea of cutting back on expensive sets so that he could afford to devote more money for lavish-looking costumes. If the costumes were eye-filling, he reasoned, filmgoers would not notice that he had skimped on the sets. He accordingly brought in Eiko Ishioka, the Japanese designer who had collaborated with him on his telefilm "Rip Van Winkle." In hiring Eiko, Coppola explains, he was confident that at least one element of the film's design, the costumes, would be totally unique and original.

Eiko's dazzling costumes were exotic, stunning creations, all exquisite silks and brocades, worthy of a museum. Since red often symbolizes blood in films, she dressed Dracula primarily in red (the red cloak Dracula wears when Jonathan Harker, a young attorney, comes to visit him at his castle demonstrates this technique). The enormous train, which trails behind Dracula as he walks, "is conspicuous when Dracula rushes about his castle like a bat. It was designed to undulate like a sea of blood."[8]

Coppola selected German cinematographer Michael Ballhaus as director of photography. Ballhaus, a favorite of German director Rainer Werner Fassbinder before coming to Hollywood, had recently shot *GoodFellows* for Martin Scorsese. Since Coppola was not in the market for the kind of elaborate sets favored by Dean Tavoularis for previous Coppola films, Coppola turned to a young production designer, Thomas Sanders.

Because many of the scenes take place at night, Coppola had Ballhaus photograph these scenes in deep, jarring shadows. Therefore, Coppola was often able to get by with simple settings, because they were shrouded in shadows. In this fashion he was spared the cost of having Sanders build lavish sets and was therefore able to stay within the budget.

Coppola states that he opted to shoot *Dracula* entirely in the studio, rather than on location as he had done *Tucker* and some other films. In the studio "we could control the settings in an artistic and unusual way." That simply was not possible on real locations, where weather conditions could spoil a scene.[9] As another money-saving device, Coppola commandeered some sets built for Steven Spielberg's *Hook,* which were still standing at the studio.

Eleanor Coppola was amazed when she visited the studio during shooting to see what marvels Sanders could produce with paint and plaster. One of Sanders's principal sets was "a grand Victorian mansion," with a front room that "opened onto a terrace overlooking a garden with a fountain and a pond."[10] The sumptuous-looking garden was actually cobbled together from an old wooden set, colored lights, and potted palms.

Coppola commissioned Peter Ramsey and his team of artists to produce nearly one thousand storyboard drawings for individual shots. He instructed Ramsey and his artists to draw not only on their research but on their own nightmares in designing the storyboards. When complete, the storyboards were correlated with the script, page by page, to produce a detailed shooting guide, which accordingly became the bible for the whole film.

Coppola wanted an impressive musical score, on a par with those Sergei Prokofieff composed for Sergei Eisenstein's Russian epics like *Alexander Nevsky* (1938). He imported Wojciech Kilar from Poland to give the underscore an Eastern European flavor. Kilar obliged him with one of the scariest film scores ever. This ghastly, frightening music, states musicologist Larry Timm, "has a certain satanic aura that leaves the listener with an uneasy, eerie feeling" since it comprises several themes scored in a variety of minor keys.[11]

When it came to casting the title role, Coppola selected the young British actor Gary Oldman. The actor rightly saw Stoker's Dracula as a fallen angel, a tortured soul. "Vampires are selfish, destructive creatures who half despise what they're doing, yet can't avoid doing it," says Oldman. "So I don't play Dracula as out-and-out evil."[12]

Winona Ryder, of course, was to play Vlad's first wife, Elisabeta, as well as Mina Murray, the later reincarnation of Elisabeta. Mina at that point is the fiancée of Jonathan Harker, played by Keanu Reeves. Anthony Hopkins, who had recently won an Academy Award for *The Silence of the Lambs,* was tagged to play Professor Abraham Van Helsing, a physician and metaphysician who dabbles in the occult and who is also the namesake of Abraham Stoker. Hopkins also was to play a Romanian priest who clashes with Vlad in the film's prologue.

Coppola assembled the actors at Castle Coppola in Napa for the customary week of preproduction rehearsals. The cast spent two days taking turns reading selections from Stoker's novel. This dramatic reading of passages from the book recalls a similar dramatic reading of excerpts from the novel that Stoker himself staged at the Lyceum Theater in London, for one performance only, shortly after it was published.

Coppola transferred the storyboards to videotape and had the script read as a voice-over to accompany the drawings on the tape. So Coppola already had a tape that told the whole story, which he could refer to during rehearsals. The movie's cast also did walk-throughs of all the scenes in the script. Hopkins, who normally frowns on extended rehearsals, found them helpful this time around. Coppola creates a great atmosphere to work in, he said afterward. The director sets up a scene and then improvises within that framework, "and talks you through the scene." He concludes, "The only way to work with somebody like him is just learn your lines, show up, and don't ask questions, because he seems to know what he wants to do."[13] Coppola then arranged for some run-throughs of the script before live audiences, a technique he had originated way back when he was making his first mainstream studio film, *You're a Big Boy Now.* These "dress rehearsals" were videotaped, and they served, Coppola notes, as his version of trying out a Broadway play in Boston.

Principal photography commenced on October 14, 1991, on the former MGM sound stages, which Columbia had taken over. Oldman chose to stay in character between takes, so he came across as morose and disagreeable when dealing with the cast and the director. Admittedly, Oldman had an abundance of helpful hints on how each scene should be played, but both Coppola and the other actors found him too bossy in seeking to impose his ideas on them. Coppola thought that Oldman was the most temperamental actor he had had to cope with since Marlon Brando on *Apocalypse Now.* When Coppola attempted to reason with him, Oldman replied that he was under a great deal of pressure, endeavoring to play such a demanding role: "I'm four hundred years old and dead; how the fuck do I get into character?"[14] One way he found was to shrewdly modify his voice so that he purred with "the perverse timbre of Bela Lugosi's inhuman intonations."[15]

Coppola became concerned about Oldman's drinking habits, and he finally confronted him about it when the actor was arrested for driving under the influence of alcohol one weekend. Nevertheless, Oldman, a gifted actor, gave an unforgettable performance as the smoldering creature of darkness.

Each take was videotaped at the same time it was photographed on motion picture film. This enabled the trio of film editors, Nicholas Smith, Glenn Scantelbury, and Anne Goursaud, to assemble a preliminary edit of each scene on videotape right after it was shot. Consequently, by the end of principal photography, Coppola had a "draft" of the final film—a process he had employed on other films, including *The Outsiders,* which Goursaud also edited.

The rather stringent budget allocated only a minimal sum of money for special effects. Coppola compensated by having his twenty-seven-year-old son Roman, who was in charge of special effects, achieve most of the visual tricks in the camera itself—without the benefit of expensive computer-generated images (CGI). Roman Coppola employed such quaint cinematic techniques as double exposures, slow fades, and dissolves to achieve spectral effects. For example, making a vampire disappear by means of a slow dissolve suggests their ability to evaporate into thin air. A close-up of Dracula's face grinning maniacally is superimposed on a shot of the sky, implying his unearthly evil presence brooding over the dark, gloomy Transylvanian landscape. Chiaroscuro lighting infuses certain interiors with vast, menacing shadows, which loom on walls and ceilings, giving a sinister, Gothic quality to a vampire's face. These artfully composed visual effects were not only economical, but they also paid homage to the magic of the earlier Dracula films of Murnau and Browning, which utilized similar effects in the days before CGI. Therefore, the present film has the look of a 1930s, studio-enclosed production.

Coppola also borrowed gimmicks that were used to produce magical effects in a stage play. For example, for the scene in which Dracula's three concubines materialize in Jonathan Harker's bedroom while he is staying in Dracula's castle, a trapdoor was constructed underneath his bed so that they would emerge from beneath it. They provocatively rise from under the sheets between his legs to rape him.

By the same token, Coppola created the illusion of a lengthy journey on horseback on a single indoor set, without the use of exterior locations. It is the sequence in which Van Helsing and his vampire killers journey through the Transylvanian mountains to Dracula's castle. Sanders employed a soundstage that was the size of a football field. He constructed an oval track around the perimeter of the stage. The actors rode their horses hell-bent-for-leather around the track in the face of a blizzard churned out by wind machines blowing artificial snow in the air. Between takes the greens crew kept moving the fake trees and plants around in different formations in order to create a variety of backgrounds. As a result, the horsemen appear to be covering hundreds of miles on different roads at breakneck speed, when in fact they are merely galloping around the circumference of the soundstage.

The shooting period finished on February 1, 1992—on budget and slightly ahead of schedule. Coppola then plunged into postproduction with his team of editors at the American Zoetrope facility in San Francisco. By April, Coppola had put together a rough cut. He then arranged for a sneak preview in San Diego, where he had previewed *Godfather II*. History repeated itself, and audience reaction to *Dracula* was no better than it had been for *Godfather II* earlier. Coppola reflected that the negative tone of several preview cards submitted by filmgoers meant that the present picture just did not meet their expectations.

The fundamental problem was that the audience found the plot, which spans four centuries, hard to follow. So the narrative clearly needed editing and tightening. In reworking the rough cut, Coppola kept in mind that he was committed by contract to deliver an R-rated picture to Columbia. As a result, he deleted some footage that he judged too gory and lurid to sustain an R. For example, in one scene Dracula's vampire brides carried an infant down a dark corridor as they prepared to suck its lifeblood away. Coppola trimmed the incident to a single shot of Dracula's concubines gathering around the baby and left the rest to the viewer's imagination.

Coppola was not unduly depressed by audience reaction to the rough cut: "On the brighter side, I also know that sometimes very good films have a low score at first," as *Godfather II* did. Consequently, "I hope I can get the audience to like it better than they did in San Diego," Coppola recorded in his journal on April 17.[16]

Another sneak was held in late summer, this time in Denver. According to the preview cards, narrative continuity was still a problem. Filmgoers thought that "as a whole, the storytelling skipped around, that transitions were bad," and "things were not explained enough," as Coppola wrote in his journal on September 2.[17] For example, why did Jonathan Harker, an inexperienced solicitor, have the temerity to visit Count Dracula at his castle in Transylvania? Viewers also wanted more character development, especially in terms of Mina's attitude toward Dracula: Did she really fall in love with him when he sought to seduce her?

Coppola's work was cut out for him. He must "eliminate the audience's feeling that . . . they don't know what is going on." He was convinced that ironing out the difficulties in the plot would involve new material that would require retakes. For example, he obviously needed to add a brief scene to establish that Jonathan, a junior attorney in a law firm, is sent to Transylvania to arrange for the count to purchase property in London, because Renfield, another lawyer, failed to complete the transaction. Coppola also decided to have Anthony Hopkins, as Van Helsing, record additional voice-over narration to knit the plot together more coherently—a technique he had utilized to clarify the plotline of *Apocalypse Now*. The front office at Columbia balked at the added expenditure for bringing back cast members to do more work, but Coppola insisted.

The cast and crew reconvened in the early fall of 1992 for retakes. On October 28, Coppola wrote in his journal that he was confident that he had corrected the flaws that had been observed by the preview audiences: "I think I did gain by doing the Denver preview, and certainly by being so stubborn about getting these changes into the final picture."[18]

Dracula premiered on November 13, 1992, and swiftly became a box-office bonanza.

Bram Stoker's Dracula begins with a prologue set in 1462. Van Helsing, the narrator, states, voice-over on the sound track, "Muslim Turks swept into Europe, striking at Romania, threatening all of Christendom." A Romanian knight, Vlad Dracula, known as the impaler, and his crusaders defend their Christian homeland against the infidel Turks. In order to film the opening battle sequence economically, Coppola used rear-screen projection, whereby the actors performed in front of a screen on which the silhouettes of additional fighting men were projected in the background. In the middle ground, he also employed puppets in silhouette, representing dead Turkish soldiers impaled on stakes, receding into the background. In this manner, Coppola was able to give a sense of depth to the scene and to suggest a much larger number of fighting men on the battlefield than was actually the case.

The victorious Vlad and his troops drive the Turkish invaders from Romania. As a parting shot the vengeful Turks shoot an arrow containing a note into the castle for Vlad's wife, Princess Elisabeta. It falsely claims that Vlad has fallen in battle. "Just like in *Romeo and Juliet*," Coppola comments, "she decides that, if Vlad was dead, she could not go on living herself," and so she commits suicide.[19] Vlad returns to his castle only to find Elisabeta's corpse lying in state in the chapel. Father Chesare and his fellow priests pronounce judgment on Elisabeta: because she took her own life, she is damned and therefore prohibited by Church law from having a Christian burial or being buried in consecrated ground. (Suicide at the time was considered "the unforgivable sin.")

Vlad responds by renouncing the Christian faith he has so valiantly defended against the infidels. Vlad the Impaler then angrily impales the enormous cross above the altar with his sword, and blood streams forth from it. He catches the blood in a sacramental Communion chalice taken from the altar and drinks it. Through "the reaction of these holy men," the scene shows the degree of Vlad Dracula's blasphemy, comments Coppola.[20] Vlad Dracula has condemned himself to becoming a vampire by cursing God and defiantly proclaiming that he is now in league with Satan, the Prince of Darkness. As one of the infamous undead, his existence will be prolonged by drinking the blood of his victims, just as he sacrilegiously consumed the blood that spurted from the cross.

The previous film versions of Stoker's book, as we know, were primarily based on the Deane-Balderston stage play, which omitted Stoker's prologue. Hence Coppola's film is the first screen adaptation to depict the historical background of the novel. After the prologue, which serves as an overture to this symphony of horror, the story leaps ahead to nineteenth-century London. Jonathan Harker, an ambitious young solicitor, travels to Transylvania to complete negotiations with Count Dracula for some London real estate. Jonathan's predecessor, Mr. Renfield (Tom Waits), had been sent to conduct this business with Dracula at his castle in the Carpathian wilds, but he inexplicably returned to London suffering from a complete mental breakdown and was summarily consigned to an insane asylum.

Jonathan sets down his harrowing experiences at Castle Dracula in a diary. We see his hand take pen to paper as he begins to narrate the events in voice-over. Jonathan initially views Count Dracula as an elderly eccentric living in a decrepit castle, but he soon discovers with increasing dread that the count is a sinister phantom. Dracula says to Jonathan at one point, "Listen to them," referring to the wolves howling at his castle gates, "the creatures of the night—what music they make!" To Jonathan's great consternation, Dracula himself is likewise revealed to be a creature of the night—a vampire. Indeed, Dracula possesses the preternatural power to transform himself into a bat or a werewolf.

When Dracula spies a photograph of Jonathan's fiancée Mina Murray, the count is amazed to recognize her as the reincarnation of his beloved Elisabeta. Dracula therefore decides to detain Jonathan in his castle, while he goes to London in search of Elisabeta/Mina. He orders his three concubines to overpower Jonathan, seduce him, and hold him captive in the castle. Jonathan eventually manages to escape from his imprisonment, however, and takes sanctuary in a nearby convent where the nuns nurse the wretched young man back to health after his dreadful ordeal. Although he later admits to having been unfaithful to Mina when he was seduced by these demonic females, he steadfastly maintains that he never once tasted their blood. He therefore was not infected by them with "the disease of Venus," the Victorian euphemism for venereal disease.

Meanwhile, Dracula voyages across the sea to London, where he searches for Mina Murray. He then reflects that he has "crossed oceans of time to find her." Coppola notes that "*Dracula* is a dark, passionate, erotic drama." It depicts "feelings so strong that they can survive across the centuries—like Dracula's love for Mina/Elisabeta."[21]

Dracula changes himself into a young Victorian dandy with a stovepipe hat. He prowls the London of foggy streets and gaslight in search of his true love. He finally discovers Mina, a demure schoolteacher, and introduces himself as a nobleman from the continent. He escorts Mina to view an early silent movie, shown on a cinematograph, a primitive version of the motion picture projector. The movie they watch is in fact the battle scene from the prologue of this film—a sly cinematic joke on Coppola's part.

Dracula woos Mina, who has lost contact with Jonathan, by plying her with absinthe in the smoky Rule Café. (He implies that absinthe makes the heart grow fonder.) "Absinthe was sort of the LSD of the Victorian era," Coppola explains. It was like a sexy seducer "who got into your brain. That's the kind of drugged, decadent, Oscar Wilde level that Jim Hurt tried to lay into the script as the spirit of Rule's Café," a bistro that Wilde did in fact frequent.[22] Just as Mina is about to succumb to Dracula's blandishments, she learns that Jonathan has been imprisoned in Dracula's castle and has escaped. She hurries off to Transylvania to marry him in an elaborate Catholic ceremony. A priest blesses the couple at the altar as they receive the sacrament of holy matrimony. Coppola offers the wedding scene as a stark contrast to the unholy seduction of Jonathan by the vampire brides and of Mina by Dracula.

When the married couple return to London, Jonathan turns over to Professor Abraham Van Helsing his account of his dreadful experiences in Castle Dracula. Van Helsing is shocked to learn that Dracula, in the guise of a foreign aristocrat, has sought to lure Mina away from Jonathan. Before Van Helsing can intervene, Dracula bewitches Mina by convincing her that she is the incarnation of his long-lost Elisabeta. He then possesses her in order to be reunited with Elisabeta. Too late, Mina finally realizes that she has fallen into the clutches of a vampire, and that Dracula's promise of "eternal love" means that she is condemned to endure the curse of living death with him.

Thereafter Mina slowly sickens and becomes listless and pale. Van Helsing suspects that she has fallen under Dracula's satanic spell. He touches her forehead with a sacred Communion wafer consecrated at Mass, and it sears her skin, leaving a red mark branded on her forehead. When Mina recoils from the sacramental wafer, Van Helsing is convinced that she is in Dracula's power. Just as Coppola incorporated elements of Catholic ritual in other films (baptism in *The Godfather*, First Communion in *Godfather II*), so, following Stoker's lead, he includes similar references to Catholic ritual in this film, for the movie, like the book, reflects a Christian outlook on sin, guilt, and redemption. Thus Van Helsing is committed to saving Mina from damnation. Van Helsing, the fearless vampire killer, vows to vanquish Dracula. He carries with him a silver cross, since Christ's cross is the adversary of Satan. Brandishing the cross, he proclaims, "Dracula's war against God is over. Now he must pay for his crimes."

Van Helsing enlists three vampire hunters, including Jonathan Harker, to pursue Dracula to his lair in Transylvania by an arduous journey through the Transylvanian Alps in a relentless snowstorm. This episode, like the prologue, has never before been portrayed in any previous movie of Stoker's book. At the film's climax, the vampire killers attack Dracula with knives, and he lies on the floor, bleeding from his wounds. There follows a brief concluding scene between Dracula and Mina, whom Dracula had spirited away with him to his castle. Coppola decided to reshoot this scene in the wake of the negative response it evoked at the previews. The original ending is printed in the published edition of the screenplay (which does not include Coppola's last-minute revisions of the script.)

As originally filmed, Mina kisses Dracula, and his youth is miraculously restored. He is once again the Vlad Dracula of four centuries before. Dracula then beseeches Mina to plunge a knife into his heart. By doing so, she thereby bestows on him at long last the eternal peace of death. The scene ends as Mina rushes into Jonathan's arms, and they embrace. The shooting script states at this point, "Jonathan holds her, understanding what has happened."[23]

Jonathan may have understood what happened, but the preview audiences manifestly did not. "The end especially let them down," Coppola wrote in his journal after the Denver preview. "They wished for a more dramatic kill of Dracula. They were vexed that it wasn't clear whether Mina was a vampire or not at the end; and they hated that she went from Dracula to kissing Jonathan at the end. . . . I will see if I can come up with a new final moment with Mina and Dracula, perhaps even involving his head being decapitated," since in folklore that is the only decisive way to make a vampire meet death and cease to be cursed as one of the undead.[24]

In conferring with Hart, Coppola revised the final scene as follows. After Dracula is stabbed by the vampire hunters, he is moved into the castle chapel. As he lies dying in the chapel where he had cursed God four hundred years before, he gasps to Mina, "Why has my God forsaken me?" He is actually uttering Christ's own words as he died on the cross on Calvary, thus implying that Dracula, who had defended Christ's cross as a crusader, may yet be redeemed by the cross of Christ. In fact, as Mina kisses Dracula, a celestial light shines down from the huge cross over the altar, transforming him into the young Vlad Dracula of four centuries past.

Mina then says, voice-over on the sound track, "There, in the presence of God, I understood how my love could release us all from the powers of darkness." After all, as Richard Corliss notes, "Dracula is a cursed soul in need of exorcism; and only Mina, the avatar of his dead wife, can provide it."[25] Dracula murmurs, "Give me peace." Mina stabs him in the heart and kisses his dead eyes. At this point Coppola makes a very crucial addition to the scene: Mina pulls the knife from his heart—and cuts off his head. She thus liberates herself from his curse by severing the bond between them, while granting him the eternal rest he craved. Then she gazes at the painting on the ceiling, which depicts Elisabeta with Vlad Dracula as they were centuries before. Vlad Dracula and Elisabeta do survive, "frozen in flight across the sky in a painted cupola, high above the carnage."[26]

Coppola was confident that the retakes represented a marked improvement in the final cut of the movie. The new ending, says Coppola, shows "that love can conquer death, or worse than death—that Mina can actually give back to the vampire his lost soul."[27] Consequently, Coppola ended the film focusing on Dracula and Mina being freed from the powers of darkness, rather than with Mina inevitably returning to the arms of Jonathan.

I have examined the alternate endings of *Dracula* in some detail because most commentators on the film have failed to do so. Clearly, Coppola did a better job of tying up loose ends in the finale that is in the movie's release prints than in the original ending in the shooting script, which left the fate of Mina in doubt.

Critics and filmgoers alike celebrated Coppola's return to form with *Bram Stoker's Dracula*. "*Dracula* is Coppola's illuminated manuscript of Stoker's classic," writes Hal Hinson, "as if the book were actually coming to life before our eyes."[28] Corliss raves that Coppola "powerfully reimagines the Victorian myth . . . and brings the old spook story alive—well, undead—as a luscious infernal romance." More recently, Carol Fry and John Craig have declared *Bram Stoker's Dracula* a closer adaptation of the novel than one finds in most Dracula films. Although Dracula remains a monster, a creature of the night, in Coppola's film, Coppola gives him a touch of sympathy, making him something of a tragic figure with redeeming qualities—for his undying, centuries-old love of Elizabeta/Mina lives in his heart. Coppola has made a stylish rendition of a musty formula, the most visually stunning of Dracula films.[29] In other words, Coppola raised the stakes for his screen version by promising the definitive version of Stoker's novel, and that is precisely what he delivered.

Bram Stoker's Dracula is an affectionate homage to the golden era of the horror film. The fabric of the eerie milieu provides a near-perfect setting for Coppola's more baroque tendencies. The bold expressionistic color scheme of the film's design is quite appropriate for a horror tale. Furthermore, the visual effects complement the story—a horror film rarity. This darkly seductive, flawlessly edited film is worlds away from most horror flicks. One can shake off the scare, but the sorrow at the heart of the picture lingers long afterward. At a time when the science-fiction genre was in the ascendancy, thanks to *Star Wars* and *Star Trek,* Coppola conjured up magic from fantasy, not technology, from swords, not lasers, and from the past, not the future.

Coppola fled to a secluded vacation spot in Guatemala before the film's premiere on November 13, "so I wouldn't have to wonder or worry about how the film opens," as he recorded in his journal on November 19. He finally had Eleanor phone the front office to get the results of the first five days. "I knew that it would have to do at least seven or eight million dollars for it not to be a disgrace."[30] She reported that the picture took in over $31 million on the first weekend, the highest opening gross for any film in Columbia Picture's history.

On June 30, 1992, just a few months earlier, Coppola had filed for personal and corporate bankruptcy. One of his principal creditors was Jack Singer, who had loaned him a substantial sum in 1981 to help finance the production of *One from the Heart,* a loan Coppola had yet to pay back. "I was being sued and pursued by this man," says Coppola.[31] Consequently, the profits from *Bram Stoker's Dracula* enabled him at long last to clear his debts and move on. American Zoetrope in San Francisco was healthy once more. The picture grossed $82 million domestically and went on to chalk up a worldwide gross of $200 million. (Furthermore, Coppola's winery, Niebaum-Coppola, was expanding, so he was finally out of the woods.)

By retelling the Dracula story in a fresh and original fashion, Coppola had "triumphed over an exhausted genre."[32] Moreover, the film was honored at the Academy Awards with Oscars for costume design (Eiko Ishioka), make-up (Michelle Burke), and sound editing (Leslie Schatz). Coppola has presented a fully realized version of Stoker's novel. As such, it is the yardstick by which all subsequent adaptations must be judged.

The only film of consequence that has been derived from the Stoker novel since Coppola's adaptation is Elias Merhige's *Shadow of the Vampire* (2000), about the making of Murnau's *Nosferatu.* This unusual, creepy movie is based on the fictional premise that Max Schreck, the actor whom Murnau cast as Dracula, was really a vampire who preyed on members of the cast and crew during production. Coppola had an implicit connection to the film in that Cary Elwes, who was cast as the cinematographer Fritz Arno Wagner in *Shadow of the Vampire,* played one of the vampire hunters in Coppola's film. Furthermore, *Shadow of the Vampire* was coproduced by Nicolas Cage, Francis Ford Coppola's nephew.

Bram Stoker's Dracula signaled that Coppola's auteurist impulse had not only survived the financial upheavals of the past decade, but had prevailed. "There's no distress for me—for the first time in thirty years, no worries," he reflected. "I can have time for repose."[33] In the decade from 1982 to 1992, Coppola had made nine feature films, averaging nearly one picture per year. It was no longer necessary for him to be a hired gun, taking on pictures like *Gardens of Stone* just to pay the bills. He could now afford to be choosy, and one film that he chose to make would bring him further critical and popular success: a courtroom drama entitled *The Rainmaker*.

13

The Vanishing Hero

The Rainmaker and Jack

Just keep your mind open and take in the experience; and if it
hurts, it's probably worth it.

—Richard, a castaway in the film *The Beach*

While waiting for his flight to Paris to take off from JFK in New York, Francis
Coppola bought a copy of John Grisham's novel *The Rainmaker*. No less
than five of Grisham's books had made it to the big screen, and so Coppola
decided to take a gander at this one. By the time his plane touched down at
Orly, he was hooked on filming Grisham's *The Rainmaker* as an American
Zoetrope production. "I was down on my knees in gratitude that I had a
book that I liked—with characters that I liked," he says.[1]

Coppola took the novel to Paramount, his old standby, and the studio
agreed to finance and distribute the film. Previous Grisham movies like
The Firm (1992) had fared well at the box office, and Coppola's films in
recent years had likewise made a bundle. In April 1996 he signed with Paramount to write the screenplay and to direct the picture. Michel Herr, who
had provided the narration for *Apocalypse Now,* would take on the same
task for *The Rainmaker.* (Coppola's *Rainmaker* should not be confused with
the 1956 movie of the same title starring Katharine Hepburn.) This is the
first script Coppola had written since *Godfather III.* He officially launched
the project with an announcement to the international press at the Cannes
Film Festival in May.

The Rainmaker (1997)

The story revolves around Rudy Baylor, an idealistic Southern lawyer who endeavors to maintain his integrity in a profession filled with too many sellouts. The main plot concerns the battle young Rudy, an eager-beaver attorney, wages against a huge insurance company that has cheated Dot and Buddy Black, a poor Memphis couple, out of the benefits they need to finance a critical operation for their desperately ill son Donny. Along the way Rudy assists an elderly widow, Miss Birdie, in coping with her greedy son, who wants to badger her into leaving him all her money. He also aids a battered wife, Kelly Riker, in escaping from her sadistic husband. Coppola sagely pared down the novel's complicated narrative by relegating the sub-plots about Miss Birdie and Kelly Riker to the background, so that he could foreground the main storyline about Rudy's fencing with the insurance company. As in *Tucker,* Coppola was once more making a picture about the little guy standing up to the establishment.

Coppola put together an impressive production team, engaging cinematographer John Toll, who had garnered an Academy Award for photographing *Legends of the Fall* (1994), to lens the movie. In addition, composer Elmer Bernstein, another Oscar winner for *Thoroughly Modern Millie* (1967), contributed the score. Barry Malkin, veteran of several Coppola movies, was secured to edit the picture.

The director cast the picture in much the same way that he cast *The Godfather*: instead of spending a big chunk of the budget on some expensive marquee names, he elected to people his cast with dependable veterans and promising newcomers. Jon Voight (*Midnight Cowboy*) was called upon to play Leo Drummond, the slick, fancy-suited chief attorney for the insurance company, Great Benefit. Roy Scheider (*Jaws*) won the part of Wilfred Keely, the sly, corrupt CEO of Great Benefit. Mickey Rourke (*Rumble Fish*) took the role of a venal shyster lawyer named Bruiser Stone, who hires Rudy right out of law school, and Danny DeVito (*Tin Men*) enacted the role of Deck Schifflet, Rudy's wily, down-at-the-heels mentor in the law office. Miss Birdie was to be played by Hollywood icon Teresa Wright, who won an Oscar for the classic film *Mrs. Miniver* (1942).

Coppola had a record of giving fresh young talent a boost dating back to *The Outsiders.* Running true to form, he selected Matt Damon to play Rudy and Clare Danes to play Kelly Riker. Neither of them had had a major role in a film up to that time. Damon found the whole idea of working for Francis Coppola intimidating: "I was so nervous that I'd let him down."[2] So Mickey Rourke made a point of encouraging Damon. Rourke had never fulfilled the promise he had demonstrated in *Rumble Fish*. The grizzled actor's notorious boozing, plus a string of flops like *Desperate Hours* (1990), had all but eclipsed his career. He hoped that Damon would profit by his mistakes: "You have a big opportunity, kid," he told Damon when they first met. "I had that opportunity and I blew it. Don't piss it away! Focus on the work, don't waste your energy acting out. It gets you nowhere."[3] The cast, as usual, spent more than a week rehearsing and improvising at Coppola's Napa estate in order "to teach the actors to be attentive and to listen" to each other, says Coppola. "You give them a chance to experiment; the goal is to get life into the camera."[4]

Coppola has a long-standing penchant for shooting films on location whenever possible. Therefore, it is not surprising that he opted to take the cast and crew to Memphis, Tennessee, where the story takes place. Filming began in September 1996. Collaborating closely with John Toll, Coppola shot a large part of the picture in and around the local courthouse. Filming in autumn, Toll used pastel colors to give the film the dreary, autumnal ambience appropriate for the essentially dark tale of some decent characters struggling, not to get ahead, but just to survive.

During shooting Coppola did not hesitate to manipulate his actors occasionally in order to evoke from them the emotional response he was looking for. For example, he took Damon aside just before the cameras rolled on a scene in which Rudy is fired by a client. Recalling the rumors that he was going to be replaced by Elia Kazan on *The Godfather*, Coppola told Damon that the front office was dissatisfied with his performance and was thinking of replacing him with Edward Norton. This news helped Damon to radiate insecurity in the ensuing scene.

As filming progressed, Coppola became concerned that the courtroom scenes were slanted too much in Rudy's favor. He worried that the audience would be able to guess what the verdict in the insurance case would be half an hour away from the ending. He therefore aimed to make it clear that an inexperienced young attorney was up against a high-priced corporation lawyer that he would find it hard to beat. Hence, during the hiatus from shooting occasioned by the Christmas holidays, Coppola cleverly reworked the last forty pages of the script. In the rewrites Rudy makes some tactical errors that jeopardize his chances of winning the case. In his revisions of the screenplay, Coppola thus injected a greater degree of uncertainty and suspense into the courtroom scenes.

For example, Rudy presents in open court some incriminating documentation against Great Benefit, which was turned over to him by a disgruntled former employee who had stolen it from the firm's files when she was fired. Drummond maintains, much to Rudy's embarrassment, that stolen evidence is not admissible in a court of law. But Deck subsequently saves the day by finding a loophole, whereby evidence that has been stolen can legitimately be presented in court, provided that it was not stolen by the attorney who makes use of it!

Like the narration Michael Herr wrote for *Apocalypse Now,* the running commentary he composed for Rudy in *The Rainmaker* casts somewhat of a jaundiced light on the events in the story. Rudy observes members of his profession who have long since abandoned the ideals he still holds dear, beginning with flashy, sleazy Bruiser Stone, who is given to fraudulent practices like jury tampering. As a result, Rudy has a penchant for lawyer jokes, and his voice-over commentary is punctuated with them. At one point he quips sardonically, "When do you know a lawyer is lying? When his lips are moving." He continues, "What's the difference between a hooker and a lawyer? A hooker stops screwing you once you're dead. Everybody loves lawyer jokes." In fact, the film's overall sense of disillusionment with the legal profession is largely conveyed through Herr's articulate voice-over narration, which is usually right on target.

During the postproduction phase, Coppola returned to American Zoetrope in San Francisco to collaborate with Barry Malkin in producing the rough and final cuts of the film on Coppola's state-of-the-art equipment. The picture previewed well, so Coppola felt he was home free.

The Rainmaker starts out with the image of the traditional statue of the Goddess of Justice standing outside a courthouse. Justice holds the scales of justice in her hands, and she is blindfolded to symbolize that, although she may be blind, she always triumphs in the end. Rudy Baylor, a greenhorn attorney with lofty ideals, still believes in Justice, although he finds himself operating out of a law office in a strip mall, working for a disreputable lawyer named Stone who is certainly no rock of respectability in legal circles.

But Rudy, an undertrained lawyer who has just graduated from a second-rate law school and is living in his car, cannot hope for a more appropriate employer at this point than Bruiser Stone. Commenting on Rourke's portrayal of Bruiser Stone, Kent Jones says that Coppola has always possessed a gift for telling character traits and audacious casting choices. Casting Mickey Rourke as a flamboyant shyster "is a stroke of genius; putting him in a turquoise suit with a white belt is nothing short of divine inspiration."[5]

Bruiser assigns Rudy to do some blatant ambulance chasing. He is to comb hospital wards for accident victims in order to drum up business for the law firm by soliciting them as clients. Rudy soon becomes involved with Kelly Riker, who is in the hospital recuperating from a beating that she endured from her husband, a professional baseball player. It seems that his aluminum bat is his weapon of choice.

Rudy's other clients include Miss Birdie, a pixilated elderly woman who is determined to disinherit her ungrateful son. She soon becomes Rudy's landlady. So Rudy takes Kelly to stay with Miss Birdie in order to provide Kelly with a sanctuary from her heartless husband. In harmony with Coppola's pervasive theme about the significance of family in people's lives, he depicts Rudy as establishing a surrogate family, with Miss Birdie as the mother figure and Rudy himself and Kelly as her two "kids." Rudy comments wryly on the sound track, "A lawyer isn't supposed to get involved with his clients, but there are all kinds of lawyers and all kinds of clients."

Deck warns Rudy that the FBI. is getting ready to close in on Bruiser for his slimy illegal practices. Rudy accordingly opens his own shoestring, storefront law office, with Deck as his right-hand man. As Deck tells Rudy when they depart from Bruiser's office, Bruiser's business was never really a law firm—"it was just every man for himself."

The neophyte lawyer then in earnest takes on a major league insurance company, Great Benefit, which is bent on denying the low-income Black family the insurance benefits for their son Donny Ray (Johnny Whitworth), who is suffering from leukemia. Indeed, the medical coverage that Great Benefit has denied Donny Ray would provide funds for a bone-marrow transplant that could very likely save his life. Great Benefit claims that such an experimental operation is an extraordinary means of treating leukemia, and no insurer is obligated to fund such extraordinary means of medical treatment. Rudy, of course, counters that in an age of advanced medical technology bone-marrow surgery is no longer "experimental," but an ordinary means of treating leukemia. Therefore, Great Benefit should provide coverage for this standard surgical procedure.

With the Black case Rudy finds himself involved in big-time litigation. His chief opponent is Leo Drummond, a high-priced, amoral attorney backed up by a battery of lawyers. By contrast, Rudy's sole colleague is his seedy sidekick Deck Shifflet, an intrepid would-be lawyer who has failed the bar exam six times. Be that as it may, Deck knows his way around courthouses and teaches Rudy the ropes. Their give-and-take is at the heart of the film. Moreover, their deft interplay exemplifies how Coppola "allows his actors, rather than his showmanship, to carry the scenes."[6] Coppola's skillful screenplay is filled with the kind of behind-the-scenes legal maneuverings that keep the story from becoming a battle of words instead of a battle of wits. As a matter of fact, Rudy discovers that his opponent, a bona fide scoundrel, is not above underhanded tactics like installing a surveillance device in Rudy's office to monitor his phone calls (shades of *The Conversation*).

Judge Tyrone Kipler (Danny Glover, in an uncredited cameo), is a black veteran of civil rights protests and is thus partial to Rudy and his downtrodden clients. But Kipler is also scrupulously fair, and he must reluctantly rule in favor of Drummond when the legal ace sometimes outmaneuvers Rudy on a point of law. Jones notes that Coppola can get fresh perspectives in any scene, "zeroing in on the possibilities of any given space." He singles out the scene in which Rudy, with Judge Kipler's permission, holds a conference in the Blacks' backyard so that Donny Ray, who is too weak to go to the courthouse, can videotape his deposition. "The outdoor deposition is a beauty, deftly juxtaposing viewpoints and moods in a few minutes of screen time. The details are superb: the courtly judge greeting all the participants and ushering them into a believably run-down backyard; the team of million-dollar lawyers led by Leo Drummond trudging through the mud and unkempt grass in their expensive shoes; a gnatlike Deck Shifflet setting up his video camera"; and Rudy introducing his cancer-ravaged client to the assembled group.[7] The scene is capped by Coppola cutting to Donny Ray's father, a sullen, withdrawn alcoholic, silently retreating with a pint of whiskey to his abandoned car in the weeds to mope. Instead of milking the heartbreaking scene for the last drop of pathos, Coppola finishes it off with a sliver of comic relief: Deck, the little shadow who has stage-managed the whole meeting, goes to the fence and offers his card to a nine-year-old black boy with a broken arm, asking him if he needs legal representation.

Meanwhile, Rudy keeps one eye on Kelly's case. He takes her back to her house to collect her belongings after he has convinced her to file for divorce. Once there, Rudy is forced into a confrontation with Cliff, her abusive mate. When Cliff begins brutally slapping his wife around, Rudy intervenes, and they engage in savage hand-to-hand combat in which a lot of furniture is smashed to pieces. This is the most harrowing depiction of domestic violence in a Coppola film since Carlo attacked Connie in *The Godfather*.

Rudy finally knocks Cliff senseless with Cliff's own ball bat. Thinking that Cliff has been subdued, he stalks out of the house. But Cliff comes to. The terrified Kelly picks up the bat that Rudy had discarded and administers what turns out to be a death blow with a resounding thud. Kelly has killed her husband, but Rudy eloquently convinces the district attorney that she did so in self-defense.

In the movie's deeply moving climax, Rudy presents documentation that proves that the life of Donny Ray Black—who has died in the course of the trial—could have been saved by the operation that the criminally negligent insurance company patently should have funded. Rudy shows in open court the videotape of Donny Ray's deposition, made shortly before his death, in which he testifies, "Leukemia was detected in plenty of time for a bone-marrow transplant to save my life." Rudy shrewdly freezes the image of the haggard, pale young man on the screen in the courtroom, and Donny Ray seems to be staring plaintively, with dark circles under his eyes, directly at Wilfred Keely, the CEO of Great Benefit. Then, for good measure, Donny Ray's wretched father strides over to Keely and silently thrusts a cherished photograph of his dead boy in Keely's face, while the CEO averts his eyes in shame.

The jury ultimately sees through the slick and manipulative legal tactics of the high-powered lawyer, Leo Drummond, while at the same time the jurors are favorably impressed by Rudy's sincere, straightforward defense of his client. The jury, accordingly, awards the Black family $50 million in punitive damages. Consequently, the movie's title refers to a lawyer who causes a deluge of cash to rain down on his client. In short, Rudy Baylor is a latter-day David, who has vanquished Goliath in the person of big-time attorney Leo Drummond, whose client, Great Benefit, is bankrupted by the verdict. Keely shortly thereafter is apprehended at the airport as he desperately attempts to flee the country.

When Rudy mulls over his triumph, he wonders if he really wants to wear the mantle of a legal eagle, which this case has conferred upon him. He considers instant retirement from the law profession: "Every client that I ever have will expect this kind of victory, nothing less," he says in a voice-over. He is not sure he can live up to such grandiose expectations. "I still love the law," he adds, "but maybe I should be teaching it, rather than practicing it." As the movie ends, Rudy and Kelly are driving away from Memphis, preparing to build a new life somewhere else.

Early in the film a client of Bruiser's notices that he has a fish tank in his office with a shark swimming around in it. He observes, "A live shark in a lawyer's office. It must be a joke." Since Bruiser is a killer shark, it is no joke. Coppola ingeniously plants this incident at the beginning of the movie so that he can pick up on it at the end. As Rudy and Kelly ride off into the sunset, Rudy says on the sound track, "I don't want to wake up some morning and find that I have become Leo Drummond. And then you're nothing but another lawyer joke—just another shark in the dirty water." The movie concludes on this thought-provoking reflection.

The Rainmaker opened on November 21, 1997, to critical hosannas and big box office. It earned $46 million in domestic rentals, rivaling the grosses of *Godfather II*. It was generally rated a well-crafted picture and by far the most satisfying adaptation of a John Grisham novel. Critics also agree that Herr's cogent running narration gave the movie its spine, providing a pithy, morally nuanced commentary on the legal profession. Jonathan Rosenbaum applauded Matt Damon's assured performance, plus the many star turns and glittering cameos by Jon Voight, Mickey Rourke, and Teresa Wright, as well as the solid work done by Mary Kay Place and Red West as Donny Ray's parents and by Johnny Whitworth as Donny Ray. He also handed a well-deserved bouquet to Elmer Bernstein for his richly textured score.[8] Bernstein's underscore is one of the most evocative scores ever contributed to a film set in the Deep South and is redolent with the colors and rhythms of old-fashioned gutbucket jazz, featuring an electronic organ and a guitar.

Besides its barb-filled dialogue and luminous cast, one notes in *The Rainmaker* the sheer vibrancy of Coppola's eye for detail and the scope of his storytelling. The film in essence affirms life in all its ambiguity and complexity, briefly banishing death even while contemplating it.

Michael Wilmington, who awarded the film his top rating of four stars, is not alone in comparing *The Rainmaker,* with its brilliant courtroom crossfire, to Otto Preminger's classic courtroom drama *Anatomy of a Murder* (1959). *The Rainmaker,* Wilmington contends, is "a richer, deeper, more enjoyable work" than most films about court cases. "Working near the top of his form, Coppola and his extraordinary cast and company turn an expert, crowd-pleasing best seller into a film of greater warmth, humanity, and humor."[9] As such, the picture richly deserves to be called, in this writer's view, one of the best courtroom dramas ever made.

There remains one other Coppola film to consider, one which is unfortunately not in a class with *The Rainmaker*. It is a minor effort that serves as a footnote to the director's illustrious career. Walt Disney Pictures, for whom Coppola had filmed "Life without Zoe" for *New York Stories,* brought him a script by Gary Nadeau and James De Monaco entitled *Jack,* in which the title character has the mind of a ten-year-old in a forty-year-old body. Coppola was immediately attracted to the material because it called up some childhood memories of his own.

Jack is afflicted with a fictitious disease that makes him age at four times the normal rate, a factor that cuts him off from normal children. The screenplay caused Coppola to remember his bout with polio as a boy: "When I was nine I was confined to a room for over a year with polio, and because polio is a child's illness, they kept every other kid away from me. I remember being pinned to this bed, and longing for friends and company," says

Coppola. "When I read *Jack,* I was moved because that was precisely his problem; there were no children in his life." Hollywood insiders wondered why Coppola involved himself in another Disney picture after the debacle of "Life without Zoe." But, aside from his affinity with the story, Coppola welcomed the opportunity to plough his director's fee back into American Zoetrope. In addition, *Jack* reminded him of an earlier film: "*Peggy Sue Got Married* was a kind of sweet fable," he explained, "and in a way *Jack* is like that." (In *Peggy Sue* the situation that obtains in *Jack* is reversed: she is a forty-year-old woman who finds herself in her teenage body. "Even though *Jack* didn't originate with me, I tried to tackle the story with as much feeling and love as I could."[10]

Jack (1996)

Coppola did not do much tinkering with the screenplay of *Jack,* but he did modify it in some interesting ways. The film begins with a pre-credit sequence in which a woman is rushed in to labor, crying, "It's too soon. It's not even two months!" She then gives birth to a premature baby. "Now that's a pretty serious kind of opening for such a whimsical movie," says Coppola. "So I added a thing where the mother is at a *beaux-arts* ball; when they rush her into the hospital," she and her husband are wearing bizarre costumes straight out of *The Wizard of Oz.* This gives a wacky kind of "Preston Sturges" feeling to the scene.

For his production team Coppola was able once more to bring back production designer Dean Tavoularis and editor Barry Malkin, with John Toll (*The Rainmaker*) as director of photography. Tavoularis and Coppola chose location sites in Northern California, in easy commuting distance from Coppola's Napa estate, just as he had done for *Peggy Sue Got Married.* As a matter of fact, the rambling old house inhabited by Jack and his family closely resembles Peggy Sue's family manse in the earlier movie.

Robin Williams was set to take the title role, and Coppola heartily approved. Williams can be childlike, Coppola stated, "but he's such an extraordinarily intelligent man that I knew he could pull off the illusion" of being a child trapped in an adult's body.[11] Diane Lane, whose association with Coppola dated way back to *The Outsiders,* took the part of Jack's mother, Karen Powell.

During the three-week rehearsal period at Coppola's Napa estate, he encouraged the children in the cast, who would play Jack's schoolmates, to improvise as they engaged in games like hopscotch and in childish pranks with Williams. By the end of rehearsals, Williams was not a superstar to them any more, but just one of the gang. "We just ran around up at his place," said Williams. "[I]t was great, because you assimilate behavior without even knowing it."[12] Principal photography started in September 1995 and proceeded in a routine fashion.

The concept of a boy with a man's body had been done before, most notably in the Tom Hanks vehicle *Big* (1988), in which a twelve-year-old gets his wish to grow "big" granted temporarily by a carnival wishing-machine. In *Jack* the boy's rapid growth is not caused by magic but by an irreversible disease. That gives the present film some poignancy. It is evident that, since Jack ages physically four years for each calendar year that he lives, he may not reach twenty.

In the film's prologue Jack is born fully developed after a two-month pregnancy. After the prologue the story leaps ahead a decade, whereby Jack is ten and looks like a robust adult of forty. His parents, Brian and Karen Powell, in the intervening years have kept him at home. A kindly school teacher, Lawrence Woodruff (Bill Cosby), has come to the house regularly to tutor Jack. Since Jack has no ordinary contact with other children, Brian, with Woodruff's support, persuades Karen to liberate Jack from his cloistered existence and let him go to elementary school with other children his age. "Just because a person is different," says Woodruff, "he shouldn't be an outcast." Be that as it may, Jack's classmates initially see him as a freak and ridicule him during class and in the schoolyard. After all, Jack towers over them, and when he sits in a school desk on his first day in the fifth grade, he is too big for the desk, which tips over and collapses under his weight. The other kids gradually accept him, however, when they realize that his size can benefit them. He is a topnotch basketball player at recess, and he looks old enough to buy them *Penthouse* at the local drugstore.

But Jack's adult body, coupled with his child's mind and emotions, can present drawbacks for him. He nurses a school-boy crush on his teacher, Miss Marquez (Jennifer Lopez), and he asks to be her escort to a school dance, since she is tall enough to dance with him. He seeks to ingratiate himself with her by offering her a bag of red Gummi Bears. She is touched but gently and tactfully declines his invitation, calling herself an elderly lady, too old for school dances.

Jack gets into real trouble when he goes to a café, hoping to find a girl tall enough for him to dance with. But first he encounters Paulie (Michael McKean), a middle-aged, confession-prone regular. He engages Jack, who looks forty, in a heart-to-heart talk about getting old, which he calls "God's cruel trick" on men. "You start losing your hair," he says, and, significantly, the toupee that he sports in a futile effort to hide his age is slightly askew.

Then Dolores Durante (Fran Drescher), a promiscuous divorcee, sidles into the club. She happens to be the mother of Louie (Adam Zolotin), Jack's best buddy at school, but she is unaware that Jack is only ten years old. So she unabashedly displays a romantic interest in Jack. Louie had earlier remarked that his mother "looks for love in all the wrong places," so she is running true to form. When she takes a shine to Jack, a jealous drunk resents the attention that she is giving him and punches him out. Jack gets into a slugfest with the drunk and knocks him flat. So he spends the night in the slammer, to the chagrin of his parents.

Todd McCarthy terms the tavern scene a high spot in the movie, "sparked by vibrant performances from Drescher and McKean." The sequence is amusing because it involves Jack in "passing" physically as an adult, which he can do effortlessly, "while desperately trying to behave as an adult as well," which is decidedly not easy for him.[13] Thus, when Jack dances with Dolores, he ineptly attempts to imitate her gyrations on the dance floor, with hilarious results.

This scene raises some serious questions for syndicated columnist Stephen Witty. For him it illustrates the path the entire movie might have taken if it had been more ambitious. After all, if Jack is chronologically and emotionally ten years old, but physically forty, "then he's a sexually adult male with a child's lack of inhibitions." Consequently, his cuddles with Dolores "take on a twisted look," and raise issues far too complex for the movie and its "feel-good story."[14] Actually, because the movie was designed to appeal to children, Coppola skirts the sexual implications that the plot might otherwise have raised. By the same token, there is no hint of pedophilia in Dolores having designs on ten-year-old Jack, since she assumes he is a mature adult.

At any rate, after Jack lands in jail, his overprotective parents consider isolating him once more from the big, bad world to spare him further travails. But his loyal chums prevail upon them to permit Jack to remain in school with them. Nevertheless, Jack's physician dutifully warns Jack's parents that "Jack's internal clock is ticking faster than normal," and that premature signs of aging will regularly occur, which will indicate that his time is running out. In short, Jack will grow old and sick and inevitably have a short life span. At this moment Coppola cuts to a butterfly landing on Jack's windowsill. Jack picks it up—it is dead. The image implies that life is short for a butterfly and for Jack too and once more demonstrates Coppola's strong visual sense, which never deserts him when he is filming.

In the epilogue, set seven years later, an aging, somewhat feeble Jack, who by this time is going on seventy, is valedictorian when his class graduates from high school. "My life has been short," he begins, "but in the end none of us has very long on this earth. Life is fleeting—it's like a shooting star: it passes quickly. But while it is here it lights up the sky. So we must live life to the fullest while we are still here. He concludes, "When you see a shooting star, think of me. Make your life spectacular. I know I did."

Jack's final speech struck a chord in Coppola: "The idea is that it really isn't how long you live; it's how completely you live your life that is important. . . . My son Gio only lived twenty-three years, but it was a complete twenty-three years. He got to do everything—he got to be a kid, he got to be an adult, got to fall in love," got to be second unit director on *The Cotton Club*.[15] The picture ends with a dedication to Coppola's granddaughter Gia, Gio's daughter: "To Gia, 'When you see a shooting star. . . .'"

Coppola was thoroughly lambasted by the reviewers for *Jack*, in much the same way he was excoriated for his previous Disney outing, "Life without Zoe." Gene Siskel, one of Coppola's biggest fans in the past, took great exception to *Jack*, as did most of his colleagues. Apparently Siskel noticed that one of the revelers at the costume party in the movie's opening sequence was dressed up as a bottle of wine from Coppola's vineyard. "Coppola has been expanding his vineyard," Siskel opines, "and my guess is that his *Jack* fee paid for a lot of grapes. But *Jack* is anything but vintage Coppola. Williams takes over the movie and basically does some talk show riffs on what it's like being a boy. . . . My advice: Buy the wine; put a cork in the movie."[16] (For the record, Coppola put his director's fee for the film back into American Zoetrope, not into the Niebaum-Coppola winery.)

Michael Wilmington's more benign appraisal of the picture called it "sunny, humane, and high-spirited," and complimented Coppola at the very least for outclassing his material: "*Jack* does manage to triumph over its likeable but derivative script, which is no more provocative or funny than it is original."[17]

Admittedly, Coppola's cast served him well throughout the movie. Robin Williams brings star charisma to the title role. Bill Cosby copes adequately with the part of Lawrence Woodruff. Fran Drescher injects some vitality into the role of the dubious, loose-moraled Dolores Durante, and winsome, wise-cracking Adam Zolotin as her son Louie proves once again W. C. Fields's adage that child actors and dogs are the best scene-stealers in the business.

On the other hand, Coppola's direction is competent but not inspired. Lacking the invention or the fluency of his other films, *Jack* suffers by comparison. Coppola has always had a predilection for youth flicks, but with *Jack* he has not progressed much beyond his earlier "coming of age" movies like *You're a Big Boy Now, The Outsiders, Rumble Fish*—or *Peggy Sue Got Married,* the picture that *Jack* most resembles as a mild fantasy. Overlong at 113 minutes, *Jack* finally wears out its welcome. The milk of human kindness has curdled in this dark comedy about a youngster who grows old before his time because of an incurable disease. Still, the movie takes some imaginative risks as it veers between stark drama (Jack growing old) and knockabout farce (the barroom brawl).

In the last analysis, Coppola's best films were used against him by the reviewers of *Jack.* Critics had come to have substantial expectations of a director with Coppola's elegant craftsmanship. "Coppola is one of the greatest of the post-war American filmmakers," Wilmington writes, "and though you can't expect him to give us a *Godfather Trilogy* or an *Apocalypse Now* every time out, you can expect more ambition and ideas" than are evident in *Jack.*[18]

As things turned out, nobody liked *Jack* but the public. When it opened across the United States on August 9, 1996, it quickly put $11 million in the Disney coffers on the first weekend, thereby becoming the top-grossing picture in the country. It obviously reached its target audience of youngsters. By the end of the year it was one of the top box-office attractions of 1996, with $60 million as a domestic gross.

The Rainmaker, the other film treated in this chapter, would likewise turn a handsome profit. But, unlike *Jack,* it would also enhance Coppola's reputation as one of the finest filmmakers of his generation. Although *Rainmaker* was never really undervalued as a major Coppola picture, its reputation has continued to grow over the years, and it has finally been recognized as one of Coppola's warmest and richest films.

Sometimes a film comes off, like *The Rainmaker,* and sometimes it does not, like *Jack.* A director cannot always predict the outcome when he makes a film. So every moviemaker's career is marked by peaks and valleys. Still a director like Coppola cannot be faulted for taking risks in his films just because the risks do not always pay off. A moviemaker who does not take risks in creating his films will surely fall by the wayside, whereas a venturesome director whose reach sometimes exceeds his grasp continues to be of interest. Critics and audiences alike too often are impatient with an artist's need to ripen and develop his talent gradually. A serious artist needs and deserves some degree of tolerance and patience on the part of critics and audiences while he refines his methods and style. In the upcoming epilogue, then, I shall make some concluding remarks about how Coppola has progressed throughout his career.

Epilogue

The State of the Artist
in the Industry Today

Some good pictures come from Hollywood. God knows how,
but they do.

—William Faulkner

You're stepping off a cliff when you start to make a film.

—Francis Ford Coppola

Francis Ford Coppola learned during his career that a director not only has
to work hard to achieve the kind of artistic independence that qualifies
him to be an auteur, but also that the director has to work just as hard to
keep it. For example, although a director like Coppola has often been looked
upon as a maverick who makes films perhaps more subjective and personal
than those of many of the other Hollywood directors, it is important to
realize that his motion pictures have often been financed by some of the
oldest and largest of Hollywood studios: Paramount, Columbia, and
Warners. That these companies have been willing to allow him such a great
degree of artistic freedom is yet another indication that the big Hollywood
studios are well aware that they must make an effort to present contemporary audiences with fresh material and not just a rehash of the old commercial formulas long since overfamiliar to moviegoers.

On the other hand, a canny director like Coppola realizes that a film-maker must cooperate with the studio that has invested in his film if he expects to get backing in the future. In other words, the cooperation must be on both sides. And Coppola does not mind meeting company demands, as long as he can meet them in his own way. Thus he has it stipulated in his contracts that any cuts the studio wants to make in a film of his are to be made under his supervision.

The relationship of artist and industry will always be a difficult one, since the director is primarily concerned with preserving his artistic integrity, while the industry is primarily interested in safeguarding its investment. This conflict of interest will inevitably lead to compromise, but, as has been seen in the films covered in this book, the compromise can often be one enabling the director to produce a film that is recognizably his own and, yet, one from which the studio can expect a return on its investment.

"I feel that I'm not reckless or crazy," says Coppola. "It's just that I'm primarily interested in making films more than in amassing money, which is just a tool" needed to make films.[1] Without the safety net provided by a Hollywood studio, not even bravery and determination can keep an independent filmmaker's dream alive—hence, the effort of going it alone and having to solicit studio backing for each film that he makes is considerable. The "Flavor of the Month" mentality of many producers—whereby they try to gauge changes in public taste—is difficult for a director to cope with. Movie executives, Coppola tells me, "can see the artist coming, cap in hand, with a project he wants to do," and they will say, "Well, he wants to do it very badly, so he's going to have to make a sacrifice because it's not a project that has been instigated by us." By contrast, if it is a project that the studio is initiating, it is possible to obtain immense amounts of money to do the film.

"I've done so much for the studios," he adds elsewhere, "and yet they resent even putting me in a position where I don't have to go to one of them with my hat in my hand and have them tell me what movies I can or cannot make."[2] As television becomes to an ever increasing degree the medium that claims the largest segment of the mass audience in the way the cinema once did, motion pictures are being thought of more and more in the same category as the legitimate theater: a medium that can afford to appeal to a more discriminating audience that wants fare a bit more challenging than what they can usually find on the tube. As this happens, film directors are more frequently being given a freer hand in making films that are more inventive and personal than has usually been the case in the past.

After all, the major studios began to extend artistic freedom to independent filmmakers in the first place because studio executives realized that they were losing touch with the moviegoing public's taste. The great virtue of a director like Coppola is that he has for the most part been able to make films his own way while at the same time remaining aware of what would appeal to his audience. He has, in short, shown his respect for the creative freedom he has achieved by working so hard to win it and by using it so well.

"There are two kinds of movies you make," Coppola explains. "There's your dream project that you are basically trying to figure out how you are going to get financing for" (like *Apocalypse Now*), "and then there's the job that's brought to you." Although *Peggy Sue Got Married* was more of a job than a dream movie in Coppola's view, he was gratified by the way that it turned out. Still Coppola admits to accepting from studios at times assignments he did not find particularly attractive in order to afford to make films of his own choosing. "The thing that unites young, inexperienced directors and older, experienced directors" is that neither type of filmmaker often gets the opportunity "to do their personal work," he says.[3]

Coppola may have the *Godfather* films to his credit, but he is still hard put to get the financing to do a project that is original. The reason is that the studios are now owned by multinational corporations who are more interested in making big bucks than in making great movies. Therefore, as Mark Caro points out, Coppola has learned to mix "the occasional pet project"—such as 1982's *One from the Heart*, which fizzled at the box office—with "bill-payers," like 1986's *Peggy Sue Got Married*. "Coppola's experience is a cautionary tale that demonstrates the increased pressure on filmmakers to deliver commercial hits." Yet Coppola has never downgraded the films he made as a "hired gun" (like *Peggy Sue*), simply because they were not personal projects of his own devising. He has always been quick to emphasize that *The Godfather* started out as a job-for-hire. Paramount asked him to adapt a routine crime novel for the screen, and Coppola turned it into an epic cinematic saga and a moneymaker in the bargain. "It's like, you bake this cake," he concludes, "and sometimes it turns out to be a wonderful cake."[4] Coppola, in his time, has made some wonderful cakes.

Coppola contends that the negative press that has persisted over the years about his cavalier attitude toward going over budget on his pictures is unfair. *The Outsiders, Peggy Sue Got Married, Gardens of Stone,* and *Tucker* were all pretty close to being brought in on budget and on schedule. Nevertheless, journalists prefer to dig up old news about his exceeding the budgets on *Apocalypse Now* and *One from the Heart*, both of which are exceptions that prove the rule.

At any rate, a milestone was reached in the ongoing tug-of-war between the film artist and the industry in 1998 when Warner Brothers reneged on a deal with Coppola's independent production unit, American Zoetrope, to film *Pinocchio*. Coppola's suit against Warners came to trial on June 3, 1998. His deposition declared, "This action arises from a dream of plaintiff Francis Coppola to bring the beloved children's story *Pinocchio* to the screen as a live action motion picture, and the efforts of defendant Warner Bros. first to grab Coppola's film at a bargain-basement price and then, when that failed, to ruin Coppola's efforts to bring his dream to life."[5] In brief, when Warners refused to agree to pay Coppola his standard directorial fee and offered him considerably less, he understandably went shopping for a better deal elsewhere. But then the front office at Warners decreed that they were still committed to the project, to the extent that they had invested development money in commissioning a screenplay by Frank Galati; therefore, they maintained, if Coppola did not make *Pinocchio* for Warners, he could not make it at all. Coppola replied, "If they had any sentiment for movies at all, you'd think they'd never stop anyone from making a film; in the end, they'd just say, 'Go ahead, make your film. We don't want to make it, but we're not going to prevent you because, after all, we're film people too.' They're not film people; they're 'money and power people.'"[6]

While detailing the scenario of *Pinocchio* on the witness stand, Coppola burst into tears. The Warners attorney dismissed Coppola's "crying jag" as a plea for sympathy from the jury. After all, we recall, Coppola pretended to have a fainting spell during a conference on *The Godfather* with Paramount's studio brass, in order to coax them into seeing things his way. Nonetheless, he contended that, in the present instance, he was not shedding crocodile tears. "I was emotional because I was describing the theme of the story, and I was very much moved by this. But it wasn't manipulative."[7]

In Coppola's behalf, Al Pacino recounted an episode during the filming of *The Godfather*: later one afternoon Coppola was filming the burial of Don Vito Corleone. "I see Francis sitting on a gravestone, and he's crying. 'Francis,' I say, 'What's the matter?' And he says, 'They won't give me another setup.' Meaning they wouldn't let him shoot the scene again. So he's sitting on the gravestone bawling, and I thought, 'This guy *cares*. . . . That's the way to live. It may be a tough ride, but something is going to come out of it.'"[8]

At all events, while Coppola and American Zoetrope were in litigation with Warners, New Line Cinema released the live-action feature, *The Adventures of Pinocchio*. This movie garnered a cool critical response and sank without a trace, thereby making it inadvisable for Coppola to make his *Pinocchio* movie at that time. "Another *Pinocchio* picture got made, and we lost millions," he says laconically. The jury ordered Warners to pay Coppola $80 million in compensatory and punitive damages. No other director has ever scored such a triumph over a major studio. To that extent, Coppola's victory is shared by every filmmaker working in the industry today. The parallel with *The Rainmaker*, "which culminates with a stunning jury award in favor of a plaintiff tackling powerful business interests," was not lost on Coppola.[9] For Coppola to take on giant Warner Brothers was once again, in his view, David conquering Goliath.

Moreover, Coppola saw some poetic justice in winning his suit against Warners, since he had lost a suit against the same studio in the late 1960s. At that time, we remember, the front office at Warners insisted that Coppola repay the studio the money it had advanced him as development funds for a package of ill-fated American Zoetrope projects they had rejected. After Warners won the case, it took Coppola years to pay off the debt (see chapter 3). Concerning the verdict in the *Pinocchio* case, Coppola gleefully commented, "Hopefully this will teach them" to treat creative people as an asset, "not as serfs."

Still, regardless of where a filmmaker works, he must reconcile himself to the fact that he is usually going to have difficulties in securing studio backing for a project he has developed. In the present setup, a director must negotiate with movie executives who operate a given studio as part of some larger conglomerate and who are therefore wary of rocking the corporate boat by providing financing for a property that departs in varying degrees from the kind of safe, commercial subject matter they tend to favor. Yet, as Coppola tells me, "it is precisely the risky, offbeat projects that often capture a large audience," and movies like *Apocalypse Now* and *Bram Stoker's Dracula* bear out this contention. Jonathan Rosenbaum has said of the latter film, "Still the overreacher, Coppola suffers at times from a surfeit of ideas (rather than a dearth, like most of his colleagues). But this is still one of the best vampire movies around—a visual feast with ideas, more disturbing than scary, and a rich experience in many other respects as well."[10]

"I've played the highwire act with regular studio pictures and gotten away with it," Coppola points out. "When you think that *Bram Stoker's Dracula* is a picture financed by Columbia, a regular studio—I mean, that's a weird movie."[11] So Coppola continues to be characterized as a Hollywood maverick, forever slugging it out with the producers, just as he was when he started making movies in the 1960s. Even then he was already pictured as the champion of the individual filmmakers against the studio system.

"No American career has had such endless turmoil or says so much about making movies in America" as the career of Francis Coppola. He revitalized the moribund gangster film genre with *The Godfather,* which "had a calm faith in narrative control that had not been current in Hollywood for twenty years. It was like a film of the 1940s in its nostalgic decor, and in Gordon Willis's bold exploration of a film noir in color." Furthermore, it rendered an uncompromising portrayal of evil.[12] The gangster genre continued to enjoy a renaissance with *Godfather II.* In imagining the early life of Don Vito Corleone, it carved out a superb recreation of "a gritty, turn-of-the-century Lower East Side" populated by raffish lowlifes.[13]

The *Godfather* trilogy inspired *The Sopranos* (1999–), a TV series about the Mafia in New Jersey, as well as the 2002 miniseries *Kingpin,* which involves a Mexican American crime family. While *The Sopranos* boasts writing, directing, and acting of a consistently high order, *Kingpin* lacks originality. If imitation is the sincerest form of flattery, then *Kingpin* is very flattering to the *Godfather* films. Miguel Cadenas is patently based on Michael Corleone, even in name (Miguel is Spanish for Michael). Like Michael, Miguel is a college-educated member of the family who marries an outsider (recall Kay Adams) and who, though reluctant to get involved, eventually takes over the family empire. Miguel intimidates a rival by slaughtering his prize dog, echoing how the Corleones killed an opponent's prize horse to scare him. Yet the characters in *Kingpin* lack the psychological complexity of the Corleones or of the Sopranos, and therefore *Kingpin* cannot be classed with either of its forerunners.

Although perhaps not as influential, the films Coppola directed after *Godfather II* continued to set precedents and to succeed in unexpected ways. *Apocalypse Now* is one of the most colossal war movies ever made. The helicopter attack on the Vietcong village is unparalleled as one of the most astounding, graphic battle sequences ever committed to celluloid. Coppola's filmography also includes some films like *The Conversation* and *The Outsiders,* which attest to his ability to make compelling movies while working on pictures conceived on a smaller scale than his cinematic epics. They qualify as chamber pieces, rather than grand opera.

Coppola has become less prolific as the years have gone on—only three films in the 1990s. The reasons for his restricted output are not hard to find. He has come to the conclusion that it was the carefully made films that would have lasting value, not those turned out on a regular basis. In his painstaking way, Coppola not only reinvented the gangster film and the war film, but, with *Bram Stoker's Dracula,* the horror film as well.

In the 1990s Coppola's wine business really took off. He engaged the distinguished enologist André Tchelistcheff as winemaking consultant. As one journalist put it, that is like hiring Stradivarius as a consultant for your fiddle factory. Coppola's vineyard in Rutherford, California, has become a tourist attraction. "He sits outside at a wooden table, the padrone, greeting tourists, autographing the labels of wine bottles."[14] (For myself, I chose a bottle of dark, dry, Coppola claret. I drank the wine but kept the autographed label.)

Even though his winery has prospered, Coppola still maintains an active interest in the film business. American Zoetrope is running efficiently and has released *The Virgin Suicides* (1999), written and directed by Coppola's daughter Sofia as her first feature. The film tells sympathetically the story of four teenage daughters of overprotective, repressive parents, who kill themselves. The cast included Kathleen Turner (*Peggy Sue Got Married*) and Danny DeVito (*The Rainmaker*). American Zoetrope also released *CQ* (2002), the debut feature written and directed by Coppola's son Roman. It is the tale of an American film editor working on a French sci-fi flick in Paris and becoming infatuated with the movie's sexy leading lady. Jason Schwartzman (the son of Roman's aunt, Talia Shire) stands out in a good cast. Sofia appears in a cameo.

Eleanor Coppola shot a documentary about the making of the film for the DVD. "I seem to have become the family documentarian," she observes at the start of her documentary. "I shot a film of my husband Francis making *Apocalypse Now* and my daughter Sofia doing her debut film, and now our son Roman is directing his first feature, *CQ*." Francis Coppola observes in Eleanor's movie that "Roman incorporated his memories of being in a family involved in filmmaking into *CQ*"—including the incident during the making of *The Godfather* when Francis got so frustrated that he put his foot through his office door (see chapter 4). In Roman's film Gerárd Depardieu, as a volatile director, punches a hole in his office door. "Roman fashioned his memories into this ingenious film," Francis concludes.

Since Coppola had directed a student production of a musical at Hofstra University before graduating in 1960, he decided to return to the stage for a month in the summer of 2000. He adapted the novel *Gidget,* about a teenaged girl who loves surfing, into a high school musical. He composed all twelve of the original songs himself. He then staged the show as a workshop production at Orange County High School for the Performing Arts in Cerritos, California, and the four-night run got raves from the locals. Coppola, as we know, was a drama counselor at a summer camp when he was in his teens. "I like to work with kids," he says, which is obvious from *The Outsiders, Rumble Fish,* and *Jack.* "It was really a nice experience for me. And that was how I spent my summer vacation."[15]

Meanwhile Coppola has continued as a member of the board of directors of MGM-UA. Indeed, he supervised (uncredited) the final edit of *Supernova* (2000) after the director, Walter Hill, walked off the picture due to artistic squabbles with the studio brass. The movie starred James Spader, who urged Coppola to pull up a chair to the editing table and rescue the picture. So it seems that Coppola's career has come full circle. Not only did he return briefly to directing student musicals, but he also reedited a movie, just as he had reedited a Russian sci-fi film, *Battle Beyond the Run,* while he was working for Roger Corman after departing UCLA's film school in the early 1960s.

Supernova casts Spader as an astronaut aboard a medical rescue ship who discovers a malevolent alien stowed away on board. MGM-UA insisted on a PG-13 rating for the film, so Coppola and his editing team had to delete some material in the love scenes between Spader and Angela Bassett (as a lady astronaut) that he would have preferred to keep. He also eliminated a confusing subplot. As a result, the release prints of the movie came in at a spare eighty-eight minutes. Still Coppola's editorial assistance helped to create a standard sci-fi movie that is an intriguing, gripping deep-space thriller. Coppola issued a statement when the film premiered, stating, "I hope that my experience in the film industry helped improve the picture and rectified some of the problems that losing a director caused."[16]

More important for Coppola personally was the release of a reedited version of *Apocalypse Now Redux* (2001), with fifty minutes of footage added to the film as originally released. The release of this new version of *Apocalypse Now* was like "the reclaiming of a child." It is a fascinating reworking of the original movie that seems "to alter the film enormously and make it into a masterpiece that left the contemporary landscape of films in 2001 looking even more threadbare." By the same token, Ryan Gilbey, in his 2003 book on the films of the 1970s, *It Don't Worry Me,* contrasts the weatherproof grandeur of *The Godfather* with the dated machismo of gangster pictures like *Dirty Harry.*[17]

In recent years Coppola has received recognition from various sectors in the film world. These acknowledgments include a Golden Lion from the Venice Film Festival in 1992 for his contribution to the art of the cinema; a Life Achievement Award in 1998, the highest honor that can be bestowed by the Directors Guild of America; and a gala tribute by the Film Society of Lincoln Center in New York on May 7, 2002, for his distinguished career in the cinema. In addition, the National Film Registry of the Library of Congress, which preserves films that are deemed culturally, historically, and aesthetically important, included *The Godfather, The Godfather Part II,* and *The Conversation* in its collection in 1995.

Moreover, the American Film Institute honored the best one hundred American films made during the first century of cinema with a TV special that aired on July 16, 1998. Included high on the list of films (which were chosen by a panel of film professionals and critics) were *The Godfather, The Godfather Part II,* and *Apocalypse Now.* Furthermore, an international poll of filmmakers and film critics, conducted in 2002 by *Sight and Sound,* the London film journal, voted Coppola one of the top ten directors of all time and listed the same three films just mentioned among the ten greatest motion pictures ever made. Furthermore, when *Premiere* magazine held a nationwide poll in 2003 for the one hundred greatest movies, *Godfather II* led the list in first place. In addition, when the AFI announced the top one hundred heroes and villains during a TV special broadcast on June 3, 2003, Michael Corleone, as played by Al Pacino in *Godfather II,* was among the legendary villains of all time. The official recognition accorded Coppola by the Directors Guild, the American Film Institute, the Library of Congress, and other organizations attests to his enduring contribution to American film.

At the close of the Lincoln Center tribute, Coppola gave a "curtain speech" in which he stated:

> At the Academy Awards in 1979 I presented the Best Director award. I don't know what got into me but I looked at that vast audience of people out there in their tuxedos (this was the entire body of the creative talent really of Hollywood) and I just broke from what I was supposed to say, and started talking about the future: how the cinema was about to change, and how it would happen in a wonderful way. But even with all this new technology, it will always be based on human talent. The people were looking at me kind of funny. Of course what I said was true. Cinema has continued to evolve, and since it's always been a marriage of technology and human talent it would be naive to think it wouldn't continue. . . .
>
> The new cinema of the last few years shows what the real potential is. Artists working together on extraordinary impossible films air the ideas and question the problems, which illuminate contemporary life and bring us to some solutions. I dream and hope the cinema in general can step forward, be something other than a means of employment. Many of my colleagues would love someone to say to them, "Gee, make a film you consider valuable, not something we have calculated with our cor-

porate budgets." If you wonder why few classics have been made in the last 20 years, that's primarily the reason.[18]

Writing on the occasion of Coppola's Lincoln Center tribute, Kent Jones notes: "There are few spectacles in American cinema more touching than the career of Francis Ford Coppola, one-time *wunderkind*, now creative grand old man of Hollywood. . . . There's something uniquely moving about Coppola's need to bring us all under his tent and waltz together to the music of the spheres." It even accounts, as stated above, for his smaller films, "where he's looking for a shortcut to grandeur." Coppola possesses "talent to burn and a precocious command of the medium," which makes him "a great director, as opposed to a calculating entertainer."[19]

In fact, Coppola is an expert storyteller capable of making riveting films with powerful performances. As such, he has sometimes been called a genius—a term he disavows: "It's embarrassing when someone calls me a genius. What is that? I would like it if it meant I was a unique person, one of a kind."[20] He prefers to think of himself as "a talented amateur," he tells me. "I'm an amateur, because being an amateur means that you make movies because you love them—not to make a living."

Coppola has always maintained that he is not interested in "soap opera psychodramas" rife with sentimentality, or the rest of "the current parade of clichés and formulas" that open every week at the multiplex. On the contrary, "I am stimulated by stories of great adventure and enterprise," films like *Apocalypse Now* and *Tucker*. "We all know what the last act will be, that we'll be looking up from a bed somewhere saying our final words. When that happens to me, I want to know that I went on some adventures. I think in those terms, and prefer stories about people like that, people who step out."[21]

Coppola ended his remarks at the Lincoln Center gala by saying that he had begun work on an ambitious, epic-scale film entitled *Megalopolis*. "Al Pacino, quoting Robert Browning has said, 'If a man's reach does not exceed his grasp, what's a heaven for?'" Actually Coppola has been nursing this pet project, which deals with "the contest of the past and the present," since the early 1980s. In it he plans to mesh a story of the corruption of ancient Rome at the time of the conspiracy fomented by the corrupt politician Catiline (108–62 B.C.) with a story about the evils of modern urban life in contemporary New York. So the movie "will swing from the past to the present, and the images of republican Rome will merge and blend with the New York of today."[22] "Clearly, a man with a phantom project called *Megalopolis* on the back burner has a whole universe in his head, far more expansive and more magical than anything possible in drab old reality. And what's touching is the way he attempts to share the oceanic vastness of his imagination with this audience."[23] Whether Coppola has another great film in him remains to be seen. That he has already proved himself to be an exceptional director is beyond question.

And the Coppola legend lives on. Sofia Coppola's second feature, *Lost in Translation* (2003), a bittersweet comedy with Bill Murray playing a Hollywood star stranded in Tokyo, was the occasion of a cover story on Sofia in the *New York Times Magazine.* The article states that Sofia promises to live up to the standard set by her father, "one of the most important American filmmakers of all time."[24] Francis Coppola served as an executive producer on the film for American Zoetrope, a company with a history as long and varied as the producer himself. Coppola now has his own American Zoetrope DVD label, which releases not only his own films but the films of other directors. As usual, Coppola runs this operation with state-of-the-art equipment that allows for the best possible transfers of film to DVD.

The reputations of filmmakers soar and sputter in the stock market of critical opinion. Reliable blue-chip directors like Coppola tend to weather the cyclical ups and downs of the marketplace with long-term returns. In 2004 *Premiere* magazine released the results of another nationwide poll, this time for the seventy-five most influential films of all time. *The Godfather* was chosen because it elevated the gangster film to the level of epic cinema. Furthermore, pictures such as Coppola's recent *Dracula* continue to be popular on TV; indeed, *TV Guide* hailed the movie upon a recent showing as "Coppola's sumptuously crafted vampire classic."[25] A Hollywood director who has helped set the gold standard for motion picture artistry with films like the *Godfather* trilogy, *Apocalypse Now, The Conversation, Peggy Sue Got Married, Dracula,* and *The Rainmaker,* Francis Coppola has forever secured his place in the pantheon of auteur directors.

Notes

Prologue: Artist in an Industry

1. Lee Lourdeaux, *Italian and Irish Filmmakers in America: Ford, Capra, Coppola, and Scorsese* (Philadelphia: Temple University Press, 1990), p. 177.

2. Richard Schickel, "Rough Cuts," *Los Angeles Times Book Review,* 13 January 2002, p. 2.

3. Jeffrey Chown, *Hollywood Auteur: Francis Coppola* (New York: Praeger, 1988), p. 214.

4. Chuck Kleinhans, "Independent Features: Hopes and Dreams," in *The New American Cinema,* ed. Jon Lewis (Durham, N.C.: Duke University Press, 1999), p. 310.

5. Michael Schumacher, *Francis Ford Coppola: A Filmmaker's Life* (New York: Crown, 1999), pp. 179–80.

6. Gerald Mast and Bruce Kawin, *A Short History of the Movies,* rev. ed. (Boston: Allyn and Bacon, 2000), p. 444.

7. Robert Johnson, *Francis Ford Coppola* (Boston: Twayne, 1977), p. 29.

1. Point of Departure

1. Ben Hecht, "Enter the Movies," in *Film: An Anthology,* ed. Daniel Talbot (Los Angeles: University of California Press, 1966), p. 258.

2. Unless noted otherwise, quotations from Coppola in this book are from the author's conversation with him.

3. Lee Eisenberg, "Francis Coppola and Gay Talese," *Esquire Film Quarterly* (July 1981): 84.

4. Joseph Gelmis, *The Film Director as Superstar* (Garden City, N.Y.: Doubleday, 1970), p. 179.

5. Peter Biskind, *Easy Riders, Raging Bulls: Coppola, Scorsese and Other Directors* (New York: Simon and Schuster, 1999), p. 149.

6. Harlan Lebo, *The Godfather Legacy* (New York: Simon and Schuster, 1997), p. 16.

7. Schumacher, *Francis Ford Coppola,* p. 19.

8. Jean-Paul Chaillet and Elizabeth Vincent, *Francis Ford Coppola,* trans. Denise Jacobs (New York: St. Martin's Press, 1984), p. 3.

9. Johnson, *Francis Ford Coppola,* p. 28.

10. Ronald Bergan, *Francis Ford Coppola: The Making of His Movies* (New York: Orion Books, 1998), p. 17.

11. Michael Goodwin and Naomi Wise, *On the Edge: The Life and Times of Francis Ford Coppola* (New York: Morrow, 1989), p. 238.

12. Ibid., p. 37.

13. Jon Lewis, *Whom the Gods Wish to Destroy: Francis Coppola and the New Hollywood* (Durham, N.C.: Duke University Press, 1997), p. 15.

14. Peter Cowie, *Coppola: A Biography,* rev. ed. (New York: Da Capo, 1994), p. 25.

15. Johnson, *Francis Ford Coppola,* pp. 29–30.

16. Roger Corman, *How I Made a Hundred Movies in Hollywood and Never Lost a Dime,* with Jim Jerome (New York: Random House, 1990), pp. 90–91.

17. Ibid.

18. Johnson, *Francis Ford Coppola,* p. 30.

19. Chaillet and Vincent, *Francis Ford Coppola,* p. 5.

20. Corman, *Hundred Movies,* pp. 110–11.

21. Cowie, *Coppola,* p. 26.

22. Corman, *Hundred Movies,* p. 114.

23. Bergan, *Francis Ford Coppola,* p. 21.

24. "*The Young Racers,*" *Variety Film Reviews: 1907–1996,* vol. 16 (New Providence, N.J.: Bowker, 1997), n.p.

25. Corman, *Hundred Movies,* pp. 113–14.

26. Michael Pye and Linda Myles, *The Movie Brats: How the Film Generation Took Over Hollywood* (New York: Holt, Rinehart, and Winston, 1979), p. 71.

27. Bergan, *Francis Ford Coppola,* p. 21.

28. Goodwin and Wise, *On the Edge,* p. 44.

29. Johnson, *Francis Ford Coppola,* p. 32.

30. Goodwin and Wise, *On the Edge,* p. 48.

31. "Video Classics: *Dementia 13,*" *American Film* 15, no. 6 (1990): 54.

32. Gelmis, *Director as Superstar,* p. 180.

33. Ibid., pp. 177, 186.

34. Goodwin and Wise, *On the Edge,* p. 55.

35. Johnson, *Francis Ford Coppola,* p. 39.

36. Chaillet and Vincent, *Francis Ford Coppola,* p. 8.

37. Johnson, *Francis Ford Coppola,* p. 89.

38. Ibid.

39. Ibid., p. 90.

40. Robert Evans, *The Kid Stays in the Picture: A Memoir* (Beverly Hills: Dove, 1995), pp. 248, 255.

41. Johnson, *Francis Ford Coppola,* p. 170.

42. Ibid., p. 174.

43. Chaillet and Vincent, *Francis Ford Coppola,* p. 41.

44. Gene D. Phillips, *Creatures of Darkness: Raymond Chandler, Detective Fiction and Film Noir* (Lexington: University Press of Kentucky, 2000), pp. 221, 222.

2. Going Hollywood

1. John Gallagher, *Film Directors on Film Directing* (New York: Greenwood Press, 1989), p. 25.

2. Chaillet and Vincent, *Francis Ford Coppola,* p. 11.

3. Goodwin and Wise, *On the Edge,* pp. 63–64.

4. Johnson, *Francis Ford Coppola,* p. 57.

5. Goodwin and Wise, *On the Edge,* pp. 63, 64.

6. Chown, *Hollywood Auteur,* p. 23.

7. Ibid., pp. 23–24.

8. Ibid., p. 26.

9. Lourdeaux, *Italian and Irish Filmmakers,* p. 176.

10. Goodwin and Wise, *On the Edge,* p. 73.

11. Chown, *Hollywood Auteur,* p. 23.

12. Johnson, *Francis Ford Coppola,* p. 61.

13. Biskind, *Easy Riders,* p. 36.

14. Goodwin and Wise, *On the Edge,* p. 75.

15. Gelmis, *Director as Superstar,* p. 183.

16. Ibid., p. 184.

17. Bergan, *Francis Ford Coppola,* p. 32.

18. Ibid.

19. Goodwin and Wise, *On the Edge,* p. 80.

20. Chaillet and Vincent, *Francis Ford Coppola,* p. 17.

21. Pauline Kael, *Going Steady: Film Writings, 1968–1969* (New York: Boyars, 1994), p. 159.

22. Goodwin and Wise, *On the Edge,* p. 82.

23. Stephen Farber, "George Lucas Hits the Big Time," in *George Lucas: Interviews,* ed. Sally Kline (Jackson: University Press of Mississippi, 1999), p. 36.

24. Dale Pollock, *Skywalking: The Life and Times of George Lucas,* rev. ed. (New York: Da Capo, 1999), p. 74.

25. Pye and Myles, *Movie Brats,* p. 82

26. Jean Valley, "*The Empire Strikes Back* and So Does George Lucas," in *George Lucas: Interviews,* ed. Sally Kline (Jackson: University Press of Mississippi, 1999), p. 96.

3. Nightmares at Noon

1. Judy Stone, *Eye on the World: Conversations with Filmmakers* (Los Angeles: Silman-James, 1997), p. 642.

2. Bergan, *Francis Ford Coppola,* p. 34.

3. Gelmis, *Director as Superstar,* pp. 187–88.

4. Ibid., p. 187.

5. Gabriella Oldham, *First Cut: Conversations with Film Editors* (Los Angeles: University of California Press, 1995), p. 326.

6. Chaillet and Vincent, *Francis Ford Coppola,* p. 21.

7. Ibid., pp. 27–28.

8. Dennis Schaefer and Larry Salvato, *Masters of Light: Conversations with Contemporary Cinematographers* (Los Angeles: University of California Press, 1984), pp. 85, 88.

9. Goodman and Wise, *On the Edge,* p. 87.

10. Johnson, *Francis Ford Coppola,* p. 73.

11. Kristin Thompson and David Bordwell, *Film History: An Introduction* (New York: McGraw-Hill, 1974), p. 710.

12. Goodwin and Wise, *On the Edge,* pp. 91–92.

13. Pauline Kael, *5001 Nights at the Movies* (New York: Holt, 1991), p. 613.

14. Chaillet and Vincent, *Francis Ford Coppola,* p. 21.

15. Pollock, *George Lucas,* p. 85.

16. David Briskin, *Inner Voices: Filmmakers in Conversation,* rev. ed. (New York: Da Capo, 1997), p. 15.

17. Chaillet and Vincent, *Francis Ford Coppola,* p. 29.

18. Pollock, *George Lucas,* p. 88.

19. Chaillet and Vincent, *Francis Ford Coppola,* p. 30.

20. Goodwin and Wise, *On the Edge,* p. 197; see Pollock, *George Lucas,* p. 99.

21. Pollock, *George Lucas,* p. 92.

22. Biskind, *Easy Riders,* p. 100. Pollock dates this meeting in November 1969, which is impossible since *THX 1138* was shot in 1969 and edited in 1970, at which point the rough cut was prepared for Warners-Seven (see Pollock, *George Lucas,* p. 99).

23. Goodwin and Wise, *On the Edge,* p. 104.

24. Pye and Myles, *Movie Brats,* p. 89.

25. Over the years the film facility that Coppola originally named American Zoetrope has undergone various kinds of reorganization with attendant variations of name (e.g., it was temporarily called Omni Zoetrope in the 1980s). For the sake of consistency and to avoid confusion, I shall refer to Coppola's production company as American Zoetrope throughout this book, especially since that has become the permanent name.

26. Schumacher, *Francis Ford Coppola,* p. 151.

27. Gene Phillips, *Creatures of Darkness: Raymond Chandler, Detective Fiction, and Film Noir* (Lexington: University Press of Kentucky, 2000), p. 199.

28. Gelmis, *Director as Superstar,* pp. 189–90.

29. Stone, *Conversations with Filmmakers,* p. 717.

30. Ibid., p. 643.

31. Anita Busch and Beth Lasker, "United We Stand: The Directors Company," *Premiere* 15, no. 4 (2002): 36, 34.

32. Bergan, *Francis Ford Coppola,* p. 44.

33. Chaillet and Vincent, *Francis Ford Coppola,* p. 43.

34. Goodwin and Wise, *On the Edge,* p. 151.

35. Richard Blake, *After Image: The Catholic Imagination of Six Filmmakers* (Chicago: Loyola Press, 2000), p. 191.

36. Foster Hirsch, *Detours and Lost Highways: A Map of Neo-Noir* (New York: Limelight, 1994), p. 171.

37. Pye and Myles, *Movie Brats,* p. 99.

38. Goodwin and Wise, *On the Edge,* p. 158.

39. Vincent LoBrutto, *Sound on Film: Interviews with Creators of Film Sound* (New York: Praeger, 1994), p. 91.

40. David Edelstein, "Gene Hackman," *New York Times,* 16 December 2001, sec. 2, p. 29.

41. Bill Desowitz, "A Still Topical *Conversation,*" *New York Times,* 2 January 2001, sec. 2, p. 28.

4. In a Savage Land

1. Mario Puzo, *The Godfather Papers* (Greenwich, Conn.: Fawcett Crest, 1973), pp. 34–36.

2. Robert Evans, *Kid Stays in the Picture,* pp. 223–24.

3. Bernard Dick, *Engulfed: The Death of Paramount Pictures and the Birth of Corporate Hollywood* (Lexington: University Press of Kentucky, 2001), pp. 126–27.

4. Evans, *Kid Stays in the Picture,* p. 225.

5. Goodwin and Wise, *On the Edge,* p. 113.

6. Marilyn Yaquinto, *Pump 'em Full of Lead: Gangsters on Film* (New York: Twayne, 1998), p. 42.

7. Biskind, *Easy Riders,* p. 143.

8. Chown, *Hollywood Auteur,* p. 63.

9. Puzo, *Godfather Papers,* p. 17.

10. The DVD edition of the *Godfather Trilogy* has both a documentary about the making of the three films and an audio commentary track by Francis Coppola on each film. I will quote both the documentary (which includes interviews with cast and crew) and Coppola's commentary in discussing the films. I will identify in each case which is the source of a given citation.

11. Edward Rothstein, "Chilling Balance of Love and Evil," *New York Times,* 3 March 1997, sec. 2, p. 26.

12. Pauline Kael, *For Keeps* (New York: Penguin, 1996), p. 434.

13. Puzo, *Godfather Papers,* pp. 42–43.

14. Ibid., pp. 60–63. See also Chown, *Hollywood Auteur,* pp. 66, 80.

15. Dick, *Death of Paramount Pictures,* p. 144.

16. Johnson, *Francis Ford Coppola*, p. 99.

17. Michael Sragow, "Godfatherhood," *New Yorker*, 24 March 1997, p. 48. See also Schumacher, *Francis Ford Coppola*, p. 100.

18. Puzo, *Godfather Papers*, p. 63.

19. Ibid., pp. 60–63.

20. Karen Durbin, "Nonstop Perfectionist: Al Pacino," *New York Times*, 12 September 1999, sec. 2, p. 52. See also Lebo, *Godfather Legacy*, p. 107.

21. Durbin, "Al Pacino," sec. 2, p. 52.

22. Schumacher, *Francis Ford Coppola*, p. 113. See also Schaefer and Salvato, *Conversations*, p. 188.

23. Biskind, *Easy Riders*, p. 156.

24. David Breskin, *Inner Voices: Filmmakers in Conversation*, rev. ed. (New York: Da Capo, 1997), pp. 41–42.

25. Peter Biskind, *The Godfather Companion* (New York; Harper-Collins, 1990), p. 76. See also Biskind, *Easy Riders*, p. 157.

26. Sragow, "Godfatherhood," p. 49. See also Michael Sragow, "*The Godfather* and *The Godfather Part II*," in *The A List: One Hundred Essential Films*, ed. Jay Carr (New York: Da Capo, 2002), p. 128.

27. Evans, *Kid Stays in the Picture*, pp. 230–31.

28. Ibid., p. 232.

29. Jon Lewis, "Francis Coppola, Paramount Studios, and the *Godfather Trilogy*," in *Francis Ford Coppola's Godfather Trilogy*, ed. Nick Browne (New York: Cambridge University Press, 2000), p. 31. See also Lebo, *Godfather Legacy*, p. 122.

30. Lebo, *Godfather Legacy*, pp. 105–6.

31. Schumacher, *Francis Ford Coppola*, p. 114.

32. Vincent LoBrutto, *Selected Takes: Film Editors on Editing* (New York: Praeger, 1991), p. 20. See Glenn Man, "Genre in the *Godfather* Films," in *Francis Ford Coppola's Godfather Trilogy*, ed. Nick Browne, (New York: Cambridge University Press, 2000), pp. 115–16.

33. Gene Siskel, "Celluloid Godfather," *Chicago Tribune*, 5 October 1986, sec. 13, p. 5.

34. Michael Jarrett, "Sound Doctrine: Walter Murch," *Film Quarterly* 53, no. 3 (2000): 5.

35. Durbin, "Al Pacino."

36. Lebo, *Godfather Legacy*, pp. 62, 165.

37. Francis Ford Coppola and Mario Puzo, "The Godfather: A Screenplay," in *Best American Screenplays Three*, ed. Sam Thomas (New York: Crown, 1995), p. 54.

38. Chaillet and Vincent, *Francis Ford Coppola*, p. 37. See also Lebo, *Godfather Legacy*, p. 170.

39. Chaillet and Vincent, *Francis Ford Coppola*, p. 37.

40. Ibid.

41. Sragow, "Godfatherhood," p. 51.

42. Naomi Greene, "Family Ceremonies in the *Godfather Trilogy*," in *Francis*

Ford Coppola's Godfather Trilogy, ed. Nick Browne (New York: Cambridge University Press, 2000), p. 144.

43. Kathleen Murphy, "Dancing on the High Wire: Al Pacino," *Film Comment* 36, no. 2 (2001): 23.

44. Lebo, *Godfather Legacy,* p. 190.

45. Evans, *Kid Stays in the Picture,* p. xiv. See also Peter Bart, afterword to *The Godfather* by Mario Puzo (New York: Penguin, 2002), pp. 447ff.

46. Evans, *Kid Stays in the Picture,* pp. 350–51.

47. Biskind, *Easy Riders,* p. 159.

48. See Julie Salamon, "A Hollywood Used-to-Be," *New York Times,* 28 July 2002, sec. 2, p. 22.

49. John McCarty, *Hollywood Gangland: The Movies' Love Affair with the Mob* (New York: St. Martin Press, 1993), p. 188. See also Jack Shadoian, *Dreams and Dead Ends: The American Gangster Film,* rev. ed. (New York: Oxford University Press, 2003), p. 271.

50. Andrew Dickos, *Street with No Name: A History of the Classic American Film Noir* (University Press of Kentucky, 2002), pp. 114–15.

51. Kael, *For Keeps,* p. 439.

52. Johnson, *Francis Ford Coppola,* p. 98.

53. John Cawelti, *Adventure, Mystery, and Romance: Formula Stories as Art and Popular Culture* (Chicago: University of Chicago Press, 1976), p. 53. See also Richard Combs, "Coppola's Family Plot," *Film Comment* 38, no. 2 (2002): 42.

54. William Pechter, "Keeping Up with the Corleones," in *Francis Ford Coppola's Godfather Trilogy,* ed. Nick Browne (New York: Cambridge University Press, 2000), p. 168.

55. Johnson, *Francis Ford Coppola,* p. 125.

5. Decline and Fall

1. Chaillet and Vincent, *Francis Ford Coppola,* p. 49. See also Biskind, *Easy Riders,* p. 182.

2. Biskind, *Easy Riders,* p. 181; Evans refers to his substance abuse in *Kid Stays in the Picture,* p. 269.

3. Chaillet and Vincent, *Francis Ford Coppola,* p. 49.

4. Chown, *Hollywood Auteur,* p. 107.

5. Goodwin and Wise, *On the Edge,* p. 162.

6. Bergan, *Francis Ford Coppola,* pp. 48, 163.

7. Mario Puzo, *The Godfather* (New York: Penguin, 2002), pp. 194–228.

8. Chown, *Hollywood Auteur,* p. 102.

9. Vincent LoBrutto, *Principal Photography: Interviews with Cinematographers* (New York: Praeger, 1999), p. 26. See Schaefer and Salvato, *Conversations,* p. 228.

10. Lebo, *Godfather Legacy,* p. 228.

11. Biskind, *Easy Riders,* p. 261.

12. Goodwin and Wise, *On the Edge,* p. 181.

13. Richard Combs, "Coppola's Family Plot," p. 44.

14. Biskind, *Easy Riders,* p. 274.

15. Stone, *Conversations with Filmmakers,* p. 644.

16. Schumacher, *Francis Ford Coppola,* p. 178.

17. Goodwin and Wise, *On the Edge,* p. 180.

18. Kael, *For Keeps,* p. 596.

19. Yaquinto, *Pump 'em Full of Lead,* p. 135.

20. Pye and Myles, *Movie Brats,* p. 106.

21. Allesandro Camon, "*The Godfather* and the Mythology of Mafia," in *Francis Ford Coppola's Godfather Trilogy,* ed. Nick Browne (New York: Cambridge University Press, 2000), p. 69.

22. See John Yates, "Godfather Saga: The Death of Family," in *Movies as Artifacts: Cultural Criticism of Popular Film,* ed. Michael Marsden, John Nachbar, and Sam Grogg (Chicago: Nelson Hall, 1982), pp. 202ff.

23. Kael, *For Keeps,* p. 595.

24. Cited by Naomi Greene, "Family Ceremonies," p. 150.

25. Nick Browne, "Violence as History in the *Godfather* Films," in *Francis Ford Coppola's Godfather Trilogy,* ed. Nick Browne (New York: Cambridge University Press, 2000), p. 14. See also Glenn Mann, "Ideology and Genre in the *Godfather* Films," in *Francis Ford Coppola's Godfather Trilogy,* ed. Nick Browne (New York: Cambridge University Press, 2000), p. 121.

26. Lebo, *Godfather Legacy,* p. 216.

27. Yaquinto, *Pump 'em Full of Lead,* p. 140.

28. Johnson, *Francis Ford Coppola,* p. 155.

29. Francis Ford Coppola and Mario Puzo, "The Godfather-Part II: A Screenplay," in *Best American Screenplays Three,* ed. Sam Thomas (New York: Crown, 1995), pp. 112–13.

30. Biskind, *Godfather Companion,* p. 114.

31. Robert Warshow, "The Gangster as Tragic Hero," in *The Immediate Experience* (Garden City, N.Y.: Doubleday, 1962), p. 132.

32. Biskind, *Godfather Companion,* p. 82.

33. Kael, *For Keeps,* pp. 595, 600.

34. A. O. Scott, "Seen This Guy Lately?: Al Pacino," *New York Times,* 20 April 2003, sec. 2, p. 11.

35. Oldham, *Conversations with Film Editors,* p. 337.

36. Breskin, *Filmmakers in Conversation,* p. 31. See also Guy Garcia, "The Next Don?" *American Film* 15, no. 12 (1990): 27.

37. Pauline Kael, *Movie Love* (New York: Plume, 1991), p. 309.

38. See David Papke, "Francis Ford Coppola and the Popular Response to the *Godfather* Trilogy," in *Legal Realism: Movies as Legal Texts* (Chicago: University of Illinois Press, 1996), pp. 15–16.

39. Breskin, *Filmmakers in Conversation,* p. 32.

40. Cowie, *Coppola*, pp. 235–36. See also Biskind, *Godfather Companion*, p. 140.

41. Stephanie Mansfield, "Andy Garcia," *GQ*, December 1990, p. 332.

42. Bergan, *Francis Ford Coppola*, p. 90.

43. Cowie, *Coppola*, p. 235.

44. Douglas Brode, *Money, Women, and Guns: Crime Movies* (New York: Carol, 1995), p. 172.

45. Cowie, *Coppola*, p. 241.

46. Dick, *Death of Paramount Pictures*, p. 146. See also Lewis, "Paramount Studios," p. 51.

47. Barbara Harrison, "*Godfather-III*," *Life*, November 1990, p. 65.

48. Biskind, *Godfather Companion*, p. 152.

49. Mansfield, "Andy Garcia," p. 341.

50. Eleanor Coppola, "Further Notes," in *Projections Six: Filmmakers on Filmmaking*, ed. John Boorman and Walter Donahue (London: Faber and Faber, 1996), p. 54.

51. Jack Kroll, "The Corleones Return," *Newsweek*, 24 December 1990, p. 58. See also Garcia, "The Next Don?," p. 27.

52. See Kroll, "Corleones Return," p. 61.

53. William McDonald, "Thicker Than Water and Spilled by the Mob: *The Godfather*," *New York Times*, 21 May 1995, sec. 2, p. 11.

54. Richard Corliss, "Schemes and Dreams," *Time*, 24 December 1990, p. 76.

55. Eleanor Coppola, "Further Notes," p. 61.

56. Schumacher, *Francis Ford Coppola*, pp. 428–29.

57. Lebo, *Godfather Legacy*, p. 253.

58. Yaquinto, *Pump 'em Full of Lead*, p. 168.

6. The Unknown Soldiers

1. Gallagher, *Film Directors on Film Directing*, p. 175.

2. Peter Lev, *American Films of the 1970s: Conflicting Visions* (Austin: University of Texas Press, 2000), pp. 118–20.

3. Dale Pollock, *George Lucas*, pp. 128–29.

4. Richard Thompson, "John Milius Interviewed," *Film Comment* 12, no. 4 (1976): 15.

5. Francis Ford Coppola, "*Apocalypse Now*: For the Record," *New York Times*, 27 May 2001, sec. 2, p. 4.

6. Karl French, *On Apocalypse Now* (New York: Bloomsbury, 1999), p. 163. See also Pye and Myles, *Movie Brats*, p. 111.

7. Brooks Riley, "'Heart' Transplant," *Film Comment* 15, no. 1 (1976): 26. Coppola states on the title page of his draft of the script: "Inspired by Joseph Conrad's 'Heart of Darkness.'"

8. Goodwin and Wise, *On the Edge*, p. 196.

9. French, *On Apocalypse Now*, pp. 109–10.

10. John Milius, "Apocalypse Now," unpublished screenplay (American Zoetrope, 1969), p. 2.

11. Riley, "'Heart' Transplant," p. 26.

12. Tony Chiu, "Coppola's Cinematic *Apocalypse*," *New York Times*, 12 August 1979, sec. 2, p. 17.

13. William Hagen, "'Heart of Darkness' and the Process of *Apocalypse Now*," *Conradiana* 13, no. 1 (1981): 49.

14. Cowie, *Coppola*, p. 120.

15. Linda Cahir, "Joseph Conrad's 'Heart of Darkness' and Francis Ford Coppola's *Apocalypse Now*," *Literature/Film Quarterly* 20, no. 3 (1992): 182–83.

16. Francis Ford Coppola, "Apocalypse Now," with John Milius, unpublished screenplay (United Artists, 1975), p. 5.

17. Ibid., p. 150.

18. Eleanor Coppola, *Notes: On Apocalypse Now* (New York: Limelight, 1995), p. 277.

19. French, *On Apocalypse Now*, p. 123. See also Chaillet and Vincent, *Francis Ford Coppola*, p. 59.

20. Jerry Ziesmer, *Ready When You Are, Mr. Coppola, Mr. Spielberg, Mr. Crowe* (Lanham, Md.: Scarecrow Press, 2000), p. 195. See also Lawrence Suid, "Hollywood and Vietnam," *Film Comment* 15, no. 1 (1979): 21.

21. Ziesmer, *Ready When You Are*, p. 234. See also Eleanor Coppola, *Apocalypse Now*, p. 103.

22. Gallagher, *Film Directors on Film Directing*, p. 135; Biskind, *Easy Riders*, p. 355, documents Hopper's drug addiction.

23. Gallagher, *Film Directors on Film Directing*, p. 135.

24. Ric Gentry, "Vittorio Storaro in Conversation," in *Projections Six: Filmmakers on Filmmaking*, ed. John Boorman and Walter Donahue (Boston: Faber and Faber, 1996), p. 265.

25. Coppola, "For the Record."

26. Eleanor Coppola, *Apocalypse Now*, p. 138. See also Michael Ondaatje, "*Apocalypse Now* and Then," *Film Comment* 37, no. 3 (2001): 45.

27. French, *On Apocalypse Now*, p. 96.

28. Schumacher, *Francis Ford Coppola*, p. 228. See also French, *On Apocalypse Now*, p. 96.

29. Ziesmer, *Ready When You Are*, pp. 26, 61.

30. "Production Log," in *Apocalypse Now*, Souvenir Program (United Artists, 1979), p. 3.

31. Schumacher, *Francis Ford Coppola*, p. 253.

32. Ibid., p. 218. See also Chiu, "Coppola's Cinematic *Apocalypse*."

33. Eleanor Coppola, *Apocalypse Now*, pp. 180–82.

34. Biskind, *Easy Riders*, pp. 360–61.

35. Breskin, *Filmmakers in Conversation*, p. 17.

36. David Thomson, "*Apocalypse* Then and Now," *New York Times*, 13 May 2001, sec. 2, p. 32. See also Breskin, *Filmmakers in Conversation*, p. 17.

37. Coppola, "For the Record."

38. William Phillips, "*Hearts of Darkness*: A Documentary," in *Film: An Introduction,* rev. ed. (New York: St. Martin's Press, 2002), p. 361. The author of the essay and book cited in this note is no relation to the author of this book.

39. Breskin, *Filmmakers in Conversation,* pp. 45–46. See also Schumacher, *Francis Ford Coppola,* p. 239.

40. Coppola, "For the Record."

41. Harrison, "*Godfather-III,*" p. 62. See also Eleanor Coppola, *Apocalypse Now,* pp. 42, 229.

42. LoBrutto, *Film Editors on Editing,* p. 116.

43. Ibid., pp. 183–84. See also Oldham, *Conversations with Film Editors,* pp. 33, 369.

44. Michael Ondaatje, *The Conversations: Walter Murch and the Art of Editing Film* (New York: Knopf, 2002), p. 63. See also Mark Cousins, "Walter Murch," in *Projections Six: Filmmakers on Filmmaking,* ed. John Boorman and Walter Donahue (Boston: Faber and Faber, 1996), p. 159.

45. French, *On Apocalypse Now,* p. 14.

46. Cowie, *Coppola,* p. 127.

47. Michelle Wallens, "Putting Films to the Test," *New York Times,* 25 June 2000, sec. 2, p. 11.

48. Goodwin and Wise, *On the Edge,* p. 257.

49. Steven Bach, *Final Cut: Art, Money, and Ego,* rev. ed. (New York: Newmarket Press, 1999), p. 126.

50. Goodwin and Wise, *On the Edge,* p. 262.

51. Thomson, "*Apocalypse* Then and Now."

52. Coppola, "Apocalypse Now," unpublished screenplay, pp. 144–45.

53. Chaillet and Vincent, *Francis Ford Coppola,* pp. 68, 62.

54. Chiu, "Coppola's Cinematic *Apocalypse.*"

55. Schumacher, *Francis Ford Coppola,* p. 208. See also Chown, *Hollywood Auteur,* p. 124.

56. Chiu, "Coppola's Cinematic *Apocalypse*"; cf. Siskel, "Celluloid Godfather," sec. 13, p. 5.

57. Louis Grieff, "Conrad's Ethics and the Margins of *Apocalypse Now,*" *Literature/Film Quarterly* 20, no. 3 (1992): 190.

58. Howard Hampton, "*Apocalypse Now Redux,*" *Film Comment* 37, no. 3 (2001): 42; cf. Wallace Watson, "Willard as Narrator," *Conradiana* 13, no. 1 (1981): 37.

59. David Sundleson, "*Danse Macabre,*" *Conradiana* 13, no. 1 (1981): 44.

60. Peter Cowie, *The Apocalypse Now Book* (New York: Da Capo, 2001), pp. 80, 156. See also John Tessitore, "The Literary Roots of *Apocalypse Now,*" *New York Times,* 21 October 1979, sec. 2, p. 21.

61. Joseph Conrad, *Youth and Heart of Darkness* (New York: Doubleday, 1925), p. 118.

62. Joy Boyum, *Double Exposure: Fiction into Film* (New York: Universe, 1985), p. 111.

63. Philip Horne, "Casualties of War," *Sight and Sound,* n.s., 11, no. 11 (2001): 14.

64. Ibid., p. 15. See also Richard Corliss, "*Apocalypse* Back Then, and Now," *Time,* 6 August 2001, p. 60.

65. Cowie, *Apocalypse Now Book,* p. 73.

66. Chiu, "Coppola's Cinematic *Apocalypse.*"

67. Peter Keough, "Coppola Carves Out a Cinematic Elegy," *Chicago Sun-Times Show,* 10 May 1987, p. 5.

68. Schumacher, *Francis Ford Coppola,* p. 382.

69. See Ziesmer, *Ready When You Are,* pp. 195ff.

70. Goodwin and Wise, *On the Edge,* p. 416.

71. Keough, "Coppola Carves Out a Cinematic Elegy," p. 5.

72. Goodwin and Wise, *On the Edge,* p. 425.

73. Jeff Silverman, "Angelica's Arrival," *Chicago Tribune,* 10 May 1987, sec. 13, p. 7.

74. Robert Lindsey, "Coppola Returns to the Vietnam Era," *New York Times,* 3 May 1987, sec. 2, p. 34.

75. Schumacher, *Francis Ford Coppola,* p. 388. See also Cowie, *Coppola,* p. 208.

76. Cowie, *Coppola,* p. 208.

77. Francis Ford Coppola, 8 August 1991, "Journal: 1989–1993," in *Projection Three: Filmmakers on Filmmaking,* ed. John Boorman and Walter Donohue (Boston: Faber and Faber, 1994), p. 17.

78. Lindsey, "Coppola Returns to the Vietnam Era." p. 34.

79. Oldham, *Conversations with Film Editors,* p. 331.

80. Keough, "Coppola Carves Out a Cinematic Elegy," p. 5.

81. Oldham, *Conversations with Film Editors,* p. 331.

82. Keough, "Coppola Carves Out a Cinematic Elegy," p. 9.

83. Richard Blake, "Overgrown: *Gardens of Stone,*" *America,* 17 June 1987, p. 506.

7. Exiled in Eden

1. Biskind, *Easy Riders,* p. 417.

2. Chaillet and Vincent, *Francis Ford Coppola,* p. 73.

3. Lillian Ross, "Some Figures on a Fantasy: Francis Ford Coppola, *New Yorker,* 8 November 1982, p. 49.

4. Lewis, *Whom God Wishes to Destroy,* pp. 10–11.

5. Francis Coppola, "Memorandum," *Esquire,* November 1977, pp. 190–96 passim.

6. Schumacher, *Francis Ford Coppola,* p. 267. See also Goodwin and Wise, *On the Edge,* p. 291.

7. Cowie, *Coppola,* p. 155. See also Chaillet and Vincent, *Francis Ford Coppola,* p. 88.

8. Ross, "Some Figures on a Fantasy," p. 49.

9. Cf. Scott Haller, "Francis Coppola's Biggest Gamble," *Saturday Review,* July 1961, p. 26.

10. Goodwin and Wise, *On the Edge,* p. 317.

11. Biskind, *Easy Riders,* p. 418.

12. Ross, "Some Figures on a Fantasy," p. 69.

13. Haller, "Francis Coppola's Biggest Gamble," p. 24. See also Ross, "Some Figures on a Fantasy," p. 69.

14. Ross, "Some Figures on a Fantasy," pp. 68–69. See also Lewis, *Whom God Wishes to Destroy,* pp. 57–59.

15. Ross, "Some Figures on a Fantasy," p. 69.

16. Pollock, *George Lucas,* p. 245. See also Ross, "Some Figures on a Fantasy," pp. 76, 81.

17. LoBrutto, *Film Editors on Editing,* p. 100.

18. Ibid.

19. Richard Jameson, "One from Coppola," *Film Comment* 17, no. 3 (1981): 4.

20. Ross, "Some Figures on a Fantasy," p. 76.

21. Richard Corliss, "Coppola Previews His New Film," *Time,* 25 January 1982, p. 70. See also Ross, "Some Figures on a Fantasy," pp. 75–76.

22. Schumacher, *Francis Ford Coppola,* p. 306.

23. Chaillet and Vincent, *Francis Ford Coppola,* p. 90.

24. Richard Corliss, "Surrendering to the Big Dream," *Time,* 25 January 1982, p. 71.

25. Pauline Kael, *Taking It All In* (New York: Holt, Rinehart, and Winston, 1984), pp. 296–98.

26. Jerome Ozer, ed., *Film Review Annual* (Englewood, N.J.: Film Review Publications, 1983), p. 859; see also pp. 858–69 for a survey of the film's reviews.

27. Chaillet and Vincent, *Francis Ford Coppola,* pp. 87–88.

28. Schumacher, *Francis Ford Coppola,* p. 278.

29. Leonard Matlin, et al., *Movie Guide,* rev. ed. (New York: Penguin, 2003), p. 570; cf. Todd McCarthy, "Michael Powell: Zoetrope's Senior Director in Residence," in *Michael Powell: Interviews,* ed. David Lazar (Jackson: University Press of Mississippi, 2003), pp. 67–70.

30. Greg Solmon, "Walter Hill's *Supernova," Film Comment* 36, no. 4 (2000): 22.

31. Gallagher, *Film Directors on Film Directing,* pp. 273–74.

32. Robert Lindsey, "Promises to Keep," *New York Times Magazine,* 24 July 1988, p. 27.

33. Goodwin and Wise, *On the Edge,* p. 410.

34. Bergan, *Francis Ford Coppola,* p. 74.

35. Keough, "Coppola Carves Out a Cinematic Elegy," p. 9. See also Lindsey, "Promises to Keep," p. 27.

36. Cited by Goodwin and Wise, *On the Edge,* p. 337.

8. Growing Pains

1. Bergan, *Francis Ford Coppola,* p. 65.

2. Lewis, *Whom the Gods Wish to Destroy,* pp. 100–101.

3. David Thomson and Lucy Gray, "Idols of the King," *Film Comment* 19, no. 5 (1983): 64.

4. Chaillet and Vincent, *Francis Ford Coppola,* p. 93.

5. Stephen Farber, "Directors Join the S. E. Hinton Fan Club," *New York Times,* 20 March 1983, sec. 2, p. 19.

6. Goodwin and Wise, *On the Edge,* p. 346.

7. Schumacher, *Francis Ford Coppola,* p. 324. See also Goodwin and Wise, *On the Edge,* p. 346.

8. Thomson and Gray, "Idols of the King," 65. See also Chaillet and Vincent, *Francis Ford Coppola,* p. 93.

9. Thomson and Gray, "Idols of the King," 62.

10. Schumacher, *Francis Ford Coppola,* p. 320.

11. Farber, "Directors Join the S. E. Hinton Fan Club," sec. 2, p. 27.

12. Goodwin and Wise, *On the Edge,* p. 343.

13. Schumacher, *Francis Ford Coppola,* p. 323.

14. Thomson and Gray, "Idols of the King," p. 65.

15. Chaillet and Vincent, *Francis Ford Coppola,* p. 93.

16. Chown, *Hollywood Auteur,* p. 165.

17. Richard Corliss, "Playing Tough," *Time,* 4 April 1983, p. 78. For the comparison with *Scorpio Rising,* see *The Advocate,* 22 April 1983, p. 40.

18. Cowie, *Coppola,* p. 170.

19. See Francis Ford Coppola, "The Outsiders," with Katherine Rowell, unpublished screenplay (Warner Bros., 1982), pp. 115–16.

20. Ibid., pp. 116–17.

21. Ibid., p. 114.

22. Corliss, "Playing Tough," p. 78.

23. Thomson and Gray, "Idols of the King," 64.

24. Farber, "Directors Join the S. E. Hinton Fan Club," sec. 2, p. 27.

25. Thomson and Gray, "Idols of the King," 65–66.

26. Ibid., 63.

27. Farber, "Directors Join the S. E. Hinton Fan Club," sec. 2, p. 27.

28. Foster Hirsch, *The Dark Side of the Screen* (New York: Da Capo, 1982), p. 54.

29. Goodwin and Wise, *On the Edge,* p. 352.

30. Farber, "Directors Join the S. E. Hinton Fan Club," sec. 2, p. 27.

31. Gallagher, *Film Directors on Film Directing,* p. 136.

32. Oldham, *Conversations with Film Editors,* p. 330.

33. Goodwin and Wise, *On the Edge,* p. 383.

34. Jon Lewis, "The Road to Romance and Ruin: *Rumble Fish,*" in *Crisis Cinema,* ed. Christopher Starrett (Washington, D.C.: Maison Elve Press, 1993), pp. 136–37.

35. Thomson and Gray, "Idols of the King," 63.

36. Cowie, *Coppola*, p. 176.

37. Lourdeaux, *Italian and Irish Filmmakers*, p. 202.

38. Francis Ford Coppola, "Rumble Fish," with S. E. Hinton, unpublished screenplay (Universal, 1982), pp. 93–94.

39. Goodwin and Wise, *On the Edge*, p. 350.

40. David Ehrenstein, "One from the Art," *Film Comment* 29, no. 1 (1993): 30. See also Ozer, *Film Review Annual* (1984), pp. 1020–32, for a survey of the film's reviews.

41. Oldham, *Conversations with Film Editors*, p. 330.

42. Bergan, *Francis Ford Coppola*, p. 69.

9. Night Life

1. Michael Daly, "A True Tale of Hollywood," *New York*, 7 May 1984, p. 46. See also Evans, *Kid Stays in the Picture*, p. 334.

2. Douglas Brode, *Money, Women, and Guns: Crime Movies* (New York: Carol, 1995), p. 97. See also Biskind, *Easy Riders*, p. 425.

3. Thomson and Gray, "Idols of the King," 74. See also Evans, *Kid Stays in the Picture*, p. 336.

4. Thomson and Gray, "Idols of the King," pp. 74–75.

5. Daly, "A True Tale of Hollywood," p. 46.

6. John Connolly, "Man of a Thousand Lives," *Premiere* 14, no. 8 (2001): 96. See also Evans, *Kid Stays in the Picture*, p. 376.

7. Thomson and Gray, "Idols of the King," 75.

8. Goodwin and Wise, *On the Edge*, p. 366. See also Lewis, *Whom God Wishes to Destroy*, p. 124.

9. Goodwin and Wise, *On the Edge*, p. 367.

10. Chown, *Hollywood Auteur*, p. 187.

11. Evans, *Kid Stays in the Picture*, p. 345.

12. Goodwin and Wise, *On the Edge*, p. 370.

13. Ibid., p. 372.

14. Bergan, *Francis Ford Coppola*, p. 72. See also Evans, *Kid Stays in the Picture*, p. 345.

15. Biskind, *Easy Riders*, p. 425.

16. Evans, *Kid Stays in the Picture*, pp. 345–47. See also Goodwin and Wise, *On the Edge*, p. 389.

17. Cowie, *Coppola*, pp. 183–85.

18. Ibid.

19. Daly, "A True Tale of Hollywood," p. 56.

20. Schumacher, *Francis Ford Coppola*, p. 349.

21. Daly, "A True Tale of Hollywood," p. 53.

22. Goodwin and Wise, *On the Edge*, p. 385.

23. Lewis, *Whom God Wishes to Destroy*, p. 130.

24. Connolly, "Man of a Thousand Lives," p. 97; see Evans, *Kid Stays in the Picture*, p. 352.

25. Oldham, *Conversations with Film Editors*, p. 332.

26. Evans, *Kid Stays in the Picture*, pp. 353, 357.

27. Lawrence Grobel, *Above the Line: Conversations with Robert Evans and Others* (New York: Da Capo, 2000), p. 46. See also Lewis, *Whom God Wishes to Destroy*, p. 133.

28. Cowie, *Coppola*, p. 186.

29. Oldham, *Conversations with Film Editors*, pp. 332–33.

30. Neil Isaacs, "*The Cotton Club*: A Reverie," *Literature/Film Quarterly* 24, no. 1 (1996): 110.

31. Chown, *Hollywood Auteur*, p. 189.

32. Ibid., p. 190.

33. Richard Corliss, "Once Upon a Time in Harlem," *Time*, 17 December 1984, p. 99.

34. Kael, *For Keeps*, p. 1037.

10. The Past as Present

1. Goodwin and Wise, *On the Edge*, p. 409.

2. Chown, *Hollywood Auteur*, p. 199.

3. Siskel, "Celluloid Godfather," p. 4.

4. Richard Corliss, "Just a Dream," *Time*, 13 October 1986, p. 104.

5. Siskel, "Celluloid Godfather," p. 4.

6. Goodwin and Wise, *On the Edge*, p. 422.

7. Siskel, "Celluloid Godfather," p. 4.

8. Ibid.

9. Oldham, *Conversations with Film Editors*, p. 335.

10. Siskel, "Celluloid Godfather," p. 4.

11. Lourdeaux, *Italian and Irish Filmmakers*, p. 206.

12. Bergan, *Francis Ford Coppola*, p. 126.

13. Stephen Farber, "Francis Ford Coppola Sallies into TV on a Fairy Tale," *New York Times*, 27 December 1984, sec. C, p. 20.

14. Ibid.

11. The Disenchanted

1. Marcia Coburn, "Car and Striver: Tucker," *Chicago Tribune*, 7 August 1988, sec. 13, p. 4.

2. The DVD edition of *Tucker*, released in 2000, has a documentary about the making of the film, as well as an audio commentary track by Coppola. I will quote from both the documentary and Coppola's commentary.

3. Coburn, "Car and Striver," p. 6.

4. Ibid.

5. Goodwin and Wise, *On the Edge*, p. 16.

6. William Murray, "*Playboy* Interview: Francis Ford Coppola," *Playboy*, July 1975, p. 68.

7. Johnson, *Francis Ford Coppola*, p. 170. See also Murray, "*Playboy* Interview," p. 68.

8. Francis Ford Coppola, "Memorandum," p. 195.

9. Bob Strauss, "Coppola, Lucas, and Tucker," *Chicago Sun-Times*, 7 August 1988, sec. 2, p. 5. See also Bergan, *Francis Ford Coppola*, p. 8.

10. Lindsey, "Promises to Keep," p. 27.

11. Ibid., p. 26.

12. Timothy Corrigan, "Auteurs and the New Hollywood," in *The New American Cinema*, ed. Jon Lewis (Durham, N.C.: Duke University Press, 1999), p. 52.

13. Lindsey, "Promises to Keep," p. 26.

14. Goodwin and Wise, *On the Edge*, pp. 445–47.

15. Lewis, *Whom God Wishes to Destroy*, p. 153.

16. Stone, *Conversations with Filmmakers*, p. 646.

17. Lewis, *Whom God Wishes to Destroy*, p. 153.

18. Patrick McGilligan, "Arnold Schulman," in *Backstory: Interviews with Screenwriters of the 1960s* (Los Angeles: University of Southern California Press, 1997), p. 324. See also Arnold Schulman, "Tucker: The Man and His Dream," unpublished screenplay (Paramount, 1987).

19. Breskin, *Filmmakers in Conversation*, p. 41.

20. Robert Lindsey, "Martin Landau Rolls Up in a New Vehicle," *New York Times*, 7 August 1988, sec. 2, p. 19.

21. Schumacher, *Francis Ford Coppola*, p. 402.

22. Lindsey, "Martin Landau Rolls Up in a New Vehicle," p. 19.

23. McGilligan, "Arnold Schulman," p. 325.

24. Bergan, *Francis Ford Coppola*, p. 86.

25. Strauss, "Coppola, Lucas, and Tucker," p. 5.

26. Lindsey, "Promises to Keep," p. 27.

27. Goodwin and Wise, *On the Edge*, p. 457.

28. Strauss, "Coppola, Lucas, and Tucker," p. 5.

29. Cowie, *Coppola*, p. 219.

30. Ibid.

31. Kristin Thompson and David Bordwell, *Film History: An Introduction* (New York: McGraw-Hill, 2003) p. 523.

32. Richard Schickel, "On the Road to Utopia," *Time*, 15 August 1988, p. 68.

33. Cowie, *Coppola*, p. 218.

34. Schulman, "Tucker: The Man and His Dream," p. 125.

35. Roger Ebert, "*Tucker* Gives Viewers the Legend," *Chicago Sun-Times*, 12 August 1988, sec. 2, p. 5.

36. Jay Scott, "Coppola's Wish Comes True," *Toronto Globe and Mail,* 12 August 1988, sec. C, p. 1.

37. Strauss, "Coppola, Lucas, and Tucker," 5.

38. Francis Coppola, "Frankly Francis," *Premiere* 15, no. 9 (2002): 20.

39. Schumacher, *Francis Ford Coppola,* p. 406.

40. Oldham, *Conversations with Film Editors,* p . 338.

41. Breskin, *Filmmakers in Conversation,* p. 36.

12. Fright Night

1. Francis Ford Coppola, *Bram Stoker's Dracula: The Film and the Legend,* with James Hart (New York: Newmarket, 1992), pp. 167, 169.

2. Ibid., p. 2.

3. Francis Ford Coppola, *Coppola and Eiko on Bram Stoker's Dracula,* with Eiko Ishioka (San Francisco: Collins, 1992), pp. 13–14.

4. Coppola, *Bram Stoker's Dracula,* p. 2. See also Coppola, *Coppola and Eiko,* p. 13.

5. Francis Ford Coppola, "Journal," pp. 17, 25. See also Coppola, *Bram Stoker's Dracula,* p. 3.

6. Coppola, *Coppola and Eiko,* p. 13.

7. James Hart, "The First Time I Met Francis Coppola," in *The First Time I Got Paid for It: Writer's Tales,* ed. Peter Leecourt and Laura Shapiro (New York: Perseus, 2000), p. 86.

8. Coppola, *Coppola and Eiko,* p. 41.

9. Coppola, *Bram Stoker's Dracula,* p. 42.

10. Eleanor Coppola, "Further Notes," p. 61.

11. Larry Timm, *The Soul of Cinema: Film Music* (Upper Saddle River, N.J.: Prentice Hall, 2003), p. 280.

12. Coppola, *Bram Stoker's Dracula,* p. 162.

13. Grobel, *Above the Line,* p. 157. See also Coppola, *Bram Stoker's Dracula,* p. 4.

14. Bergan, *Francis Ford Coppola,* p. 96.

15. Hal Hinson, "*Bram Stoker's Dracula,*" in *Flesh and Blood: Film Critics on Violence and Censorship* (San Francisco: Mercury House, 1995), p. 168.

16. Coppola, "Journal," p. 24.

17. Ibid., pp. 24, 31–32.

18. Ibid., pp. 32, 34.

19. Coppola, *Coppola and Eiko,* p. 14.

20. Coppola, *Bram Stoker's Dracula,* p. 96.

21. Coppola, "Journal," pp. 18–19.

22. Coppola, *Bram Stoker's Dracula,* p. 96.

23. James Hart, "Bram Stoker's Dracula: A Screenplay," in Francis Ford Coppola, *Bram Stoker's Dracula: The Film and the Legend,* with James Hart, (New York: Newmarket, 1992), p. 163.

24. Coppola, "Journal," pp. 31–32.

25. Richard Corliss, "A Vampire with a Heart," *Time,* 23 November 1992, p. 71.

26. Cowie, *Coppola,* p. 249.

27. Coppola, "Journal," p. 19.

28. Hinson, *"Bram Stoker's Dracula,"* p. 169.

29. Corliss, "Vampire with a Heart," p. 71. See also Carol Fry and Robert Craig, "The Genesis of Coppola's *Dracula,*" *Literature/Film Quarterly* 30, no. 4 (2002): 272–75.

30. Coppola, "Journal," pp. 37–38.

31. Lewis, "Paramount Studios," p. 50.

32. David Cook, "Auteur Cinema and the Film Generation in the 1970's Hollywood," in *The New American Cinema,* ed. Jon Lewis (Durham, N.C.: Duke University Press, 1999), p. 19.

33. Schumacher, *Francis Ford Coppola,* p. 455.

13. The Vanishing Hero

1. Mark Caro, "Francis Coppola: An Interview," *Chicago Tribune,* 20 November 1997, sec. 5, p. 1.

2. Schumacher, *Francis Ford Coppola,* p. 474.

3. Steven Daly, "Matt Damon," *Details,* September 1998, p. 225.

4. Schumacher, *Francis Ford Coppola,* p. 474.

5. Kent Jones, "Mythmaker: Francis Ford Coppola," *Film Comment* 38, no. 2 (2002): 34.

6. Bruce Diones, *"The Rainmaker,"* New Yorker, 5 January 1998, p. 22.

7. Jones, "Mythmaker," p. 34.

8. Jonathan Rosenbaum, "Southern Accents," *Chicago Reader,* 28 November 1997, sec. 1, p. 40.

9. Michael Wilmington, "Courting Success," *Chicago Tribune,* 21 November 1997, sec. 7, p. O.

10. Bergan, *Francis Ford Coppola,* pp. 13, 99.

11. Schumacher, *Francis Ford Coppola,* p. 464.

12. Bergan, *Francis Ford Coppola,* p. 100.

13. Ibid., p. 140.

14. Schumacher, *Francis Ford Coppola,* p. 469.

15. Bergan, *Francis Ford Coppola,* p. 99.

16. Gene Siskel, "Tiresome *Jack,*" *Chicago Tribune,* 9 August 1996, sec. B, p. B.

17. Michael Wilmington, "Trapped in the *Jack* Box," *Chicago Tribune,* 9 August 1996, sec. B, p. CI.

18. Ibid., sec. B, p. I. See also Ozer, *Film Review Annual* (1997), pp. 713–18, for a survey of the film's reviews.

Epilogue

1. Timothy Corrigan, "Auteurs and the New Hollywood," p. 57.

2. Ibid.

3. Caro, "Francis Ford Coppola: An Interview," p. 1.

4. Ibid., p. 9.

5. Stephen Galloway, "Coppola Sues Warners over *Pinocchio*," *Hollywood Reporter,* 14 September 1995, p. 1.

6. Schumacher, *Francis Ford Coppola,* p. 467.

7. Judy Brennan and Chris Nashawaty, "Coppola Bucks," *Entertainment Weekly,* 24 July 1998, p. 25. See also "Won by a Nose," *Sight and Sound,* n.s., 8, no. 9 (1998): 5.

8. Cal Fussman, "Al Pacino," *Esquire,* July 2002, p. 49.

9. Claudia Eller and James Bates, "Coppola: Verdict is Vindication," *Chicago Sun-Times,* 22 July 1998, p. 51. See also Caro, "Francis Coppola: An Interview," p. 9.

10. Jonathan Rosenbaum, "Movies: *Bram Stoker's Dracula,*" *Chicago Reader,* 21 February 2003, sec. 2, p. 4.

11. Caro, "Francis Ford Coppola: An Interview," p. 5.

12. David Thomson, *The New Biographical Dictionary of Film,* rev. ed. (New York: Knopf, 2002), pp. 176–77.

13. Yaquinto, *Pump 'em Full of Lead,* p. 147.

14. Biskind, *Easy Riders,* p. 426.

15. "Leave the Gun, Keep the Libretto," *Time,* 21 August 2000, p. 78.

16. John Horn, "First Take: *Supernova,*" *Premiere* 13, no. 6 (2000): 36.

17. Thomson, *New Biographical Dictionary of Film,* p. 178; Ryan Gilbey, *It Don't Worry Me* (London: Faber and Faber, 2003).

18. Francis Ford Coppola, "Coppola Speaks," *Film Comment* 38, no. 4 (2002): p. 78.

19. Jones, "Mythmaker," p. 30, 36.

20. Breskin, *Filmmakers in Conversation,* p. 14.

21. Strauss, "Coppola, Lucas, and Tucker," p. 5.

22. Coppola, "Coppola Speaks," p. 78.

23. Jones, "Mythmaker," p. 30.

24. Lynn Hirschberg, "The Coppola Smart Mob," *New York Times Magazine,* 31 August 2003, p. 35. See also Mark Olson, "Sofia Coppola: Interview," *Sight and Sound* 14, no. 1 (January 2004): 15.

25. Glenn Kenny, "The 75 Most Influential Movies," *Premiere* 12, no. 4 (January 2004): 5; "This Week's Scary Movies," *TV Guide,* January 2, 2004, p. 7

Selected Bibliography

(N.B.: Only the most significant research materials are included here. Some books and articles alluded to in the text are not listed below.)

"*Apocalypse Now.*" *Film and Broadcasting Review,* 15 September 1979, 95–96.

Apocalypse Now. Souvenir Program. United Artists, 1979.

"*Apocalypse Now*: Special Section." *Conradiana* 13, no. 1 (1981): 35–58.

Bach, Steven. *Final Cut: Art, Money and Ego.* Rev. ed. New York: Newmarket Press, 1999.

Beaver, Frank, ed. *100 Years of American Cinema.* New York: Macmillan, 2000.

Bergan, Ronald. *Francis Ford Coppola.* New York: Orion Books, 1998.

Biskind, Peter. *Easy Riders, Raging Bulls: Coppola, Scorsese, and Other Directors.* New York: Simon and Schuster, 1999.

———. *Godfather Companion.* New York: Harper-Collins, 1990.

Blake, Richard. *After Image: The Catholic Imagination of Six Filmmakers.* Chicago: Loyola Press, 2000.

———. "Overgrown: *Gardens of Stone.*" *America,* 27 June 1987, 506–8.

Blum, David. "The Reign Maker." *Time,* 1 December 1997, 79–80.

Boorman, John, and Walter Donohue, eds. *Projections Six: Filmmakers on Filmmaking.* Boston: Faber and Faber, 1996. [Includes recollections on Coppola's films by Eleanor Coppola, cinematographer Vittorio Storaro, and editor Walter Murch.]

Boyum, Joy Gould. *Double Exposure: Fiction into Film.* New York: New American Library, 1985.

Breskin, David. *Inner Views: Filmmakers in Conversation.* Rev. ed. New York: Da Capo, 1997.

Browne, Nick, ed. *Francis Ford Coppola's The Godfather Trilogy.* New York: Cambridge University Press, 2000.

Bruni, Frank. "In the Name of the Father: Francis Ford Coppola." *New York Times Magazine,* 19 May 2002, 26–28.

Busch, Anita, and Beth Laski. "United We Stand: The Directors Company." *Premiere* 15, no. 4 (2002): 34–37.

Cagin, Seth, and Philip Dray. *Born to Be Wild: Hollywood and the Sixties Generation.* Boca Raton, Fla.: Coyote, 1994.

Cahir, Linda. "Joseph Conrad's *Heart of Darkness* and Francis Coppola's *Apocalypse Now.*" *Literature/Film Quarterly* 20, no. 3 (1992): 181–87.

Canby, Vincent. "Anthologies Can Be a Bargain." *New York Times,* 12 March 1989, sec. 2.

———. "Obsession with Technique." *New York Times,* 21 February 1982, sec. 2.

———. "A Tale of Two B Movies." *New York Times,* 23 December 1983, sec. 2.

Carnes, Mark, ed. *Past Imperfect: History According to the Movies.* New York: Holt, 1995.

Caro, Mark. "Francis Coppola: An Interview." *Chicago Tribune,* 20 November 1997, sec. 5.

Chaillet, Jean-Paul, and Elizabeth Vincent. *Francis Ford Coppola.* Translated by Denise Jacobs. New York: St. Martin's Press, 1984.

Chiu, Tony. "Coppola's Cinematic Apocalypse." *New York Times,* 12 August 1979, sec. 2.

Chown, Jeffrey. *Hollywood Auteur: Francis Coppola.* New York: Praeger, 1988.

Clarens, Carlos. *Crime Movies: A History of the Gangster Genre.* Rev. ed. New York: Da Capo, 1997.

Coburn, Marcia. "Car and Striver: Tucker." *Chicago Tribune,* 7 August 1988, sec. 13.

Combs, Richard. "Coppola's Family Plot." *Film Comment* 38, no. 2 (2002): 38–44.

Connolly, John. "Man of a Thousand Lives: Robert Evans." *Premiere* 14, no. 8 (2001): 93–97, 119.

Conrad, Joseph. *Youth and Heart of Darkness.* 1902. New York: Doubleday, 1925.

Coppola, Eleanor. *Notes: On Apocalypse Now.* New York: Limelight, 1995.

Coppola, Francis Ford. "Apocalypse Now." Unpublished screenplay. With John Milius. United Artists, 1975.

———. "*Apocalypse Now*: For the Record." *New York Times,* 27 May 2001, sec. 2.

———. *Bram Stoker's Dracula: The Film and the Legend.* With James Hart. New York: Newmarket Press, 1992. [Includes Hart's final shooting script.]

———. "The Conversation." Unpublished screenplay. Paramount, 1972.

———. *Coppola and Eiko on Bram Stoker's Dracula.* With Eiko Ishioka. San Francisco: Collins, 1992.

———. "Coppola Speaks: Life Achievement Award." *Film Comment* 38, no. 4 (2002): 78.

———. "Frankly Francis: Coppola on the Coppolas." *Premiere* 15, no. 9 (2002): 20.

———. "*The Godfather*: A Screenplay and *Godfather II*: A Screenplay." With Mario Puzo. In *Best American Screenplays Three,* edited by Sam Thomas, 7–113. New York: Crown, 1995.

———. "Journal: 1989–1993." In *Projections Three: Filmmakers on Filmmaking,* edited by John Boorman and Walter Donohue, 3–43. Boston: Faber and Faber, 1994.

———. "Memorandum." *Esquire,* November 1977, 190–95.

———. "The Outsiders." Unpublished screenplay. With Katherine Rowell. Paramount, 1982. [This is Coppola's revision of Rowell's original draft.]

———. "Patton." Unpublished screenplay. Twentieth Century-Fox, 1965. [Edmund North's subsequent revisions of the script are not included in this version of the script.]

———. "The Rain People." Unpublished screenplay. Warner Brothers, 1968.

———. "Rumble Fish." Unpublished screenplay. With S. E. Hinton. Universal, 1982.

Corliss, Richard. "Just a Dream: *Peggy Sue Got Married.*" *Time,* 13 October 1986, 104.

———. "Once Upon a Time in Harlem: *The Cotton Club.*" *Time,* 17 December 1984, 97.

———. "Playing Tough: *The Outsiders.*" *Time,* 4 April 1983, 78.

———. "Schemes and Dreams: *Godfather III.*" *Time,* 24 December 1990, 76–77.

———. "Surrendering to the Big Dream: *One from the Heart.*" *Time,* 25 January 1982, 71.

———. "Time Bomb: *Rumble Fish.*" *Time,* 24 October 1983, 90–91.

———. "A Vampire with Heart: *Dracula.*" *Time,* 28 November 1992, 71.

Corman, Roger. *How I Made a Hundred Movies in Hollywood and Never Lost a Dime.* With Jim Jerome. New York: Random House, 1990.

Corman, Roger, et al. "The Ten Best Movies of All Time." *Sight and Sound,* n.s., 12, no. 9 (2002): 24–50.

Cowie, Peter. *The Apocalypse Now Book.* New York: Da Capo, 2001.

———. *Coppola: A Biography.* Rev. ed. New York: Da Capo, 1994.

Daly, Michael. "A True Tale of Hollywood: *The Cotton Club.*" *New York,* 7 May 1984, 43–60.

Denvir, John, ed. *Legal Realism: Movies as Legal Texts.* Chicago: University of Illinois Press, 1996.

Desowitz, Bill. "A Still Topical *Conversation.*" *New York Times,* 2 January 2001, sec. 2.

Dick, Bernard. *Engulfed: The Death of Paramount Pictures and the Birth of Corporate Hollywood.* Lexington: University Press of Kentucky, 2001.

Dickos, Andrew. *Street with No Name: A History of the Classic American Film Noir.* Lexington: University Press of Kentucky, 2002.

Diones, Bruce. "*The Rainmaker.*" *New Yorker,* 5 January 1998, 22.

Durbin, Karen. "Nonstop Perfectionist: Al Pacino." *New York Times,* 12 September 1999, sec. 2.

Ebert, Roger. "*Dracula*: Looks Good." *Chicago Sun-Times Weekend,* 13 November 1992, 35.

———. "The Great Movies: *The Godfather.*" *Chicago Sun-Times,* 12 September 1999, sec. B.

———. "*Jack* Stunts Growth." *Chicago Sun-Times,* 9 August 1996, sec. 2.

———. "*New York Stories.*" *Chicago Sun-Times,* 3 March 1989, sec. 2.

———. "Stylistic Devices in *Outsiders.*" *Chicago Sun-Times,* 25 March 1983, 49.

———. "*Tucker* Gives Viewer the Legend." *Chicago Sun-Times,* 12 August 1988, sec. 2.

Edelstein, David. "Gene Hackman." *New York Times,* 16 December 2001, sec. 2.

Ehrenstein, David. "One from the Art: *Dracula.*" *Film Comment* 29, no. 1 (1993): 27–30.

Eisenberg, Lee. "The Conversation; Francis Coppola and Gay Talese." *Esquire Film Quarterly,* July 1981, 78–87.

Eller, Claudia, and James Bates. "Coppola Verdict Is Vindication." *Chicago Sun-Times Showcase,* 22 July 1998, 51.

Entertainment Weekly. Special Film Issue. 24 September 1999.

Evans, Robert. *The Kid Stays in the Picture: A Memoir.* Beverly Hills: Dove, 1995.

Farber, Stephen. "Directors Join the S. E. Hinton Fan Club." *New York Times,* 20 March 1983, sec. 2.

———. "Francis Coppola Sallies into TV on a Fairy Tale." *New York Times,* 27 December 1984. sec. C.

French, Karl. *On Apocalypse Now.* New York: Bloomsbury, 1999.

Fry, Carol, and Robert Craig. "The Genesis of Coppola's *Dracula.*" *Literature/Film Quarterly* 30, no. 4 (2002): 271–78.

Fussman, Cal. "Al Pacino." *Esquire,* July 2002, 44–48, 110–12.

Gallagher, John. *Film Directors on Directing.* New York: Greenwood Press, 1989.

Garcia, Guy. "The Next Don?" *American Film* 15, no. 12 (1990): 24–29, 47.

Geist, Kenneth. "*Gardens of Stone.*" *Films in Review* 38, nos. 8–9 (1987): 423–24.

Gelmis, Joseph. *The Film Director as Superstar.* Garden City, N.Y.: Anchor, 1970.

Gianetti, Louis, and Scott Eyman. *Flashback: A Brief History of Film.* Rev. ed. Upper Saddle River, N.J.: Prentice Hall, 2001.

Gilbey, Ryan. *It Don't Worry Me: The Films of the 1970s.* London: Faber and Faber, 2003.

Goodwin, Michael, and Naomi Wise. *On the Edge: The Life and Times of Francis Coppola.* New York: Morrow, 1989.

Grant, Edmund. "*Godfather III.*" *Films in Review* 42, nos. 3–4 (1991): 102–7.

———. "*Bram Stoker's Dracula.*" *Films in Review* 44, nos. 3–4 (1993): 131–32.

Greiff, Louis. "Conrad's Ethics and the Margins of *Apocalypse Now.*" *Literature/Film Quarterly* 20, no. 3 (1992): 188–98.

Grisham, John. *The Rainmaker.* 1995. New York: Dell, 1996.

Grobel, Lawrence. *Above the Line: Conversations with Robert Evans and Others.* New York: Da Capo, 2000.

Haller, Scott. "Francis Coppola's Biggest Gamble." *Saturday Review,* July 1981, 20–26.

Halliwell, Leslie. *Film Guide.* Edited by John Walker. Rev. ed. New York: Harper Collins, 2003.

Hampton, Howard. "*Apocalypse Now Redux.*" *Film Comment* 37, no. 3 (2001): 36–42.

Harrison, Barbara. "*Godfather III.*" *Life,* November 1990, 50–65.

Hart, James. "The First Time I Met Francis Ford Coppola. In *The First Time I Got Paid for It: Writers' Tales,* edited by Peter Leecourt and Laura Shapiro, 82–87. New York: Perseus, 2000.

Hart, Marion. "Home Guide: *The Conversation.*" *Premiere* 14, no. 7 (2001): 114.

Hirschberg, Lynn. "The Coppola Smart Mob." *New York Times Magazine,* 31 August 2003, pp. 35–39, 50, 57.

Horn, John. "First Take: *Supernova.*" *Premiere* 13, no. 6 (2000): 35–36.

Horne, Philip. "Casualties of War: *Apocalypse Now Redux.*" *Sight and Sound,* n.s., 11, no. 11 (2001): 12–16.

Isaacs, Neil. "*Cotton Club*: A Reverie." *Literature/Film Quarterly* 24, no. 1 (1996): 109–10.

James, Caryn. "Film View: *Dracula.*" *New York Times,* 11 November 1992, sec. 2.

Jameson, Richard. "One from Coppola." *Film Comment* 17, no 3. (1981): 3–4.

Jarrett, Michael. "Sound Doctrine: Walter Murch." *Film Quarterly* 53, no. 3 (2000): 1–9.

Jones, Kent. "Mythmaker: Francis Ford Coppola." *Film Comment* 38, no. 2 (2002): 30–36.

Kael, Pauline. *5001 Nights at the Movies.* Rev. ed. New York: Henry Holt, 1991.

———. *For Keeps.* New York: Penguin, 1996.

Keough, Peter. "Coppola Carves Out a Cinematic Elegy." *Chicago Sun-Times Show,* 10 May 1987, 5.

———. *Flesh and Blood: Film Critics on Sex, Violence, and Censorship.* San Francisco: Mercury House, 1995.

Kline, Sally, ed. *George Lucas: Interviews.* Jackson: University Press of Mississippi, 1999.

Kobel, Peter. "Hollywood's Honeymoon with Time: *Peggy Sue Got Married.*" *New York Times,* 20 January 2002, sec. 2.

Kolker, Robert. *A Cinema of Loneliness: Coppola and Other Directors.* Rev. ed. New York: Oxford University Press, 1988.

Kroll, Jack. "The Corleones Return." *Newsweek,* 24 December 1990, 58–61.

Lebo, Harlan. *The Godfather Legacy.* New York: Simon and Schuster, 1997.

Lev, Peter. *American Films of the 70s: Conflicting Visions.* Austin: University of Texas Press, 2000.

Lewis, Jon, ed. *The New American Cinema.* Durham, N.C.: Duke University Press, 1999.

———. "The Road to Romance and Ruin: *Rumble Fish.*" In *Crisis Cinema: Postmodern Narrative Film,* edited by Christopher Starrett, 129–46. Washington, D.C.: Maison Elve Press, 1983.

———. *Whom God Wishes to Destroy: Francis Coppola and the New Hollywood.* Durham, N.C.: Duke University Press, 1997.

Lindsey, Robert. "Coppola Returns to the Vietnam Era." *New York Times,* 3 May 1987, sec. 2.

———. "Martin Landau Rolls Up in a New Vehicle." *New York Times,* 7 August 1988, sec. 2.

———. "Promises to Keep." *New York Times Magazine,* 24 July 1988, 23–27.

LoBrutto, Vincent. *Principal Photography: Interviews with Cinematographers.* New York: Praeger, 1999.

————. *Selected Takes: Film Editors on Editing.* New York: Praeger, 1991.

————. *Sound on Film: Interviews with Creators of Film Sound.* New York: Praeger, 1994.

Lourdeaux, Lee. *Italian and Irish Filmmakers in America: Ford, Capra, Coppola, and Scorsese.* Philadelphia: Temple University Press, 1990.

Macnab, Geoffrey. "*Apocalypse Now Redux.*" *Sight and Sound,* n.s., 11, no. 12 (2001): 41–42.

McCarthy, Todd, "Michael Powell: Zoetrope's Senior Director in Residence." In *Michael Powell: Interviews,* edited by David Lazar, 57–70. Jackson: University Press of Mississippi, 2003.

McCarty, John. *Hollywood Gangland: The Movies' Love Affair with the Mob.* New York: St. Martin's Press, 1993.

McGillian, Patrick, ed. *Backstory Three: Interviews with Screenwriters of the 1960s.* Los Angeles: University of California Press, 1997.

Maltin, Leonard, Cathleen Anderson, and Luke Sader, eds. *Movie Guide.* Rev. ed. New York: Penguin, 2003.

Mansfield, Stephanie. "Andy Garcia." *GQ,* December 1990, 272–77.

Maslin, Janet. "*Dracula* Doesn't Scare Coppola." *New York Times,* 15 November 1992, sec. 2.

Messenger, Chris. *The Godfather and American Culture.* Albany: State University of New York Press, 2002.

Milius, John. "Apocalypse Now." Unpublished screenplay. American Zoetrope, 1969.

Murphy, Kathleen. "Dancing on the High Wire: Al Pacino." *Film Comment* 36, no. 2 (2000): 19–31.

Murray, William. "*Playboy* Interview: Francis Ford Coppola." *Playboy,* July 1975, 53–68+.

Nash, Jay, and Stanley Ross, eds. *The Motion Picture Guide: 1927–1983.* Chicago: Cinebooks, 1985.

Nowlan, Robert, and Gwendolyn Nowlan. *The Films of the Eighties: A Complete Qualitative Filmography.* Jefferson, N.C.: McFarland, 1991.

Oldham, Gabriella, ed. *First Cut: Conversations with Film Editors.* Los Angeles: University of California Press, 1995.

Olsen, Mark. "Grisham Movies." *Film Comment* 34, no. 2 (1997): 76–79.

Ondaatje, Michael. "*Apocalypse Now* and Then." *Film Comment* 37, no. 3 (2001): 43–47.

————. *The Conversations: Walter Murch and the Art of Editing Film.* New York: Knopf, 2002.

Ozer, Jerome, ed. *Film Review Annual.* Englewood, N.J.:Film Review Publications, 1980–2000.

Phillips, Gene D., and Rodney Hill, eds. *Francis Ford Coppola: Interviews.* Jackson: University Press of Mississippi, 2004.

Phillips, William. "*Hearts of Darkness*: A Documentary." In *Film: An Introduction,* 353–61. Rev. ed. New York: St. Martin's Press, 2002.

Pollock, Dale. *Skywalking: The Life and Times of George Lucas.* Rev. ed. New York: Da Capo, 1999.

Puzo, Mario. *The Godfather.* 1969. With an Afterword by Peter Bart. New York: Penguin, 2002.

———. *The Godfather Papers.* Greenwich, Conn.: Fawcett Crest, 1973.

Pye, Michael, and Linda Myles. *The Movie Brats: How the Film Generation Took Over Hollywood.* New York: Holt, Rinehart, and Winston, 1979.

Riley, Brooks. "'Heart' Transplant." *Film Comment* 15, no. 5 (1979): 26–27.

Roquemore, Joseph. *History Goes to the Movies.* New York: Doubleday, 1999.

Rosenbaum, Jonathan. "Movies: *Bram Stoker's Dracula.*" *Chicago Reader,* 21 February 2003, sec. 2.

———. "Southern Accents: *The Rainmaker.*" *Chicago Reader,* 25 November 1997, sec. 1.

Ross, Lillian, "Some Figures in a Fantasy: Francis Coppola." *New Yorker,* 8 November 1982, 48+.

Rothstein, Edward. "Chilling Balance of Love and Evil." *New York Times,* 23 March 1997, sec. 2.

Salamon, Julie. "A Hollywood Used-to-Be: Robert Evans." *New York Times,* 28 July 2002, sec. 2.

Schaefer, Dennis, and Larry Salvato. *Masters of Light: Conversations with Cinematographers.* Los Angeles: University of California Press, 1984.

Schickel, Richard. "On the Road to Utopia: *Tucker.*" *Time,* 15 August 1988, 68–69.

———. "Recess Yet?: *Jack.*" *Time,* 12 August 1996, 64.

———. "Tales of Young Men: *The Rainmaker.*" *Time,* 6 March 1989, 68.

———. "Three's Company: *New York Stories.*" *Time,* 6 March 1989, 68.

Schoell, William. *The Films of Al Pacino.* New York: Carol, 1995.

Schulman, Arnold. "Tucker: the Man and His Dream." Unpublished screenplay. Paramount, 1987.

Schumacher, Michael. *Francis Ford Coppola: A Filmmaker's Life.* New York: Crown, 1999.

Scott, A. O. "Seen This Guy Lately?: Al Pacino." *New York Times,* 20 April 2003, sec. 2.

Scott, Jay. "Coppola's Dream Comes True: *Tucker.*" *Toronto Globe and Mail,* 12 August 1988, sec. C.

Shadoian, Jack. *Dreams and Dead Ends: The American Gangster Film.* Rev. ed. New York: Oxford University Press, 2003.

Siskel, Gene. "Celluloid Godfather." *Chicago Tribune,* 3 October 1986, sec. 13.

———. "Coppola's Sumptuous *Dracula.*" *Chicago Tribune,* 13 November 1992, sec. C.

———. "It's Not Auto Biography: *Tucker.*" *Chicago Tribune,* 7 August 1988, sec. 13.

———. "Tiresome *Jack.*" *Chicago Tribune,* 9 August 1996, sec. B.

Skow, John. "Coppola Previews His New Film: *One from the Heart.*" *Time,* 25 January 1982, 70.

Solmon, Greg. "Uncertain Glory: The Director's Cut." *Film Comment* 29, no. 3 (1993): 19–27.

Sragow, Michael. "*The Conversation.*" *New Yorker,* 27 March 1995, 33.

———. "Godfatherhood." *New Yorker,* 24 March 1997, 44–52.

———. "*You're a Big Boy Now.*" *New Yorker,* 11 May 1998, 32.

Stoker, Bram. *Dracula.* 1897. The Annotated Edition. Edited by Leonard Wolf. New York: Potter, 1975.

Stone, Judy. *Eye on the World: Conversations with Filmmakers.* Los Angeles: Silman-James, 1997.

Storaro, Vittorio. *Writing with Light.* London: Aperture, 2003.

Strauss, Bob. "Coppola, Lucas, and Tucker: The Men and Their Dreams." *Chicago Sun-Times,* 7 August 1988, sec. 2.

Suid, Lawrence. "Hollywood and Vietnam." *Film Comment* 15, no. 5 (1979): 20–25.

Tessitore, John. "The Literary Roots of *Apocalypse Now.*" *New York Times,* 21 October 1979, sec. 2.

Thompson, Kristin, and David Bordwell. *Film History: An Introduction.* New York: McGraw-Hill, 2003.

Thompson, Richard. "John Milius Interviewed." *Film Comment* 12, no. 4 (1976): 10–21. [Contains extracts from the first draft of Milius's scenario for *Apocalypse Now.*]

Thomson, David. "*Apocalypse* Then, and Now." *New York Times,* 13 May 2001, sec. 2.

———. *The New Biographical Dictionary of Film.* Rev. ed. New York: Knopf, 2002.

Thomson, David, and Lucy Gray. "Idols of the King: Francis Coppola." *Film Comment* 19, no. 5 (1983): 61–75.

Timm, Larry. *The Soul of Cinema: Film Music.* Upper Saddle River, N.J.: Prentice Hall, 2003.

Variety Film Reviews: 1907–1996. 24 vols. New Providence, N.J.: Bowker, 1997.

Warshow, Robert. "The Gangster as Tragic Hero." In *The Immediate Experience,* 127–33. Garden City, N.Y.: Doubleday, 1962.

Whalen, Tim. "Romancing Film: Images of *Dracula.*" *Literature/Film Quarterly* 23, no. 2 (1995): 99–101.

Wilmington, Michael. "The Best of 2001: *Apocalypse Now Redux* and Other Films." *Chicago Tribune,* 16 December 2001, sec. 7.

———. "Courting Success: *The Rainmaker.*" *Chicago Tribune,* 21 November 1997, sec. 7.

———. "Trapped in the *Jack* Box." *Chicago Tribune,* 9 August 1996, sec. B.

Yaquinto, Marilyn. *Pump 'em Full of Lead: Gangsters on Film.* New York: Twayne, 1998.

Ziesmer, Jerry. *Ready When You Are, Mr. Coppola, Mr. Spielberg, Mr. Crowe.* Lanham, Md.: Scarecrow Press, 2000.

Zuker, Joel. *Francis Ford Coppola: A Guide to References and Resources.* Boston: G. K. Hall, 1984.

Filmography

Tonight for Sure (1961)

Screenplay: Jerry Shaffer and Francis Ford Coppola
Direction: Francis Ford Coppola
Photography (color): Jack Hill
Art Direction: Albert Locatelli
Editing: Ronald Waller
Music: Carmine Coppola (credited as Carmen Coppola)
Produced by Francis Ford Coppola. 75 minutes.

The Bellboy and the Playgirls (1962)

Screenplay: Fritz Umgelter and Francis Ford Coppola
Direction: Fritz Umgelter and Francis Ford Coppola
Photography (color): Jack Hill
Art Direction: Albert Locatelli
Produced by Wolfgang Hartwig. 94 minutes.

Dementia 13 (1963)

Screenplay: Francis Ford Coppola
Direction: Francis Ford Coppola
Photography (black and white): Charles Hannawalt
Art Direction: Albert Locatelli
Editing: Mort Tubor, Stuart O'Brien
Music: Ronald Stein
Cast: William Campbell (Richard Haloran), Luana Anders (Louise Haloran), Bart Patton (Billy Haloran), Mary Mitchel (Kane), Patrick Magee (Justin Caleb), Ethne Dunn (Lady Haloran), Peter Reed (John Haloran), Karl Schanzer (Simon), Ron Perry (Arthur), Derry O'Donovan (Lillian), Barbara Dowling (Kathleen)
Produced by Francis Ford Coppola for Roger Corman Productions. 97 minutes.
Premiere: September 25, 1963.

You're a Big Boy Now (1966)

Screenplay: Francis Ford Coppola, based on the novel by David Benedictus
Direction: Francis Ford Coppola
Photography (Eastmancolor): Andy Laszlo
Art Direction: Vassele Fotopoulos
Costumes: Theoni V. Aldredge
Choreography: Robert Tucker
Editing: Aram Avakian
Music: Bob Prince; songs by John Sebastian; performed by The Lovin' Spoonful
Cast: Peter Kastner (Bernard Chanticleer), Elizabeth Hartman (Barbara Darling), Geraldine Page (Margery Chanticleer), Julie Harris (Miss Thing), Rip Torn (I. H. Chanticleer), Tony Bill (Raef), Karen Black (Amy), Michael Dunn (Richard Mudd), Dolph Sweet (Francis Graf), Michael O'Sullivan (Kurt Doughty).
Produced by Phil Feldman for Seven Arts, released by Warner Bros. 96 minutes.
Premiere: March 20, 1967.

Finian's Rainbow (1968)

Screenplay: E. Y. Harburg and Fred Saidy, based on the Broadway play (book by E. Y. Harburg and Fred Saidy, lyrics by E. Y. Harburg, Music by Burton Lane)
Direction: Francis Ford Coppola
Photography (Technicolor, Panavision): Philip Lathrop
Production Design: Hilyard M. Brown
Costumes: Dorothy Jenkins
Choreography: Hermes Pan
Editing: Melvin Shapiro
Music Direction: Ray Heindorf
Associate Music Supervisor: Ken Darby
Sound: M. A. Merrick and Dan Wallin
Cast: Fred Astaire (Finian McLonergan), Petula Clark (Sharon McLonergan), Tommy Steele (Og), Don Francks (Woody Mahoney), Barbara Hancock (Susan the Silent), Keenan Wynn (Senator "Billboard" Rawkins), Al Freeman, Jr. (Howard), Ronald Colby (Buzz Collins), Dolph Sweet (Sheriff), Wright King (District Attorney), Louil Silas (Henry), Brenda Arnau (Sharecropper), Avon Long, Roy Glen, Jerster Hairston (Passion Pilgrim Gospellers)
Produced by Joseph Landon for Warner Bros.-Seven Arts. Associate producer: Joel Freeman. 145 minutes.
Premiere: October 9, 1968.

The Rain People (1969)

Screenplay: Francis Ford Coppola
Direction: Francis Ford Coppola

Photography (Technicolor): Bill Butler
Art Direction: Leon Erickson
Editing: Barry Malkin
Music: Ronald Stein
Sound: Nathan Boxer
Sound Montage: Walter Murch
Cast: James Caan (Kilgannon), Shirley Knight (Natalie Ravenna), Robert Duvall
    (Gordon), Marya Zimmet (Rosalie), Tom Aldredge (Mr. Alfred), Laurie Crews
    (Ellen), Andrew Duncan (Artie), Margaret Fairchild (Marion), Sally Gracie
    (Beth), Alan Manson (Lou), Robert Modica (Vinny)
Produced by Bart Patton and Ronald Colby for American Zoetrope, Warner Bros.-
    Seven Arts. Production associates: George Lucas and Mona Skager. 101 minutes.
Premiere: August 27, 1969.

The Godfather (1972)

Screenplay: Mario Puzo and Francis Ford Coppola, based on the novel by Mario
    Puzo
Direction: Francis Ford Coppola
Photography (Technicolor): Gordon Willis
Production Design: Dean Tavoularis
Art Direction: Warren Clymer
Costumes: Anna Hill Johnstone
Editing: William Reynolds and Peter Zinner
Music: Nino Rota, with additional music by Carmine Coppola
Sound: Christopher Newman
Cast: Marlon Brando (Don Vito Corleone), Al Pacino (Michael Corleone), James
    Caan (Sonny Corleone), Richard Castellano (Clemenza), Robert Duvall (Tom
    Hagen), Sterling Hayden (McCluskey), John Marley (Jack Woltz), Richard Conte
    (Barzini), Al Lettieri (Sollozzo), Diane Keaton (Kay Adams), Abe Vigoda
    (Tessio), Talia Shire (Connie), Gianni Russo (Carlo Rizzi), John Cazale (Fredo
    Corleone), Rudy Bond (Cuneo), Al Martino (Johnny Fontane), Morgana King
    (Mama Corleone), Lenny Montanna (Luca Brasi), John Martino (Paulie Gatto),
    Salvatore Corsitto (Bonasera), Richard Bright (Neri), Alex Rocco (Moe Greene),
    Tony Giorgio (Bruno Tattaglia), Vito Scotti (Nazorine), Tere Livrano (Theresa
    Hagen), Victor Rendina (Philip Tattaglia), Jeannie Linero (Lucy Mancini), Julie
    Gregg (Sandra Corleone), Ardell Sheidan (Mrs. Clemenza), Simetta Stefanelli
    (Apollonia), Angelo Infanti (Fabrizio), Corrado Gaipa (Don Tommasino),
    Franco Citti (Calo), Saro Urzi (Vitelli).
Produced by Albert S. Ruddy for Paramount. Associate producer: Gray
    Frederickson. 175 minutes.
Premiere: March 11, 1972.

The Conversation (1974)

Screenplay: Francis Ford Coppola
Direction: Francis Ford Coppola
Photography (Technicolor): Bill Butler and Haskell Wexler (uncredited)
Production Design: Dean Tavoularis
Set Decoration: Doug von Koss
Costumes: Aggie Guerard Rodgers
Supervising Editor, Sound Montage, and Rerecording: Walter Murch
Editing: Richard Chew
Music: David Shire
Technical Advisers: Hal Lipset, Leo Jones, and Jim Bloom
Cast: Gene Hackman (Harry Caul), John Cazale (Stan), Allen Garfield (Bernie Moran), Frederic Forrest (Mark), Cindy Williams (Ann), Michael Higgins (Paul), Elizabeth MacRae (Meredith), Harrison Ford (Martin Stett), Robert Duvall (the Director), Mark Wheeler (Receptionist), Teri Garr (Amy), Robert Shields (Mime), Phoebe Alexander (Lurleen).
Produced by Francis Ford Coppola and Fred Roos for American Zoetrope, Paramount. 113 minutes.
Premiere: April 7, 1974.

The Godfather Part II (1974)

Screenplay: Francis Ford Coppola and Mario Puzo, based on events in the novel by Mario Puzo.
Direction: Francis Ford Coppola
Photography (Technicolor): Gordon Willis
Production Design: Dean Tavoularis
Art Direction: Angelo Graham
Set Decoration: George R. Neison
Costumes: Theadora van Runkle
Editing: Peter Zinner, Barry Malkin, and Richard Marks
Music: Nino Rota and Carmine Coppola
Sound Montage and Rerecording: Walter Murch
Cast: Al Pacino (Michael Corleone), Robert Duvall (Tom Hagen), Diane Keaton (Kay Adams), Robert De Niro (Vito Corleone), John Cazale (Fredo Corleone), Talia Shire (Connie Corleone), Lee Strasberg (Hyman Roth), Michael V. Gazzo (Frank Pentangeli), G. D. Spradlin (Senator Pat Geary), Richard Bright (Al Neri), Gaston Moschin (Fanucci), Tom Rosqui (Rocco Lampone), Bruno Kirby Jr. (Clemenza), Frank Sivero (Genco), Francesca de Sapio (Young Mama Corleone), Morgana King (Mama Corleone), Mariana Hill (Deanna Corleone), Leopoldo Trieste (Signor Roberto), Dominic Chianese (Johnny Ola), Amerigo Tot (Bodyguard), Troy Donahue (Merle Johnson), John Aprea (Tessio), Joe Spinell (Willi Cicci).

Produced by Francis Ford Coppola for American Zoetrope, Paramount. Associate
Producer: Mona Skager. Coproducers: Gray Frederickson and Fred Roos. 200
minutes.
Premiere: December 12, 1974.

Apocalypse Now (1979)

Screenplay: John Milius and Francis Ford Coppola, based on "Heart of Darkness"
by Joseph Conrad (uncredited). Narration by Michael Herr.
Direction: Francis Ford Coppola
Photography (Technicolor, Technovision): Vittorio Storaro
Second-Unit Photography: Steven H. Burum
Insert Photography: Caleb Deschanel
Production Design: Dean Tavoularis
Art Direction: Angelo Graham
Costume Supervision: Charles E. James
Supervising Editor: Richard Marks
Editing: Walter Murch, Gerald B. Greenberg, Lisa Fruchtman, and Barry Malkin
(uncredited)
Offscreen Commentary: Michael Herr
Music: Carmine Coppola and Francis Ford Coppola
Sound Montage/Design: Walter Murch
Cast: Marlon Brando (Col. Walter E. Kurtz), Robert Duvall (Lt. Col. Bill Kilgore),
Martin Sheen (Capt. Benjamin L. Willard), Frederic Forrest ("Chef" Hicks),
Albert Hall (Chief Phillips), Sam Bottoms (Lance B. Johnson), Larry Fishburne
("Clean"), Dennis Hopper (Photojournalist), G. D. Spradlin (General Corman),
Harrison Ford (Colonel Lucas), Jerry Ziesmer (Civilian), Scott Glenn (Capt.
Richard Colby).
Produced by Francis Ford Coppola for American Zoetrope, United Artists. Asso-
ciate Producer: Mona Skager. Coproducers: Fred Roos, Gray Frederickson, and
Tom Sternberg. 153 minutes.
Premiere: August 15, 1979.

One from the Heart (1982)

Screenplay: Armyan Bernstein and Francis Ford Coppola, from the original screen-
play by Armyan Bernstein.
Direction: Francis Ford Coppola
Photography (Technicolor): Vittorio Storaro
Special Visual Effects: Robert Swarthe
Electronic Cinema: Thomas Brown, Murdo Laird, Anthony St. John, and Michael
Lehmann, in cooperation with Sony Corporation
Production Design: Dean Tavoularis

Art Direction: Angelo Graham
Costumes: Ruth Morley
Choreography: Kenny Ortega and Gene Kelly (uncredited)
Editing: Anne Goursaud, with Rudi Fehr and Randy Roberts
Songs and Music: Tom Waits; sung by Tom Waits and Crystal Gayle
Sound Design: Richard Beggs
Cast: Frederick Forrest (Hank), Teri Garr (Frannie), Raul Julia (Ray), Nastassia
    Kinski (Leila), Lainie Kazan (Maggie), Harry Dean Stanton (Moe), Allen Garfield
    (Restaurant Owner), Jeff Hamlin (Airline Ticket Agent), Italia Coppola (Woman
    in Elevator), Carmine Coppola (Man in Elevator).
Produced by Gray Frederickson and Fred Roos for Zoetrope Studio, Columbia
    Pictures. Associate producer: Mona Skager. Executive producer: Bernard
    Gersten. Coproducer: Armyan Bernstein. 101 minutes.
Premiere: January 15, 1982.

The Outsiders (1983)

Screenplay: Kathleen Knutsen Rowell and Francis Ford Coppola (uncredited), from
    the novel by S. E. Hinton
Direction: Francis Ford Coppola
Photography (Technicolor, Panavision): Steven H. Burum
Special Visual Effects: Robert Swarthe
Production Design: Dean Tavoularis
Costumes: Marge Bowers
Editing: Anne Goursaud
Music: Carmine Coppola
Sound: Jim Webb
Sound Design: Richard Beggs
Cast: Matt Dillon (Dallas Winston), Ralph Macchio (Johnny Cade), C. Thomas
    Howell (Ponyboy Curtis), Patrick Swayze (Darrel Curtis), Rob Lowe (Sodapop
    Curtis), Emilio Estevez (Two-Bit Matthews), Tom Cruise (Steve Randle), Glenn
    Withrow (Tom Shepard), Diane Lane (Cherry Valance), Leif Garrett (Bob
    Sheldon), Darren Dalton (Randy Anderson), Michelle Meyrink (Marcia),
    Gailard Sartain (Jerry), Tom Waits (Buck Merrill), William Smith (Clerk).
Produced by Fred Roos and Gray Frederickson for Zoetrope Studios, Warner Bros.
    Associate producer: Gian-Carlo Coppola. 91 minutes.
Premiere: March 25, 1983.

Rumble Fish (1983)

Screenplay: S. E. Hinton and Francis Ford Coppola, based on the novel by S. E.
    Hinton
Direction: Francis Ford Coppola

Photography (black and white): Steven H. Burum
Production Design: Dean Tavoularis
Costumes: Marge Bowers
Editing: Barry Malkin
Music: Stewart Copeland
Sound: David Parker
Sound Design: Richard Beggs
Cast: Matt Dillon (Rusty-James), Mickey Rourke (the Motorcycle Boy), Diane Lane (Patty), Dennis Hopper (Father), Diana Scarwid (Cassandra), Vincent Spano (Steve), Nicolas Cage (Smokey), Christopher Penn (B. J. Jackson), Larry Fishburne (Midget), William Smith (Patterson), Michael Higgins (Mr. Harrigan), Glenn Withrow (Biff Wilcox), Tom Waits (Benny), Herb Rice (Pool Player), Maybelle Wallace (Late Pass Clerk), Nona Manning (Patty's Mother), Domino (Patty's Sister), Gio (Cousin James), S. E. Hinton (Hooker).
Produced by Fred Roos and Doug Claybourne for Zoetrope Studios, Universal. Executive producer: Francis Ford Coppola. Associate producers: Gian-Carlo Coppola and Roman Coppola. 94 minutes.
Premiere: October 7, 1983.

The Cotton Club (1984)

Screenplay: William Kennedy and Francis Ford Coppola, from a story by William Kennedy, Francis Ford Coppola, and Mario Puzo, suggested by a pictorial history of James Haskins
Direction: Francis Ford Coppola
Photography (Technicolor): Stephen Goldblatt
Production Design: Richard Sylbert
Art Direction: David Chapman and Gregory Bolton
Costumes: Milena Canonero
Principal Choreographer: Michael Smith
Tap Choreographer: Henry LeTang
Sound Editing: Edward Beyer
Montage and Second-Unit Director: Gian-Carlo Coppola
Editing: Barry Malkin and Robert Q. Lovett
Music: John Barry and Bob Wilber
Cast: Richard Gere (Dixie Dwyer), Gregory Hines (Sandman Williams), Diane Lane (Vera Cicero), Lonette McKee (Lila Rose Oliver), Bob Hoskins (Owney Madden), James Remar (Dutch Schultz), Nicolas Cage (Vincent Dwyer), Allen Garfield (Abbadabba Berman), Fred Gwynne (Frenchy), Gwen Verdon (Tish Dwyer), Lisa Jane Persky (Frances Flegenheimer), Maurice Hines (Clay Williams), Julian Beck (Sol Weinstein), Novella Nelson (Madame St. Claire), Larry Fishburne (Bumpy Rhodes), John Ryan (Joe Flynn), Tom Waits (Irving Stark).
Produced by Robert Evans, for Zoetrope Studios, Orion. Coproducers: Silvio Tabet

and Fred Roos. Executive producer: Dyson Lovell. Line producers: Barrie M. Osborne and Joseph Cusumano.

Premiere: December 14, 1984.

"Rip Van Winkle" (1985)

Screenplay: Mark Curtis, Rod Ash, and Francis Ford Coppola (uncredited), from the story by Washington Irving

Direction: Francis Ford Coppola

Photography (color): George Riesenberger

Production Design: Michael Erler

Artistic Consultant: Eiko Ishioka

Costumes: Sam Kirkpatrick

Editing: Murdo Laird, Arden Rynew

Music: Carmine Coppola

Cast: Harry Dean Stanton (Rip Van Winkle), Talia Shire (Wilma Van Winkle), Henry Hudson (John P. Ryan), Mayor (Tim Conway), Ed Begley, Jr., Christopher Penn, Roy Dotrice, Sofia Coppola.

Produced for HBO's *Faerie Tale Theatre* television series by Fred Fuchs and Bridget Terry. Executive producer: Shelley Duvall. 48 minutes.

Peggy Sue Got Married (1986)

Screenplay: Jerry Leichtling and Arlene Sarner

Direction: Francis Ford Coppola

Photography (Deluxe): Jordan Cronenweth

Electronic Cinema: Murdo Laird, Ted Mackland, and Ron Mooreland

Production Design: Dean Tavoularis

Art Direction: Alex Tavoularis

Costumes: Theadora Van Runkle

Editing: Barry Malkin

Music: John Barry

Supervisory Sound Editing: Michael Kirchberger

Cast: Kathleen Turner (Peggy Sue Kelcher), Nicolas Cage (Charlie Bodell), Barry Miller (Richard Norvik), Catherine Hicks (Carol Heath), Joan Allen (Maddie Nagle), Kevin J. O'Connor (Michael Fitzsimmons), Jim Carrey (Walter Getz), Lisa Jane Persky (Dolores Dodge), Lucinda Jenney (Rosalie Testa), Wil Shriner (Arthur Nagle), Barbara Harris (Evelyn Kelcher), Don Murray (Jack Kelcher), Sofia Coppola (Nancy Kelcher), Maureen O'Sullivan (Elizabeth Alvorg), Leon Ames (Barney Alvorg), with Helen Hunt and John Carradine.

Produced by Paul R. Gurian for American Zoetrope, Tri-Star, Executive producer: Barrie M. Chase. 104 minutes.

Premiere: October 5, 1986.

Gardens of Stone (1987)

Screenplay: Ronald Bass, based on the novel by Nicholas Proffitt
Direction: Francis Ford Coppola
Photography (Deluxe): Jordan Cronenweth
Production Design: Dean Tavoularis
Art Direction: Alex Tavoularis
Costumes: Will Kim and Judianna Makovsky
Editing: Barry Malkin
Music: Carmine Coppola
Sound Design: Richard Beggs
Cast: James Caan (Clell Hazard), Anjelica Huston (Samantha Davis), James Earl
    Jones (Sgt. Maj. Goody Nelson), D. B. Sweeney (Jackie Willow), Dean Stockwell
    (Homer Thomas), Mary Stuart Masterson (Rachel Feld), Dick Anthony Will-
    iams (Slasher Williams), Lonette McKee (Betty Rae), Sam Bottoms (Lieuten-
    ant Webber), Elias Koteas (Peter Deveber), Larry Fishburne (Flanagan), Casey
    Siemaszko (Wildman), Peter Masterson (Colonel Feld), Carlin Glynn (Mrs.
    Feld), Erik Holland (Colonel Godwin), Bill Graham (Don Brubaker).
Produced by Michael I. Levy and Francis Ford Coppola for Tri-Star. Executive
    producers: Stan Weston, Jay Emmett, and Fred Roos. Coexecutive producer:
    David Valdes. 111 minutes.
Premiere: May 8, 1987.

Tucker: The Man and His Dream (1988)

Screenplay: Arnold Schulman and David Seidler
Direction: Francis Ford Coppola
Photography (Technicolor, Technovision): Vittorio Storaro
Production Design: Dean Tavoularis
Art Direction: Alex Tavoularis
Costumes: Milena Canonero
Editing: Priscilla Nedd
Music: Joe Jackson
Sound Design: Richard Beggs
Cast: Jeff Bridges (Preston Tucker), Joan Allen (Vera), Martin Landau (Abe Karatz),
    Frederic Forrest (Eddie), Mako (Jimmy), Elias Koteas (Alex), Christian Slater
    (Junior), Nina Siemaszko (Marilyn Lee), Anders Johnson (Johnny), Corky
    Nemec (Noble), Marshall Bell (Frank), Jay O. Sanders (Kirby), Peter Donat
    (Kerner), Lloyd Bridges (Senator Ferguson), Dean Goodman (Bennington),
    John X. Heart (Ferguson's Aide), Don Novello (Stan), Patti Austin (Millie),
    Sandy Bull (Stan's Assistant), Joseph Miksak (Judge), Scott Beach (Floyd Cerf),
    Roland Scrivner (Oscar Beasley), Dean Stockwell (Howard Hughes), Bob Safford
    (Narrator), Larry Menkin (Doc), Ron Close (Fritz), Joe Flood (Dutch).
Produced by Fred Roos and Fred Fuchs for Lucasfilm Ltd., Zoetrope Studios, Para-

mount. Executive producer: George Lucas. Associate producer: Teri Fettis. 111 minutes.

Premiere: August 12, 1988.

"Life Without Zoe" (Segment Two in *New York Stories* [1989])

Screenplay: Francis Ford Coppola and Sofia Coppola
Direction: Francis Ford Coppola
Photography (Technicolor): Vittorio Storaro
Production Design: Dean Tavoularis
Art Direction: Speed Hopkins
Costumes: Sofia Coppola
Editing: Barry Malkin
Music: Carmine Coppola
Sound Recording: Frank Graziadei
Songs: Kid Creole and the Coconuts
Cast: Heather McComb (Zoe), Talia Shire (Charlotte), Gia Coppola (Baby Zoe), Giancarlo Giannini (Claudio), Paul Herman (Clifford), James Keane (Jimmy), Don Novello (Hector), Bill Moor (Mr. Lilly), Tom Mardirosian (Hasid), Jenny Bichold (Lundy), Gia Scianni (Devo), Diane Lin Cosman (Margit), Selim Tlili (Abu), Robin Wood-Chapelle (Gel), Celia Nestell (Hillary), Alexandra Becker (Andrea), Adrien Brody (Mel), Michael Higgins (Robber), Chris Elliott (Robber), Thelma Carpenter (Maid), Carmine Coppola (Street Musician), Carole Bouquet (Princess Soroya), Jo Jo Starbuck (Ice Skater).
Segment producers: Fred Roos and Fred Fuchs for Touchstone Pictures. 34 minutes.

Premiere: February 26, 1989.

The Godfather Part III (1990)

Screenplay: Mario Puzo and Francis Ford Coppola
Direction: Francis Ford Coppola
Photography (Technicolor): Gordon Willis
Production Design: Dean Tavoularis
Art Direction: Alex Tavoularis
Costumes: Milena Canonero
Editing: Barry Malkin, Lisa Fruchtman, and Walter Murch
Music: Carmine Coppola
Additional Music and Themes: Nino Rota
Sound Design: Richard Beggs
Cast: Al Pacino (Michael Corleone), Diane Keaton (Kay Adams), Talia Shire (Connie Corleone Rizzi), Andy Garcia (Vincent Mancini), Eli Wallach (Don Altobello), Joe Mantegna (Joey Zasa), George Hamilton (B. J. Harrison), Bridget Fonda (Grace Hamilton), Sofia Coppola (Mary Corleone), Raf Vallone (Cardi-

nal Lamberto), Franc D'Ambrosio (Anthony Corleone), Donal Donnelly (Archbishop Gliday), Richard Bright (Al Neri), Helmut Berger (Frederick Keinszig), Don Novello (Dominic Abbandando), John Savage (Andrew Hagen), Franco Citti (Calo), Mario Donatone (Mosca), Vittorio Duse (Don Tommasino), Enzo Robutti (Lucchesi), Michele Russo (Spara), Al Martino (Johnny Fontane), Robert Cicchini (Lou Pennino), Rogerio Miranda (Armand), Carlos Miranda (Francesco), Jeannie Linero (Lucy Mancini).

Produced by Francis Ford Coppola for Zoetrope Studios, Paramount Pictures. Executive producers: Fred Fuchs and Nicholas Gage. Coproducers: Fred Roos, Gray Frederickson, and Charles Mulvehill. Associate producer: Marina Gefter. 161 minutes (170 minutes, final version [2001]).

Premiere: December 26, 1990.

Bram Stoker's Dracula (1992)

Screenplay: James V. Hart
Direction: Francis Ford Coppola
Photography (Technicolor): Michael Ballhaus
Visual Effects: Roman Coppola
Production Design: Thomas Sanders
Art Direction: Andrew Precht
Costumes: Eiko Ishioka
Editing: Nicholas C. Smith, Glenn Scantlebury, and Anne Goursaud
Music: Wojciech Kilar
Sound: David Stone
Cast: Gary Oldman (Dracula), Winona Ryder (Mina/Elisabeta), Anthony Hopkins (Abraham Van Helsing), Keanu Reeves (Jonathan Harker), Sadie Frost (Lucy Westenra), Richard E. Grant (Dr. Jack Seward), Cary Elwes (Arthur Holmwood), Billy Campbell (Quincey Morris), Tom Waits (Renfield), Monica Bellucci (Dracula's Bride), Jay Robinson (Mr. Hawkins), I. M. Hobson (Hobbs), Laurie Frank (Lucy's Maid).

Produced by Francis Ford Coppola, Fred Fuchs, and Charles Mulvehill for American Zoetrope, Columbia Pictures. Executive producers: Michael Apted and Robert O'Connor. Coproducer; James V. Hart. Associate producer: Susie Landau. 123 minutes.

Premiere: November 13, 1992

Jack (1996)

Screenplay: James DeMonaco and Gary Nadeau
Direction: Francis Ford Coppola
Photography (Technicolor): John Toll
Production Design: Dean Tavoularis
Art Direction: Angelo Graham

Costumes: Aggie Guerard Rodgers
Editing: Barry Malkin
Music: Michael Kamen
Sound: Agamemnon Andrianos
Cast: Robin Williams (Jack Powell), Diane Lane (Karen Powell), Jennifer Lopez (Miss Marquez), Brian Kerwin (Brian Powell), Fran Drescher (Dolores Durante), Bill Cosby (Lawrence Woodruff), Michael McKean (Paulie), Don Novello (Bartender), Allan Rich (Dr. Benfante), Adam Zolotin (Louis Durante), Todd Bosley (Edward), Seth Smith (John-John), Mario Yedidia (George), Jeremy Lelliott (Johnny Duffer), Rickey O'Shon Collins (Eric), Hugo Hernandez (Victor).
Produced by Ricardo Mestres, Fred Fuchs, and Francis Ford Coppola for American Zoetrope, Buena Vista. Executive producer: Doug Claybourne. 113 minutes.
Premiere: August 9, 1996.

The Rainmaker (1997)

Screenplay: Francis Ford Coppola, based on the novel by John Grisham; narration by Michael Herr.
Direction: Francis Ford Coppola
Photography (Deluxe): John Toll
Production Design: Howard Cummings
Art Direction: Robert Shaw, Jeffrey McDonald
Costumes: Aggie Guerard Rodgers
Editing: Barry Malkin
Music: Elmer Bernstein
Sound: Nelson Stoll
Cast: Matt Damon (Rudy Baylor), Claire Danes (Kelly Riker), Jon Voight (Leo F. Drummond), Mary Kay Place (Dot Black), Mickey Rourke (Bruiser Stone), Danny DeVito (Deck Schifflet), Dean Stockwell (Judge Harvey Hale), Teresa Wright (Miss Birdie), Virginia Madsen (Jackie Lemancyzk), Andrew Shue (Cliff Riker), Red West (Buddy Black), Johnny Whitworth (Donny Ray Black), Danny Glover (Judge Tyrone Kipler), Wayne Emmons (Prince Thomas), Adrian Roberts (Butch), Roy Scheider (Wilfred Keeley), Randy Travis (Billy Porter), Michael Girardin (Everett Lufkin), Randall King (Jack Underhall), Justin Ashforth (F. Franklin Donaldson), Michael Keys Hall (B. Bobby Shaw).
Produced by Michael Douglas, Steven Reuther, and Fred Fuchs for American Zoetrope, Paramount Pictures. Coproducer: Georgia Kacandes. Associate producer: Gary Scott Marcus.
Premiere: November 21, 1997.

Apocalypse Now Redux (2001)

An expanded version of *Apocalypse Now,* with fifty-three minutes of additional footage.

Editor: Walter Murch
Supervising Sound Editor: Michael Kirchberger
Cast: The French Plantation: Christian Marquand (Hubert DeMarais), Aurora
    Clément (Roxanne Surrault).
Produced by Kim Aubry for American Zoetrope, Miramax Films. 202 minutes.
Premiere: August 15, 2001.

Index